FLORENCE 1900

1   Hans Thoma, *The Park at the Hildebrand Villa* (Monastery of San
Francesco di Paola) with a statue by Adolf von Hildebrand (1887)

'It was like a glimpse into a Golden Age' (ISOLDE KURZ)

Florence 1900
The Quest for Arcadia

BERND ROECK

Translated by Stewart Spencer

YALE UNIVERSITY PRESS
NEW HAVEN AND LONDON

For information about this and other Yale University Press publications, please contact:
U.S. Office: sales.press@yale.edu   www.yalebooks.com
Europe Office: sales@yaleup.co.uk   www.yaleup.co.uk

Set in Bembo by IDSUK (DataConnection) Ltd.
Printed in Great Britain by T J International Ltd., Padstow, Cornwall.

Library of Congress Control number: 2009920123

ISBN 978-0-300-09515-9

A catalogue record for this book is available from the British Library.

10 9 8 7 6 5 4 3 2 1

Contents

Illustrations

2   Aby Warburg in Florence in December 1898

'*To locate a thought is child's play, to express it means work*' (HERMANN USENER)

Preface

The great mirrors whose expanse in the past has reflected images and scenes long since vanished . . . (Lilian Whiting)

This book tells of people who have come to terms with the present by attempting to flee from it. The men and women who travelled to Florence at the end of the nineteenth century were seeking a faraway country very different from their own. They already bore its image within them even before their train left Hamburg, Berlin, London or Paris or before their ocean liner had set sail from New York. Like many visitors to Italy before and since, they wanted to find Arcadia.

For them, 'Arcadia' was not just the mountain region of the Peloponnesian peninsula but also the symbol of a Garden of Eden that is older than the moon. Hermes and Pan were born here, herdsmen and shepherds live here in peaceful innocence and in harmony with nature. It is a mythical place beyond history, a place that foreigners seek on the deepest level, believing that they have found an idea of it in the hills of Tuscany and in the narrow winding streets of Florence. And they were no less convinced that emanations of it had been captured in the slides that the private scholar Aby Warburg – the main character in our narrative – projected on to the walls of a Hamburg lecture room in 1899. Our tale, which Hayden White would no doubt have classified as a tragedy, deals in 'Images and Shadows', to quote the title given to her autobiography by Iris Origo, another of the foreigners who chose to live in Tuscany. It tells of the shadows of objects and of images in the brain and, as such, of the only realities that cannot entirely escape from appropriation.

The idea for the present book came from Maurizio Ghelardi. Between cala-mari and *macedonia* at a Venetian trattoria, he suggested that I might write a slender volume on Aby Warburg's years in Florence for an Italian publishing house. Readers will find before them the fruits of this conversation.

The German Research Council supported the project, while a fellow-ship from the British Academy paid for a study trip to London. Work on 'Italia Germania' – a project by the German Ministry for Education and Research – provided me with further opportunities to explore the history of German–Italian relations.

I am particularly grateful to Nicholas Mann, the Director of the Warburg Institute in London, and his predecessor, Joseph B. Trapp, for granting me access to Warburg's unpublished papers. It was Nicholas Mann, moreover, who proposed me for the British Academy fellowship. I was able to discuss various aspects of Warburg's life with the late Sir Ernst H. Gombrich.

I should additionally like to thank the staff of the Warburg Institute, especially Elizabeth McGrath and Susanne Meurer. Expert assistance also came from Anne Marie Meyer and Dorothea McEwan, who helped me to decipher Warburg's handwriting. Special thanks are further due to Belinda Shand and Michael Molnar (London), Peter Clark (Leicester) and Michael Mallett (Warwick).

In Florence I received all the support that I could have asked for from Max Seidel, the Director of the German Art Historical Institute. Maja Häderli and Jan Simane were also of great assistance, as were Maurizio Bossi and the archivists at the Gabinetto Vieusseux. I should also like to place on record my gratitude to the Harvard Center for Renaissance Studies at the Villa I Tatti. It is not the Center's fault that none of Warburg's letters is lodged here. The late Harry Brewster, Adolf von Hildebrand's successor as owner of San Francesco di Paolo, allowed me to experience at first hand one of the mythical sites from turn-of-the-century Florence.

Francisco Bethencourt (Paris), the Calouste Gulbenkian Foundation Museum (Lisbon), Andreas Beyer (Aachen), Anchise Tempestini (Florence) and Hermann Hipp and Hans Meyer-Veden (Hamburg) all helped in obtaining illustrations and in locating sources. I am particularly grateful to the Bode Museum Archives in Berlin for their unbureaucratic assistance.

This book could not have been written without the support of my colleagues at the Villa Vigoni in Menaggio and at the Universities of Bonn and Zurich: Christine Tauber, Christiane Liermann, Simona Della Torre, Stefanie Hanke, André Weibel and Daniela Hacke. Natalie Bräker (Zurich) organized the illustrations and assumed responsibility for the final editing. My working relationship with Karin Beth at C. H. Beck was as agreeable as it was efficient.

Above all, however, I must express my gratitude to Vera and Joachim Burmeister of the Villa Romana on the Via Senese. If the Germans who have settled in Florence over the years have a presiding genius who deserves to have garlands woven in his honour and incense burnt in sacred groves, it is Commendatore Burmeister. The present book owes much to his suggestions, while his hospitality has taught me that the stories of stars and fireflies and Chianti that are found throughout the nineteenth century's more effusive accounts of Arcadian Florence can indeed still come true on warm June nights.

Throughout my work on this book, my family has had to endure my tribulations rather than share in my pleasure in it. I dedicate it to my wife, in memory of our travels in Italy, and to my children.

Zurich, June 2001
Bernd Roeck

Abbreviations

AGV	Archivio del Gabinetto Vieusseux, Firenze
AWI	Archive of the Warburg Institute, University of London
BCF	Biblioteca comunale, Firenze
BNF	Biblioteca nazionale, Firenze
BStBM	Bayerische Staatsbibliothek, Handschriftenabteilung, München
Diaries	Aby Warburg, Diaries, in GC
DLA	Deutsches Literaturarchiv/Schiller-Nationalmuseum, Marbach
FC	Family correspondence (London, AWI)
GC	General correspondence (London, AWI)
NL Bode	Nachlaß Bode (The Bode Estate), Staatliche Museen zu Berlin – Preußischer Kulturbesitz, Zentralarchiv

3 View of Florence

'In the morning, in the gleam of a hundred hopes, almost shimmering with impatient expectation' (RAINER MARIA RILKE)

1

The mirror of Florence

F LORENCE, Sunday 31 December 1899. The weather is mild,[1] the temperature of fifteen degrees positively spring-like. To mark the end of the year, the city's mayor, Pietro Torrigiani, is hosting a reception at the Palazzo Vecchio, while elsewhere in the city, at the prefecture of police and the archbishop's palace, local dignitaries are bidding farewell to the old year and indeed to the old century. Popular attractions include a cinematograph show featuring the Lumière brothers' latest invention and a panorama of the Holy Land. The evening's entertainments include cabarets and *cafés chantants* and performances of Wagner's *Lohengrin* at the Teatro alla Pergola and Mascagni's *Cavalleria rusticana* at the Pagliano. From there audiences make their way to the cathedral for midnight mass, celebrated by the archbishop. In the streets outside, people are waiting for the sound of the bells in the Bargello to mark the end of the year.

Some distance away, in an apartment overlooking the Mugnone, a small party has gathered.[2] Those inhabitants of the Via Lungo Mugnone who have not gone into the city centre will have been able to hear loud singing coming through the closed windows of the property at number twenty-three. The tune is that of Beethoven's setting of Schiller's ode 'To Joy':

Hail! O nineteenth century that / Did into the world us send,
Much reviled and much admired / As you now approach your end:
Greatness you yourself achieved, / Greatness too was thrust on you,
You, the hero, who in armour / Built this house of peace so true.
You have tamed both steam and lightning / In our state of slavery
And from earth's profound depressions / Sunlight now is plain to see.[3]

With the last stroke of midnight, the revellers clink their glasses, wishing each other good health and a happy new year in German, after which they file out into the street. A shortish man with a black walrus moustache is hopping around and holding a doll dressed as a babe in arms, which represents the new century. From a bottle he shakes little scraps of paper, each containing lines of poetry and horoscopes that he reads out to his guests, while at the same time distributing diaries for 1900 and in general carrying on like some caricature of a Florentine *mascalzone*, his undetectable Hamburg accent replaced by stilted Tuscan, each inimitable 'ch' sounding as if he is clearing his throat. And so the nineteenth century comes to its boisterous end as a theatrical extravaganza.

At least when seen from the standpoint of the history of ideas, the little community which gathered under Florence's night sky that winter evening in 1899 must be regarded as fairly select. The high-spirited man who could easily be mistaken for a local is the cultural historian Aby Warburg. Also present are his wife, Mary; a mutual friend, Tilli Mönckeberg from Hamburg; the Dutch writer André Jolles; and, finally, Robert Davidsohn, a historian best known for his work on medieval Florence. It was he who wrote the patriotic anthem on the end of the nineteenth century.

This rite of passage had begun with a meal in the Warburgs' apartment on the Via Lungo Mugnone, while its high point had been the performance of a play organized by Jolles and probably based on Jacob van Maerlant's *Merlijn*.[4] Jolles himself played the magician Merlin, who wakes up from his sleep just once, at the end of the century. Tilli Mönckeberg – who, according to Mary Warburg, was 'as pretty as a picture' – took the part of the Goddess of Fortune, her costume modelled on that of a figure in one of the paintings of Piero della Francesca.

Aby Moritz Warburg was what was then known as a 'young man from a good house'. He was born in Hamburg in 1866 and had had a sheltered adolescence, free from material cares. An oft-reported family legend[5] claimed that, as the oldest of the five sons and two daughters of the Hamburg banker Moritz Warburg, he had renounced his rightful inheritance on the curious condition that his family must instead buy him all the books he needed. Whether or not the story is true, it remains a fact that Aby Warburg did not become a banker. After a certain amount of hesitation, he decided to study archaeology and the history of art, but his interests soon took him beyond the narrower confines of art and into the realms of myth, psychology and biology.[6] A particularly formative influence on his subsequent career was his encounter with the art of the Florentine Renaissance and its sources in the archives of the city, which he visited for the first time after completing his military service in 1888. On that occasion he attended a course organized for a small group of students by the Breslau art historian August Schmarsow, a course that laid the foundations for his lifelong interest in Florence. It was later said that, right up to the end of his life, the people of Florence continued to regard Warburg as a local on the strength of his accent and gesticulatory language, and indeed of his whole demeanour. According to his later assistant, Gertrud Bing, 'physiognomically, too, he stood out less than he did in Hamburg with his slender build and expressive, dark-skinned features'.[7]

Emotionally speaking, Warburg was drawn to more than just the painted beauties of Florence. During the winter of 1888/9 he had been introduced to the young woman from Hamburg whom we have already met and with whom he returned to the Arno in 1897 with the aim of settling there at least for a time. At that period in the city's history he was merely one of the many foreigners who chose to live in Florence. His international fame still lay in the future, and for the present the people around him regarded him only as a well-read, eloquent and indeed witty member of the group of historians and art historians who often met for lectures and excursions and, even more frequently, for leisurely meals and visits to the theatre. A small group of specialists knew his name from his dissertation, which he had just completed and which had taken him deep inside the world of the early Florentine Renaissance and of the poetry of the period – which he compared in masterly fashion with the stylistic features of painting at this time. In poetry he explored in detail the idiosyncratic and often cryptic language of its imagery.

Now, on New Year's Eve 1899, the revellers looked forward confidently to the new century. None the less, there is little doubt that Aby Warburg's behaviour was a little too manic. The truth of the matter is that he was plagued by phobias which were deeply rooted in his troubled psyche. For him, to conjure up the image of Fortuna at the end of the century was entirely typical of his state of mind: Fortuna, after all, was the goddess of fortune but she also summed up the fate of a godless, chaotic world whose inhabitants had begun to navigate the world without the help of the stars. Time and again Warburg scribbled a triple W in his diary, meaning *Was wird werden?* – 'What will happen?'

His fears were probably grounded in the first instance in individual psychological and emotional factors, but they were made worse by his experience of the upheavals that were taking place all around him. Transport and communications were evolving with breathtaking speed, tightening their grip on the world and enclosing it within a cocoon of net-like structures with more and more points of intersection. Social and demographic conditions were changing even more dramatically, while failing to produce any clear solutions to the problems they were causing. Although technological progress made life much easier and gave hope for the future, the key word that sums up the *fin de siècle* was not so much 'new' as 'end', leaving traditional spheres of existence profoundly affected.

The years around 1900 were also a turning point in terms of science and learning. This was the year in which Freud laid the foundations for psycho-analysis and published his study on *The Interpretation of Dreams*. Increasingly insecure, modern individuals descended into the depths of their own soul, while at the same time setting out to measure the dimensions of the universe. Max Planck formulated the fundamentals of quantum mechanics, and in 1905 Albert Einstein published his special theory of relativity. The old picture of the world was thus turned upside down by two great theories which were as yet incompatible. The reader may recall parallels in literature and art. 'There are truths, but no truth,' Robert Musil noted in 1902. 'I can very easily maintain two completely contradictory things and in both cases be right.'[8]

In this way the nineteenth century witnessed the culmination and end of the basic positions of the Enlightenment. It continued to believe in the infinite possibilities of progress, continued to believe that all things were knowable – even if that belief was no longer held with the same degree of conviction as before. Already there was a growing insight into the limitations of human potential. Irrationality and superstition were as widespread as before: this was the age in which great and dangerous ideologies came into being, ideologies that jostled for contemporaries' attention alongside the world's religions.

One extreme conclusion to be drawn from the death of God was man's liberated attitude to death. The late nineteenth century developed a literary and philosophical interest in suicide that no previous era had evinced: it is sufficient in this context to recall Dostoevsky's *Devils*. Suicide became a revolutionary act, a sign of rebellion directed against the world and proof that mankind does indeed lead an autonomous existence.[9] Something that materialistic nihilism sought theoretically to think through to its logical conclusion now found an echo in life. This age was at the same time an age of suicide, and Florence, for all its brilliance, would emerge as one of its principal settings. Of central concern was the question of our attempts to come to terms with change by means of our intellect and the possibility of building something new on the ruins of old Europe. In this context, the recourse to art and its elevation to the status of an object of religious veneration was of considerable significance.

This brings us to the subject of the modern tourist's pilgrimages to Florence – for there is no doubt that the road to Florence took the traveller away from the heart of darkness, away from modern civilization and its unfathomable mysteries, and to Arcadia.

Florence is a good place from which to observe the radical changes between the old world and its modern counterpart. Our subject is this symbolic city, reflected twice over. Florence is a mirror in which we may see elements of our modern world emerging and which is for this reason a prime object of historical analysis; it is the embodiment of a new outlook on life, which had become increasingly clear from the fourteenth century onwards and was later to break open the encrusted shell that enclosed it and to overwhelm the antiquated reality from which it had emerged: and this time it would destroy it for good. Tradition would be left with no more than a wraith-like existence confined within the cocoons of historical monuments, a life cordoned off from present-day existence and able to form constructs only in the 'blessed isles' of archives and libraries. From the standpoint of the present, *fin de siècle* Florence was a miniature old world that saw itself exposed to a belated and shocking modernization process. The view from the tower of the Palazzo Vecchio provided particularly clear evidence of the way the city was bursting out of its shell.

Even today, Florence is an object of longing for many – and not only for the rearguard of the educated middle-class movement of the nineteenth century. The way in which *fin de siècle* observers looked at the city, at its art and surrounding countryside, and even at the cloud formations in the skies above it reveals patterns which, more or less consciously, continue to affect our perception of Florence today.

Our principal means of viewing *fin de siècle* Florence is Aby Warburg's perception of the city, as conveyed through a veritable treasury of letters, diary jottings, published writings and notes. But we shall also consider the things which did not interest the hero of our tale and escaped his observations – most notably, the social movements of the time. His blinkered view reflects that of the middle classes and the perceptions of the artists, art historians and aesthetes who visited Florence with a particular aim in mind and whose interests were correspondingly limited. In all, our account tells of only a few days in the life of turn-of-the-century Florence, and it shows the city largely from the outside, as seen through the eyes of foreigners. Their texts do not produce a film whose thousand images might merge together to create a sense of movement. Rather, they depict a whole series of separate scenes, snapshots whose significance lies in their ability to tell us something about an age of dramatic upheavals. In this age the arts created a sense of meaning and provided a prop in life, acquiring importance in the emotional lives of a bewildered generation.

It is very much through its art that Florence – like Athens and Alexandria – has become one of the mythic sites of world culture. Against the backdrop of the uncertain situation of the arts (a situation which appears to reflect the rapid change in conditions in general) and of the confused mass of Impressionists, Pre-Raphaelites, adherents of *verismo*, Symbolists and early supporters of the *art nouveau* movement, the historical art of Florence seemed to offer a rare degree of stability. Specific forms of aestheticism developed here and a theory of art was proposed which, while not dispensing with certain aspects of modernity, sought to ground itself in a more classical outlook. The work in question was Adolf von Hildebrand's *The Problem of Form in Painting and Sculpture* of 1893. Conrad Fiedler's pioneering theory of art likewise presupposed its author's stay in Florence.

Aby Warburg was later to describe Florence as a 'blessed isle' for the 'cultivated but weary modern men and women', – the tourists who made the pilgrimage to Florence. The city was an aesthetic utopia before whose radiant art the tourists who sought refuge from a hectic and ugly present could sink to their knees in rapt and relieved adoration. Here they could rediscover what had been lost in their own worlds, surrogates for saintliness, focal points for transcendence. The poet Theodor Däubler provides a good example of this.[10] In 1898 – almost certainly in Florence – he drew up a plan to write a 'Divine Comedy' of his own: *Das Nordlicht* (*Aurora Borealis*) was to become a vast and yet comic epic of around thirty thousand lines, its aim being to provide a comprehensive interpretation of existence, a universal panorama. In this monumental *pasticcio* of Christian and mythological set pieces, sun and light are metaphors for the pure spirit, to which the poet hopes to guide his readers from the darkness of the present. The clear minds of the Florentines and the beauty of their city give Däubler his first presentiment of all this,[11] turning him into an eloquent orator prepared to stand his ground against the prophets of doom: myth could offset materialism.

Florence was a kind of Lourdes for enthusiasts, who found rapture and a real awakening here. In the Uffizi, in the Bargello, in the Accademia and in the faintly lit churches with their clouds of incense stood altars to beauty, the magical fetishes of the religion of art whose high priests were Jacob Burckhardt, John Ruskin and Bernard Berenson, spiritual guides on the road to beauty.

The city was a stimulus not only for artists but also for philosophers and scientists. It is arguably no accident that Bertrand Russell started to write what is probably his most famous essay, 'A free man's worship', in Florence around Christmas 1902. It was here that the thirty-year-old philosopher set out to answer the question of humankind's potential in a godless universe and in a world whose very reasons for existing were as inaccessible to human knowledge as was its goal:

That Man is the product of causes which had no prevision of the end they were achieving; that his origin, his growth, his hopes and fears, his loves and his beliefs, are but the outcome of accidental collocations of atoms; that no fire, no heroism, no intensity of thought and feeling, can preserve an individual life beyond the grave; that all the labours of the ages, all the devotion, all the inspiration, all the noonday brightness of human genius, are destined to extinction in the vast death of the solar system, and that the whole temple of Man's achievement must inevitably be buried beneath the debris of a universe in ruins – all these things, if not quite beyond dispute, are yet so nearly certain, that no philosophy which rejects them can hope to stand.[12]

It is clear from his later reminiscences that Russell came to this bleak conclusion in the midst of the most enchanting landscape and the most beautiful art imaginable: at Bernard Berenson's villa on the hillside around Fiesole, surrounded by pine trees, cypresses and holm oaks still decked in their autumn colours. The air, Russell wrote, had been filled with the deep tolling of Italian church bells: 'The human surroundings were ideally the worst, but I spent long days alone on the hillsides & in the groves of olive & cypress, with the Arno below & the austere barren country above.'[13]

Did not this situation already imply an answer to the question raised by Russell? He himself was aware of the distance that separated his puritan upbringing from the art and beauty around him. The world of the aesthetes and art critics was not his, even though he cannot have been unaffected by the charms of the Villa I Tatti and the gardens surrounding it. Russell contrasted the enjoyment of the senses with the work of the intellect, 'pure contemplation' and freedom of thought:

In action, in desire, we must submit perpetually to the tyranny of outside forces; but in thought, in aspiration, we are free, free from our fellow-men, free from the petty planet on which our bodies impotently crawl, free even, while we live, from the tyranny of death. Let us learn, then, that energy of faith which enables us to live constantly in the vision of the good; and let us descend, in action, into the world of fact, with that vision always before us.[14]

It is remarkable that a writer like Russell – a positivist and, as such, someone opposed to all speculative philosophy – should have celebrated a kind of mysticism of pure thought when confronted by a Tuscan country-side echoing with the sound of church bells. He rejoices in the freedom of a mind which, released from all material fetters, is able to contemplate the good. From here, humans can return to the world and prove themselves through the active life. How remote such a view is from the attitude of the Franciscan who, standing before the side altar in his monastery church, sinks to his knees in silent contemplation of a golden image of the Madonna in his search for God, before going forth and doing good works! Russell's superficially rational reaction to the breakdown of accustomed order is seen to be close to mystic thought, the only difference being that the certainties he is looking for are intended to be empirically and logically ascertainable. For him, those certainties do not lie in metaphysical realms accessible only to faith.

Berenson was one of the first to read Russell's essay, but his response was reserved, a reserve he ascribed on a superficial level to questions of style. But the differences between the two men went deeper. For the aesthete, the masterpieces of art that engaged his interest undoubtedly provided a possible answer to the question of existence. This answer was to be found in the very city he could look down at from the heights of Fiesole.

Florence is ultimately a city full of monuments that seem to have been erected as a bulwark against transience and death: the Duomo and the Campanile, embodying the timelessness of the commune; Michelangelo's *David*, defying a more timorous view of the world and symbolizing our self-assertion in the face of all adversity; Santa Croce, housing the mortal remains of the city's great sons, pantheon of the immortal spirit of Florence; San Lorenzo, paying tribute to life everlasting; the Gates of Paradise, leading to salvation – the whole of Florence can be read as a statement against modern pessimism, against all positivist philosophy and against a material-istic view of the world which sees mankind as part of an accidental collo-cation of atoms. Of course, the composition of the Fonte della Fata Morgana centuries earlier had sprung from a spirit that was still assured of great truths. By the years around 1900, the context in which these external forms appeared was different, as they were now divorced from their reli-gious base. If they were worshipped, it was because of their beauty, not because of God, to whose existence they had once attested.

According to Arthur Schopenhauer – by the end of the nineteenth century arguably the most widely read of German philosophers – art featured alongside compassion and philosophy as a preliminary stage leading to the mystery of the pure denial of will and, as such, was one of the ways of rising above human unhappiness and misery. In the blissful, will-less contemplation of art, the blind, instinctual, material will is momentarily overcome: 'We celebrate the Sabbath of the penal servitude of willing; the wheel of Ixion stands still.'[15] It is here that the religion of art of the educated middle classes and the modern aesthetic movement found their most powerful philosophical fundament. The contemplation of beauty was felt to offer the possibility of drawing closer to the absolute, however that term was defined. The beautiful no longer had to point beyond itself to something higher, or even to something divine. Just as all art allows us to feel a desire for sensual gratification, so it is able in principle to assuage that desire, even if it cannot do so always and for everyone. 'Sensuality without sexual attraction in an aesthetic state,' Heinrich Mann noted in his edition of Nietzsche's *On the Genealogy of Morals*.[16]

Tension and its resolution lie at the heart of every aesthetic experience. Or, to be more precise, the essence of a work is to be found in the permanent dialectics between the presentiment of an ideal possibility and the process of gradually coming closer to its realization, when desire is satisfied in a state of disinterested pleasure. For Berenson and many of his contemporaries, this was the most that could be hoped for in the world. Beyond it there was nothing, the sublation of the subject, object and individual – or another form of the religious.

As a result, the meeting between Russell and Berenson on the hillside overlooking Florence has a symbolic significance for our theme. In the art connoisseur and in the philosopher we see two possible attitudes to a world that seemed to be out of joint: on the one hand there is the withdrawal, typical of the educated middle classes, into an aesthetic ambiance which is seen as an absolute; and on the other hand there is the philosophical retreat, exemplified by Russell, to an altar of thought and contemplation.[17]

Although Aby Warburg was to find himself, at least initially, in a different situation from Russell, he too was concerned to identify a space in which he could think, and it was in Florence that he first sought that space. It was a search, moreover, that required years of effort on his part. He was afraid of beauty because it stirred his emotions and in consequence jeopardized the state of equilibrium to which he aspired. For much the same reason he avoided religion. And yet Florence acquired a metaphorical status for him too, as a real and yet ideal, not actual centre of the world. In its intimations of history and beauty lay the possibility of dealing with the modern world.[18] Few of his contemporaries had Warburg's ability to see this connection.

4 Franz von Stuck, *Sin* (*c.*1893)

'Beautiful! – Seductive! – Sensual! – Poisonous! – Consuming brain and veins!
– Unsuspecting! – Ungainly! – Cruel! – Incalculable! – Psychologically tainted!
– Naïve!' (Oskar Panizza)

Trials and tribulations

AT the time of his first visit to Florence in 1888, Aby Warburg was still leading the life of a student with well-lined pockets. That year alone he received over three thousand marks – nearly nine thousand pounds at today's prices – most of which he invested in books which, as he wrote to inform his family in Hamburg, were increasingly becoming good friends.[1] On his very first night in the city he encountered a torchlit funeral procession, an unsettling and yet picturesque experience that would surprise every new visitor to Florence with its sooty torches and its coffin bearers, members of Misericordia, their black cassocks leaving only their wearers' eyes visible – Warburg, too, must have been reminded of a scene from the Middle Ages.[2]

Warburg took rooms at 20 Lungarno delle Grazie for forty-five lire a month (approximately one hundred pounds a month at today's prices). The apartment consisted of a 'large bright south-facing room with a wonderful view through its three windows'.[3] From this apartment Warburg could gaze across the Arno to the hills around San Miniato, the façade of which glittered above a sea of houses. In the evenings especially, the city struck him as relatively tedious. He claimed – rather unfairly – that it was not even possible to get drunk on the heavy, 'undrinkable' Chianti, before going on to report: 'Everything is cooked in oil here, and everything possible – kidneys, spinal cord, brain, feet – everything has a name here and figures as a special dish: this motley society initially amuses one, but it's not long before one prefers a plain honest German to these Italian Harlequins.'[4]

In spite of this, the shorthand jottings in his diary paint an impressionistic picture of a carefree existence divided between his studies and the high life. He and his friends dined at the Giotto and at Paoli's behind Or San

Michele, although their favourite haunt was the Etruria. His diary also mentions circus performances ('the trapeze artiste') and, during the winter of 1888/9, visits to the theatre. There was also work. He earned his first money as a student by revising the local Baedeker, and we often find him in the city's museums, checking locations and names.

Among the older art historians who had settled in Florence, Warburg occasionally met Adolf Bayersdorfer,[5] who had come to the Arno from Munich and who frequented the company of Arnold Böcklin and his circle. He was also a die-hard member of 'Götterdämmerung', a group of Germans who met on a regular basis at one of Florence's hostelries.[6] 'In spite of our many differences, a circle of aesthetes formed of its own accord at that time,' Bayersdorfer recalled: 'Victor Müller, Böcklin, Marées, Thoma, Hillebrandt, Hildebrand, Theodor Heyse, Speidel, Fiedler *et moi*. Art historians of the future may one day discover this group of artists.' Böcklin painted his friend and patron in the style of Hans Holbein, inscribing the portrait *Florence 1875*.

Bayersdorfer is known above all for the position he took in the argument over Holbein that flared up in Dresden in 1871.[7] At stake was the question as to which of the two surviving copies of the *Madonna of Burgomaster Meyer*, in Dresden and Darmstadt, should be attributed to Holbein the Younger and which to a later copyist. The argument is of interest chiefly from a methodological standpoint. Warburg considered the scholarly thrust of Bayersdorfer's views not very profound, describing his elder as a 'whimsical rough diamond'.[8] Essentially he had no time for what Burckhardt, too, had dismissed with not a little irony as 'this childish game of attribution'.

Another art historian whom Warburg occasionally met in Florence was Henry Thode.[9] The two men had already become acquainted while Warburg was studying in Bonn and Thode was about to move to Frankfurt to take up his new position as director of the Städel Institute of Art. Thode had come to prominence as the author of a book on Francis of Assisi which aimed at revising the traditional view of the Renaissance proposed by Burckhardt and saw Saint Francis as the first representative of a new era, an age of 'humanity' when the individual first became free and a subjective 'harmonious and emotional understanding' of nature and religion had evolved. Thode may well have been the first person to alert Warburg to the problem of the transition between the Middle Ages and the modern period, but he also appears to have warned him of the dangers lurking in the overwhelming amount of material available to researchers in Florence.[10]

Thode owed his position in German society not least to the fact that he was Wagner's son-in-law, having married one of the composer's stepdaughters. Thode lectured on Wagner in Bonn, his veneration for the 'tremendous artist' being boundless. On one occasion Thode mentioned Beethoven, Goethe and Wagner in the same breath, hailing all three as representatives of a 'Christianity of the future' and in Warburg's view demonstrating extraordinary arrogance in placing his father-in-law among the gods.[11] At least during his student days, Warburg evidently felt an affinity with the elegant, well-connected Thode, whose darker side – his anti-Semitism and a militant nationalism which formed a remarkable, if by no means rare, alliance with his Protestant Christianity – may have been less pronounced in his university lectures. Within a decade, however, Thode had delivered himself of an anti-Semitic and nationalist tirade against Impressionist art in general and against Max Liebermann in particular.[12]

Together with August Schmarsow and his fellow students, two of whom – Max Semrau and Max J. Friedländer[13] – were already on their way to becoming brilliant art historians, Warburg visited the city's churches, *palazzi* and museums.[14] Even at this early date, he already seems to have taken an interest in the subjects that were to be of importance to him in his later research. On one occasion, for example, his diary mentions an invitation to have tea with Schmarsow, when the two men discussed Botticelli, whose *Birth of Venus* and *Primavera* were later to be the topic of Warburg's dissertation.

It was in the presence of these masterworks of the early Florentine Renaissance that Aby Warburg's love affair with Mary Hertz pursued its poetical course.[15] Warburg acted as guide for the young woman at the Uffizi and probably also at the Accademia. She had come to the city with her father on an educational visit and found in Warburg a knowledgeable, lively and even brilliant companion. In the evening they talked by the hearth in the luxury hotel where the Hertzes were staying. The result was a great nineteenth-century love story whose turning point was set in Florence. Warburg described Mary as his first pupil, and on the evening of one of their initial meetings he wrote the following entry in his diary, encoding it in Greek characters: 'Eos, I thank you for allowing me to see the pure blossoming splendour of her soul!'[16]

Mary Hertz had just turned twenty-two at the time of her first meeting with Aby Warburg in Florence. She was an exceptionally pretty, flaxen-haired young woman from one of the leading families in Hamburg, the daughter of a ship owner and senator, Adolph Ferdinand Hertz. Her family was regarded as strict and puritanical. According to Aby's brother Max, the only luxury they allowed themselves was red wine. 'All the courses arrived on the table at the same time, so afraid were they that the servants might commit some indiscretion.'[17] Mary Hertz was known for her sometimes tomboyish sense of humour, but she must also have been very gentle by nature, a woman of 'the purest heart', as one of the Warburgs' biographers says.[18] A female friend claimed to have learnt from her 'that simplicity and silent grandeur are worth more than the wittiest coquetry and the most winning way of serving tea'.[19] Intelligent and unaffected, she chafed against the constraints imposed on any daughter from a good family – or at least she did so within certain limits. Ernst Gombrich called her a 'young artist', on which point he was correct, as Mary had had painting lessons and later turned her hand to sculpture. It is clear from her best-known piece – the portrait bust of her husband that she made around 1930 – that she was genuinely talented. 'As an artist' was a phrase she sometimes used when referring to herself. It seems that through her art she hoped to rise above the grey conformity of her middle-class surroundings and allow her higher self to express itself. She felt that in her everyday life her 'wings had been clipped' and that she was 'tied by ropes to the ground and to everyday existence'.[20]

'O my dear, dear art!' she wrote on one occasion:

> What an incalculable treasure has been given to me here! It has just struck me yet again what a thoroughly undeserved gift it is from our dear Lord, a gift capable of making me blissfully happy! There was one such moment yesterday when Herr Thiele praised my composition and called me a divinely gifted artist, and I felt that he understood me and that I was his equal – moments like that weigh a great deal with me.[21]

These candid remarks reveal a woman who, although well cared for and sheltered from life, hoped to fulfil some 'higher' purpose, at least until marriage brought her a predictable sense of fulfilment. Like Tonio Kröger in Thomas Mann's short story of the same name, she sought to escape from the dull and lowly life of bourgeois existence. Mary, too, would seek the south, whose sun promised a more luxuriantly mature art.

Following his first visit to Florence, Warburg resumed his studies in Bonn and then at the Imperial University in Strasbourg,[22] where he worked on his dissertation with Hubert Janitschek, who held a chair in art history. But Mary Hertz had been unable to forget the young art historian from Hamburg ever since their first encounter at the Uffizi, and the couple had remained in contact. A further meeting in Hamburg was followed by a tentative rapprochement, attended by veiled references to their emotions and disclosures of various kinds. For the present, their most extreme form of intimacy was to refer to each other as 'comrades', Mary having had the idea of passing herself off as a boy to Aby, a ploy which made it easier to articulate ambiguities and provided them with a screen behind which more intimate confidences could be spoken.

Aby Warburg was not particularly happy in Strasbourg. Not only did he have to work hard, but on more than one occasion he was faced with crude expressions of anti-Semitism,[23] with the result that memories of the time he had spent with Mary Hertz in Florence were correspondingly transfigured. He wrote of the 'golden days' when they had read Vasari 'among roses'. Now he found himself contending with what he called 'armies of ghosts' from the past.[24]

The science of history was now seen as an act of conjuring up ghosts: the scholar's critical understanding and creative imagination fashioned a new world of his or her own from texts and images. This was all that mattered. The profane and often unedifying reality of everyday life sank into nothingness. But Warburg had to remain in control of the ghosts, otherwise his work as a researcher would be threatened. As he saw it, there was the risk that he would become lost in the other world, which was a product of his imagination, and he would be robbed of his reason by dint of a romantic liaison. Much later, in a seminar he gave in Hamburg in 1927 on the subject of Jacob Burckhardt, Warburg was to speak of the dangers that beset the professional historian and of the 'eerie halls' temporarily inhabited by the man who chooses to confront the demons of the past.

Warburg was at risk in this way. Struggling to concentrate, he sought emotional stability in scholarly activity – 'when I have some research to work on, then everything is in order,' he once wrote.[25] At this period in his life, Warburg was still generally able to retain his composure towards the outside world and to regard the inner disquiet that drove him on as a sign of creative strength. 'What is called inner calm', he once opined with feigned contempt, 'always has something of the peace of the graveyard about it.'[26]

Only with the passage of time did Mary Hertz realize that she was dealing with a 'neurotic'. But in the end she decided to be open and to help him, while always remaining concerned to show tact and anxious not to overstep the mark. For the present everything was still in a state of flux, the outcome of their liaison being unclear. The young woman confided her doubts and hopes in a diary, an extremely intimate document which preserves an internal perspective on a difficult relationship and at the same time reveals an astute woman who, emancipated in her own way, ended by humbly submitting to traditional role models.

Mary Hertz's diary is one of those logbooks recording the life of the self that were so popular in the nineteenth century. By the second half of the century, people's preoccupation with their own state of mind and the cult of self-perception had become a veritable obsession.[27] The manic way in which they examined the creviced landscapes of their souls, being now motivated by vanity, now by self-torment, now in a spirit of awestruck hesitation, was inspired in the main by the breakdown of order in nineteenth-century Europe and by the profound uncertainty triggered by technological innovations, social upheavals and the increasing rate of change in all areas of life. Help was promised not only by religion, which retained its importance, but also by mysticism and esotericism. Race, nation and folk became objects of cultic veneration. So too did the 'beautiful' – the least dangerous of all these options. In short, contemporaries were spoilt for choice and, given the threat to the self, were very much driven to self-examination. Diagnosis was the necessary precursor to therapy. Aby Warburg's voluminous diaries – the most important source for the present account – are just as much a part of this wider context as is the diary of his wife. But Warburg's fate also reveals the limitations of therapy. Self-reflection, neurosis, psychosis and ultimately suicide as an extreme position to adopt in response to the question of how to deal with the world – all of this finds its place within this overall context. Never before had such questions been discussed with a comparable degree of intensity.

Mary Hertz's diary jottings similarly revolve around their writer's own inner life and around the highs and lows of her feelings for Aby Warburg. But they also deal with her work as an artist. A preoccupation with her own emotional life and her attempts to express beauty in art – these were two of the answers that could be given to what had become urgent questions as to the meaning of life in a world that had been turned on its head. Mary's diary became a discreet conversationalist who never had cause to blush, a guide through the mansion of the soul. 'O beloved book,' Mary thanked her paper companion on one occasion, 'that I can confide everything, everything in you!'[28]

And how many pages she filled with her musings during the early days of their love! 'I cannot quite understand myself,' she noted in early September 1890: 'I am really not in love with him, and yet I forget everything else when he is there.'[29] A few weeks later, doubts begin to assail her: 'I am starting to think that I am really not capable of any true, deep feelings and that sister Charlotte is right to put forward her butterfly theory! . . . O God! I would give anything in the world not to have such a superficial, fickle heart!'[30] Once we find her jubilant: 'I have been so happy in recent days; everything is so beautiful & sunny & golden, everything is turning out well with my art . . . & my heart is full to overflowing.' And in the very next sentence she goes on: 'Am I really in love with him?'

Mary also had a tendency to start by looking for shortcomings and failings in herself rather than others. (According to Stendhal, those who are in love underestimate their own good qualities and overestimate the least merits of the people they love.) Like any woman of the time, she looked up with feelings approaching awe to her learned 'comrade', and she was proud whenever he initiated her into his scholarly projects.[31] Yet the problem was not only that Mary was not at all sure of her own feelings but that the man she so desired was Jewish, whereas it is clear from her letters and diary entries that she herself was a devout Protestant. As a result she found herself torn between her Christian convictions – which she still identified as the 'good' in her – and the suspicion that she was not free of the anti-Jewish and, indeed, anti-Semitic sentiments that were widespread at this time. In short, she was concerned about what she described as 'prejudices' and 'superficialities'.

For the young Mary Hertz, there were thus many difficulties to be overcome before she could consider any further approach to the fascinating intellectual whom she had met in Florence. The Warburgs were certainly not less well-off than the Hertzes, but they were undoubtedly beneath them socially. For a Christian to marry a Jew was far from self-evident at the turn of the century. For the present it mattered little that Warburg had sought to distance himself from the religion of his forebears. Moreover, his own family could be expected to resist the match. It should not be forgotten that in Germany at this time Jewish families in particular still set great store by traditional forms of marriage-broking and made every attempt to remain within their own cultural and religious circles.

Of course, the nineteenth century was not the first to discover romantic relationships, but there was certainly a greater tendency at this time to move away from the centuries' old principle of the arranged marriage, and not just in the upper echelons of society. The literature of the late eighteenth century, the texts of the Romantics and their imitators and periodicals such as *Die Gartenlaube* all proposed patterns of behaviour in matters of love that were increasingly accepted in real society, and the relationship between Aby Warburg and Mary Hertz turns out on closer examination to exemplify a particular phase in the history of human emotions – so much so, indeed, that Mary Hertz felt obliged to protest that her love was really not the kind that was found in novels.[32]

But ancient traditions still held sway, and both Aby Warburg and Mary Hertz knew that they were violating the rules of the game. Once the matter had become more serious and the question of marriage entered the realm of possibility, the two families took part in discussions and negotiations as if they were still part of some pre-industrial European society. The conflict had several overlapping aspects and was of central importance to all the parties, for the family was still worshipped as sacrosanct in the nineteenth century. No longer principally an economic partnership of convenience, it was a sentimentally transfigured form of existence, a psycho-social institution.

This sanctification of the family is the obverse of those moves towards greater individuality whose expression was romantic love, with all its joys and sorrows. But it could also entail the lascivious and voluptuous view of the erotic embodied by Franz von Stuck's 1893 canvas, *Sin*.[33] All that had been suppressed in reality returned in literature as the only object of colour to have been left in modern life, or so Oscar Wilde insisted. Often it would come in Renaissance garb and in the company of death. The arm briefly revealed through the gauze of a summer dress or momentarily divested of its elbow-length kid glove, revealing delicate purple veins beneath its skin, had been a recurrent topos of nineteenth-century literature but was now felt to be increasingly inadequate as a symbol of the erotic. More powerful stimuli were necessary, hence the image of the beautiful woman who brings death with her in Oscar Panizza's *Council of Love* of 1893: 'Beautiful! – Seductive! – Sensual! – Poisonous! – Consuming brain and veins! – Unsuspecting! – Ungainly! – Cruel! – Incalculable! – Psychologically tainted! – Naïve!'[34]

All this steamy suggestiveness is the very opposite of the burgeoning relationship between Aby Warburg and his 'comrade'. For her part, Mary kept asking herself whether the pyrotechnical energy of the passion they were shameless enough to prefer to conventionality was sufficient to remove the obstacles that lay in their way. Bourgeois convention was showing signs of breaking down, but this is far from saying that the son of a Hamburg banker could be compared with Romeo and a senator's daughter with Juliet. They had difficulties handling romantic love. The object of Mary Hertz's sentimental interest, Aby Warburg, could sometimes be surprisingly unfeeling in his dealings with the woman who was revealing her love to him. His diary entries show him to be discouraged, anxious and plagued by bouts of depression.[35] He travelled a great deal, visiting Florence among other places, in an attempt to find peace of mind and stability in his academic work. One such trip meant that he was out of town when a cholera epidemic broke out in Hamburg.

Warburg in fact spent his whole life running away from himself and from his inner demons. Sometimes he would describe his attempts to come to terms with his own psyche as a titanic struggle, a battle between the highly gifted scholar and his genius: 'To get through it as best they can, to enjoy the life that offers them more than they deserve – only those with below-average gifts succeed in doing this. . . . Finer organisms exist only to be destroyed, but this is a thoroughly decent profession.'[36] He directed his comrade's attention to Carlyle's book on heroes and hero worship, and Mary proved to be fascinated by it: 'What a man! You once called him a moral giant; that describes him. My dear, I don't know, but since I've started reading this book, I again feel much, much closer to you; I mean, I now understand you better . . . Does one not think that one would become a better person as a result? Could one remain in a Carlylean mood in daily life? My God, what an imperfect stick of furniture one is!'[37]

The aim, then, was to come to grips with everyday life by adopting a Carlylean mentality. This passage from Mary Hertz's letter to Aby Warburg also suggests one of the reasons for the Renaissance-like mood of the *fin de siècle*, when a world without heroes sought those heroes in history or in the imagination. Unrealizable fantasies opened up a way of escaping from the tribulations of bourgeois existence: people dreamt that they could rise above the trivial and the vapid, ignore convention and, with a hero's strength, cut the Gordian knot that had tightened around their most private problems. The 'hero' was a brain-spun ideal in a complex world that could not be controlled, or else the individual's own psychosis was defined as a heroic confrontation with life. In Florence, Warburg himself would one day make fun of the 'supermen on their Easter holidays' who came to the city with a copy of Nietzsche's *Thus Spake Zarathustra* in the pocket of their loden coats. In doing so, he was ridiculing exactly the same attitude of helplessness that Mary Hertz had invoked in her letter as a way of facing up to everyday life.

With the passage of time, Mary Hertz became Aby Warburg's closest confidante. She met him during his return visits to Hamburg and wrote long letters to him: 'I know', he explained to her, 'that I have not shown myself worthy of the best and that I am changing from a giver of life into someone who needs another's light – and who knows how soon this will be? You, my dearest, are the only person who has any presentiment of this. Others think me eccentric but on the whole content. But in your flight upwards you have stopped being a comrade and become a nurse. This is eating away at me!'[38]

And yet Warburg did not really want to be helped. For him, there was no alternative to existential suffering. He was more of a Hamlet figure than Carlylean hero or Feuerbach's God. He used his psychological state as a pretext to delay any decision about marriage, a decision that Mary Hertz wanted him to reach. He was anything but decisive by nature, and so we find him writing about a lack of resolve and complaining about his hay fever or observing that he had forfeited all claims to life. On another occasion he wondered about studying medicine,[39] only to announce a few weeks later that he wanted to become a monk as soon as possible – 'but the statutes are too complicated'.[40]

Mary Hertz eventually lost all patience. As she admitted,[41] she had long been content to think as little of herself as she could and to want as little as possible for herself, in other words, to behave as any young woman from a good family was expected to behave. And yet doubts finally began to assail her, and she started to ask herself if this was enough. Was she – she wondered – not increasingly falling into the role of a victim in her curious relationship with Aby Warburg? And a woman who had been so tomboyish in her attitude and so articulate in her dealings with others began to grow unstable in turn. As she later explained,

> I saw that I too had some merit, that my life at home was really one big sacrifice, that the person I loved thought only of himself and that instead of giving me consolation and happiness he brought me only renewed torment. It seemed to me to be unworthy, as he really did not need me at all to continue doing things by halves. It was like throwing myself away.[42]

And so Mary Hertz underwent a course of psychiatric treatment with Kurt Richard Großmann, a hypnotist well known in his day.[43] Warburg thought that this was something really only for sick people and that for their healthy counterparts it amounted to a brutal violation of their will.[44] But all this indicates how isolated Mary Hertz felt in an ocean of feelings that was still largely uncharted at the end of the nineteenth century. Things had certainly been easier in an age when marriages were discussed above the heads of the partners themselves, even if the situation was even more humiliating for the woman. Mary Hertz saw herself faced with the challenge of having to struggle to be accepted as a woman – and an independent woman at that – and to break free from her role as a nurse who could be activated at any moment; and she had to do so, moreover, in her dealings with a neurotic partner who, without realizing it, had assimilated social stereotypes regarding the woman's role in life. However open Warburg may have been to unorthodox methods in art history, he remained conservative, or rather conventional, in his attitude to women's emancipation. Later he even tried to prescribe what his wife should wear.[45] And yet her own attempts at emancipation remained entirely symbolic and were never very far-reaching – for a time she stopped wearing corsets and other unnaturally tight-fitting clothes, but that was all. Marriage was all she strove for in her attempts to resist a world of opposing forces. Aby Warburg was in Florence when he promised to marry her in 1892, but within a year he had already forgotten the date of their official engagement, 26 August.

In September 1894, while they were out walking in Berlin, their conversation took a distinctly dramatic turn.[46] Warburg spoke of a 'disastrous erotic shift' in their correspondence, something for which he assumed complete responsibility. Marriage was now out of the question: Mary could either 'simply destroy' her engagement ring or throw it away, or she could 'destroy it *and* throw it away'. But Mary refused to give up. In a long and revealing letter she tried to find a new basis for her relationship with Warburg: 'You no longer want me to be your wife but prefer me as your best friend instead? . . . Kindly let me have your new address.'[47]

And so they remained in contact, even though Warburg tried to escape from his problems and from the constraints of having to reach a decision by resuming his travels. By now he had completed his dissertation. It was a demanding subject but one that could hardly have been more appropriate to Florence, inasmuch as it revolved around the two main Quattrocento masterpieces that Warburg had shown Mary Hertz on their first meeting: Botticelli's *Birth of Venus* and *Primavera*, both of which embodied the Florentine Renaissance in the eyes of the late nineteenth century.

5   Evelyn De Morgan, *Flora* (1994)

'How Botticellian!' (W. S. GILBERT)

In the realm of Venus

I found in dreams a place of wind and flowers,
Full of sweet trees and colour of glad grass,
In midst whereof there was
A lady clothed like summer with sweet hours.

Swinburne's 'Ballad of life' conjures up a picture of a carefree Garden of
Eden far from any hideous modern industrial setting. The scene is a place
of the imagination, a reflection of the radiantly coloured dream sequences
of the Pre-Raphaelite painters. This place of beauty had its real-life equivalent in Florence, in the Galleria dell'Accademia, in the form of Botticelli's
Primavera. Also known as *Flora, Primavera* forms a pendant to the painter's
Birth of Venus and by the nineteenth century had acquired positively mythical significance.

Both *Primavera* and *The Birth of Venus* were icons of the English Pre-
Raphaelites. In Edgar Jepson's sometimes deeply ironical reminiscences,
Primavera features as the epitome of Victorian taste:

> The Oxford day I enjoyed would be a day in May, with the sun shining
> and a west wind blowing. . . . I would read Pater, slowly, till I had finished
> my pipe, then stroll up to the market to buy some flowers, for the
> Æsthetic Movement was waxing to its height, and I wore my hair long
> and was striving, as Pater prescribed, to become a monochronos [*sic*]
> hedonist. I had hidden the pier glass in my sitting-room under Liberty
> silks, draped round a skull, and my chief picture was the large photograph
> of the Flora, in Botticelli's Primavera.[1]

6   Sandro Botticelli, *Primavera* (*c*.1478)

The critical fortunes of Botticelli's two main works are extraordinary by any standards.[2] In 1880, when he was working as piano tutor to Nadezhda von Meck in Fiesole, Debussy was inspired by the *Primavera* to write an orchestral suite, while Botticelli quite literally haunts the novels, short stories and poems of the period. Many writers felt that satire was the only appropriate response to the effusive enthusiasm for 'Sandro'. 'How Botticellian!' simpers Lady Saphir in *Patience* by Gilbert and Sullivan, a hugely successful parody of the esoteric world of flowers associated with the Pre-Raphaelites, and in particular with Oscar Wilde. The Victorians did not merely rediscover Botticelli, they positively reinvented him.

The way in which contemporaries were to see Botticelli may be found in John Ruskin's Oxford lectures on the painter, and above all in Walter Pater's widely read study of the Renaissance.[3] Ruskin described Botticelli as 'the most learned theologian, the most perfect artist, and the most kind gentleman whom Florence produced'.[4] Botticelli knew everything – certainly more than Dante knew about theology. Ruskin's religious Botticelli was also the Botticelli of the Pre-Raphaelite artists, foremost among whom were Edward Burne-Jones, John Everett Millais, Walter Crane and Evelyn De Morgan.[5]

Pater's view of Botticelli differed substantially from that of his mentor. He saw in Botticelli a poetic, visionary painter 'with a sentiment of ineffable melancholy', an artist who, amoral to the point of blasphemy, embodied the 'freshness, the uncertain and diffident promise' of the early Renaissance in its purest form, making it 'perhaps the most interesting period in the history of the mind. In studying his work one begins to understand to how great a place in human culture the art of Italy had been called.'[6]

The reader needs to be aware of the way in which Botticelli had been overburdened with historical roles and accorded the function of an aesthetic model in order to understand the challenge that Warburg faced when deciding to write his dissertation on two of this painter's greatest works. He wanted to reconstruct the historical Botticelli in contrast to the mythical figure created by men of letters and aesthetes. And Warburg had a very clear picture of the Renaissance, a picture closely associated with aesthetic – and moral – standards. Under the influence of his teacher in Bonn, Karl Lamprecht,[7] he believed that it was possible to relate the course of history to developments in art. The masterpieces of the high Renaissance in the form of the art of Raphael and Leonardo, in whom he was to take an interest during his years in Florence, were in his view the expression of a cultural process. With the harmony of their colours and the balanced proportions of their forms, they represented for him not only the breakthrough of humanity and rationality but also a superior, reserved approach to things. In them it was possible to discern that clear view of the world and of mankind that Jacob Burckhardt declared the hallmark of the period in his famous study *The Civilization of the Renaissance in Italy*, in which the author describes mankind awakening at the dawn of the modern age. Beneath the blue sky of Italy, a veil of 'childish diffidence and delusion' still wafted through the air, a veil that had lain over medieval men and women in their half-dreaming, half-waking state. The classical beauty of antiquity and the accurate observation of life are an expression of a process which is important in terms of world history.

Warburg tries to locate Botticelli within this cultural process. In his dissertation, he argues that, as a result of his particular predilection for calm emotional states, Botticelli was persuaded to give the faces of his figures a 'dreamy, passive beauty': 'One could say of many of Botticelli's women and young men that they have just woken up from a dream and become conscious of the world around them, and even though they engage actively with the outside world, dreamlike images continue to permeate their awareness.' This echoes Burckhardt's view of the Renaissance. Botticelli stands on the cusp between the two ages. There are already signs of a break-through to the modern period, to humanism and the Enlightenment, all of which is adumbrated in the work of art with its soothing beauty, but this development is not yet complete. As Walter Pater puts it, Botticelli still represents an age of 'mournful maturity'.

Warburg saw signs of the older dispensation, above all, in those aspects of Botticelli's art which had so fascinated the Victorians: his ornamental manner of depicting objects and figures and the apparent *naïveté* of the pure and prematurely born artist. Here in particular Warburg saw relics of that 'medieval pleasurableness' that the high Renaissance was to overcome as its principal contribution to civilization. But Warburg also sought in his hero another, more forward-looking aspect. This was the liberation of the figure of Venus who, no longer a planetary icon or token of dark superstition, appears before the observer as pure and naked as a classical statue. Above all, however, he believed that in a number of details in both paintings he could see signs of a more accurate observation of reality – features, in short, of a naturalistic interpretation of objects that was to point the way forward in the direction of the modern period.

Only against this background does it become clearer why Warburg took such a detailed interest in the question whether it is possible to prove that Botticelli's masterpieces reflect literary conventions, concrete classical models or 'real life'.[8] His dissertation represents an attempt to decode their specific historical context, and he believed he had discovered that context in a tournament that Giuliano de' Medici organized in honour of his lover Simonetta Vespucci Cattaneo on 28 January 1475. The young woman in question died only shortly afterwards. A poem – 'Giostra' – by Angelo Poliziano, a writer closely associated with the court of Lorenzo the Magnificent, provides the missing link; for Poliziano mentions the death of the beautiful nymph Simonetta, in whom Warburg sees a literary reflex of Simonetta Vespucci. Warburg even makes it seem likely that Poliziano's description of the nymph anticipates important aspects of Botticelli's depiction of the goddess of spring. But he also posits a link between Poliziano's poem and *The Birth of Venus*, arguing that the representation of the goddess on the seashore spreading a cloth over the newly born Venus is a transfigured portrait of Simonetta. *The Birth of Venus* features Simonetta in the idealized form of a nymph and with her actual facial characteristics.[9] In such naturalism Warburg saw a distinctly forward-looking feature.

On the other hand, Warburg took exception to the manner in which Botticelli appeared not to subscribe to Winckelmann's ideal of a calm and harmonious antiquity. In particular, the billowing garments with which the artist clothed his figures pointed to classical models such as dancing maenads. These 'accessories in motion' – to use Gombrich's translation – seemed to be intended as a way of indicating agitation and 'the semblance of intensified life', which suggested the echo of an unbridled 'Dionysian' antiquity. In Warburg's eyes the use of this element was dangerous, requiring careful thought and considerable moral awareness. It seemed to him that

Botticelli was wrestling with his surroundings and with the seething world of incipient modernity. It was a struggle which, in Warburg's view, Botticelli had not entirely won, as he had slipped into the purely ornamental – which led Warburg to conclude that Botticelli was still one of those artists who had been too 'flexible'.

But Warburg also believed that Botticelli's naturalistic features placed him in the evolving tradition of mankind's increasing liberation from our 'medieval' shackles. 'Is our admiration and respect for Sandro Botticelli diminished by our realization that he is complicated as an artist?' he later summed up his thinking. 'Is it not perhaps a gain if we can feel that his mythological images also document the struggle of an enlightened individual? A fellow combatant fighting alongside his brave precursors in the intellectual field, poets and thinkers who, like him, dared to look for a new, classical, ideal way of expressing inner and outer movement in words and images for the new humanism that was very much of this world?'[10]

If *The Birth of Venus* was closer to nature than it seemed to be at first sight, then this clearly had consequences for its aesthetic assessment. In the present case, the painting was 'more truthful' than one cobbled together from traditional formal elements. In a word, Botticelli was not at all 'Botticellian' but in Warburg's eyes was more naturalistic than his admirers, brought up in the school of Pater and Ruskin, would have us believe. Herein lay the artist's true significance. In Warburg's view, the aspects of Botticelli's work that *fin de siècle* audiences liked most of all were precisely the ones which, being traditional, deserved most to be thrown into the lumber room of aesthetics.

As a historical study, Warburg's dissertation was pioneering, even if today's readers will no more share his view of the Middle Ages than they will subscribe to his conception of the Renaissance. Its importance lay in the fact that Warburg used written sources to interpret works of art, placing those works in a concrete relationship with a specific patron and in that way helping to revise the 'mythical' picture of Botticelli. This did not, of course, make Botticelli a representative of naturalism, but it did at least allow him to appear to be modern within the context of his own particular age. In adopting this approach, Warburg was also attempting to break out of the vicious circle that circumscribed the artist's work. The Pre-Raphaelites thought that they shared Botticelli's principles, while *Jugendstil*, *art nouveau* and the Italian Liberty style could all claim something in common with their great Renaissance forebear. As a result, the quality of the model[11] was retrospectively justified. 'Is it really possible that he was so like us?' mocked a number of sceptics at this time.[12]

Warburg was aware that his research had contemporary relevance.[13] On one occasion, for example, he asked if a friend could point him towards writings 'in which Botticelli is idolized or criticized'. In particular, he was interested in 'semi-belletristic remarks by foreign contemporaries such as Anatole France in *Le Lys rouge*, Zola in *Rome* and Léon Daudet in *Kamchatka*'. From the manner in which turn-of-the-century writers responded to Botticelli, Warburg drew conclusions not only for some of their own artistic criteria, which Warburg believed were misguided; he also judged the products of the present day by the same standards. He was devastatingly critical of *Jugendstil* and of the Pre-Raphaelites, dismissing them for being even more 'flexible' than Botticelli had been with regard to the spirit of the times. Walter Benjamin went even further when discerning a 'line of vice' in *Jugendstil* and contrasting it with those of emancipation and of priesthood.[14]

In a review he submitted to the periodical *Pan*, Warburg attacked what he called the '*fin de siècle* pose of self-indulgent languor',[15] by which he meant a lack of resistance to the purely 'pleasurable' elements that he so disliked in Botticelli's work. He also took this opportunity to proclaim his high regard for an uninhibitedly artistic view of 'life'. To contrast this with 'our humourless, rushed daily routine' was 'a task that could almost be described as ethical'. On another occasion he drew a parallel between his own age and the Quattrocento, a century capable of preferring Benozzo Gozzoli to an Andrea Castagno or a Donatello. 'The situation was no different then from what it is today: the affably conciliatory was preferred to the emotionally impressive, the Lutteroths occupying the position that should have been taken by Segantini.'[16]

In Warburg's view, ornament was a sign of decadence with the moderns, too. Artists pleaded for the use of the Corinthian order in architecture, for example, because it was closest to the spirit of an age that demanded the greatest possible accumulation of details within the available space.[17] But, Warburg argued, the task of any 'true' and great artist was not simply to reproduce contemporary taste. *Jugendstil* – or indeed any ornamental view of things – was suspect in his eyes because it seemed to him to be a mere construct and hence untrue, a product of a defective sense of artistic morality: 'There is nothing comparable in nature, with the result that in the course of time the mere repetition of the form will reveal its lack of truthfulness, allowing us to see its creator as a stylizing, finite individual.'[18] At the heart of the ornament is the repetition of forms, but this, Warburg felt, was profoundly unnatural. His was a contemporary aesthetic evaluation, a clear stance towards the *fin de siècle* debates about art history, debates in which – as in the Arts and Crafts Movement and in *Jugendstil* – there were signs that the gap between the fine arts and the decorative arts was beginning to close.

But the opposing position was already being formulated. According to this view, the beauty of a form should lie above all in its functionality. Anyone familiar with the writings of Nietzsche could appeal to the case of Botticelli to draw up the equation: the ornament = female = decadent. Adolf Loos's famous remark about ornament as a 'crime', first articulated in 1908, was already in the air at this time.[19]

But Warburg's critical examination of the ornament was concerned with more than just an aesthetic problem. The suspicion that the 'pleasurable' and the ornamental indicated a lack of artistic resolve and a failing sense of artistic morality demanded closer investigation in order to discover why this should be so. Warburg did not attempt to explore this new line of enquiry in his dissertation, but surviving notes show that he none the less grappled with it in detail.[20] His enquiry culminated not in a history of taste or in an examination of the art market but in speculations on the psychology of the ornament based on the theories of the nineteenth-century German writer on aesthetics Friedrich Theodor Vischer.

This brings us closest to Warburg's inner world of experience, as he was dealing here with questions that exercised him on the profoundest level. 'Only those objects are reproduced in the visual arts', he noted, 'which are ordered or mastered either in our imagination or in practice and which are no longer to be feared.'[21] The '*pleasingly* animated' seemed to him to be the least dangerous of all forms.[22] The ornamental flourish, being 'pointless or self-referential', could never run the suspicion of approaching the observer as something 'hostile'.[23] To observe the ornament was to take 'pleasure in contemplating the unthreatening plenitude of life'.[24] The 'pleasingly animated' reckoned on our ability 'to control the world around us and to delight in a controlled existence'.[25] This is a recurrent and central idea, which plays a leading role in Warburg's later writings but still remains in the background in his study of Botticelli.

Warburg's remarks suggest an anthropological interpretation of the ornament, which is seen as a cure or remedy in dealing with a world which is felt to be confused and dangerous. In Bonn, Warburg's teacher was the mythographer Hermann Usener, who had shown him that in primitive societies images could be amulets against fear and that they could serve as a way of coming to terms with a dangerous world. Warburg's interpretation was also inspired by ideas drawn from the contemporary behavioural sciences and from developmental physiology. Writings on the subject were readily available to him in Florence, which was then a stronghold of Darwinism.[26] It is tempting to speculate that these considerations were also bound up with Warburg's own phobias.[27]

But how was it possible to come to terms with the horrors of the world? Certainly not by means of ornamental flourishes. The only practicable route, in Warburg's eyes, was science and logical, discursive thinking. Writing to Mary Hertz, he stressed the superiority of the scientific approach in dealing with the world over all artistic attempts to find one's bearings.[28]

Mary Hertz's reply took the form of a long letter which is also interesting for the way it documents the relationship between the sexes at the end of the nineteenth century. On the one hand we have a young woman who admits to her intellectual inferiority ('only now do I notice how unused I am to keenly focused thinking and how much I have to trespass on your patience & forbearance') and, on the other, the 'revered' scholar who gives pleasure to his correspondent by telling her about his intellectual work. But she would like to speak as someone who 'herself has a bit of artist' in her and who writes defensively and with the forcefulness of a person directly affected by the accusation that art is merely a 'transitional state' leading to a third stage in the explanation of the world:

> If the situation were as you think it is, why would an artist find such perfect satisfaction in his art as soon as he approaches his ideal or even achieves it? . . . Why does the mere exercise of his art make him so utterly happy? . . . Does an artist know why he paints? (I mean a genuine artist.) Does he know why he has interpreted & created something in one way rather than another? Even I myself, a bungling beginner, have on occasions stood before my own botched effort & wondered how I'd done it; there is something inside me that forces me – without any effort on my part – to do it in such and such a way, rather than any other. Of course, this effortlessness ends as soon as it becomes a matter of executing the idea or the draft; I don't think that any amount of hard work or teaching can help with this first fleeting indication of what lies in the depths of the mind, still less can it help to achieve the genuine warmth of feeling that is created by such an idea. But it is mainly only energy, lasting hard work and care that are needed to realize this idea and to visualize it according to the ideas of our great mistress, Nature, without harming the original individual idea.

Mary Hertz's description of the artist's creative work is thus based on experience. Without actually expressing the idea as such, she saw inspiration as a higher force, something that came from deep inside her – certainly she did not regard it as the reflex of some phobia or other, or as the reflection of social conditions. As a result she confessed that she could not really see the contradiction that Warburg felt was the constitutive element in any artist's work.

Warburg's attempts to interpret works of art from a biological standpoint were bound to fail, as they ignored tradition and the weight of convention and omitted to take account of the complex and subtle way in which societies differ from one another. After all, it is extremely doubtful that the function of Renaissance works of art or ornaments can be grasped by means of categories such as 'banishment', 'appropriation',[29] the act of 'being threatened' and 'the overcoming of one's fears'. Renaissance Florence was not the home of Stone Age men and women who used pictorial imagery to 'appropriate' parts of the world around them or who were afraid of the creatures striding towards the observer in the pictures under review.

A scholar who saw it as his business to wrestle with 'armies of ghosts' must have found such ideas less wayward. Warburg evidently took the matrix of the neurotic, instinctual individual as the yardstick for his anthropological speculations. This was a type of person who was abundantly familiar to contemporaries in an age as 'neurotic' as Warburg's own. Around 1900 he expressed a wish to write the definitive 'book about "primitive man" '.[30] At the same time, we have to admit that behind his efforts lay a serious attempt to use the methods of what was then the new discipline of psychology to question more or less woolly aesthetic categories such as the concept of 'empathy', which had been central to Vischer's aesthetic.

In her letter, Mary Hertz drew attention to the possibility of stylistic developments which do not need to be justified as reflexes of collective psychological facts. 'You justify your view by arguing that art goes into decline as soon as it becomes ornamental, and this certainly makes sense to me,' she conceded, while at the same time wondering if this was not an inevitable stage in the history of art.

> People cannot bear to remain for any length of time on a very lofty standpoint once it has been finally achieved; in some way or other we must once again descend to a lower level; people cannot go beyond this lofty standpoint, they can achieve nothing better and so they resort to imitation – ultimately only purely superficially and in respect of form – & because they miss something in this mindless form, they attempt to replace it with a multiplicity & volatility of forms until everything becomes flat and superficial, & this lasts until a rebirth takes place, a rebirth that starts out from pure Nature.

In writing this, Mary Hertz provided a relatively precise description of the situation in the arts around the turn of the century, in other words, at the very moment when modernism was making its breakthrough. In Florence, too, there was much talk of a renaissance in art at this time, and the columns of the *Marzocco*, for example, were full of articles on the subject. But there was no clear idea as to what this rebirth should look like.

As for Warburg's dissertation, it is hardly surprising to learn that Florence's writers on aesthetics had little idea what to make of it.[31] The University of Strasbourg dignified it with the description '*docte et acute*', while the scholarly community reacted favourably to it. Above all, Warburg must have been pleased that the great Renaissance scholar Jacob Burckhardt dropped him a line, thanking him for sending him a copy[32] and encouraging Warburg to turn his attention to Botticelli as a 'mystic theologian'. No doubt he was alluding to Ruskin's assessment of Botticelli as 'the most learned theologian', although this was in fact the aspect of Botticelli that interested Warburg the least, inasmuch as it reflected the more traditional, backward-looking aspect of the painter. This was the only direct contact between Warburg and Burckhardt.

On completing his doctorate, Warburg did his military service in Karlsruhe, then treated himself to another visit to Florence, where he studied sixteenth-century pageantry.[33] His diaries indicate that he also undertook a number of visits to neighbouring towns, including Arezzo, Perugia and Siena. In addition, he made contact with a number of his fellow countrymen and other foreign nationals. He called on the Wagnerian Jessie Hillebrand, née Laussot, and attended an evening at the German Club at which Arnold Böcklin was also present.[34] He also saw a lot of the English art dealer and writer Herbert Horne and spent Thanksgiving Day 1894 with a group of American friends.[35]

Warburg travelled to the United States in September 1895, a visit which, at least on a superficial level, was prompted by the wedding of his brother Paul and Nina Loeb. In the event his journey was to become a part of the Warburg myth, when he attended a snake-dance by the Pueblo Indians in New Mexico and watched the dancers attempt to make it rain, convincing himself that figurative art played a functional role in 'primitive' cultures.

7 Mary and Aby Warburg (*c.*1900)

'The twilight deepens, yet the fantastic rock formations still shine brightly in a muted roseate glow like an echo of the vanished sun' (MARY WARBURG)

4

Judaeo-Christian *divan*

Wɪᴛʜ the passage of time, the tensions between Aby Warburg and Mary Hertz that had come to a head in Berlin began to ease, or, rather, Mary Hertz decided 'not to make a fuss' and fell in with the ways of her 'comrade', accepting his whims because she suspected how sick was the mind which concealed itself behind the pretence of hard-heartedness.

Following his return from America, the question as to Warburg's professional future assumed a greater urgency. He was now thirty, but, although he had no permanent appointment in prospect, he was not really looking for one. There was, however, one decision that he did take at this time, when he finally made up his mind to marry Mary Hertz. Conceivably an unsettling experience with a woman he met on his visit to America may have confirmed him in his decision finally to sort out the matter.

Since 1868, there had no longer been any legal obstacles to a marriage between a Jew and a non-Jew in Hamburg. Throughout the Reich the Jews had full civic rights, even though many positions in the army, judiciary and civil service, and even at universities, were still barred to them in practice.

Objections to their marriage came less from Mary Hertz's Protestant family than from Aby Warburg's father. Moritz Warburg had been born in 1838,[1] but it was not until the death of his brother Siegmund in 1889 that he took over as head of the family bank. By that date the Warburgs were among the financial elite of Hamburg. Aby Warburg grew up in an elegant house on the Mittelweg, where the family's lifestyle was distinctly upper-class. The fact that he had no regular profession and as a result had no income of his own was no serious impediment to his marriage. M. M. Warburg & Co. was a well-respected enterprise with a hand in the city's economic policies, even if its image was relatively middle-class. Even so, the firm had been involved in the establishment of the Commerz- und Disconto-Bank in 1870 and through a series of astute marriages had forged its first contacts with European high finance. The bank had begun to expand in Moritz's lifetime and already enjoyed an international reputation, a development in which Aby's two brothers, Max and Paul, played a not insignificant part.[2]

Moritz Warburg was a thoughtful individual, to whom probity mattered more than anything. He is said to have summed up his business maxim under the claim that it was easier to earn money with one's behind than with one's head.[3] At the same time he was not lacking in vanity and always ensured that he maintained a reputable appearance. He was an amateur musician and revered Brahms. Even on the most superficial level, he was a bon vivant who regarded fine wines, good food and aromatic cigars as essential to his lifestyle. But there was far more to his character than this. His most salient character-istic was the bond he felt with Jewish religion and Jewish culture. He gave considerable financial help to Hamburg's Jewish community,[4] establishing an orphanage and supporting the Jewish Hospital and the Talmud Torah School. He was uncompromising in upholding the laws which were important in his daily life, ensuring, for example, that on Friday evenings only non-smokers were invited to his home: he had no wish to offend visitors who smoked by preventing them from doing so after midnight, when no fires could be lit.[5] He took great care to ensure that only kosher food was eaten, and even his children were forbidden to carry books on the Sabbath. For tasks that they themselves were prevented from undertaking on the Sabbath, the family employed Christian servants whom they called 'Sabbath boys'.[6]

Of course, religion was uppermost in Moritz Warburg's mind when he resolved to stick rigorously to the precepts of his forefathers, but he was also concerned to preserve the Jews' sense of identity in the face of threats from the likes of Wilhelm Marr, whose anti-Semitic rabble-rousing was rife in Hamburg, while the Court Chaplain Adolf Stoecker was inveighing against the 'Jewish cancer' in Berlin. In their everyday lives, by contrast, it seems that the Warburgs rarely encountered anti-Jewish outbursts, and Moritz Warburg even appears to have deluded himself about the prevailing mood.[7] The Zionist leader Chaim Weizmann felt that the German Jews of this period were living in a world of total make-believe, being convinced that their position was secure and feeling inordinately proud of their achieve-ments.[8] Only later did it become clear to him that, even at this time, a powerful anti-Semitism was evolving which, backed by a theoretical thrust, was to have ultimately fatal consequences.

But the identity of the Jewish community was threatened not only from outside. In the first instance it was not a socially or culturally cohesive group, as there were vast differences between the poor Jews who had come from the east and the rich bankers who had lived in the city for generations, and between orthodox Jews and those who wanted reform. As a result, it is impossible to speak of the Jews as a unified stratum or group. Many wanted integration or, to be more accurate, they aspired to acculturation with the norms and values of bourgeois culture. According to Aby's nephew Eric, the Warburgs' only ambition was to be 'a respected bourgeois family'.[9] No doubt they would have concurred with the view of Walter Rathenau who, in his 1897 article 'Listen, Israel!', saw the goal of the assimilation process to be 'Jews who, German by nature, are brought up to be Germans'. Equally certainly they regarded themselves as the 'Jewish patricians' of the 'intellectual and physical culture' that Rathenau was hoping for.

Other Orthodox Jews had to struggle to prevent themselves from being cut off from non-Jewish bourgeois society in Hamburg.[10] Aby Warburg once complained bitterly that it was only in his imagination that his father had connections in Hamburg; and he certainly did not share the latter's view that traditional Jewish culture was superior to its German counterpart.[11] Members of the older generation in particular were faced by the dilemma of wanting to advance socially while at the same time maintaining their sense of Jewish identity.

The young Aby Warburg found himself in a difficult position here. Occasionally he and his brothers and sisters would make fun of the customs in their parental home, but he was conscious of a certain 'otherness' and aware that, purely physically, he conformed to his contemporaries' stereotype of the Jewish physiognomy. He must have a 'very pronounced oriental veneer', he wrote on one occasion. Physically – and therefore inescapably – he felt closer to the despised Orthodox Jews than he liked.[12] Every day he would take special care to be well shaved, being determined at all costs to avoid even a shadow of a 'Jewish beard'. In much the same way he sought to distance himself from his co-religionists, speaking of 'ghetto Jews', for example, and referring to others as 'parvenus' and 'Jewish snobs'.

It is entirely symptomatic of Warburg's ambivalent attitude towards the social world of German Jews from which he was growing apart that he thought he could see the roots of anti-Semitism, above all, in the behaviour of these very same 'snobs'. Arguably the most difficult thing for a German brought up as a Christian, he once wrote, was not to follow one's basic instincts and not 'to pull a sour face when registering the provocatively repellent behaviour of the newly propertied classes'.[13] As for the German Jews who had emigrated to France, and 'above all the Levantine Jews', he thought that, 'even if they had not caused the general state of corruption, they had at least added to it'.[14] During his student days, Aby Warburg still remained loyal to his father, yet even at that time he was already drawing a clear line between himself and Jewish Orthodoxy.[15] Later he rejected all religious rites, dismissing them as an expression of irrationality and wherever possible refusing to take any part in them.

The specific problem of the Jews in the German Reich was bound up with a more general crisis in religious attitudes at this time. Paradoxically, one of the causes of modern anti-Semitism lay in the breakdown of older Christian denominational certainties: precisely because the Christian picture of the Jew as an enemy was now obsolete, a new 'theoretical' justification for anti-Semitism was needed, a justification which was ultimately found in obscure racist teachings. Not even Aby Warburg was entirely remote from all this,[16] and it was only his critical attitude to the Judaism practised by his father that enabled him finally to aspire to a 'mixed marriage' with Mary Hertz. The letters he wrote her in the mid-nineties speak of a profound scepticism towards the more superficial aspects of religion: 'I do not believe that God is concerned very much with the detailed execution of our life's plan,' he wrote on one occasion.[17] No doubt he did not dare tell Mary Hertz that the God of the Old Testament struck him as just as improbable a phenomenon as that of the New.

The casual tone that Warburg customarily adopted when discussing matters of religion within the family circle emerges from a conversation about death with his little daughter Marietta that took place some years later and that he recorded in his diary: 'Pippus, how do people actually die?' the child had asked. 'They fall asleep.' 'Do people learn how to do that at school?' 'I don't think so, because people don't have such a precise answer to the question.' 'I wouldn't like to fall asleep like that because everyone becomes angels, and I'd like to play with the angels; then you fly like that – and then our dear Lord receives more and more angels and then everywhere is full, and there's nowhere left.' 'But', Warburg comforted his little daughter, 'heaven is so big that it never gets full.'[18]

Warburg once provided us with a deeper insight into his own inner life when he described Ludwig Feuerbach's *Theogony* as one of the finest human achievements. This essay was written towards the end of the philosopher's life and treated the 'wish' – the product of the gulf between wanting and being able to do something – as the object of a psychological theory.[19] Here the gods appear as creatures of the imagination for whom wanting to do something and being able to do it are one and the same thing. They are products of our wishes and appear to grant us what is denied to limited human possibilities on their own. For Feuerbach, there is no existence beyond the natural world. The critic of religion does not even share the general belief in immortality, but sees it as the expression of our egoistic struggle to assert our own independence.

All of this was diametrically opposed to Jewish orthodoxy, of course, just as it was at odds with the attitude taken by Warburg's father, an attitude from which Warburg sought increasingly to distance himself. 'In casting aside the formulaic nonsense of my inherited religion, I have forfeited the right to purely religious uplift: without forcing myself to do so through any act of sentimental self-mortification, I can no longer bring myself to pray. Anyone who devotes himself to science and to the world will find his reward there.'[20] Warburg, too, was 'God-forsaken', a metaphysically isolated representative of modernity, and this was a burden that he had to bear as best he could.

In May 1897, Mary Hertz and her father travelled to Lyme Regis in Dorset for a few weeks' holiday. In Mary's case the trip no doubt represented an attempt to distance herself from the trials and tribulations attendant upon her engagement. She wrote to Warburg from Land's End, painting an atmospheric portrait which was also a metaphor of her own situation in life:

The sun has just set, a red-hot ball in a purple haze. A diminutive figure leaps nimbly out of one of the low-silled windows of the small, lonely house on the cliff and jumps quickly down the steep slope, then stands leaning against one of the great boulders projecting over the abyss, entirely alone, a single speck in a vast landscape. Beneath it the breakers roar unceasingly, thundering black waters and bluish white spume, a seagull floats gently past, and beyond it another, while single sails glide over the watery surface in the twilit distance. . . . The twilight deepens, yet the fantastical rock formations still shine brightly in a muted roseate glow like an echo of the vanished sun; but in the opposite direction the moon is already rising, round and golden in its bluish twilit surroundings. The small figure is still standing there, thinking and dreaming, its hair flying around its head, before it too finally feels the cold night wind that has sprung up. The figure wakes up and disappears along the path by which it had come, silent and noiseless.[21]

The small figure is Mary Hertz, her romantic song of destiny a symbolic image of her own situation – whether or not she was conscious of this, we cannot say. The reader may imagine the scene as a landscape in the style of Charles-François Daubigny: in it we can see the small figure of a woman, alone beside the storm-tossed sea. The seagulls above her are like dreams. Then there is the cold night wind that draws her back from the golden light of a self-absorbed setting and restores her to a less poetical reality. It is difficult not to interpret her portrait as an allegory of the 'modern loneliness' that its artist felt all around her.

But there was still her religion. Could the basis of her own character really remain a closed book to her lover, she once asked herself.[22] Mary contrasted the certainty of her Protestant faith with Warburg's doubts. 'Formulae have never helped anyone in life,' she wrote to him.[23] Even their love for each other, she said on another occasion, came from God; it all depended on believing that God was more powerful than the world or the devil.[24] A number of Mary's letters became regular sermons, and in some cases she must have had a Bible open beside her when she wrote them. In the early days of her love she confided to her diary the hope that her God would one day be Aby's God, but this hope was never to be realized.[25]

Meanwhile the question of their marriage took a decisive turn when two of the couple's relations intervened: John Hertz, a brother of the fiancée and a friend of Aby's since their time together as students in Bonn; and then Aby's mother, Charlotte. But the real problem was the attitude of Moritz Warburg. As Aby explained to Mary's family, he had 'in the sixty years of his life, against wind, weather, and passing currents, stood for the principle that Jews had their own ideals and shouldn't give them up'.[26] Aby Warburg was not seriously thinking of converting to Protestantism, even though his fiancée seems to have broached the subject on more than one occasion. The Hertz family, for its part, remained remarkably tolerant, neither Mary's parents nor her brother placing any obstacles in the way of the planned union in spite of the fact that, as a prominent member of Hamburg's Lutheran Synod, Senator Hertz was far from moderate in his views.[27]

Towards his own father, Aby refused to compromise. During this period we find him writing to his friend Paul Ruben,[28] an Old Testament scholar, asking for detailed information about the significance of circumcision, which he had been told represented 'the minimum of concrete Judaism'. Even in Oxford, Ruben wrote back, 'a good half of all the boys' were circumcised: 'If an educated town in a "civilized nation" does not find this so terrible – for all I know, for health reasons – then we do not need to be so very alarmed if it is demanded for other, respectable reasons.'[29] But the reference to Oxford made no impression, and Warburg vigorously rejected his father's suggestion that his sons should be circumcised and brought up in the Jewish faith. Although he did not convert to Protestantism, it is noteworthy that when his father died in late January 1910 he refused to fulfil the first-born's obligation to say the Kaddish – the Jewish prayer for the dead: 'It lacks all style, especially if you respect your father; my own respect for him lies in the fact that I am not hushing up a fundamental difference in our philosophies by means of a superficial ritualistic act, for I am a dissident.'[30]

The moving conflict that was triggered by Aby Warburg's decision to marry Mary Hertz reflects the contradictions that existed between the old,

8   Jan Pieter Veth, *Charlotte and Moritz Warburg* (*c*.1900)

self-contained Jewish world and its modern equivalent; for Moritz Warburg, too, remained inflexible. In mid-April 1897 we find him writing to his first-born son in his laborious, deliberate script:

> Never have I felt the truth of the poet's words 'Two souls, alas! dwell here within my breast' as clearly as I do now, so difficult is this time for us all. I am fully justified in wishing that right up to the end of my life I may be able to tell myself that I have been honest with myself + my family. If my views are a cause of sorrow to many, including my nearest and dearest, that saddens me, but I can also say: 'Here I stand, I cannot do otherwise.'[31]

As a result of this, Aby Warburg decided to dispense with his father's permission to marry Mary Hertz, while complaining to his mother about her husband's 'patriarchal sentimentality'. His father had grown unworldly, he went on; he had no real friends willing to tell him the truth. 'The most ridiculous part of it all', he continued, 'is that you want everything to be done or not done out of consideration for the outside world, and yet you have practically no contact with this world. Society is an extremely crude construction in which "sensitive souls" are exposed to ruin or unproductiveness.'[32] He was not acting out of frivolousness or egoism, he insisted, but was being honest with himself, convinced as he was that he was fulfilling a lofty, ethical duty.[33] Was his father prepared to support him in the future, something that he, Aby, could hardly expect him to do? Moritz Warburg merely added a reluctant note to the letter to the effect that Aby would of course continue to receive 6,500 marks a year. His brother Max, who was increasingly turning into the real head of the bank, was instructed to inform Aby of this arrangement. Money was not to be a means of exerting pressure in this psychological drama.

The engagement was officially announced in July 1897. Now that her in-laws had finally been won over, Mary wrote to assure them that all she could do from now on was to direct all her 'thoughts and actions' to her 'one great aim in life: to make Aby happy'.[34] And, as a good son, the bridegroom-to-be wrote to assure his mother of his abiding love for her.[35] Towards his father, he stressed that he was no 'turncoat' and would never convert to Christianity.[36] 'Do you know of a similar case in German society where in similar circumstances a mixed marriage was conceded by the Christian side?' he asked. This in itself proved 'how much people respect our position'.

Moritz Warburg ended the correspondence with a touching letter whose awkward phraseology barely conceals the sender's profound emotion, not to say his disturbed state of mind:

> I must have peace and quiet for a while, and so I would ask you not to demand from me *anything* that I would not give of my own free will. The thought that it was always a source of supreme happiness for me to bear aloft the flag of noble Jewry, whereas from a distance I can now see that flag at half-mast, is naturally still so overwhelming that I cannot write very much.

But he assured his son that he loved and respected Mary Hertz and asked Aby to pass on his best wishes to her and her family. 'The Almighty', he concluded, 'will give me the strength to get over this most difficult period in my life.'[37]

The wedding finally took place on 8 October 1897. It was a quiet affair, held as it was at the Hertzes' family home outside Hamburg. The participants did not want to compromise themselves in the eyes of the Jewish community. Neither Moritz Warburg nor Charlotte attended the ceremony, an absence that Charlotte must have found particularly painful. But Moritz wrote a friendly letter.[38] The young couple decided to set up house in Florence, a decision which set the seal on their flight from a vague and questionable reality. It remained an open question, however, whether it would usher in the paradisaical existence promised by the name of the city: Florence was, in Lilian Whiting's words, the city of flowers and the flower of cities.

9   Giorgio Sommer, View of Florence from the Boboli Gardens (*c.*1868)

*'One stands on a higher level, can see further behind one, but from the front
the prospect always remains infinite, and the journey begins anew'*
(ADOLF VON HILDEBRAND)

Wonderful light:
A city at the dawn of the modern age

Florence at this period was home to a man whose art and life epitomize the fault lines and transitions between the older type of society and the modern world: that man was the painter Arnold Böcklin. His arrival on the banks of the Arno is bound up with a curious episode, for in his interest in technology he had taken it into his head to build a flying machine.[1] He may also have been motivated by the wish to demonstrate that, like his great predecessor Leonardo da Vinci, he was a *uomo universale*. He worked on the project for years, and even petitioned the military airship division in Berlin. As early as 1881 he had travelled into the countryside around Florence with a number of fellow artists with whom he was friendly, in order to test the machine: they camped, cooked and caroused on the hillsides around the city. But the episode was no boy-scout adventure, and Böcklin and his friends appear to have managed to build at least a glider before a summer storm shattered all their hopes and the howling winds tossed the machine through the air and destroyed it. It is said that the peasants who lived in the area suspected that behind all the noise and campfires and attempts at flying lay some kind of witchcraft, with the result that the local priest had to exorcize the scene by means of a solemn procession with banners and crosses, the traditional resources of magic being used to resist the demon of modern technology. Weeks later, the local peasants were still picking up the pieces of Böcklin's pioneering achievement, seeing in them infernal meteoric particles from the future.

It was a different, much older world that lay outside the city in the villages of Tuscany and Romagna and in the remote fastnesses and farmsteads of the Apennines. The American writer Charles Godfrey Leland, who was a friend of the Pre-Raphaelite painter Edward Burne-Jones as well as being a noted translator of Heine's poetry and the author of a number of humorous books on the lives of German Americans, visited the countryside around Florence in order to study local customs and to demonstrate that a knowledge of magic had survived there since the days of the Etruscans. Whatever the historical basis to his findings, readers of his voluminous studies have always discovered themselves in a strange, archaic world which seems to anticipate D. H. Lawrence's romantic picture of the Etruscans.[2]

At the same time, however, Florence was becoming a modern city, even if its newspapers were still reporting stories from the old world that included ghostly apparitions at the local cemetery, for example:[3] clairvoyants and faith healers could rely on a good trade. By the end of the nineteenth century attempts were made here too to take stock of the situation: statistics began to accumulate and the figures started to make sense.

By the final decade of the nineteenth century this sizeable provincial town numbered more than 190,000 inhabitants. It was still a banking centre, albeit less internationally influential than it had been during the late Middle Ages and early Renaissance. It supported numerous trades and crafts as well as publishing houses, metal-processing works, foundries and a number of instrument builders and clockmakers, including the famous firm of the Officina Galileo, which was founded in 1867. In Doccia, beyond the city gates, was the no less famous Richard Ginori porcelain works, which in the years around 1896 employed fourteen hundred workers in grounds extending over an area of 75,000 square metres. There were also straw workers who made fans, mats, the typical Florentine hats or *monachine* and, of course, countless thousands of straw containers for bottles of Chianti. The largest employer within the city itself was the state-owned cigarette factory which employed two thousand workers. Everything could still be encompassed within a single overview. By far the majority of Florentines worked in traditional crafts, although tourism was already demanding its due, and there were numerous service industries supporting thousands of people.

The city's craftsmen, together with a veritable army of handymen, day labourers and a growing number of factory workers, completely outnumbered the burghers of Florence, who comprised a relatively small stratum of society. Even so, the level of literacy was comparatively high and certainly above the average compared with the rest of Italy.[4] The tone was set by a small elite:[5] by the local aristocracy, with its extensive possessions in the surrounding area; by bankers, landowners, businessmen and lawyers; by the 'classic' middle classes, made up of literary figures, artists, teachers and journalists; and, finally, by the civil servants, who worked in local and national government. The key political positions were in the hands of the city's leading families, who treated those positions like inherited fiefs.

Florence at this time contained around four hundred rich or well-to-do households, each of which employed an average of five servants. A man like Pier Francesco Rinuccini – the second-richest man in Florence after Prince Corsini – had no fewer than twenty servants on his payroll.[6]

Tuscany, and more especially Florence, were still largely untouched by industrialization. This was no accident, but the result of the local aristocracy's unwillingness to invest. Rome's economic policies became a retarding factor, playing into the hands of the traditionally minded and paternalistic ruling classes, which – at least within certain limits – wanted the historic picture of Florence to remain unspoilt. The '*arti rumorose e dannose all' igenie pubblica*' – those trades that were 'noisy or injurious to public health' – were to be kept well away from the city centre.[7]

Herein lay the deeper reasons for the fact that, as one contemporary observer noted, the waves of modern life lost their elemental force on the banks of the Arno: 'Anyone who has just arrived in Florence from the outside world and who still has the tempo of modern life in their limbs feels like a ball falling into a woolsack.'[8] The English writer Thomas Hardy described the city, quite simply, as 'soothing'. And yet by the end of the nineteenth century conditions were changing fundamentally.

At this date the city had still retained its clear contours, outlines which, evident from the famous fifteenth-century *View of Florence with the Chain*, had barely been obscured. A town plan from 1895 shows where modernism was already beating at the gates in the guise of the gasometer not far from the Porta San Frediano, the clear-cut lines of the railway that swept into the town to the west of the Fortezza da Basso, terminating at the Stazione Centrale, and, only a short distance away, the buildings that housed the railway management and workshops and where the Stazione Porta al Prato was later to be built.

As before, entrance to the city was still largely effected through the vast late medieval gates on whose walls painted saints watched over the inhabitants' welfare and spiritual well-being. Administratively, too, a tax barrier where the *dazio* – a customs duty – was levied divided the city from the surrounding area. The old ditches and ramparts had been replaced by broad streets, boulevards and squares: from the Viale Umberto to the Viale Principessa Margherita and beyond it to the Viale Carlo Alberto, the city was girdled by a belt of ring roads, all of which bore patriotic names. Parks were laid out in the shadow of the old city walls, in some cases on the site of those very walls. And new squares such as the Piazza Beccaria were opened up. Close to the Piazza Cavour was the Parterre, while the Parco delle Cascine extended along the Arno to the west. The Florentine nobleman and popular novelist Carlo Placci called the latter Florence's 'Bois de Boulogne', while the German writer Theodor Fontane earlier described it as 'half Rotten Row in Hyde Park, half Hofjägerallee in Berlin'.[9] But the city had already begun to outgrow its old confines, extending as far as the Mugnone in the north and the railway line in the east. The first industrial quarter was established in the suburb of Cure in the north-east.

In the south, the famous Piazzale Michelangelo, with its 1875 monument based on bronze replicas of Michelangelo's *David* and figures from the Medici Chapel, offered a superb view of Florence and continues to this day to present visitors with a picture-postcard perspective on the city. Symbols of Florentine power, art and faith tower up above the confused mass of houses and narrow streets, while at the heart of the city stands the stark tower of the Palazzo Vecchio and the unique group of buildings that includes the Campanile and the Duomo, with its famous cupola. From up there the observer scarcely suspects the far-reaching changes that the old inner city underwent during the final decades of the nineteenth century.

Yet the number of Florence's inhabitants – 190,000 – had increased dramatically.[10] Even as recently as 1861, that number had been no larger than 114,000. In the years around 1900, considerable social inequalities were becoming apparent. Demographic structures, too, revealed differences. On the whole – and this is a sign of the simultaneity of the non-simultaneous – the traditional types of family remained largely intact,[11] the relevant statistics revealing that the old structures continued in existence until after the Second World War. To all intents and purposes, the number of typically modern 'nuclear family' households with between two and three members did not increase between 1810 and 1936, while at the same time the number of larger households of the 'old European' type, with six or seven members, likewise remained virtually the same. At least in terms of family structures, the turn of the century did not prove to be a watershed.[12] In the working-class quarters of Florence, in particular, conditions were still those of the pre-industrial age, with high birth rates and equally high mortality rates.

At the same time, the violent swings in mortality rates and the temperature curve of epidemics and famines now grew more infrequent, inasmuch as they had been characteristic features of the population structures of the older type of society.[13] In general – and for the most part this explains the growth in population – mortality rates fell considerably in the course of the nineteenth century, a more detailed analysis revealing that there was no comparison between the mortality crises of the late Middle Ages and those of the early modern period. To a certain extent we are witnesses here to the final convulsions of the dying demographic body of old Europe, for circumstances in general were changing out of all recognition, changes which from a secular point of view found particularly clear expression in Florence, where the mortality rate – 41.1 per thousand between 1791 and 1860 – had sunk on average to 26.3 per thousand by 1890. Only in the centre of the city did the figure remain higher than the average for Tuscany as a whole. The reasons for this discrepancy are to be found in the inner city's poorer sanitation.

Contemporaries were well aware that one of the main reasons for the fall in mortality rates lay in better sanitation and improvements in the provision of drinking water. Indeed, the main purpose of a wide-ranging statistical survey was to furnish proof of the links between the two. The trend clearly began to gather pace during the 1880s, when the number of individual households with access to drinking water rose from two hundred to three thousand, and the length of the city's sewers increased from five hundred metres to twelve kilometres.[14] The writer Isolde Kurz recalls a noisy pump which forced water into a large container, providing her work with a disruptive accompaniment – 'at this date there was still no plumbing in houses in Florence'.[15] This was the 1880s. Somewhat later, Aby Warburg wrote to Karl Baedeker, whose guide to Florence he had agreed to revise, suggesting that in the new edition there should be a specific reference to the improvements in sanitary conditions in the city: 'The mortality rate of 21.85 achieved in 1896 places Florence on a par with the best rates found in other modern metropolises.'[16]

A modern metropolis? The suspicion that Florence had not yet achieved that distinction fuelled an inferiority complex in many of the city's inhabitants.[17] The loss of its function as a capital – a brief five-year intermezzo in the city's history that was regarded as one of its most brilliant periods – formed the background for many of the sensitivities that made up the Florentine mentality, its specific *campanilismo* fed by countless resentments. The age of the glamorous salons in which statesmen and intellectuals gathered around *grandes dames* such as Emilia Peruzzi and Maria Ratazzi was drawing to a close. The city's inhabitants had earlier felt that they were at the heart of Italy not just geographically, and regretted that the political centrality that seemed to them to be appropriate to the city's position had moved to the south. It is significant in this context that in 1897 the Florentines agonized over whether or not the great Eleonora Duse would honour '*questa nostra povera Firenze*' – 'our poor Florence' – with a visit.[18] They hoped to dispel the accusation of provinciality by means of grand gestures which were sometimes visibly exaggerated. The resentment felt by those who thought they had come off badly remained plain for all to see.

The city's architectural heritage at its medieval centre underwent a radical transformation in the final decades of the nineteenth century.[19] The urban changes pioneered by Baron Haussmann in Paris were associated with the name of Giuseppe Poggi in Florence. He was a great urban developer and the

single most important figure in the rebuilding of the old city. Considerations
of hygiene and the need to improve the traffic infrastructure were adduced
as reasons for destroying the medieval *palazzi* and for building straight wide
roads. This plan also provided for a reparcelling of the agricultural land, a
project that was without precedent in the whole history of Fiorenza. The
ghetto was forcibly cleared, the old buildings torn down and the inhabitants
relocated. At the same time, the Baptistery was fully revealed for the first time
when the historic buildings surrounding it were removed.

The most significant and – even now – the most egregious example of
this redevelopment was the destruction of the Mercato Vecchio, a picturesque conglomeration of patrician towers and palaces, small shrines, loggias,
workshops, banks and courtyards in which canaries could be heard
singing.[20] They were replaced by the showy Piazza Vittorio Emanuele II –
now the Piazza Repubblica – which, heavy with symbolism, rose up over
the forum of ancient Florentia. The Arcone was built in 1895 and provided
access to the Via Strozzi. One of the local councillors, Isidoro del Lungo,
wrote a resplendent inscription, which seems wholly out of place in the
context of the square's sterile Risorgimento architecture: *'L'antico centro
della città da secolare squallore a nuova vita restituito'* – 'The old centre of the
centre restored to new life after centuries of squalor'. Augustus Hare's guide
to Florence adds its own dry and more appropriate comment to this: 'This
most interesting part of Florence was doomed to destruction by its ignorant and short-sighted municipality in 1889.'

Some observers found it difficult to conceal their emotion when
lamenting the city fathers' radical redevelopment of its historic centre.[21]
Isolde Kurz, for example, was able to see the old heart of the town before
its destruction: 'I lived on the Viale Margherita, and from there my journey
took me along the Via Strozzi,' she recalled. 'At that date it was still a long,
narrow, and unimaginably dirty alley lined with market stalls and tables and
dominated by a constant screeching and by all the bustle of a fairground. I
have never again smelt the odours that combined there to produce an
asphyxiating miasma that quite literally took your breath away. It is impossible to list everything that sweltered and roasted on open fires, combining
its smells with those of the musty junk laid out on the vendors' tables.'[22]

Kurz's account of the ghetto is no less impressive, albeit tainted by the
inevitable anti-Semitic undertow. She describes it as 'a hotbed of crime and
the breeding ground of all epidemics', before recalling one final, ghostly
'resurrection' of the old Jewish quarter during the 1886 carnival, when
the empty houses were used as a backdrop for a spectacle like something
out of the *Arabian Nights*: camels were driven through the narrow streets,
bazaars, coffee houses, caravanserais, and flower-filled courtyards were built

as oriental perfumes rose above them, creating a veritable *fin de siècle* fresco. Immediately afterwards workmen arrived with their shovels and pickaxes: 'And years later, when the scaffolding finally came down, old Florence was no longer there but had been replaced by a new one.'

This was the new Florence: a city of modern sewers and paved roads – a major topic of discussion at council meetings in the closing years of the century. It was also a much brighter city, with public lighting – night was being progressively conquered as the old paraffin lamps were replaced by gas street lamps. Such progress was of course very slow on the edges of the city and in the suburbs. Gas was favoured above all because of its lower cost. According to calculations drawn up by one of the city's civil servants, a Signor Lenci, it cost 140 lire a night to light the city by gas, whereas the equivalent figure for paraffin was 220 lire. Moreover, gas light was forty per cent brighter, in addition to which it was switched off at midnight rather than at eleven o'clock at night. By his own admission, Lenci had made it a point of principle to wage war on paraffin lighting.[23] Others, including the town councillor Giovanni Rosadi, protested at the way in which the city was being ruined through the introduction of gas street lighting.[24]

At the same time, *fin-de-siècle* Florence was turning into a city of public clocks. Until recently, a cannon shot from Fort Belvedere had informed the local population when it was midday.[25] In 1897 the town council debated the question whether a clock with an illuminated dial should be incorporated into the restored tower of the Palazzo Vecchio, so that residents could tell the time at night as well as during the day. (In the event aesthetic considerations prevailed, and the council decided not to illuminate the dial.) The city's chief planning officer suggested that, as in Milan and Genoa – after Turin, the most obvious models on which Florence could base its modernizing ideas – ten to fifteen electric clocks should be positioned in prominent public places. This made sense, the speaker went on, not least because, in recording infringements of local bylaws, the police generally did not know what time to enter in the charge sheet.[26]

The problem of dividing up the day into exact units and, more especially, the question of the availability of information about such matters emerges as one of the most basic aspects of the modernization process.[27] Three concepts – those of increasing precision, increasing objectivity and increasing availability of information to the general public – have influenced modern attitudes to time since the church's method of dividing up the day was replaced by a middle-class and, finally, a mechanical way of defining time. This was a development which in late nineteenth-century Florence moved with exceptional speed thanks to its close correlation with the increase in traffic and other forms of communication. A curious painting in the Boston Public Library symbolizes the transition from the old world to the new in terms of communications: *Physics* is a mural depicting two female figures floating on telegraph wires, one a figure of light, the other veiled. According to the artist: 'By the wondrous agency of Electricity, Speech flashes through Space and swift as lightning bears tidings of good and evil.' The contrast between the depiction of modern technology and ancient allegorical imagery inevitably strikes today's observer as unintentionally comical. In spite of this, the artist, Pierre-Cécile Puvis de Chavannes, was much revered by the aesthetes of Florence.[28]

The telegraph and telephone spread their web-like network over the whole of the country, inevitably taking in Florence too. By 1901 it was connected by direct lines to five other towns and cities. By way of comparison, Milan had eleven such lines, Rome only two. A light-hearted *festa del progresso* was held to inaugurate the new line between Florence and San Casciano, and in his speech Sidney Sonnino invited his fellow citizens to complete their country's 'third Risorgimento' by embracing technology and modernization.[29] By 1901 there were telephone lines between Florence, Pisa, Lucca and Pistoia, as well as with Siena. By November 1903 a direct line from Florence to Rome and Naples had finally been completed.

Despite all this, Italy remained hopelessly backward when compared with other countries, as many contemporaries were acutely aware. By 1900, as one observer complained, there were only a little more than one thousand kilometres of private and state-owned telephone lines on the peninsula, whereas France had sixty thousand and Germany more than eighty-two thousand.[30] The Italian telegraph network was equally incomplete,[31] although by 1895 it was possible to send telegrams from Florence to towns and cities in every continent apart from Australia.[32]

Meanwhile, Italy too was shrinking. By 1895 Florence was a rail terminus for lines from Arezzo/Rome, Faenza, Pistoia and Livorno. In 1900 the city council tried to establish a direct rail link between Florence and Siena. A bridge over the Arno at Signa, for which the council set aside funds in its 1900/01 budget, was to cut the journey time to Empoli.[33] After the turn of the century efforts were redoubled to provide a direct rail link between Rome, Florence and Bologna.[34] Further examples could be given: attempts to shorten journeys, to link up with other networks and to increase speeds are all part of a single, almost unbroken development which was moving at breakneck speed.

Within the 'new' Florence, one of the principal means of reducing distances was the bicycle. In the years around 1900 this was still a luxury object, a means of transportation that conferred great prestige on its owner inasmuch as it cannot have cost much less than a horse.[35] Hiring a bicycle was also relatively expensive, at up to two lire an hour.[36] It comes as no surprise, therefore, to discover that this object is invariably found in turn-of-the-century photographs as a refined and fashionable accessory, literally held up for inspection by its proud owner. A curious piece in *Nuova Antologia* even expressed the fear that young people might be so fascinated by the bicycle that they would not even shy away from robbery and murder in their desire to possess a velocipede and thus enjoy the cachet granted to cyclists.[37] Luigi Masetti cycled from Florence to Yasnaya Polyana in order to visit Tolstoy, who gave him a signed photograph with a personal inscription. Masetti's feat was reported in the local papers.

The car still played a largely insignificant role in turn-of-the-century Florence, although council debates at this period already considered the question whether the city should invest in a form of technology that might soon be outmoded if cars took over from trams.[38] By 1903 car registration plates had become compulsory,[39] although trams remained the main means of transport. At this date Florence's trams were still operated by three different forms of energy, horse power, steam and electricity, which together symbolized the coexistence of three different periods in the evolving history of technology.

Debates about local roads and their impact on the city were intense and even violent. One particular source of controversy was the impact of introducing electrically operated trams, a subject which was especially delicate as some of the roads led through the city's historic heart. Central to the debate was the establishment of an *anello centrale* designed to run from the cathedral to the new Piazza Vittorio Emanuele II and from there to the Piazza del Signoria and hence to the station.[40] One councillor argued that, however beautiful they tried to make the electricity masts in the Piazza del Duomo, they would still look hideous next to the Campanile. And in the debate over the installation of electricity cables in the Piazza SS Annunziata another councillor expressed his amazement that anyone could have had the temerity to fix electricity cables beneath Andrea della Robbia's ceramic reliefs.[41] 'Let's stop destroying our city,' Councillor Edoardo Philipson exclaimed.[42]

The town council's discussions surrounding overhead electricity cables can be followed in detail in council minutes preserved in the city's archives and include an aspect that might easily be overlooked by today's reader in so far as it reveals a sensitivity to detail alien to the present age. Time and again we encounter signs of an 'old European' urban aesthetics which was not for a moment prepared to accept a tangled mass of traffic signs and traffic markings, to say nothing of masts and cables or the thoughtless asymmetries that we encounter in all our towns and cities today, even in their historic centres. In the course of one of these debates, Lenci had to draw his fellow councillors' attention to the fact that the steel cables were barely visible, being only a few millimetres thick and seven metres above the ground.[43]

By modern standards, the Florence of the tramways was undoubtedly still a picturesque city, with none of today's queues of cars blocking the streets, no buses and no motor scooters racing up and down the narrow alleyways. Even so, Isolde Kurz felt that the changes brought about by the new means of transport were already distressing.[44] In the 1880s traffic users had still been as considerate and polite as in the corridors of an ancient *palazzo*. Above all, she noticed that all this reflected the new sense of time discussed above. 'Everyone had time in abundance,' she noted immediately before the introduction of the latest means of transport. 'Never again shall I see such vast amounts of time as I did in Florence at that period. People had not yet heard of a "tranvai" and not even of the most modest horse-drawn tram.'[45]

By the turn of the century old and new were rubbing shoulders, one such example occurring at San Domenico in Fiesole, where we find Aby Warburg and André Jolles one winter's morning in 1900. In the distance they could hear the chimes of the old Cunefrana del Populo, which had been ringing for centuries. The idyllic setting inspired the two men to attempt to sum up the previous century.[46] At the time, Warburg still felt that the conquest of time and space, the opening of the Suez Canal and the invention of the telegraph and telephone were major achievements, and it was not until much later that the new media made him bewail the loss of a 'space for thinking' – a development he regarded as a sad symptom of modernity.[47]

A few weeks later, Hermann Hesse found himself in more or less the same setting. His report on his visit suggests that the new perception of time had still not been generally accepted. Following a heady excursion – 'the whole valley of the Arno, including Florence, surrounded in a pink haze, while the mountains were a deep purple' – he wanted to return to Florence by tram: 'As I was somewhat exhausted, the tram driver kindly waited until I had finished my glass of wine.'[48]

The intrusive advance of the new century's novel media was a subject unto itself. Foremost among them were the panorama,[49] the gramophone and the cinema. In January 1897, for example, the Lumière brothers gave a spectacular demonstration of their new cinematograph in Florence in the presence of the Neapolitan royal couple,[50] repeating the presentation in the winter of 1899–1900. 'Living photographs' were projected on to a huge screen measuring up to twenty-five by thirty metres. A similar demonstration at the Paris World Exhibition in 1900 elicited an equally enthusiastic response.

Sometimes modernity arrived quietly and inconspicuously, as with the pneumatic tyres which were fitted to Florence's cabs in 1900.[51] The reporter

10   Visitors walking through the Cascine

of *La Nazione* tested the invention, much as we nowadays test cars: '*una gita veramente deliziosa!*' Scarcely noticed by contemporaries, countless lesser steps in the direction of modernization resulted cumulatively in completely different living conditions. But the city was still surrounded by a customs barrier. Here as elsewhere, affairs of honour were still settled by duels,[52] between three and six cases being reported each year. Old and dangerous epidemics such as bubonic plague were still feared in the city.[53] And the advantages and disadvantages of another new invention – the typewriter – were the subject of lively debates.[54]

A more isolated example of modernization was the plan, documented from 1898 onwards, to build a factory for artificial ice in Florence. Its initiators wanted to levy protective tariffs on ice in order to make the scheme financially viable,[55] ice still being imported from the Apennines in Tuscany, as it had been for centuries. During the summer of 1897, which was especially hot, carts laden with blocks of ice were attacked. Ice was demanded at any price and had to be imported from Moncenisio.[56]

A brilliant essay by the English novelist Violet Paget, who lived in Florence and wrote under the pen name of Vernon Lee, describes the whole world of the Apennines, a world as close as it was remote, reflecting the gap that had opened up between tradition and modernity:

> My San Marcellese friends told me, what I can perfectly believe (for I could catch the gleams of the gilding of Florence Cathedral), that the shepherds up there, among the wind-warped beeches, and the snow-stunted junipers, look down of a night on the while flare of Florence, of gas and electricity; boys who, in all probability, have never been as far as Pistoia, and for whom San Marcello is the capital of the universe.[57]

Florentine society, including the city's *jeunesse dorée* and the visitors sipping their *granita* on the boulevards, will scarcely have given a moment's thought to the fact that the way in which refreshments of this kind were produced was another example of the rift opening up between old Europe and the modern world. It was not until the middle of the nineteenth century that the technology existed for producing machines that manufactured ice.[58] The Florence that these people saw and wanted to see – *their* Florence – generally proves to differ significantly from what emerges after a glance at local newspapers such as *La Nazione* or at the minutes of council meetings and other sources which document the city's history. The Florence of their perception was not the city of tramways and bicycles, not the city of new sewers and electrically operated clocks. It was not even the clean and chic Florence of Giuseppe Poggi. The Florence of these cultural tourists had its own, highly selective reality: it was a place where a past regarded as great and significant appeared to take on actual form. Florence had never been old, argued the writer Louise de la Ramée, who published under the name of 'Ouida'. Its history was of an enchanting presence: 'If you buy a posy of anemones in March or a bouquet of lilies in April, you can carry them around in the same part of the city in which Ghirlandaio as a boy once played between the garlands of gold and silver that his father had made for the young heads of the Renaissance.'[59]

Few visitors were unimpressed by the city, although their number naturally included writers keen to provoke their readers by consciously distancing themselves from the usual clichés mindlessly repeated by Florence's enthusiastic advocates. The classic example of this is the English writer and journalist Arnold Bennett, who, adopting an arrogant, blasé tone, offers harsh and apodictic views of carefully stylized ignorance:

> I walked through the Court of the Uffizzi [*sic*] without knowing that it was the Uffizzi.... Mancinelli concert last night in the Cinquecento Hall of the Palazzo Vecchio. Vast sala. Brutal and sanguinary frescoes of battle on a gigantic scale.... I went out at 10.30 to S. Maria Novella, and was

not much impressed by it as a church. Certain frescoes good. . . . I went as far as the Carmine, to see the Masaccio frescoes, which did not powerfully impress me.'

In the Uffizi he was impressed above all by Lucas Cranach and the Dutch school, his high estimation of Cranach's work apparently stemming from the fact that the artist was not mentioned by Baedeker. That he also liked Benozzo Gozzoli merely confirms what we already suspect about his taste in art.[60]

For the majority of visitors, however, the stones of Florence provided the backdrop to a Romantic play, sometimes with the unthreatening horrors of staged dramas filled with violence and passion, sometimes with sublime Renaissance settings, beautiful conversations and tender contacts beneath amethyst-coloured skies, all of them images permeated by the scents of summer.

There is scarcely a traveller's tale, scarcely a short story set in Florence that does not refer leitmotivically to the scent of orange and lemon blossom, jasmine and magnolia, mistletoe, roses and lilies as a means of evoking a view of a city whose very name implies the idea of flowers and growth. 'And when I thought of Florence,' wrote Proust, 'it was of a town miraculously scented and flower-like, since it was called the City of the Lilies, and its cathedral, Our Lady of the Flower.'[61] Proust never set foot in Florence, and so the image he offers is one that he distilled from his readings. The same is not true of Paul Klee, a great painter who was also a great writer and one whose picture of Florence is surprisingly Romantic, for all its ironic language. He describes himself walking down into the town from Fiesole beneath the April moon, the city lying spread out at his feet in a cloud of perfumes. 'Overpowering smell of wisteria & lilac, which grow here in vast numbers. Also the singing of my first nightingales. Only an envious cur was still of this world.'[62] Hermann Hesse looked at Florence from the Boboli Gardens, gazing through the translucent air at the distant mountains, where snow gleamed on the highest peaks. He wandered through the 'dense, high, dark lines of laurel', waxed lyrical over the bright green leaves of the chestnut trees and flower-filled meadows and imagined young boys playing ball and elegantly dressed patrician women of the Cinquecento listening to Ariosto read from his own works.

The paradisaical landscape conjured up images of the past, enhancing what Theodor Fontane in his *Walks through the Brandenburg Marches* called the 'wonderful light' by making observers aware of objects' ability to bear witness to that past. Soon after his arrival in Florence in 1894, André Gide noted how happy he was to be in the city of the Medici and of Savonarola – two examples of the extremities of which the city was capable.[63] And in her effusive

The Florence of Landor, Lilian Whiting wrote that the Florence of the present was always the Florence of the past:

> The narrow, winding streets with their arcades, their overhanging loggias, the glow of color in niches and arch that surprises the eye, are thronged with invisible forms, and the irregular stone pavements echo to the tread of invisible footsteps. Every turn is invested with poetic legend; every hour is filled with beauty. A morning atmosphere, clear as crystal, reveals the mountain ranges in tints of rose, purple, and azure, veined with colors that sparkle and change before the gaze like the flash of jewels. Again a wraith-like haze veils valley and mountains in the softest blue air, that half reveals and half conceals the towers and the ancient walls.[64]

This way of seeing Florence was typical of visitors to the city. They hid its modern and unattractive aspects – the two were often synonymous – behind a gauze woven from historicism and aestheticism. Old objects became set pieces in historical scenes while history was transfigured as poetry, Florence dissolving into metaphors and conceptualized images on the part of its observers. Only then did it become real for them.

Even the camera was freely used to conjure up a picture of the past, modern technology serving to create worlds of the imagination. Thomas Mann, for example, used photographs to transport himself back in time. While working on his play *Fiorenza*, he asked a friend to make notes on the world of Lorenzo the Magnificent in Careggi.[65] The set pieces in the drama were all carefully researched from a philological standpoint, an aspect of the piece that puzzled contemporary critics. Its background was supplied by the framework created by Gobineau, Nietzsche and Burckhardt, a framework featuring prefigurations of what one wants to see.

And so the present was systematically excluded, a point that sets these writings apart from the work of Italian naturalists such as Giovanni Verga and Luigi Capuana, who saw only the Florence of their own day. Readers hoped they would assimilate something of the spirit of old Florence and were inclined to rapt astonishment. The 'afternoon lights', wrote Henry James,

> carry you close to these admirable elevations, which hang over Florence on all sides, and if in the foreground your sense is a trifle perplexed by the white pavements dotted here and there with a policeman or a nurse-maid, you have only to reach beyond and see Fiesole turn to violet, on its ample eminence, from the effect of the opposite sunset. Facing again then to Florence proper you have local colour enough and to spare –

which you enjoy the more, doubtless, from standing off to get your light and your point of view.[66]

It was necessary to have chosen to live in Florence and to have experienced the city's day-to-day life for oneself in order to achieve the sort of insight that Aby Warburg was to express when commenting that Florence was 'beautiful only very indirectly', because it was 'too dirty'.[67]

The Piazzale Michelangelo, the terraces in front of San Miniato and the hills around Fiesole were all concrete vantage points from which to gaze down on Florence as it lay spread out along the valley of the Arno. Visitors would climb up the steep paths and steps to reach those places from which the city as a whole could be appreciated as a work of art that acquired its 'wonderful light' from the darkness of the past. The sculptor Adolf von Hildebrand arrived in Florence in May 1872 and almost immediately wrote to his friend Conrad Fiedler to answer his question as to whether Florence could offer him what he missed in Berlin. 'Yes,' Hildebrand replied unequivocally, adding a geographical metaphor: 'One stands on a higher level, can see further behind one, but from the front the prospect always remains infinite, and the journey begins anew.'[68]

The aura created by radiation rays from a distant age was mixed with the atmospheric moods of the present, changes in the weather as well as the time of day and seasons. The best example is arguably Rilke's 'Florence diary'. Rilke arrived in the city in April 1898 and moved into a garret in the 'Scandinavia' guest house on the Lungarno Serristori, not far from the Ponte delle Grazie. From there he had a panoramic view of the surrounding area that was all he could wish for: the Arno and the Ponte Vecchio and the Uffizi in the foreground and, beyond them, the whole vast city. Rilke's was the usual view of Florence, the foreigner's perspective, contemplated from a height:

> In the morning in the gleam of a hundred hopes, almost swimming with impatient expectation, rich at midday, full, showered with gifts and heavy, and bespeaking a simple clarity and holy majesty as the evening dies away. Then begins the hour when the air becomes like blue steel, and the many objects are ground sharp on it. The towers seem to rise up yet more slender from the seething mass of domes, and the crenellations of the Palazzo della Signoria are as if hardened in their ancient defiance, until the silence is finally covered over by the stars, and the soft light makes everything calm again with its gentle, timorous tenderness.[69]

Rilke's picture of Florence illustrates a type of account that seems more of an imaginary, idealized portrait than a reflection of reality on the part of the person committing it to paper. His text bursts with a very real longing for beauty and grandeur and for a Renaissance conceived of as significant and unique. It is the diary of a pilgrimage in search of art, attesting to the twenty-two-year-old writer's search for his own artistic genius. Above all, we have an interior view of the writer telling his tale, a text which says more about Rilke than about Florence and its art. Hesse's Florence differs from Rilke's by dint of the fact that it has more varied skies, skies full of clouds and light. It is surrounded by nature and teems with life. And it differs, finally, because it contains an impressive number of trattorie serving more or less good Chianti, which the writer consumes with gusto.

Rilke would regard all this – like the 'Grünwald & Bauer' cutlet in Venice – as the product of a narrower culture.[70] Isolde Kurz, for her part, was the poet of a historical Florence, a city of famous dead men and women filled with the relics of the past, and a place where thoughts could take wing. Imagination was her time machine, and it took her to realms shimmering with gold and crimson, or else out into the Tuscan country-side 'with its austere cypress backdrops and its radiantly smiling meadows, where even now La Bella Simonetta wanders through the springtime splendour in the company of the Graces'.[71]

Florence's mirror reflects back at us the reflections of foreigners. They see themselves in it, and we ourselves see their likeness. Warburg, too, must be seen illumined by the light of Florence. He sensed that every perception of the city led deep inside himself. More than that, he was the first to attempt with any real seriousness to deconstruct the myth of Florence.

11   Jessie Hillebrand (*c*.1900)

'*A galaxy of spirits on this small plot of ground*' (WALBURGA, LADY PAGET)

Florentine circles

AT least for Mary Warburg, Florence had remained what it had been from the time of her first visit: a place of dreams, an object of yearning and a world 'filled with the golden clouds of memory'.[1] As early as 1891, when she and Aby Warburg were still referring to one another as 'comrades', Warburg had suggested by way of a joke that the two of them should meet in Florence. 'Too sweet of him,' she wrote in her diary at the time, adding: 'Ah, Florence, Florence, O summertime!'[2] The romantic fantasy had now become a reality. The newlyweds arrived in the city on 27 October 1897, at a time when Florence was revealing its most alluring aspect. The city lay bathed in the light of a radiant late autumn sun, which obscured the fact that winter was already on its way. Even more beautiful, wrote Mary Warburg, striking a poetical note, was the 'inner sunlight' on which she was able to warm herself with Aby.[3] Warburg himself was happy to be back in Florence: 'My old Florentine "business contacts" welcomed me back with evident joy, and I am indeed more at home here or, rather, "better placed" than anywhere else in the world,' he wrote to Charlotte Warburg in Hamburg.[4]

A few weeks after their move to Florence, Mary Warburg recalled that it was now exactly nine years since her first meeting with Aby: 'How beautiful it is', she wrote, 'that one does not have to be afraid of waking from this glorious dream!'[5] Quite the opposite: it was a question of setting up house. The couple had rented a spacious apartment at 42 Viale Principessa Margherita, only a short distance from the building housing the German Art Historical Institute.[6] They presumably took over the apartment from their friend Alice Hallgarten, the daughter of a New York financier, who had been living there until 1896.[7]

This part of Florence had been developed only in the final decades of the nineteenth century, following the establishment of a national state. The old town walls had been torn down, their former presence recalled only by the Porta San Gallo of 1284, not far from the Warburgs' apartment. Along the new ring roads, elegant villas surrounded by grass sprang up, their upper storeys affording views that extended across the city to San Miniato, and even as far as the hills around Fiesole. This whole area was redeveloped in the years around 1900. The roads were paved, and street lamps were erected.[8] According to Henry James,

> Such modern arrangements as the Piazza d'Azeglio and the *viale* or Avenue of the Princess Margaret please not a little, I think – for what they are! – and do so even in a degree, by some fine local privilege, just because they are Florentine. The afternoon lights rest on them as if to thank them for not being worse, and their vistas are liberal where they look toward the hills.[9]

There is little doubt that the first weeks and months that Mary Warburg spent in Florence, setting up her new home, were among the happiest in her life. Warburg resumed his research into sixteenth-century pageantry, while Mary did the 'handiwork', as she herself called it, regaling her mother-in-law with little genre scenes: 'If you had seen how eagerly my orderly little husband sorted out his finances & triumphantly announced the glorious fact that everything tallied right down to the very last franc, your maternal heart, so fond of order as it is, would undoubtedly have been delighted. I am still unashamedly in love with my little Abyman.'[10]

The Warburgs set about making the apartment 'a little more homely'. It was in fact almost baronial in size, with an anteroom, salon, dining room, two studios, a bedroom, bath and kitchen in addition to a breakfast room, a guest room and a room for the female servant. Unfortunately, few photographs of the Warburgs' private surroundings have survived. Warburg owned a Kodak and is known to have taken lots of photographs with it, including a street scene which, according to the photographer, was shot in Settignano. It shows a late nineteenth-century villa and in front of it, on a still unpaved road, a two-wheeled donkey cart from which bundles of brushwood are being unloaded. There may have been a basket-weaver's on the ground floor. The scene is still entirely rustic. Even in Florence itself many of the streets were still unsurfaced, so that it is hardly surprising that Warburg initially complained about the terrible dust that forced its way through every crack and cranny.[11]

Another photograph undoubtedly depicts the couple in Florence, as it was cut out and stuck to a letter to Warburg's parents. Warburg himself can be seen peering into the camera while striking the attitude of a man suffering from melancholia. In front of him, on a table with a neo-Baroque curved base, lies a thick book as a scholar's attribute. Mary is seen looking over her husband's shoulder, with a bouquet of flowers as her emblem.[12]

Mary's letters, invoices and drawings convey an idea of the couple's domestic arrangements: salon furniture, including a sofa and divan, oriental rugs, a Japanese runner, wallpaper from Brussels; an easel, steps for a model and a tripod for the lady of the house's studio, and bookshelves and a desk for that of her husband. The beds were made of walnut with ornamental carvings. Mary Warburg herself created the designs for some of these objects. New armchairs, covered in a green fabric, arrived at the end of December, causing Mary to exclaim in jubilation that their living room could now stand comparison with a creation of Schneider & Hanau.[13] The couple also ordered fine porcelain – *a fiori porpora* – from Richard Ginori and twelve crystal tumblers described as 'Modello 977 C Maria Antonietta'. All these objects reflect the philosophy underpinning late nineteenth-century furnishings, which were intended to radiate an 'artistic atmosphere'. 'Imagination, plenty of imagination' was the motto proclaimed by Henri de Noussanne in his article 'Le Goût dans l'ameublement' of 1896: elements from the Middle Ages, the Renaissance and China were all to be included, while symmetry was to be avoided as far as possible. Above all, the emphasis should be Japanese: '*Les Japonais sont tous artistes*.'[14] The western and oriental traditions were combined in the form of symbolic artefacts. Creativity was revealed by the art of selection, by combining *pasticcii* to produce a kind of panorama of the European history of style.

The Warburgs were able to spend considerable sums of money on rent – two thousand lire a year – and on furnishing their apartment.[15] They received generous bills of exchange to pay not only for furnishing the flat, which must have cost around ten thousand marks, but also for their living costs. Warburg's annuity amounted to fifteen thousand marks a year – about £45,000 at today's prices. If the money was not enough, Moritz Warburg helped to smooth things over.[16] The generosity of Aby Warburg's annuity emerges from various comparisons:[17] a grammar-school teacher would have earned some two thousand marks a year at this time, while freelance professionals, relatively well-off businessmen and university teachers could earn as much as six thousand – about ten times the income of the average workman.

The couple gradually surrounded themselves with an appropriate degree of comfort. Of course, they had to make do with gaslight, whereas Charlotte Warburg was able to write to them from Hamburg as early as May 1898: 'Since last Tuesday we have also had electric light and so we are altogether *fin de siècle*',[18] a comment which also provides evidence of the fact that the phrase '*fin de siècle*' had associations of modernity at this time. A further photograph, which was taken in Florence and is dated December 1898, shows Warburg at his desk in the light of a desk lamp (see p. viii). 'To locate a thought is child's play, to express it means work': Warburg added these words by his teacher, Hermann Usener, as a motto to the photograph.

The Warburgs' stays in Florence were mostly interrupted by absences lasting several months at a time. They would spend the hot summer months in Hamburg, although on some of these occasions Aby remained on his own in Florence. At other times he would travel in Italy, either to Venice, which he visited in May 1898, or to the Umbrian countryside.[19] The Warburgs spent only a single season in the Viale Margherita, moving the following year to another apartment a few streets away, in the Via Lungo Mugnone, at the edge of the city. It was here that they celebrated New Year's Eve in 1899. The Mugnone flows down from the Apennines, passing this way as it joins the Arno. At the time in question, there were plans for the river's canalization, costing an estimated two hundred thousand lire, and a start was also made on increasing the number of gas lamps in the street.[20] Situated not far from the site of the Russian Church, these rooms, too, were worth seeing: the apartment was 'on the first floor in a gloriously free-standing building on the Mugnone, with an enchanting view over the whole of the hills surrounding Fiesole,' Mary reported. '4 rooms with a view at the front, 3 at the back which catch the sun and look out over some small gardens.'[21] By contemporary standards, the apartment was the ultimate in modernity, having both gas light and a hot-water supply.[22] Early in the new century, the Warburgs moved again, this time to the tiny Via Paolo Toscanelli, close to their old apartment. They were 'bright rooms, with no decorative staircase', Warburg characterized the place.[23] The apartment had seven large rooms overlooking a garden to the south and the Piazza Cavour – now the Piazza della Libertà. Of all the places where the Warburgs lived in Florence, this is the only one that is still standing.

Mary Warburg was meticulous in her housekeeping. The various entries and the rows of figures in her housekeeping book are fragments of the everyday world of an upper middle-class household, the cook Carlo, for example, receiving fifty-five lire a month, while Lucia, the housekeeper, received twenty-five. Expenditure on flowers, sweets and chocolate, clothes, heating, newspapers, caviar, champagne, vermouth and wine – from Montepulciano, St Julien and Brolio – is listed in no particular order. Remarkably, the local Chianti did not find favour with the head of the household.[24] Payments were also made to a dressmaker and a copyist, who transcribed source material in the city archives for Warburg. The entries indicate that he did not abandon his habit of being shaved at the local barber's and that their tired bodies were sometimes entrusted to the ministrations of a masseur. Books and photographs were naturally a large item of expenditure. Other entries relate to the payment of a piano tuner, while the purchase of a hammer and chisel makes it clear that Mary was continuing with her work as a sculptor.

And then there are entries for leisure activities of every kind: dinners, visits to the theatre, celebrations, concerts, and once – in 1901 – four lire for entry to a panorama. We also encounter the Warburgs at the carnival celebrations organized by Florence's artistic community, presumably at the Palazzo Pucci not far from the cathedral, where the *Circolo degli artisti* had its headquarters from 1887.[25] Aby was a founding member of the Florence branch of the Naval Association,[26] and he was invariably present when members of the German colony met either at the elegant Capitani Restaurant on the Via Tornabuoni or at the Grand Hôtel Continental de la Paix, where a bust of Wilhelm II would be framed by the flags of Italy and Germany and the assembled company would celebrate the Kaiser's birthday to the accompaniment of a splendid banquet, speeches and toasts to the German ruler and King Vittorio Emanuele, ending with patriotic songs and telegrams congratulating both their majesties.[27]

Jews had only recently been accepted into such circles, membership of these associations giving them the feeling that they had arrived socially. Warburg in particular represented the typical 'Kaiser Jew', as ardent an admirer of Wilhelm II as he had previously viewed Bismarck through critical eyes. An eloquent entry in his diary reflects his admiration for Wilhelm II's bravery in undergoing surgery for polyps: 'May he return to himself and to us in joy! Otherwise the shadows of evening will descend on our European culture.'[28]

The lives that the Warburgs led in Florence were affluent and even luxurious. Soon after settling in the city, Mary had already admitted to what she called her 'terrible' addiction to pleasure: 'In general we have of late been living more for our enjoyment than for our work, but this seems to do us both good. . . . We've been out a terrible amount of time all this week. The theatre (Duse in *La locandiera*), concerts (with the violinist Thompson) & parties follow hard on each other's heels (today we're attending a musical soirée at the Pension Laurent).'[29]

The Warburgs were thus in the audience for one of the three long-awaited appearances by Eleonora Duse in Florence in late February 1898, performances that the inhabitants of Florence felt set the seal on their cultural standing. She played the title role in Goldoni's *La locandiera* and, according to another eyewitness who was almost certainly present at the same performance, she was 'a mature woman, lightly touched by old age but all the more enchanting in consequence, an actress who knows all the tricks of her trade, the archetype of Italian grace and *malizia*.'[30]

Warburg must have responded coolly to the famous actress' notoriously histrionic performances. Of course, they were aimed at other listening and viewing habits and at a mode of perception fundamentally different from today's. Alice Hallgarten, who had attended several of Duse's performances in Rome shortly before the actress' visit to Florence, wrote to the Warburgs: 'This great actress is the only one who allows me to forget the theatre, the form, the wretched play etc. and enables me to live and suffer in the milieu that she has created.'[31] As a member of the audience, Alice Hallgarten felt that there was no longer a gap between acting and real life, finding herself transported from everyday reality into a world full of drama and passion that acquired the character of a 'second reality' thanks to the great actress' artistry. Florence's press responded warmly.[32]

From the outset, the Warburgs had no lack of social contact with their compatriots. 'Both of us are doing unashamedly well,' Aby Warburg was able to write home in January 1898. 'By day we work hard and in the evening visit Brockhaus, the Davidsohns or Dorens or take up a short story by Keller with pleasure and as a reward for our youth. Mary is busy working on a design for Paul Hertz's grave.'[33] But the Warburgs also made contact with collectors, artists and writers, largely ignoring the local Jewish community and the local rabbi, Samuel Hirsch Margulies, who was from Hamburg, while preferring to get to know artists, writers and journalists of every description.[34]

Central to Warburg's work was the German Art Historical Institute,[35] and he frequently met its director, the Leipzig art historian Heinrich Brockhaus, and the latter's family, on a social basis too. With time, relations between the two families cooled, however, and Warburg even went so far as to join forces with the influential Wilhelm Bode – later to become the general director of the Art Collections in Berlin – to intrigue against Brockhaus,[36] calling the series of publications superintended by Brockhaus a 'salad bowl' and caricaturing the institute as a 'rescue centre for itinerant art lovers'. In general, he discussed many of his colleagues in thoroughly unflattering terms, calling his old teacher August Schmarsow a 'theatrical intriguer' and claiming that his colleague Georg Gronau produced nothing but 'journalistic spider's webs' stretching from the *Burlington Magazine* to the *Gazette des beaux arts*.[37]

But it was Ernst Steinmann who was the particular butt of his contumely.[38] Steinmann, who was to play a leading role in the establishment of the Biblioteca Hertziana in Rome, had been a member of the circle of friends surrounding Henriette Hertz in Florence in 1894, when he had conducted research into both Ghirlandaio and Botticelli, but it was his monograph on the Sistine Chapel that first drew his name to the attention of a wider audience. 'For my private pleasure,' Warburg wrote to Bode,

> I am now reading E. St. on the Sistine Chapel, having overcome an almost physical revulsion at his complacent manner (I mean: see above). It is arguable whether money from the German Reich has ever been thrown at a scholarly project to less felicitous effect. It is couched in a half-hearted and coquettishly simpering language lacking in imagination and enthusiasm and suited only to old maids from polite society, while on points of detail it reveals a positively brutal superficiality.

The letter culminates in an outburst of sheer silliness:

> I shall calmly and objectively shove this right under the nose of the Reich's official guide. But what is the point of it all? This young lad will still accompany the Crown Prince to Italy or be appointed to the staff of the Faculty in Bonn. . . . But that is all right: at least in this way we know what we have to become: a spineless subject of Catholic appearance (not forgetting a secret and ardent love of Anton von Werner), and anyone who does not have this at his disposal will remain a private lecturer.

These outbursts are far from exceptional with Warburg. In order to understand them, we need to know more about his deep-seated reservations towards established colleagues and his envy of all who achieved quick success by wielding a facile pen, while he himself published his writings only under the greatest difficulties. Mentally, he suffered from his luxury lifestyle as a permanent beneficiary of his father's bank.

Irrespective of the resentment that Warburg felt towards a number of his colleagues, he and his wife held open house in Florence. In time, André Jolles – man of letters and aesthetician – became one of Warburg's closest friends. We have already met him and the medieval historian Robert Davidsohn at the New Year's Eve party in 1899.

Like Warburg, Davidsohn was Jewish.[39] He was born in Danzig in 1853 and was one of the few Germans living in Florence who succeeded in forging closer links with the locals and achieved a certain standing in the municipal life of the town. Warburg described him as the only German scholar in Florence who enjoyed the unquestioning respect of the Italians, a respect 'due to the selflessness and superiority of his work'.[40] Davidsohn also corresponded with Renato Fucini, the author of travel books and short stories set in rural Tuscany. On one occasion he visited the writer on his estates at Empoli:

We shall never forget this Alpine view of the majestic Apennines crowned with snow-covered peaks! Your Dianella is a treasure unto itself, but what makes it so twice over are the people who live there. For those of us who have a whole world of connections, all the affection and love that we feel for Tuscany takes on physical form in you. I number the hours that we spent with you last Sunday as some of the most beautiful in my life.[41]

Davidsohn's book on the history of Florence conferred on him membership of numerous academies.[42] *La Nazione* reported that in early August 1898 he presented the first volume to the local mayor, later calling him a 'concittadino illustre', a famous fellow citizen.[43] The paper quoted from the preface in which Davidsohn explained that he had interpreted the history of Florence first and foremost as the history of its people and their resistance to everything that stood in the way of progress. This same powerfully progressive spirit also finds expression in the patriotic New Year poem that he declaimed on New Year's Eve in 1900. Like Warburg, he was a nationalist in his thinking. Following an unguarded comment on Italian foreign policy, he was for a time banned from the Società Patria. In fact he was no less critical of German foreign policy, as is clear from his essay on Wilhelm II's *éminence grise*, Friedrich von Holstein.[44] Basically liberal in outlook, he took an optimistic view of the future, telling Warburg that more and more pleasures would become available to more and more people. Warburg, of course, thought differently.[45] Davidsohn's correspondence with Alessandro Chiappelli reveals an enlightened thinker who pinned his hopes on the power of reason and the freedom of science.[46]

On this point Warburg will have felt a certain affinity with his colleague. Indeed, he freely admitted to having learnt a great deal from Davidsohn, who was what Burckhardt once ironically called a 'documentarian': 'Davidsohn is sitting in his seat like a warmed-up mummy and not moving', Warburg described his colleague working in the bitterly cold archives in Florence.[47] In turn, Warburg tried to persuade Davidsohn, who normally employed assistants for such jobs, to copy out the inventories of the Medici's artistic possessions himself, because 'only in this way is it possible to enter into the "spirit of the age" '.[48]

Another foreigner with whom Warburg became friendly during his early years in Florence was the Belgian art historian Jacques Dwelshauvers, who had written on Gabriele D'Annunzio, publishing a book on the Italian socialists in 1896 under the pseudonym Jacques Mesnil and following this up in 1897 with a study of the various anarchist movements.[49] He also wrote anti-military texts, a piece inveighing against the political power of the church and articles on historical subjects and art history. Among his friends was the anarchist Elisée Reclus.[50] He later made contact with Romain Rolland. His monograph on Masaccio and his later work on Botticelli also received widespread attention.

Mesnil's interest in Renaissance civilization was fuelled in part by his antipathy to the modern industrial world. For a time he lived with a family of peasants on the slopes of the Monte Morello. His political views were coloured by the Romantic utopias of early socialism. His love of Tuscany, whither he fled from the hideousness of the hectic present, recalls Rousseau's infatuation with nature. As Fritz Saxl noted, Tuscany was for Mesnil the land of the noble savage.[51]

Mesnil was one of the few writers with whom Warburg exchanged views on contemporary events. Among the topics on which they corresponded was Gabriele D'Annunzio, whose hollow aestheticism Warburg held in low regard.[52] But Mesnil was also a welcome correspondent when it came to relations between Italian and Flemish art. Warburg also did what he could to help his friend, who eked out a living in financially straitened circumstances, although he was unable to find him a post at the institute in Florence in 1897. The institute's limited resources had to be spent on books and, as he wrote to inform Mesnil, there was no money left over for a second appointment.[53]

Warburg was also in frequent contact with the economic historian Alfred Doren, who is also mentioned in Mary Warburg's letter quoted above. In their later correspondence Warburg even refers to him jokingly as 'Alfresco'. Written at the very time when Warburg was living in Florence, Doren's monumental study of Florence's woollen industry of the early modern period is still regarded as the standard work on the subject. In the contemporary arguments over the methods and objects of historical research, Doren saw himself as the champion of a type of economic history that relied heavily on archival sources, and he mocked the well-established representatives of that guild of historians who admired trivial truths such as the demonstration that 'some medieval monk, writing in his monastery and unknown to the world at large,' had been the object of some forgery or other. Never for a moment did he think of switching to political history.[54]

Doren dedicated the first volume of his magnum opus to Warburg. 'Will you be cross with me, dear Aby, if I dedicate the first volume to my faithful companion in good times and bad in this city on the banks of the Arno?', Doren asked Warburg at Christmas 1900, 'or will you not be afraid to descend from the sublime heights of the select band of people with whom you consort and mix with my plebeian cronies and slave labourers?'[55] Warburg could not refuse a friend, but at bottom he considered his colleague's work as no more than useful at best. His own interests were indeed aimed at higher things – not in the sense that he was grappling with elite groups and with 'great individuals', but that he was concerned to test his 'psycho-historical' hypothesis. Doren had merely become a kind of Schmoller, he once noted, alluding in the process to the political economist and economic historian Gustav von Schmoller.[56]

As we have seen, there were few friends, colleagues or acquaintances about whom Warburg spoke only in the most glowing terms, and it was not long before the institute's line no longer suited him: 'Deeply disgusted by the whole Institute business,' he noted in his diary. 'A snobbish and indifferent commission: Marcuard, the typical social show-off; Krauss, the Duse among the art historians; the abbé of the previous century who has to be fêted . . . and Gentle Heinrich as the dull head.'[57] 'Heinrich' was Heinrich Brockhaus. Conversely, 'Brockhaus' young man', Georg Swarzenski, who became director of the Städel Institute in Frankfurt in 1906, impressed Warburg with his professional competence.[58]

The establishment of the German Art Historical Institute marked a turning point in the history of Florence's expatriate German community. Isolde Kurz notes in her memoirs that something akin to a sea-change took place in the social life of the Germans in Florence at the end of the nineteenth century. There had been no real literary salon since the death of Ludmilla Assing – the niece of Rahel Varnhagen and the German colony's last socialite.[59] Instead, the arrival in the city of leading scholars and the establishment of the Art Historical Institute meant that intellectual concerns of a different kind now came to the fore.[60]

These concerns signalled something more basic, the foundation of the institute representing a process of historicization both for the city and for its art. Its older history was coming to an end. Florence or, rather, the essence of Florence and all that constituted its true identity, namely its art, was emerging from the Romantic world of dreams and gradually being distilled as a petrefact that was now amenable to analysis. Florence was no longer merely a place of inspiration and, indeed, was less and less such a place. By the turn of the century it had become instead an object of scientific enquiry.[61] At the same time this immersion in the past soon brought a sense of security and calm. Warburg clothed this idea in a convoluted play of words: 'What can keep these (somatically, morally and intellectually) unequal and even contradictory elements in a state of balance? The language that controls them demands a memory: *ricordiamoci!* As an instinctive action, this addictive desire to remember leads to the "Institute", an act of civilization because it constitutes a demand for balance!'[62]

Most of the Warburgs' dealings were with historians and art historians, and yet the couple had arrived in Florence only just in time to experience for themselves a pale reflection of the old splendours of Florence as an intellectual and cultural centre and to make contact with the survivors of those groups of people who had made the city one of the main centres in the nineteenth-century history of European art and ideas. Their meeting with Jessie Hillebrand, the widow of Karl Hillebrand, was an event of particular importance in their lives. One of their first priorities on arriving in Florence was afternoon tea with 'this most enchanting of all old ladies', as Mary Warburg called her. Like everyone else, Mary admitted to having fallen completely in love with her. But 'it is a pity that she is so deaf, so that it is impossible to talk to her unhindered'.[63]

Born Jessie Taylor, Jessie Hillebrand had been married *en premières noces* to a wealthy but tedious wine dealer by the name of Eugène Laussot. Her life was in many ways a reflection of the century as a whole, so closely had she been associated with its intellectual developments – a point that emerges with peculiar clarity from a letter preserved in the National Library in Florence. In it she forwards to Pasquale Villari a letter from Ugo Foscolo addressed to her father.[64] Music was the great love of her life. In her youth she had been introduced to Felix Mendelssohn, and Wagner had fallen in love with her after she had succeeded in luring him to Bordeaux with the promise of an annuity.[65] She was living there, an elegant, pallid woman of youthful charm, a *wagnérienne avant la lettre*. She was also an excellent pianist, and it was her piano playing that drew her and Wagner together. Somewhat hysterical by nature, she persuaded herself that she must be the Master's 'swan's bride', and the couple resolved to elope to Asia Minor, only for the affair to come to nothing, leaving both parties with no alternative but to return to their respective marriage beds. Wagner must have been piqued above all by the fact that he had forfeited an annual allowance of three thousand francs.

But Jessie tired of her wine dealer and in the late 1850s she moved to Florence, where we soon find her at the side of another leading figure in European cultural history, the essayist Karl Hillebrand.[66] Hillebrand was something of an institution in Florence, one of the few foreigners to become famous in Italy during his lifetime. Condemned to death in the Baden Uprising of 1848, he escaped to Paris, where he worked as secretary to the by now bed-ridden Heinrich Heine, who dictated his *Romancero* to him. The Franco-Prussian War of 1870–1 forced Hillebrand to resume his wanderings, which this time took him to England, where he gained access to the circles around William Gladstone, Lord Odo Russell and Lord Aberdeen. He then turned his attention to Italy, settling in Rome and writing for *The Times* on the demise of the Papal States. But it was in Florence that he finally found what he described in his diary as 'the *bel ovile* that I almost yearned for like the poor exile'.[67] From 1875 he lived here in a prestigious *palazzo* with Jessie Laussot, whom he had got to know in France. But it was not until after Eugène Laussot's death some years later that the relationship could be legitimized.

Karl and Jessie Hillebrand were in contact with half the intelligentsia of Europe, including even Nietzsche, while their friends numbered many of the leading figures of the Risorgimento. Their salon was a meeting place for an older generation of artists and writers who had helped to establish Florence's reputation as one of Italy's cultural and intellectual centres: the painters Arnold Böcklin, Hans von Marées and Karl Stauffer-Bern, the writer Isolde Kurz and her colleagues Theodor and Paul Heyse, and the sculptor Adolf von Hildebrand. Other guests included statesmen and aristocrats, from Crown Prince Friedrich Wilhelm of Prussia and his wife Viktoria to the Grand Duke of Saxony, and there seems little doubt that another of the Hillebrands' habitués was Malwida von Meysenbug, an admirer of Giuseppe Garibaldi and a friend of Mazzini, Wagner and Nietzsche. Wagner himself paid his last visit on Jessie Hillebrand in December 1876.

A passionate music lover, Jessie Hillebrand not only wrote a handbook on music, she also founded the Società Cherubini. Famous musicians such as Hans von Bülow and Franz Liszt came to visit her in Florence, playing whist, chatting with her and belabouring her pianoforte. 'Many terrible shrivelled-up old maids came in the evening as usual, and Liszt played,' Adolf von Hildebrand noted after one such soirée. 'First some Chopin, all manner of tricks on a trivial motif, and then something Viennese by Strauß, full of life and grace, designed to make the women fall at his feet.'[68] Following the death of her husband in 1884, Jessie continued to cultivate the social manners which, already disappearing, could look back on a tradition originating in the salon culture of old Europe.

A photograph found among Aby Warburg's papers shows Jessie Hillebrand leafing through a book. It was presumably taken in the salon in her apartment, a room with dark wallpaper, an armchair and a divan with long fabric tassels, a Second Empire porcelain stove and a painting in a heavy gilt frame. We know from her last will and testament that she surrounded herself with mementos and trinkets, including a writing-table set, a present from the empress; a bust of Karl Hillebrand by Adolf von Hildebrand; and the plaster cast of a bust of Beethoven that Hans von Bülow once gave to Giuseppe Buonamici as his 'best pupil' and a 'most outstanding interpreter of Beethoven's piano works'. There were also paintings, including a Fragonard that may have been a reminder of Hillebrand's years of exile in France. 'Like her husband's, hers was a mind that always took the wider view,' wrote Isolde Kurz, 'and she continued to live entirely within his circle of ideas. We would find this invariably sociable woman at her five-o'clock tea amidst a pile of English, French, German and Italian newspapers and valuable literary publications. Her child's face indestructible, she still had pearly white teeth even in old age and was always surrounded by a group of friends who either lived locally or were merely passing through and with whom she conversed by means of an ear trumpet and, by the end of her life as she grew increasingly deaf, with the help of a pencil.'[69]

The writer Isolde Kurz,[70] whom we have often had occasion to quote and who knew Jessie Hillebrand well, was the great chronicler of *fin de siècle* Florence, her memoirs containing many a biographical tribute not only to local men and women but also to foreigners, especially Germans. Her brother, Edgar, was one of the foreign doctors in the town, with the result that his house at 12 Via delle Porte Nuove, which also doubled as his surgery, became a natural meeting place for many Germans, his sister regretting only that there was not enough space to hold a large salon. 'Even though my dreams of a large function room came to nothing, there was still no lack of the noblest society. Apart from Hildebrand and Böcklin, who used to be accompanied by the imaginative painter Victor Zurhelle, other leading figures from the German colony also came: the celebrated essayist Karl Hillebrand and his friend Heinrich Homberger.'[71] Isolde Kurz was herself friendly with Homberger,[72] a little-known writer and critic who, as editor of *Die Tribüne*, published one of her earliest stories, but she maintained a certain distance towards Hillebrand, describing him as a 'sophisticated man of the world' in whom she missed 'a sense of experience and genuine individuality'.[73]

Another frequent visitor was the writer Paul Heyse, who as a member of the Munich League of Poets was an important figure in the exchange of ideas between German and Italian literature. He wrote for Hillebrand's journal *Italia*, other contributors to which included Alfred von Reumont, Leopold Witte and Woldemar Kaden, as well as Italians such as Angelo de Gubernatis and Ruggero Bonghi. He was introduced to Jacob Burckhardt by members of the group who gravitated around the art historian Franz Kugler in Berlin. He spent every winter at Gardone on Lake Garda, and indeed many of his short stories are set in Italy. He features in our narrative as Isolde Kurz's mentor, a fatherly friend who remained in epistolary contact with the younger writer until the final years of his life. At the turn of the century the two of them adopted the familiar *du* in their correspondence.[74] Their friendship went back a long way, Isolde Kurz's father having been friendly with Heyse since 1859 and the two men having published numerous collections of short stories together. But the intellectual affinities ran even deeper, and there is no doubt that the would-be poetess felt a commitment to stylistic ideals similar to those held by her much older friend.

The Warburgs soon began to see more of Isolde and Edgar Kurz, choosing the latter as their family doctor. Mary wrote to her mother-in-law to report on their new friends:

> We spend virtually every Tuesday evening at the Davidsohns' and it was there, some time ago, that we met Isolde Kurz with her elderly mother, an extremely wrinkled old lady. We shall be seeing her again on Shrove Tuesday. I don't think it will be easy to get much closer to her. There is something extremely touchy about her, but I believe she is a splendid character. But old Frau Kurz would be someone for you – what a cheerful and sprightly old woman she is![75]

Edgar Kurz had settled in Florence in 1877 and set up in practice as a doctor, treating the German expatriate community. He was soon followed by Isolde and by their brother Erwin, a sculptor who studied with Adolf von Hildebrand. Brothers and sister hailed from a liberal Swabian family. Their father, Hermann Kurz, came to prominence during the Baden Uprising as the editor of the democratic *Der Beobachter*, an incumbency that led to three weeks' imprisonment at Hohenasperg. In 1851 – in circumstances that can only be described as romantic – he married the twenty-seven-year-old Baroness Maria von Brunnow, a novelist in her own right. This was the 'elderly Frau Kurz' who left such an impression on Mary Warburg. She was certainly an unorthodox woman. Classically educated, she was a free-thinking, sceptical individual and, as her daughter noted in an account of her career, was engaged in a permanent search for the meaning of life.[76] Her views came closest to those of Nietzsche. A vegetarian, she grappled with Buddhism – no doubt under the influence of Nietzsche's writings. Politically speaking, she was marked by the ideals of the 1848 revolutions and open to the ideas of French socialism. Her hero was Garibaldi, whom she saw in the flesh in Florence and after whom she named her youngest child. Maria Kurz was the lynchpin of the family, gathering around her children and grandchildren with a love that was almost desperate.

Something of the democratic spirit of the revolutionary period also seems to have survived in her eldest son, Edgar, who is said to have become a socialist under the influence of a friend who had manned the barricades during the Paris Commune.[77] Certainly he remained an independent thinker to the point of brusqueness, a man who refused to kowtow to others. Indeed, he even managed to offend the heir to the throne of Prussia, the later Emperor Wilhelm II, who turned up at Kurz's surgery in Florence on one occasion when the royal couple was travelling in Italy and his wife fell ill. Kurz remained unimpressed by the noisy insistence of his adjutants as he was treating another emergency.[78] It is also significant that Edgar Kurz was unwilling to comply with the customs adopted by Emilia Peruzzi and her circle and as a result made no attempt to gain admittance to the most famous of Florence's surviving salons. His friend Adolf von Hildebrand described him as a 'freethinker far from all convention, aristocratic and reserved by nature, remote from all that was trivial and with a tendency to set himself apart, a tendency that extended to the curious and bizarre rather than to the average and usual'.[79] Somewhat cryptically, Warburg called him a splendid and attractive person, 'albeit subject to bouts of "originality" too extreme for domestic consumption'.[80] Above all, he was a brilliant physician with a scholarly and yet practical mind.[81] Not only did he invent some new surgical equipment, he also wrote romantic poems and on his death was praised as a philanthropist. Together with an Italian colleague and friend, Carlo Vanzetti,[82] he ran an outpatients' clinic at the Palazzo Buondelmonti, which from its inception in 1889 provided free medical treatment for thousands of impoverished men, women and children.[83] His sister recalled visits to the sick that took Kurz and his colleague out into the Tuscan countryside, with its glittering olive trees. Here a celebratory *pranzo*, accompanied by Chianti and German student songs, would be held out of doors once the operation had been successfully completed. As with the older Karl Hillebrand and many other visitors to the country, Edgar Kurz's journey to Italy had a more general significance, representing, as it did, the return to the south of a humanist and idealist, escaping from the cramping confines of Germany and fleeing to a seemingly more beautiful, more poetical world.

Edgar Kurz's sister Isolde was another person hard to categorize.[84] Like her brother, she was born in 1853 and enjoyed what for the time was an unusually varied education. A university graduate, she was also a trained equestrian. She must have come into contact with classical literature while still living at home, while her mother will have introduced her to socialist writings. Versed in foreign languages, she collaborated with her father and Paul Heyse on a number of different translations while she was still a young girl. In Florence she tried to make a living as a freelance writer, keeping her head above water with translations and short stories. Karl Hillebrand proved to be a pillar of support, and in a letter to Paul Heyse we even find her describing him as her 'literary factotum'.[85] It was thanks to Hillebrand, for example, that she gained access to the columns of *Die Gartenlaube*. In 1878 the writer and literary scholar Angelo de Gubernatis, who was then the editor in chief of *Rivista Europea*, invited her to contribute to a lavishly produced collection of biographies of famous international figures from every period in history. He described it effusively as a '*monumentum aere perennius*' – a 'memorial more lasting than bronze'.[86] She also planned a series of texts to illustrate a collection of watercolours of historical Florence and had already prepared for the task by reading Burckhardt and other historical works, only for the artist in question to become mentally ill and die. From this period dates a photograph – reproduced on p. 94 – which shows the young and attractive woman in front of a southern backdrop, in a high-necked dress with her skirt gathered up, a feather-festooned hat concealing her blonde hair. It is a studio photograph, the background having been touched up. Her smile seems fixed, no doubt because she had to remain still until the plate was exposed.

It was, initially, far from easy for Isolde Kurz to make a living in Florence, and her letters are full of complaints about returned manuscripts and unduly low fees. Her correspondence with Heyse makes it abundantly clear that in her memoirs she saw events in a transfiguring light, concealing her daily hardships beneath the brilliance of her style and a series of romantic images. In her letters she writes of the bitter cold and of the most straitened circumstances in her first apartment in the Viale Margherita, where one of the residents died of smallpox. In spite of opposition from suspicious neighbours, the house had to be disinfected, during which time Isolde Kurz was moved into a hotel. The family was treated like lepers, and Edgar's medical practice suffered in consequence.

Other letters tell of the early death of Isolde's brother Garibaldi, who had suffered from a weak heart since childhood, and of the mother's bravery at her young son's sickbed:

> We gave Mama as much morphine as possible, but she still remained awake. And yet our darling's death was not disturbed by a single sigh. On the morning of the ninth [of February 1882] we buried him in a wonderful spot at San Miniato. The cathedral with the Campanile & Fiesole look across at him. He was extraordinarily beautiful in death, the colours & expression of life were fully retained & a light, humorous smile played about his lips.[87]

Tensions within the family circle were exacerbated during these difficult times, perhaps because there was no longer an object on which to lavish their care. Isolde Kurz grew desperate, feeling oppressed, confined and exploited. She fled to Forte dei Marmi on the coast, with its 'marmoreal mountains and mile upon mile of forest', where the Hildebrands had a holiday home. But the 'ghosts of Florence' followed her even there. 'I began to hate the southern light,' she wrote in her memoirs of her situation at this time, 'this implacably gleaming light that does not ask after human destiny and even robbed my soul of its suffering, filling the empty space with nothing but brightness.'[88]

Like countless other exiles before and since, Isolde Kurz found her life in Florence torn between the fascination of the south and the adversities of the daily round in Italy; between the relatively free existence of colourful towns and dazzling beaches and her longing to return to Germany; between her delight in the beauty of the light and the leaden lethargy which creeps over bodies and minds with the heat of summer and discourages creative work. Warburg, too, made a similar discovery, and there is no doubt that everything was turned upside down whenever misfortune and personal suffering entered the world of appearances that these foreign visitors had created for themselves.

Following one particularly stormy night, Isolde Kurz finally came to a difficult decision of which she informed Paul Heyse in a long letter, four drafts of which she destroyed before finding the words to tell him that it was all over: she was resolved to leave Italy for good. Could he find any work for her? 'You know more or less what I'm good at,' she wrote to Heyse from Forte di Marmi:

A companion, a reader, a teacher of four modern languages (not Russian, which I have lost), literature etc. I would be no use as a governess, as I have no real systematic knowledge. Northern Germany would be my preferred place to settle, but I would also be prepared to travel overseas, possibly to another part of the world, except that it would have to be a temperate zone. . . . I shudder at the idea of spending the winter in Florence.[89]

Heyse did indeed manage to obtain a post for her in Berlin, but she then decided against leading the life of an 'office girl' and instead pursued her calling as a writer, generally using the summer months to work, when she largely had the house in the Via delle Porte Nuove to herself. Later she moved to Poggio Imperiale, where conditions were more relaxed and she could at least distance herself a little from Florence, as she needed to do at this time. After frequent changes of address, she finally found the place of her dreams in the Via de' Bardi, by which date she was already financially independent. It was physical objects, paintings and bric-a-brac that remained her constant companions throughout these changing circumstances, lending a sense of permanence to her life at a time of upheaval. She furnished each new apartment with loving care, filling it with books, oriental shawls and a large Japanese rug, realizing her own *filosofia dell'arredamento* and embracing the exoticism of the turn of the century. On one occasion she even turned up for the carnival in a Japanese costume and found Warburg and Jolles dancing enthusiastically, the latter dressed up as a 'Malayan'.[90]

Writing provided Isolde Kurz with an adequate income. She was an occasional contributor to *Die Gartenlaube*, with whose editor, Rosalia Braun-Artaria, she was on friendly terms. Her works are written in a polished, 'classical' style, many of them being set in Italy at the time of the Renaissance. Their backdrop is the Tuscan countryside, the high-ceilinged rooms of gloomy *palazzi*, glittering marble villas and the narrow streets and squares of old Florence. In her own words, her short story *The Humanists* depicts 'the apostles of the mind and of beauty drunk on the spirit of ancient Greece and Rome'. It takes as its starting point the search for a lost Cicero manuscript, adumbrating the subject matter of Eco's *Name of the Rose*.

Isolde Kurz eventually became a genuinely successful writer, and virtually all her books went into several editions.[91] 'Let no one believe it was easy at that time for a woman to carve out a niche for herself in the world of German literature,' she later wrote. Whenever people complimented her 'as a *woman*', she could become argumentative. There was nothing, she said, that was 'more repulsive than such condescending praise by literary moles, I'd rather they showered me with their contempt'. With the passage of time she ceased to see her sex as a problem. 'The angel was accepted once it had fought its way through.'

She had no time for contemporary trends in literature such as naturalism and Expressionism, but regarded herself as a 'singer of the eternally human' that remained the same over time.[92] On this point, her aesthetic convictions coincided with those of her mentor Adolf von Hildebrand. In those of her short stories which are set at the time of the Renaissance, she paints an idealized portrait of the period inspired by her reading of Burckhardt, offering readers edification, showing them places of refuge and allowing them – in her view – to come to terms with their own fates, to which she gave literary form.

Isolde Kurz's novels and short stories are good examples of the way in which Renaissance tales and effusive descriptions of Italy could become vehicles for a flight from reality. Writing of her collection of short stories *Cora*, the reviewer of the *Wiesbadener Tagblatt* noted that 'through the classical purity of her style the poet depicts humans and landscapes with that Apollonian sense of beauty that transfigures even what is bitter and painful'.[93] Italy, beauty and history all became cult objects, allowing Isolde Kurz and her readers to immerse themselves in them. Those readers can scarcely have suspected the depths of bitter irony of which Isolde Kurz was capable when it came to her views on Christianity. Her unpublished papers include a satirical text on a nation of ants that worships a human being as its creator and as the keeper of all life until he tramples the ant hill underfoot. Presumably she did not dare to publish it.[94]

On one occasion she refers to Guy de Maupassant as a writer from whom she learnt narrative technique and a sense of form.[95] It is impossible, none the less, to overlook the fact that her style was inspired by the Swabian Romantics, including Eduard Mörike, whom she had met in person.[96] It seems that this contact was the subject of a conversation between her and Aby Warburg that the latter recorded in his diary: '11 o'clock with Isolde Kurz, supper in the arbour, glow-worms, spoke about Möricke [*sic*] and Hölderlin; shared dislike of Janitschek.'[97]

Maria Janitschek was the widow of Warburg's supervisor Hubert Janitschek, who died in 1893. As is clear from his own marriage, Warburg's views on women were conservative, and so it seems unlikely that he felt any enthusiasm for the emancipatory tendencies in the writings of someone so closely associated with the middle-class women's movement of the years around 1900. Warburg in any case had no time for *belles lettres*, least of all for the sort of 'sultry' Renaissance short stories turned out by Isolde Kurz. He regarded all such texts as expressions of the irrational, as Romantic threats to his mental equilibrium, and he kept them under lock and key in his library. As a result, his conversations with 'Isolde', as he occasionally refers to her in his diary, were never particularly deep, still less were their relations especially friendly. None the less, he occasionally provided her with information and sought her advice as a stylist.[98] Perhaps, too, the numerous nymphs that people Isolde Kurz's writings took shape in the course of her conversations with Warburg, for whom the classical *ninfa* had great significance.[99] During their later years in Florence, the two had a falling-out of entirely trivial import.[100]

In spite of all this, Isolde Kurz's contacts with the Warburgs undoubtedly had a stimulating effect on her short stories. On one occasion Mary Warburg must have given her a particularly vivid account of a scene that she was then able to use in a short story published in *Die Zeit*.[101] And one of the characters in *The Night in the Room of Carpets* reminds the reader irresistibly of Warburg: 'But he was not only a visual person to whom only the visible world belonged, he was also capable of conjuring up ghosts, who would account for themselves to him. . . . There was no past, he used to say: what people called the past had merely sunk down to a deeper layer but would be pleased to re-emerge if only it was correctly invoked.'[102]

12   Florence, Piazza Vittorio Emanuele II (*c*.1900)

'An American city built in the style of the Italian Renaissance' (VALÉRY LABAUD)

The Florence of foreigners

THE flood of foreigners that descended on Florence at the turn of the century included another figure famous for conjuring up and exorcising spirits: in September 1896, the founder of psychoanalysis, Sigmund Freud, spent a week in the city, although at that date in his career Freud was just another visitor. In a long letter to his wife Martha he describes the average day of a tourist in Florence:

> The novelty and beauty of art and nature more than make up for everything else, but as far as the art is concerned, there comes a moment when one is awash with regular enjoyment and thinks that this is how it must be and can summon up no further ecstasy, when the churches, Madonnas and Lamentations of Christ become a matter of total indifference and one longs for something else, without really knowing what.

The impressions jostled for attention and ultimately became overwhelming. Historical memories, Freud went on, were so numerous that it was no longer possible to keep them apart: 'The people of Florence kick up the most infernal racket, shouting, cracking their whips and playing trombones in the street. In a word, it's unbearable. Our feet were shot to pieces' – the visitors sought refuge in the Boboli Gardens, which Freud described as 'a kind of Schönbrunn for the Medici'.[1]

For a few days Freud even lived a life of chic and sophisticated pleasure,[2] staying at the Villa Il Gioello, where Galileo had lived under house arrest from 1633 until his death in 1642. The founder of a revolutionary new discipline which was soon to prove fiercely controversial, Freud may well have relished the symbolism of his stay here: 'It was dark when we arrived, the curator lit a lamp and showed us Galileo's room, including portraits of him, his telescope and the like. Later we heard that there were rooms with other collections, we saw a self-portrait of Michelangelo, a letter from Cromwell to Charles I, an autograph letter by Benvenuto Cellini.'They had lunch beneath a portrait of Galileo and sat facing another painting, this one of Cardinal Francesco de' Medici. The curator waited on them at table, the meal consisting of beef and produce from the villa's own garden, including figs, peaches and almonds. 'The garden is extensive but uneven,' Freud continued,

> half park and half vineyard, stretching 1/2 an hour all round the house in every direction, laurel, chestnut, olive trees (a local variety, the so-called Carafe Foundling Tree, on which wine grows), almond trees, in short the whole dizzying range of southern beauty familiar from Lovrana. One can look down at Florence from many points. Even as I'm writing these lines, there's a sea of glittering lights similar to the one afforded by the view from the Bellevue, except that this is Florence, not Vienna.

Thus the description of one prominent 'eternal tourist'. Freud combined elements of the average visitor with those of a member of a small but financially powerful elite. But how did the city strike foreigners in general? An excellent source is the loan journals in which visitors to the Gabinetto Vieusseux entered their names and other personal details. Founded in 1819, the Gabinetto was one of the leading public libraries in turn-of-the-century Florence, while also functioning as a place to meet and talk. The library was especially popular with foreigners who were staying in Florence and who could borrow novels and other volumes in return for a modest fee. There were constant comings and goings in the rooms on the Via Tornabuoni.[3]

According to the entries in the loan journal for 1897, the vast majority of users were from Britain and America,[4] with other nationalities represented by only a handful of names. A few Russian entries reflect the fact that there was a Russian colony in the city – a colony that Isolde Kurz described as 'generous and free to a fault'.[5] Dostoevsky wrote part of *The Idiot* in a guest house not far from the reading rooms in 1867–8.

The visitors' books also include the addresses of people who used the library. Most of the tourists sought rooms or apartments on the banks of the Arno along the Lungarni – as we have already seen, Rilke and Gide fall into this category.[6] But others preferred the more salubrious quarters on the edge of the town, with their better air quality. One such quarter was the Viale Margherita, where the Warburgs lived, as did Isolde Kurz during her early months in the city. Indeed, this was a favourite haunt for foreigners.[7] The *crème de la crème* of the users of the Gabinetto Vieusseux stayed at the grandest hotels and in villas both within the city itself and in the surrounding countryside – at Prato, Fiesole and Poggio a Caiano. In the case of some eighty entries, a villa is named as the user's elegant address, a place where they could hold banquets, soirées and cocktail and tea parties.

Of course, a tourist like Freud had his hands full with sight-seeing: he came, saw the sights and left again. And one will search in vain for the names of other famous visitors to Florence in the columns of the Gabinetto Vieusseux's users' books, although it is impossible not to be struck by some of the names that *are* found here. In 1896 and 1897, for example, we find the names of the sculptor Adolf von Hildebrand, the painter Ernst Sattler and the art collector Charles Loeser, who was closely associated with the work of Paul Cézanne and who in 1910 used his connections with the Durand-Ruel Gallery in Paris to help Florence to organize a large-scale exhibition of Impressionist art.[8] Warburg, too, frequented the Gabinetto Vieusseux, whose visitors' book contains an entry dated 10 December 1897, 'Dr A. Warburg – 42 Viale Margherita', together with a note that he had paid his dues for three months.[9]

The loan journals of the Gabinetto Vieusseux also reflect the presence of an international public that brought a certain air of chic sophistication to the city.[10] Valéry Labaud noted maliciously that Florence was 'an American city built in the style of the Italian Renaissance',[11] while Paul Klee thought that the impression left by Florence was not Italian but international, summing up the city as 'small but delectable'.[12] The needs of well-to-do foreigners encouraged the development of a cultural infrastructure that raised Florence to the status of a place of pilgrimage for art lovers far above the level of the average Italian town of similar size. To a certain extent, the Florence of these foreigners compensated the local population for the loss of their status as a capital, a loss that they never fully accepted.

How far tourism had come is clear from a report by a British visitor that English was the most frequently spoken foreign language in the Via Tornabuoni and was almost as common as Italian, the only difference being that it was spoken much more loudly, 'both from the chest and through the nose'.[13] With British firmness, groups of civilian and military strollers were moved on in this way from the narrow pavement outside the confectioner Giacosa's. On the Piazza della Signoria was a Birreria Viennese,[14] while the Bierhaus Troller on the Palazzo Strozzi and the Birreria Mucke behind Or San Michele both served Bavarian beer. The Birreria Mucke was additionally notable for its scenes of fauns, painted by Adolf von Hildebrand. Reinhold Begas also appears to have painted frescos there.

The best restaurant in town was Doney et Neveux,[15] which, in spite of its name, was English. The *Circolo degli artisti* mentioned in the previous chapter met in one of its back rooms,[16] but it was above all a place for foreigners to foregather. It was here that Theodor Fontane treated himself to a lavish meal of consommé, fried sole, steak and a bottle of St Julien for around four thalers, a sum he considered by no means excessive 'given the elegance of the place'.[17] The eccentric ethnologist Charles Godfrey Leland had several cups of coffee brought over to his rooms each day, while other famous customers included the artist Sir William Spence and the author of *Moby Dick*, Herman Melville.

All trace of the countless regular haunts of foreign nationals in the old town's trattorie and the quarters beyond the Arno has long since disappeared, although we know that the German artists met at the Café Gambrinus, which Florence's intellectuals referred to – significantly – as the 'Gambrinus-Halle'. Here they would drink beer and discuss the concerns of the day.[18] Arnold Böcklin and his circle could be found at the Cantina Strozzi[19] or in the delicatessen run by the Swiss restaurateur Giovanni Marugg, while at the Café Reininghaus there were occasional sightings of the dishevelled Bohemian figure of Theodor Däubler, described by Ernst Barlach as 'the majestic, overweight incarnation of the spirit of the stars' and as 'a fleshy oriental potentate in disguise'.[20]

A little more light is shed on the Buca Lapi by a publication produced by the Halcyon Academy for Unapplied Sciences at Salò. The Buca Lapi was a wine cellar beneath the Palazzo Antinori that remains famous even today. According to the publication in question:

> The cellar reflects its lofty or, rather, its base designation. A chicken ladder leads down into the world's most remarkable art gallery, more remarkable than the Uffizi and the Pitti. Walls and vaults are covered in brightly coloured posters featuring décolleté circus artistes, Michelangelo's *David* and caricatures of every description. To the left, on one of the sections of the ladder, is the microscopic kitchen, where Moro, the perfect cook with the face of an Othello, presides over his seething office. Generally packed, the room echoes with the chinking of glasses and the noise of diners and teems with Lapi's countless children of all shapes and sizes, the scene as a whole dominated by the merry landlord's stentorian voice. . . . In spring the cellar is turned into a bower of roses, and May men and women flirt in all the languages of the world.[21]

Around the turn of the century, a happy band of revellers gathered here over bottles of shimmering red Chianti. It included not only Arnold Böcklin but also the writer Otto Erich Hartleben,[22] who was as well known for his writings as for his Bohemian lifestyle as president of the

Verbrechertisch (literally 'Criminal Table'), a literary circle based in Berlin. In June 1900 he wrote a humorous poem for the landlord's daughter, describing her as 'the daintiest snake'. A number of surviving postcards recall his intoxicatedly enjoyable stays in Florence. Cäsar Flaischlen, a successful novelist and poet in the years around the turn of the century, scribbled a postcard to his fellow writer Arno Holz, punning on the German word for a night-club and referring to the 'delightful Florentine rhyme, Michelangelo–Tingeltangelo'.[23]

In addition to the restaurants and trattorie, Elvira Grifi's guide to Florence also mentions eleven public baths and gyms, as well as dance schools, riding schools and language colleges, to say nothing of more than two hundred music teachers, who helped the women and children of international high society to while away their weekends and rainy days. During the 1880s, the young Lizzie Boott from Boston engaged models for would-be artists, mainly from England and America, at the Villa Mugnone, where she also hired out space for use as studios.[24] Other visitors would meet at the city's *cafés chantants*, which lined its streets and squares, shopping at fashionable emporia and visiting its art galleries. There were also workshops which produced mosaics and majolica. And, on the Piazza Antinori, Janetti's sold products of the craft industry from Paris, London and 'Japan', while Raffaello Fontana dealt in Delft porcelain and Chinese art.

The Via Tornabuoni was the most fashionable shopping street in Florence. Thomas Mann bought some 'Iris' perfume there for 1.25 lire in 1901. A contemporary novel describes the atmosphere there on a March morning: tourists carrying guidebooks, tramps and gossips with missals and, above them all, the 'young, mild sun from which rays of sunlight pour down, obliquely angled and full of specks of dust, striking the *palazzi* and the fragrant flowers'.[25] Everywhere there were flower girls with their huge baskets of flowers – a traditional part of the townscape by the middle of the nineteenth century – selling their wares along the wall of the Palazzo Strozzi and in doing so symbolizing Florence itself: 'Against the old grey stone, long branches of apple and almond blossom rose up, together with daffodils and jonquils.'

And then there was the world of music, the theatre and brilliant opera performances; fairs; the unveiling of monuments; and historical pageants. Guidebooks went out of their way to mention them, and of course they were invariably an attraction for the city's tourists. But we would be guilty of misjudging this culture of fairs and festivities, which remains a vital force in Italian towns and cities to this day, if we were to overlook the fact that *calcio* and – on Easter Saturday – the famous *scoppio del carro* (literally, the 'exploding cart') were not enjoyed as much, or even more, by the local population.[26] In 1898 Aby and Mary Warburg followed one such spectacle from the Campanile, and Mary later wrote enthusiastically of the view of the 'multicoloured swarm of activity' above the city and above the sunlit hills of Tuscany.[27]

Among local customs was the practice of attaching a paper ladder – the *scala di mezza quaresima* – to passing women twenty days before Easter. And on Ascension Day the city's inhabitants would walk to the Cascine, where the *grillo* – a kind of flea market – was held. On the first of May the symbolic Flower Festival was celebrated. In his novel *Le Lys rouge*, which is set in Florence, Anatole France draws a parallel between the city's coat of arms, which depicts a *fleur de lys*, and the real flowers of the festival, the delicate colours of Fra Angelico's altarpieces and the flowers in Botticelli's *Primavera*, all of them images which anticipated the floral *Jugendstil* of Florence.[28]

The Feast of San Giovanni, the city's patron saint, was celebrated on 24 June with lights, processions, music and a magnificent firework display, while San Lorenzo was honoured on 10 August, when the bakers of the Borgo San Lorenzo decorated their shops. Lasagne was sold throughout the day; then, with the descent of night – the night of nights of the Italian summer – the townspeople would wander out of the city over the sable-coated hills, to watch the shooting stars and make a wish.

It was not least with an eye to tourism that the city fathers went out of their way to organize lavish celebrations designed to commemorate historical events, although in the end their plans gave rise to at least one argument over the celebrations in honour of Amerigo Vespucci and Paolo Toscanelli,[29] when the unveiling of the two monuments, a night-time pageant on the Arno, horse racing in the Cascine, a meeting of cyclists who were members of the Touring Club Italiano and much else beside cost ninety thousand lire instead of the projected ten thousand. The mayor, Pietro Torrigiani, defended his decision by pointing out that the celebrations for Dante, Michelangelo and the unveiling of the façade of the Duomo had attracted six thousand foreigners who had remained in Florence throughout the month of May. He also reminded his critics that Florence was a large city and 'not some anonymous commune'.

The local theatres could certainly be cited as proof of Torrigiani's claim and, indeed, were an extremely controversial topic in council debates. Elvira Grifi's guidebook lists no fewer than twelve theatres, including the Politeama Fiorentino Vittorio Emanuele and the Arena Nazionale, which was open for ten months of the year and which, according to the contemporary journalist Gabardo Gabardi, was the '*teatro fiorentino per eccellenza*', with its low entrance prices, plays, dance theatre, ballets and, above all, the cancan. In a wonderful piece of writing, Gabardi paints a picture of the Arena which is like a painting by Toulouse-Lautrec, while his description of the cancan there could sum up the closing years of the century:

> What seems impossible at such a blasé *fin de siècle* as ours is that the sight of those bootees, those legs, calves, garters and thighs still has the power to provoke a real sense of delirium that I have no hesitation in describing as lascivious. Go there during the waltz from *Madame Angot*, the chorus of servants from *Corneville* or the cancan from *Orpheus in the Underworld*, look and tell me what you see! To the leaping rhythms of the orchestra, the first hems are raised, the first curves can be seen, the first grunts can be heard, and time and again the men's sticks are banged feverishly against the tiles. The music presses on, and the witches' dance grows yet wilder, and flesh is exposed, and the Bacchantes stir, and their clothes ride higher and higher and yet higher. The eyes of the lads are fired with desire, they catch their breath, they shout and applaud and call out 'more', 'more', 'more'.[30]

For Gabardi, the cancan was a staple ingredient of a 'nervous' age. He describes the climax of the spectacle, when the police had to be called to prevent instinctual urges from overflowing, a 'psychological, nay pathological moment',[31] which may imply a certain cultural criticism. Certainly, it is apparent that the performance, which Gabardi saw as an expression of Bacchantic frenzy, was felt by the contemporary observer to symbolize an uninhibited present which precisely for that reason was regarded as sick.[32]

The Pagliano, too, was seen as a 'theatre for all'. This was one of the largest theatres in Italy, the scene of brilliant performances of Verdi's *Aida* and Mascagni's *Cavalleria rusticana* as well as of recitations and great balls with banquets and dancing. When Paul Klee visited it in the spring of 1902, it struck him more as a 'people's opera'. It was 'shaped like an elongated church, as large as it was filthy'.[33]

The 'aristocratic' Teatro della Pergola was Florence's leading theatre. Here Klee saw a performance by the Sadda Yakko company from Japan and was deeply impressed by it. In comparison, Loie Fuller, who was also appearing in Florence in the spring of 1902, struck him as 'purely decorative' and concerned with 'pure technique'.[34] The Pergola programme also shows the extent to which Wagner's works were already dominating the repertory to the disadvantage of home-grown operas, a point noted by Jacob Burckhardt. Both *Lohengrin* and *Tannhäuser* were staged here during the 1899/1900 season.[35]

The Pergola also hosted gala performances by candlelight, including the famous *veglione* which ended the annual carnival.[36] Everyone who was anyone in Florence was invited to the gala dinner and ball in the auditorium, which was specially decorated for the occasion. By the end of the nineteenth century, however, these events were starting to lose their lustre. The leading spoken theatre of the time was the Niccolini, not far from the Duomo. Formerly the Teatro del Cocomer, this was the theatre where Eleonora Duse famously appeared.

And yet even the theatre was losing its appeal and forfeiting its traditional role in the life of the city, so manifold were the attractions offered by the new age. Writing in 1897, Eugenio Checchi argued that many other more or less dangerous passions had replaced the impassioned delight which found expression in some ardent enthusiasm for a piece of music, a light comedy or a singer or actress. No more battles were fought over the Romanticism of a writer like Victor Hugo; and another King Ludwig of Bavaria would probably never appear on the scene, to provide a counterpart to Wagner's mystically minded patron.

The case of the theatre – an ancient institution which has always been a focus of social discourse and rituals – exemplifies the rapidly changing conditions in turn-of-the-century Europe and, more particularly, the change in sensibility, with its shifting barriers between the normal and the exceptional. In Checchi's view, it was the new themes, the more garish sensations and, above all, the constraints of hectic modern life that spelt the death of the older type of theatre. He contrasted this death agony with the idealized picture of a theatre of the people in which the class differences of modern society are no longer symbolically reproduced in the layout of the auditorium, with its class-conscious seating arrangements. Checchi's text describes a type of theatre at which audiences would foregather between six and seven in the evening and engage in light-hearted conversation with their neighbours in the diffuse light of little lamps:

> Time and again people would cast their eyes upwards to a round hole in the ceiling, because it was here that the first sign would appear that the moment had come – initially a faint glimmer, a vague light that gradually increased in intensity: a radiant star in a dark sky, the '*j'atans mon astre*' of the old Savoyard legend, a star that shone with all its splendour at ten minutes to eight, when the ceiling would open and reveal the lower side of a chandelier already completely ablaze with oil lamps. By now there was not a single member of the audience who was not gazing upwards to look. Slowly, majestically, solemnly, the chandelier was lowered on its tight hempen ropes until it stopped halfway down; an 'Ah!' escaped from

the audience's lips, and a few minutes later the orchestra would give the signal to begin.[37]

Checchi's melancholy text recalls a past that in 1900 was still relatively recent, a past when even a bright light could cause a sensation: this was the transitional period between the pitch-black night of old Europe and the artificial light produced first by gas and then by electric lighting. The result was that turn-of-the-century Florence was swamped by a flood of spectacular productions of every description, all of them attempting to outdo the last one, beginning with the play of light which was the basis of the Lumière brothers' cinematograph[38] and ending with guest appearances by world-famous artists such as Eleanora Duse and the dancer Isadora Duncan. Visiting artists included Carolina Otero – 'La Belle Otero'[39] – and Cléo de Mérode, while the city's annals also record a remarkable encounter between the American dancer Loie Fuller and Gabriele D'Annunzio, who was a frequent visitor to the banks of the Arno. But there were also more curious episodes such as the appearance of the Wild West hero Buffalo Bill, the living embodiment of the American myth, who came to Florence for the first time in 1890 to present his show on the Campo di Marzio, a pitiful spectacle comprising real and fake North American Indians. Contemporary reports claim that the performers came from all over the world and included Russian Cossacks, Mexicans and Scotsmen. There were re-enactments of buffalo hunts and battles from the Indian wars of the period, including the Battle of the Little Bighorn, in which General Custer was defeated by Sitting Bull. The show was a popular reflex of the exoticism of contemporary literature.[40]

More and more sensations and more and more colourful spectacles followed each other with increasing frequency, as all who could afford to do so attempted to offset their feelings of tedium and the paralysing ennui that threatened their very souls. In their constant quest for new stimuli and novel distractions, contemporaries were caught up in a downward spiral and endlessly driven on. Cultural commentators of the time argued that there was no longer any real creativity, the triumph of realism being held up as proof of this claim. The love of experimentation and the search for more and more new forms of entertainment was leading to a loss of individual identity. A world which had denied the absolute was pursuing the shadow of things.

Many of Florence's pilgrims simply refused to believe this: in beauty and great art they saw no mere shadows, but the highest form of human achievement. At least they had been told that this was so, and they did what they could to live up to the norm formulated by those who preached the gospel of a religion of art. A lira gained them entry to the Uffizi, to the gallery at the Palazzo Pitti and to the Accademia with Botticelli's *Primavera* and Michelangelo's *David*, which had stood there since 1882 on a podium erected by Emilio de Fabris.

Numerous churches and monasteries passed into the hands of the Commune between 1868 and 1871, and this in turn meant that the works of art which they contained were now owned by the city.[41] The Monastery of Santa Maria Novella was converted into a museum between 1905 and 1907. Meanwhile, numerous loans, private donations and legacies added to the city's art collections. The important collections of Louis Carrand, Costantino Ressman and Giulio Franchetti, including paintings, armour, bronzes and examples of the 'minor' arts, found their way into the Bargello;[42] there one of the main sights since 1888 had been Donatello's *Saint George*, which had been removed from its niche at Or San Michele. Donors and lenders included countless foreigners such as Walter Savage Landor and Anthony Trollope, who had chosen to settle in Florence and had a weak spot for these lesser arts. Etruscan vases and other pieces of pottery from the possession of Baron Vagnonville were housed at the Museo Archeologico, while other pieces finished up in the Palazzo Pitti, which was jointly owned both by the city and by the state. Such foundations document Florence's desire to assert itself culturally in the face of the centralized tendencies of the united state.

The city's sights also included those places where famous foreigners had been active in Florence in the past. In the days before Florence became the country's capital, a visit to the houses occupied by the Trollopes and the Brownings was as much a part of the standard programme of English-speaking visitors as a public audience with the grand duke. And even as late as the turn of the century, Landor's villa at Fiesole, variously known as the Villa Gherardesca and La Torraccia, was still a place of pilgrimage. A later owner, Willard Fiske, the Professor of North European Languages at Cornell University, restored the building to the state in which it had been at the time of the writer's death in 1864.[43]

Most of the private galleries and collections were open only to a limited extent: Elvira Grifi mentions six: the Martelli, Panciatichi, Capponi, Torrigiani, Strozzi and Corsini galleries.[44] Of these, it seems that only the Galleria Strozzi had regular opening times, although the Galleria Torrigiani could be visited by special permission. Heinrich Brockhaus and – presumably – the other members of the German Art Historical Institute had an opportunity to see Prince Corsini's collection at the end of April 1898.[45] Arnold Bennett provides a graphic account of the atmosphere there, with liveried custodians regarding themselves as consciously superior to ordinary state officials, in a vast space covering some five thousand square feet which resembled 'a sort of throne room' with 'very ugly candelabra', to quote Bennett's typically supercilious description:

> The other rooms large and ugly with chiefly ugly furniture and poor old pictures. A simply vast quantity of bad art. Spectacular proof of the general low level of painting etc. even in the greater centuries. When one reflects that there must be hundreds, perhaps thousands, of such collections the idea appals. But the central room on the river front had a few pictures of the first-class. Botticelli etc.[46]

The *palazzi* of Florence and of the surrounding area contained fine collections that were mentioned in none of the guidebooks of the period. One example was the exquisite collection of Frederick Stibbert, which included some pieces from the legendary holdings of Prince Anatoli Demidov.[47] Warburg mentions a visit to the collection of Rosa Piatti, the mother of Count Nobili. Here he saw 'some wonderful things, a little statuette of David, without a hat, like Donatello's with the hat, Robbia's *Mary and Child* . . . Cellini, Raphael (freehand drawing), *Madonna and Child, en face* with indications of colours'.[48] Donatello's *David* had a particularly prominent admirer in the person of André Gide, who recalled the 'oriental graces' of the statue when he encountered scantily dressed young fishermen on the banks of the Arno. One of them showed Gide tattoos on his arms and penis, offering him an opportunity to become better acquainted with these real-life embodiments of the art of the Quattrocento.[49]

13 Isolde Kurz (*c*.1890)

*'We need Italy for our spiritual sustenance, this country and its art, a country that
has been the object of our yearning and of our love for almost 1,500 years'*
(WILHELM BODE)

North and South:
Germans and Florentines

THE end of the nineteenth century witnessed the continuation of a trend which had begun with the earliest visits to Italy by German travellers, who had crossed the Alps with their heads full of Goethe's *Italian Journey* and Jacob Burckhardt's voluminous guide to Italian art, *The Cicerone*, in their luggage.[1] Once in Italy, they admired the art galleries, *palazzi,* churches and landscapes of the 'blessed' peninsula, imagining pictures of moon-lit ruins or sun-drenched gardens surrounded by pine trees, their leaves providing shade for marble statues, while lemon trees bore their heavy fruit and deities created by Giovanni da Bologna disported themselves on the glittering surfaces of the country's fountains. They thought of the sweeping bays nestling around the towns of the Adriatic and of the Tyrrhenian Sea; of distant hills and domes lit by the rays of the setting sun; and of the shimmering red wine in which all this beauty was refracted and transfigured. The views of Florence afforded by Hesse, Rilke, Isolde Kurz and others reveal this perspective from a more specific standpoint. At the same time, visitors from abroad sought the tangible reality of an ideal image which, open to physical appropriation, was made up of elements drawn from the classical tradition.

Then there was the 'lightness of being' associated with life in Italy, the enjoyment of existence being the very essence of all that was summed up by the word *italianità*. 'Human beings are often more blessed than the gods,' wrote Alice Hallgarten in a letter to the Warburgs, 'for the blessed gods are in heaven, but heaven is in the blessed human being, heaven with all its gods.'[2] She had just settled in Rome, where she was later to marry a government official with property in Umbria and to be numbered among those capable of enjoying life in Italy to the full. Isolde Kurz was only one out of many observers to regard 'refined and spiritualized sensuality' as the basis of Italian civilization. She noted a powerfully developed sense of beauty in every social class, giving rise to care over clothing and an elegant appearance, to say nothing of the ability to deal with everyday life and all its adversities and to organize life around hedonistic goals.[3] In 1911 Heinrich Mann described 'a naïve delight in the emotions' and 'gestural freedom' as the salient features of the Italian people,[4] and other foreigners noted similar findings. Max Beerbohm, for example, found a country in which everything was agreeably 'easy' and people could be 'quite alone'.[5] Even the laconic Arnold Bennett, with his conscious reserve, was unable to resist this initial impression.[6] And the no less realistic Henry James thought that 'the sum of Italian misery is, on the whole, less than the sum of the Italian experience of life'.[7]

In short, visitors compared Italy with their own country, regarding the latter as shrouded in mist in a literal and figurative sense and feeling that in Italy they were in an alternative world, sun replacing rain, chafing constraints giving way to freedom, and a Grecian blue sky usurping the place of the low-hanging clouds which mixed with the smoke of factory chimneys to produce banks of drifting smog back at home. Here was beauty instead of a hideous industrial landscape, harmony instead of the fissured modern world. It is significant that, at least as far as Italy went, there were far more nineteenth-century landscape painters from Germany (and England) than from Italy itself – and not only when we consider artists of any importance. It is worth asking, therefore, why there were so few Italians who adopted a genuinely Romantic view of the landscape.

Of some significance in this context is the whimsical correspondence which passed between Wilhelm Jensen and Paul Heyse. Jensen, whose daughter married into the upper echelons of the German aristocracy in 1892, visited Florence in November 1896, when he and his wife attended the wedding of the future King Vittorio Emanuele III and Elena of Montenegro. He dropped his fellow writer the following lines on a postcard:

In golden sunlight's late autumnal days
I cast my eyes San Miniato-wards
And often opened up your book of verse
And let my soul refresh itself thereon.
In beautiful defiance came the sound
Of ancient and proud-hearted poetry.
Thus may this *cartolin' di nozze* bear
These fleeting words of thanks to you, my friend.

Heyse replied:

In northern Europe's greyish twilit mist
A lovely ray of southern sun shines forth,
A song that long ago had died away
Now brings a friendly echo back to us,
A warming greeting from a far-off land
In times of frost and dismal disaccord.
It fortifies the heart. How heartily
We shake the friendly hand that sent it here.[8]

The Germans could look back on a long tradition in this regard. Their medieval rulers had crossed the Alps, and centuries later Goethe had been the spiritual guide *par excellence* of every visitor to Italy. As a result, we may suspect a special relationship between them and their southern neighbours. At the end of the nineteenth century, Sigmund Münz claimed that Berlin's wine list had become a map of Italy, while broccoli was the favourite vegetable of the fashionable man about town. 'We Germans still have a sentimental attachment to Italy,' he wrote, before going on to qualify that remark: 'But we shall always strive in vain to make the spirit of the Medici our own, a spirit that continues to lead its vibrant life in your brighter air, in your clearer heads and in your natural forms and customs.'[9]

The German public had adopted a reserved attitude to Italian unification at least since 1859, while evincing an effusive enthusiasm for the largely depoliticized Garibaldi.[10] Among the older generation of Germans who chose to settle in Florence, we do, however, find a whole series of individuals who did not share this attitude, notably Isolde and Edgar Kurz, Adolf von Hildebrand and his wife and, of course, Karl and Jessie Hillebrand. Hillebrand in particular seems to have gone out of his way to see the Florentine aristocracy as traditionally republican, even democratic, and in that way to trace a direct line of descent from the idealized picture of late medieval middle-class Florence to the present day.[11] For many Catholics, the Risorgimento was the work of the devil, and it is certainly striking that there were few Catholics among the famous visitors to Italy during the post-Romantic period, a handful of exceptions such as Alfred von Reumont and Franz Xaver Kraus merely serving to confirm the rule. After 1848, however, visits to Italy were more obviously politically motivated than had previously been the case – in which respect these visits resembled British pilgrimages to Florence.

One of the few Germans who were not prompted to visit Italy by the beauty of its nature and art was the journalist Henrich Homberger, who was friendly with Isolde Kurz and Karl Hillebrand.[12] When he settled in Florence, he was, in his own words, 'examining the political challenge facing Germany':

I want to see how Neapolitans, Tuscans and Lombards have merged to become one nation with one fatherland within the space of five years, and by seeing this for myself, I want to teach myself and – if possible – others, too, to understand how on both sides of the Alps the happy son of a great country may live 'standing on freedom's soil, a people free'.

Homberger wanted to play a part in bringing together two countries which already had so much in common.

Whether we are entitled to make more generalized claims on the basis of such an attitude is a question that cannot be answered here. Even writers such as Cavour's biographer Heinrich von Treitschke and the philosopher Friedrich Theodor Vischer, both of whom regarded Austria as their natural enemy and who supported Italian unification, adopted an attitude of reserve, at least for a time, preferring to side with their Habsburg 'brethren'.[13] During the wars of the Risorgimento, more Germans may well have fought on the side of the Habsburgs, and even under the command of the Pope, than for the opposing forces.[14] Only after 1866 is there evidence of an increasing sympathy for the cause of unification among German observers.[15] And the most significant expression of that support may well have been Viktor Helm's book on Italy, a study which is also the first attempt to examine Italy as a contemporary political entity.[16]

Once the German Reich had been established as a unified country, the Risorgimento lost its charismatic appeal for German observers, and by the turn of the century it had become customary to regard the relationship between Germany and Italy in a light which adumbrates worrying later developments – a point well illustrated by Houston Stewart Chamberlain, who, although born in England, became Wagner's son-in-law.[17] First published in 1899, his book *The Foundations of the Nineteenth Century* evidently struck a chord with contemporaries, as is clear from its best-seller status: by 1942 it had gone through no fewer than twenty-eight editions. Consciously dismissing the humanist tradition in culture and education, Chamberlain posited a 'Germanic' cultural awareness associated with 'race'. In his eyes, the troubling phenomena of the modern world – capitalism, industrialization, rationalism and democracy, which for unclear reasons are invested with an anti-Italian thrust – threatened *völkisch* German culture, which was said to have developed organically, and called into question the natural order of all that was Germanic. Romance elements, by contrast, were regarded as 'poisonous'. The Mediterranean world was said to represent a disastrous example of miscegenation, an unhealthy 'chaos of nations'. The ancient metropolises of southern Europe prefigured modern civilization with all its noxious side effects. The picture of the effeminate Roman necessarily enfeebled by his blood and contrasted with the superior Teuton has its roots here.

In real-life Italy, such a view was reinforced by the lordly attitude affected by many Germans and by their brusque 'Prussian' manner, which was generally felt to be disagreeable. Gino Capponi ridiculed the behaviour of many German academics, who carried on as if they had single-handedly produced all the world's culture and civilization and shown the way to other nations.[18] Even Warburg aptly described his fellow Germans as '*parvenus* of national sentiment'. And, availing herself of what is, of course, a problematic terminology, Isolde Kurz claimed that the Germans had rushed on to the scene as members of a master race whose mastery was still far too new to be easily forgiven.[19] Contemporaries called it 'new German'. When compared to the Italians, this social type acquired particularly sharp relief. On the other hand, Isolde Kurz was conscious of Germany's 'inadequate cultural standing', as she expressed it in the course of a conversation with Cosima Wagner.[20] She drew up a long list of differences between the mentality of the Italians and that of the Germans, including inappropriate tourist clothing, knee breeches, hobnailed boots and badly fitting women's dresses; indiscreet intimacies between lovers within sight of Andrea Orcagna's *loggia*; and the singing of German folksongs in the Gulf of Naples.

In spite of all this, Isolde Kurz saw the end of Italy as a sunset of radiant beauty:

> The sun was just going down over the city on the banks of the Arno, the sky was clear, the corona was on fire, towers, domes and *palazzi* stood in a sea of flames. . . . We were sitting in a room that opened on to the garden, our conversation happened to turn to the question of nationality. It was long before the Great War, the downfall of the culture and civilization of the old Latin nations was one of those doctrines that those nations themselves believed in more eagerly than any other. One of our party wanted to see in the setting sun a symbol and emblem of the beautiful country in which we were living: in just such eventide serenity Italian culture and racial identity were disappearing in order to make way for more vigorous modern nations.[21]

Talk of 'poor' Italy and a dismissive attitude to its cultural diaspora is found time and again, even if it never acquires the force of an all-pervasive leitmotif.[22] The wrath of the Florentine newspaper *Il Marzocco* was roused by an essay by Richard Muther in the Berlin-based *Der Tag* in which the writer dismissed the art of present-day Italy as derivative when compared with that of 'the chosen and dominant races', and he concluded that 'Italy has had its day'.[23]

Even those Germans who crossed the Alps often, and even settled in the country, had no real links with contemporary Italy. (Here we may also include Swiss artists and writers such as Böcklin and Burckhardt.) The case of Thomas Mann is typical. It was not until 1920 that he made contact with the Italian intelligentsia of the period, a contact he owed to his acquaintance with the Milanese Germanist Lavinia Mazzucchetti.[24] Twenty years earlier, Italy had still been the Italy of the past for him. His Savonarola – the true hero of his play *Fiorenza*[25] – represents all that is deepest and most extreme. In short, he is a profoundly German hero who rebels against the seductive, iridescent and yet dangerous sensuality of Italy.[26] The 'sultry lethargy of the orient' is said to blight the land.[27] The orient is a place of sensuality, but also a place of danger inasmuch as it is the source of the plague.

For the readers of Burckhardt, Nietzsche, Thomas Mann and other northern writers, Italy was Janus-faced. On the one hand there was the 'great' Italy of the past and, in particular, the Florence of the Renaissance, with its artists and 'supermen', while on the other hand there was a second Italy which, if it incorporated the relics of bygone greatness, offered a beguiling but dangerous alternative to all that was German.[28] The South was fascinating, but in the way a beautiful whore is fascinating. A heavy sky hung low over the country, a sky filled with the scent of magnolia and jonquil, and Arcadia was unexpectedly displaced to the far North: 'Oh God, Lisaveta, don't talk to me of Italy,' Tonio Kröger exclaims at one point in Mann's narrative:

> I am bored with Italy to the point of despising it. It's a long time since I thought I felt at home there. The land of art! Velvet blue skies, heady wine and sweet sensuality . . . No thank you, that's not for me. I renounce it. All that *bellezza* gets on my nerves. And I can't stand all that dreadful southern vivacity, all those people with their black animal eyes. They've no conscience in their eyes, those Latin races.[29]

For foreigners, the Italians of the turn of the century were generally no more than background figures in the 'magic garden of the Hesperides', dead models of marmoreal beauty, perhaps still the object of sensual desire. 'Italy really is a glorious country,' Adolf von Hildebrand wrote to Conrad Fiedler: 'the people play no part here, or least the clothed ones.'[30] The Italians were regarded as picturesque components in a dream landscape, preferably as the peasant girls and shepherds in paintings by the Germans living in Italy or in the engravings of Luigi Rossini. Other foreigners such as Ruskin regarded them with contempt and even hatred, an attitude summed up by Enrico Nencioni when he wrote with reference to the English: 'For these dear visitors, Italy is a museum or at least it ought to be, a museum of which we Italians are the custodians. . . .They would like us to wear large brigands' hats and enclose our feet in the straps and sandals of the *ciociari* in order to make us more Italian.'[31] Visitors sought not so much reality as an Arcadian genre painting. For most of them, Italy remained less a country of physical encounters than an Elysium where the transmigration of souls could take place. If they occurred at all, physical encounters were generally limited to the tourist's basic needs: landladies, hoteliers, waiters, cab drivers and the like. In a poem on the 'Genius of Old Florence' which Aby Warburg, for example, carried around with him and which he may even have written himself, we read: 'Those two who are so dear to you seek me, the old man, not the modern *italiano*.' At one point, the Genius of Old Florence says:

> Within your hand, you Friesians, Lower Saxons,
> I like to see my legacy: you take
> It not as flotsam or as spoils of war
> But as the heirloom of a dear dead friend
> Whose voice and likeness one recalls in dreams . . .[32]

Warburg's diaries mention Italian names only sporadically, generally in the context of invitations to the homes of German colleagues and friends. Nor are the contacts always friendly. On 8 October 1898, for example, we find Warburg referring to 'Carlotta, the silly young housemaid'. Of another of his servants he writes: 'Adelia's food is better than that of that Carlo swine, but the service provided by Rosina is scandalously rustic; it wouldn't surprise me if she secretly eats hay; she certainly has manners more suited to the great outdoors.'[33] Inevitably Warburg had closer contacts with the assistants whom he periodically employed to help him copying out various documents. He was also in touch with the leading art historian Adolfo Venturi.

The Warburgs' economic position and their cultural interests naturally cut them off from their Italian environment. But they had no more contact with the Italian aristocracy or the cultural elite of Florence. Instead, they lived on a kind of Anglo-German space-ship. It seems unlikely that Warburg's Jewishness played any role in this relative isolation: at all events, contemporary sources give no indication that this was the case. He and his wife maintained a good relationship with the evangelic community and its pastor, Eugen Lessing. All that we can say for certain is that Warburg knew the Florentines of the Quattrocento better than he knew those of his own time.

Even Böcklin and Hildebrand,[34] both of whom had lived in Florence for many years and acquired a certain status in the city, seem to have spent far more time with their fellow countrymen than with the people of Florence or with Italians in general. Among the exceptions were the Contessa Gabriella Spalletti Rasponi and the writer Carlo Placci. A mere handful of Germans had closer links with the Italians. Ludmilla Assing was married to an Italian, and Italians stood by her deathbed. The musician Baron Alexander Kraus, a native of Frankfurt, played a major role in the cultural life of Florence during its days as a capital and later, too, by establishing a number of schools of music and organizing concerts.[35] Arguably the leading figure in mediating between the two cultures was Karl Hillebrand who, as editor-in-chief of *Italia*, sought to elucidate Italy to his fellow Germans. But Hillebrand was a European rather than a specifically German figure.

Isolde Kurz and Paul Heyse could similarly be said to enjoy dual nationality. In her memoirs, Isolde Kurz sketches miniature portraits of numerous Italians, while Heyse busied himself translating works of Italian literature, including verse by the Florentine poet Angelo Orvieto. He was also in contact with the Italian intelligentsia. Prominent among his Italian friends was the Turin-born poet, linguist, ethnologist and journalist Angelo de Gubernatis.[36]

De Gubernatis had studied in Berlin and, European in outlook, corresponded with many Germans, including Warburg's teacher, Hubert Janitschek, and the Indologist Ferdinand Justi, whose brother was the art historian Carl Justi.[37] Ferdinand Justi had an excellent knowledge of German literature, which he wrote about in the columns of *Nuova Antologia*, repeating various negative clichés about the German folk character which included its craving for status, lack of refinement and love of the colossal, but also revealing his respect for German culture and science.[38] A prolific writer, he invariably worked on several projects at once and is generally regarded as the founder of Italian Indology, in which capacity he established the Indian Museum in Florence in 1886. He also wrote works on the sexual symbolism of plants and animals, founded newspapers and was politically extremely active. For a few months he was a member of the group of anarchists around Mikhail Bakunin[39] and went on to marry Bakunin's cousin, Sofia Besobrasova. Later still, his views became even more idiosyncratic and we find him writing pacifist texts, others which are hostile to the working classes, and yet others pleading in favour of Italy's colonial policy in Libya – a stance he evidently considered compatible with his views on pacifism.

He was also a tireless dramatist, some of his plays indicating Schiller and Goethe as his models. On one occasion he tried to persuade no lesser a composer than Wagner to set one of his plays to music, but Wagner declined on the grounds that he was preparing for the celebrations marking the laying of the foundation-stone of his Festival Theatre in Bayreuth and had no time, while he took the opportunity to ask de Gubernatis for a donation to his festival.[40] A visiting card found among the Italian's unpublished papers – '*Monsieur et Madame Wagner*' – suggests that there was also personal contact between him and the Wagners.[41] Conceivably they met when the family visited Florence in December 1876, although Cosima Wagner's diaries make no mention of such an encounter.[42] Cosima was often in Italy with Eva and Siegfried Wagner. Alice Hallgarten met them frequently in Rome and wrote to tell Warburg: 'It's funny hearing Wagner described as "Papa" and Liszt as "Grandpapa" .'[43]

De Gubernatis spent many years in Florence, where Heyse will have been introduced to him either by Karl Hillebrand or by the Kurz family. Entirely typical of 'old Europe', their correspondence records an intensive exchange of ideas and a genuinely warm relationship, its tone recalling the Age of Sensibility and the sort of bond of friendship that had been common a century earlier.[44] But, rather than sending an ivory miniature, Heyse asks for a picture of de Gubernatis and sends him a photograph in return, adding that it lacks the sunny mood attributed to its sender but that it would hardly redound to his credit if forty-four years had left no furrow on his brow.

Their correspondence also revolved around literary matters. Writing from Alexandersbad near Wunsiedel, Heyse complains about the 'dank martyrdom' and 'nervous tension' induced by his work on a translation of Manzoni's *Inni sacri*. He also reports on Munich, where he is cut off from court life by his friendship with the poet Emanuel Geibel, whose sympathies lay with Prussia, and where the good times associated with 'good King Max' are now over. He also expresses his resentment at the violent criticism of his work by adherents of the new school of Naturalism.[45]

Like many observers, Heyse also saw a profound gulf between his own literary world and that of Italy and, indeed, Romance literature in general, a point which emerges from two letters written in 1902.[46] Politely but emphatically he turns down an invitation to become a member of the Società Elleno Latina, justifying his decision by pointing out that he sees too great a divide between himself and the literary tendencies represented by de Gubernatis. German profundity that can be compared to a Faustian struggle to scale the greatest heights and a striving to achieve the ideal, are contrasted with Latin 'dabbling' and flightiness and even with the virtuosity which, for him, was exemplified by the work of Victor Hugo. These are the stereotypical opposites that Heyse thinks he can discern. For him, the question of what art can achieve – and he is profoundly convinced by its power to triumph over the world and conquer our pain – helps to define the dividing line between Italian and German literature. For all his love of Italy, he regards German literature as superior inasmuch as it gives, whereas Italian literature can only receive. He condescendingly sums this up as follows: 'We certainly do not begrudge the Latin nations the spiritual uplift that they may be able to achieve though literary fraternization.' The Italians should be grateful for any ideas they may receive, but he himself feels disinclined to collaborate with them, as he is not 'one of the family'. In any case, the Italians have shown disconcertingly little interest in German literature, although he has to admit that, for their part, the Germans have always demonstrated 'an incredible indifference to all things Italian, the only exception being their traditional *Wanderlust* that takes them to the land of Mignon'.

Heyse's comments on the Italian reception of German literature contain an element of truth, but in other respects he is simply wrong. Anyone leafing through magazines and newspapers on general sale in Florence in the years around 1900 will find that there was a widespread awareness of German-language texts. This is true not only of such German classics as Goethe and Heine, but also of the literature of the present day.[47] Historiography and philosophy encountered considerable interest, the most popular philosophers being Nietzsche and Hegel, the latter mediated through the writings of Benedetto Croce and Giovanni Gentile. Schopenhauer, by contrast, was relatively ignored.[48] There was also a wide range of articles in Italian newspapers dealing with matters German,[49] including reports on German universities and on the growth of the workers' movement. Even the Oberammergau Passion Play was discussed, while *Il Marzocco*, which normally dealt with more aesthetic issues, featured an article on the steel baron Friedrich Alfred Krupp under the heading 'Ruler of a new empire'.[50]

Most Italian readers will have got to know German literature only at second hand, either through articles in literary magazines or through French translations – the Italians' links with French culture and civilization have been always been closer than they have with their German equivalent.[51] Goethe – the classic case of a German visitor to Italy – played an insignificant role in the Italian national consciousness when set beside that played by Byron, for example. Only occasionally was Goethe seen as a German 'Romantic',[52] although the erection of a statue of him on the heights of the Pincio in Rome was none the less celebrated in the most overblown rhetoric by Angelo Orvieto: 'Crown it with laurel, O Romans, in the sweet-scented wind that blows beneath the blue heavens.'[53]

The Italian attitude to the Germans vacillated between fear and astonished, even awestruck admiration. Both reactions were reasons for the interest in Germany that the Italians showed; for all that, their interest rarely stretched to the point where they acquired any real knowledge of the Germans. Indeed, many observers noted that the political sympathies of the Italians for their neighbours to the North remained within discernible limits.[54] Even Cavour had warned of the dangers of a 'Germanicization' of Europe. Italy was afraid of becoming a satellite of Bismarck's empire and of having the latter's authoritarian structures imposed upon it. There was even talk of the threat of German world supremacy.[55]

Intellectuals drew a comparison between the two countries, a comparison that did not always redound to Italy's advantage. 'What a contrast between Germany and Italy,' wrote *La Nazione*'s correspondent in his 'Letters from Berlin':

> What a contrast between this nation which, without any natural barriers, was decimated by the Thirty Years' War, Napoleon I, the wars of 1864, 1865 [*sic*] and 1870–71, a nation that lives in a mere handful of fertile tracts of land, worn down by its inclement climate and with a literature of only recent date – and the Italian nation, which until yesterday was divided into thirty or more small states! What a difference between the former and the people of Italy, with their ancient culture, cheered by the smile of God, benefiting from an abundance of fertile soil and protected by the sea and by the Alps! Rivals of the English in trade and industry, the Germans are the leading nation in science, including the science of war; they are clever and strong and, above all, extremely serious. And us?[56]

The economic advances made by the Reich were immense,[57] the industrial development of turn-of-the-century Italy being roughly on the level of that of Germany fifty years earlier. The majority of Italians were still working in agriculture,[58] while the number of Italians unable to read and write was markedly higher than comparable figures for Germany – this being the negative aspect of the country's bucolic image, with its shepherds and dancing peasant girls who so inspired the Germans. On the other hand, the Italians had a higher proportion of students and academics,[59] and there were far more doctors and lawyers than in Germany. Inasmuch as the Italian economy was underdeveloped, these professions were obvious ways of earning a livelihood and climbing the social ladder.

Although there were many Italians who observed Germany's economic advances and its powerful military machinery with a sense of real astonishment, there were others who adopted a critical or at least an ambivalent view of German 'constitutionalism', which was regarded as 'immature'.[60] Prussia was described as a '*caserma*', or barracks, Berlin was Sparta,[61] the Germans the 'Romans' of the present day.[62] Sigmund Münz was merely repeating an Italian commonplace when he recalled an Italian woman saying that the Germans whom she had encountered north of the Alps were more notable for their sabre-rattling bellicosity than for their humanitarianism.[63] At the same time, however, the German state, being under the rule of law, was felt to be an admirable theoretical model. Certainly Italy took over numerous elements of Germany's welfare legislation.

Many saw the figure of Wilhelm II as the guarantor of German greatness,[64] the Kaiser's ostentatious self-aggrandizement inevitably leaving its mark on a society responsive to bombastic sentiments and operetta-like spectacle. Germany was held up to the Italians as an example of a country which, although inhospitable and subjected to a despotic regime, was well organized, for all that it was peopled by a somewhat philistine race. Germany's outward physiognomy seemed to reflect its intellectual and spiritual life: the Germans were admired for the depth of their thinking, but that thinking was also criticized for being dark, with something of the night about it.[65] German science, by contrast, was felt to be a model of its kind: '*Germania docet*' – 'Germany teaches us' – Italy's liberal ruling elite used to say.[66]

Few Italians had formed a picture of Germany on the basis of personal contacts and of a first-hand knowledge of the country.[67] Even as late as the nineteenth century, traffic across the Alps was almost all in a north–south direction. As for the inhabitants of late nineteenth-century Florence, the writer, journalist and tireless friend of friends Carlo Placci was very much the exception to the rule. He was a member of Adolf von Hildebrand's circle, and it was presumably Hildebrand who prepared the ground for him when he set off for Germany in December 1903. In this way he met Herbert von Bismarck and the conductor Michael Balling and was a guest of Prince Rupprecht of Bavaria during his visit to Munich. His acquaintances included Wilhelm Dilthey, Adolf von Harnack and Gerhart Hauptmann, whom he may have got to know in Florence. In spite of all this, Placci's opinions on the Germans were all couched in traditional clichés: he considered them tenaciously hard-working, while German professors struck him – a prolific writer with a keen mind – as over-specialized, inspired amateurs. Houston Stewart Chamberlain – 'a dilettante whom I like', as he noted in his diary – was one of the few Anglo-Germans to be exempt from his condemnation.[68]

For all their self-conscious elitism, the German artists and writers active in Florence were generally unresponsive to Chamberlain's unspeakable references to 'the blood of the South' that was 'poisonous to the Germanic nations'. Although Isolde Kurz had a tendency to rant about the 'blood soul' that constituted the self,[69] she none the less stressed the distance between herself and Chamberlain, drawing a dividing line between her group of acquaintances in Florence and 'pallid, bloodless aesthetes' of *fin de siècle* decadence. But she also sought to distance herself from the naturalist movement in art.[70] The circle of writers and artists around her seemed to her to preserve a threatened humanist tradition which resisted realism in art and opposed the dangers of decadence by upholding authentic, original values of its own.

The foreigners who lived in Florence saw the starkest of contrasts between themselves and the tendencies of their age. They felt safe in a place which seemed to lie beyond the present day. 'In the calm of this city,' wrote Isolde Kurz, 'the German lived as if on an island of spirits, raised above the noise and bustle of the age.'[71] These Florentine Germans may have been in Italy, but in a sense they were not. They had *their* Florence, a beautiful, spiritual place that had little in common with the Italian city of the same name. In an unpublished text, Isolde Kurz recalled the dreamlike search for this idealized place and for the 'souls' of the great Italians whose works she saw in Florence. But then, sated on historic culture, she longed to hear 'natural sounds' again: 'I felt comfortable only with children, peasants and fisherfolk. . . . I dreamt of the Wild West with its buffalos and cowboys and of hut villages in Africa and Australia.'[72]

Having elected to live in Italy, the remarkably contemplative Isolde Kurz had learnt that not even the historical Italy, with its sentimental *pasticcio* of real-life experiences in museums and libraries and all manner of fantastical and romantic ideas, was the Arcadia that she had expected to find on leaving the complex realities of her German homeland. The hope of finding paradise had drawn her to Italy, but once there she was forced to realize that longing is an abiding factor in human existence. Arcadia is always somewhere else. For those Germans who travelled to Italy, the country turned out to be no more than a stopping-off place, the antithesis in a dialectical process, rather than the synthesis in an evolving Hegelian process. It offered merely the illusion of such a synthesis.

14   Giorgio Sommer, The Loggia dei Lanzi, Florence (before 1873)

'And then, oh, I left Florence when youths, rising up in revolt, threw stones at the Loggia dei Lanzi' (RAINER MARIA RILKE)

May 1898

T URN-OF-THE-CENTURY Florence was not at all the isle of the blessed of which aesthetes and art pilgrims rhapsodized, and the lives of its foreign visitors could hardly have been further removed from the real world. Instead, they had their own remote islands, from which harsh reality appeared to them as if through a veil of mist. At best, they encountered the darker side of life in Florence only in the form of beggars, whom they accepted as a picturesque attribute befitting of a southern city. Outbreaks of violence were greeted with incomprehension, as if they were an aesthetic problem. Hardly any of the writers who were living in Florence at the end of the nineteenth century addressed the social questions of the day or considered the implications of the radical upheavals that were taking place around them as modernism asserted its sway. One exception was the English novelist Louise de la Ramée, who wrote under the name of 'Ouida' and who describes the life and struggles of the poor inhabitants of a village near Florence in her novel *A Village Commune*. Robert Davidsohn wrote about 'Ordinary people from Florence's recent past', by which he meant the craftsmen and manual workers of the period.[1]

Rainer Maria Rilke witnessed the May disturbances in 1898 and brooded on the impact of Florence's manifold splendours on the people who lived in their shadow:

The first day I was in Florence, I said to someone: 'A certain beauty, a certain grandeur must none the less feed down into a man's difficulties and wretchedness and grow up with him together with his other qualities.' I can now answer this objection myself: The common people grow up beset by this beauty much as the lion keeper's child grows up in the lion's cage. The child's thinking towards the animal is always: 'I won't do anything to you as long as you do nothing to me.' But art sometimes harms the rabble . . . and then, oh, I left Florence when youths, rising up in revolt, threw stones at the Loggia dei Lanzi.[2]

The letter that Mary Warburg wrote home in early May 1898 reflects the utter bewilderment felt by these 'exiles' in the face of certain aspects of life in Florence: 'Also, some parts of the city have been difficult to pass through since yesterday as the Social Democrats are getting up to all manner of nonsense.' She reports on rioting and on broken windows in the Palazzo Strozzi and the surrounding area, adding that in the end the army stepped in, which resulted in injuries. 'But the whole business seems to have been started by adolescent youths, who are always the biggest troublemakers.'[3] And that is all that the Warburgs have to say on the events of 1898, events that represented a brief but violent flaring up sparked by arguably the most dramatic clash between old and new in the history of late nineteenth-century Florence.

In order for us to be able to understand the background of the strikes and unrest that beset Florence at this time, we need to go back to the years following the city's loss of its function as a capital and, more generally, the period that came after Italian unification. The economic and social injustices of the final third of the century were not a 'unification crisis', but there is no doubt that they were made worse by the radical change which took place once the country had been unified. In the case of Florence itself, there were additional factors in the form of the economic, social and psychological consequences of the loss of its status as a capital, while the complex political scenario of the Crispi era was also an intrinsic part of the difficult situation of this period.

From the 1870s and 1880s onwards social developments were marked by contradictory tendencies. We have already mentioned a general improvement in living standards, as the modernization of the country's towns and cities, improved hygiene and a regular supply of drinking water brought a reduction in the mortality rate. Parts of the population fared noticeably better than others, and incomes rose slightly. Between 1861 and 1889/90 tobacco consumption more than doubled in Tuscany, and savings deposits grew. Many small speculators and some larger ones profited from the urban measures of the Poggi era.[4] Even so, it would be wrong to overestimate the importance of the middle classes in the towns and cities, for even as late as the middle of the nineteenth century one English observer insisted that there was no real middle class in Florence.[5] On the one hand there was the great mass of day labourers, craftsmen and retailers, while on the other there was an extremely wealthy aristocracy committed to traditional values. Between them were those three small groups which made up the bourgeoisie and which may be described as 'humanist', 'economic' and 'bureaucratic'.[6]

Any positive developments, therefore, were only one side of the coin. For the vast majority of the population, living standards had fallen dramatically. During the 1860s and 1870s, southern Italy and Venetia suffered a long period of agricultural decline as a result of competition from American grain imports. Production fell, as did prices. Traditional proto-industrial branches of the economy such as straw-working still employed large numbers of people, but those numbers were already in decline. Industrialization was a slow process in Italy, initially affecting only the north of the country, which resulted in unemployment and wide-scale poverty. One indication of the growing social tensions was the increase in property crimes. Many Italians sought to escape from these mounting pressures by emigrating in ever greater numbers, either to other parts of Europe or, more especially, overseas. None the less, the level of emigration from Tuscany was far lower than that from the south of the country.[7]

In Florence, too, the *Mezzogiorno* problem manifested itself in various ways, including the appearance of beggars who banded together to form an army of indigenous paupers. In her diary, Laura Cantoni Orvieto describes the peasants of Naples begging:

> They found neither a roof over their heads nor bread in Caserta, and so they took to the open road. There are six of them in a cart, but in the course of their journey the father has fallen ill as a result of the cold and the water that penetrates from all sides. Now they do not know what to do or where to go; in summer they work in the fields, in the winter their two sons play the concertina.[8]

The situation became worse during the final decade of the nineteenth century. Economically speaking, the years between 1889 and 1894 have been described as the 'blackest' of the new kingdom.[9] The 'trade war' with France prevented exports and resulted in job losses. There were also worrying developments in the banking sector, including the bankruptcies of 1891, which affected even such venerable institutions as the Florence firm of Fenzi. Many were the families that lost their entire savings.

The situation in the labour market was extremely tense, and it was no accident that vast numbers of willing workmen flocked from Mugello to Janet Ross' villa at Poggio Gherardo twelve miles away as soon as it became known that she was planning to rebuild the property.[10] Figures for the whole of Italy – in Tuscany they may have been a little lower – indicate a desperate situation among large sections of the population. One contemporary statistic puts the proportion of unemployed youths aged between fourteen and twenty in towns of more than one hundred thousand inhabitants at almost 20 per cent,[11] while the figure rises to between 32 and 35 per cent in the age group between twenty and fifty. In June 1895, almost 36 per cent of heads of families in Italy were without work, and by December that year the proportion had gone up to more than 41 per cent – undoubtedly more than just a seasonally conditioned increase. In 1892, some seventy-two thousand Florentines – far more than a third of the population – were officially registered as poor, and by the end of 1898 that figure would be eighty thousand.[12] And in Florence in particular, appearances must have encouraged a feeling of rapid and uncontrollable change and the perception of a far-reaching modernization process: after all, the very walls of the old city were literally seen falling down. Thousands lost their homes and were often forcibly resettled.

One sign of the depressed situation of the masses was the universal increase in welfare arrangements.[13] In Tuscany they virtually doubled in the last two decades of the nineteenth century, from 628 to 1,116. At the same time, the amount of money spent by the different communes on poor aid rose unstoppably, and yet not even this was enough to defuse the situation. In 1890 the state confiscated charitable foundations as its last great act of secularization, turning them into *Congregazioni di carità*, which were unable, however, to make up for the disappearance of older, traditional institutions. Rather, the measure served only to put the state's finances back on an even keel. It was for the same reason that the Italian chancellor, the Tuscan-born Sidney Sonnino, squeezed the country's taxpayers in his attempt to reduce the national debt. But, at a time of growing unemployment, this merely led to a drop in public investment.[14]

A further element in this destabilization process, finally, was the failure of Crispi's imperialist foreign policy. The defeat of Italian troops in the Battle of Adua in Ethiopia on 1 March 1896 brought a temporary end to the country's colonial ambitions and sealed Crispi's political fate. There followed the unstable government of the Marchese Antonio de Rudinì, who did, however, succeed in putting an end to the conflict in East Africa. The Peace of Addis Ababa, which was signed in late October, left Italy with only the coastal province of Eritrea. At the same time Rudinì sought a settlement with France, and the tariff war between the two countries was finally resolved. At home, too, Rudinì adopted a policy of appeasement, especially in Sicily, where Crispi had declared a state of emergency following riots by the *fasci siciliani*, who were joined above all by agricultural workers and day labourers from the sulphur mines. But the continuing strikes and disturbances, chiefly in the industrialized north of the country, had led to calls for a return to a constitutional government as early as 1897. The labour movement saw itself exposed to further repressive measures.

It has been said that Florence at this time was the capital of anarchism in Italy.[15] Certainly, the anarchists' strongholds were in the city itself, and above all in the coastal regions of Massa and Carrara. The Socialists were proving hugely popular, and by 1895 Tuscany alone had fifty-six socialist organizations with more than two thousand members. In the 1895 elections the socialist share of the vote was 9.3 per cent, a figure that rose to 16.2 per cent in the 1900 elections, nearly doubling during that period.[16] At the same time, trade union organizations were gaining in influence. The first *Camera del lavoro* was founded in Florence in 1893 and within five years numbered eight thousand members.[17]

The 1898 disturbances were preceded by strikes and protest meetings.[18] In February 1897, a student gathering at the *Circolo socialista* was broken up by the police, after which *carabinieri* prevented the Socialist – and later Fascist – Alfredo Frilli from making a speech. In October rioting broke out on the Ponte Rosso, and a *brigadiere* was killed.[19] A particular threat was felt to come from the strikes by straw-workers on the outskirts of Florence that began in May 1896 and spread rapidly. They were an anti-modernist revolt in a dying branch of the craft industry, a struggle on the part of thousands of destitute women to earn a little extra money. They were then earning between ten and twenty *centesimi* for a laborious day's work – the price of a pound of bread. And it was not long before even the price of bread had risen and bread could no longer be bought for so little.[20]

True, there were fewer strikes in Tuscany when compared with the industrialized north of the country – a situation directly related to the low level of industrialization.[21] During the period in question there were forty-eight strikes in Piedmont and seventy-two in Lombardy but only sixteen in Tuscany, a figure more reminiscent of conditions in the agricultural south.[22] On the other hand, the number of striking workers in Florence and the surrounding area was remarkably high, considering that straw-weaving was the region's key craft. Of the 43,500 strikers, almost 29,000 came from this sector, while the number of women – for obvious reasons – was well above the average. With the passage of time, the number of strikes fell, but the number of striking workers rose as the strikes gradually affected small and medium-sized businesses.[23]

So tense was this situation that a shortage of cereal produce and an increase in prices proved to be the harbingers of revolt. There was an extremely poor harvest in 1897, and the Florence city council discussed the sort of measures that had characterized municipal welfare policies centuries earlier: there was talk of a reduction in the corn tax – the *dazio sul grano* – and an appeal was made to the hearts and patriotic instincts of the city's bakers and millers. A commission was set up to look into prices and the relationship between the cost of flour and bread on the one hand and the price of corn on the other. The council even considered imposing a maximum price.[24] Demonstrations against the high price of bread broke out at the end of January, and stones were thrown in the inner city. The army was called in, and the Palazzo Vecchio cordoned off. The ringleaders were thrown into prison and promptly arraigned. '*Abbasso la borghesia!*' – 'Down with the bourgeoisie!' – shouted the crowds. For them, at least, there was no doubt as to who was to blame for their problems.[25]

The *dazio* was indeed lifted on 23 January 1898 under the shocking impact of the disturbances. But the move was only temporary. Time and again during the period that followed, council and parliamentary debates were dominated by the question of abolishing the customs barriers that surrounded Italian towns and cities like invisible remains of medieval walls. Of course, the measure made little difference, not least because the outbreak of the Spanish–American War over Cuba had again caused the cost of food to shoot up throughout the whole of Italy. In the argument over whether or not to dispense completely with this tax on consumers, it was suggested that such a measure would reduce the amount of money available for public works. At the height of the famine, Giovanni Rosadi countered this suggestion by arguing that, in order to find work for the unemployed, the council should press ahead with rebuilding the National Library, a project which had been debated since October 1896 but which had been shelved on account of the estimated cost of two million lire.[26]

The attitude of the city's elite remained ambiguous, repressive measures and welfare concern maintaining a precarious balance. As early as 1897 there had already been extensive lockouts,[27] but in January 1898 a welfare organization calling itself *Il pane quotidiano* – 'Our Daily Bread' – was summoned into existence. By mid-February bread was already being handed out, and it was not long before the new charity had five hundred members.[28] But then the city again took to rounding up beggars – on one occasion there were around three hundred of them[29] – and yet not even this restored calm to the streets. The price of bread continued to rise inexorably.[30] By early April it was the turn of workers in the tobacco industry to go on strike. The tense situation in other parts of Italy added to the disquiet, and by the end of April there were disturbances prompted by the widespread famine – known locally as *proteste del stomaco* – in the south of the country.[31] The crisis came to a head in Milan,[32] where the death of the radical parliamentarian, Felice Cavalotti, in a duel with a conservative member of parliament led to demonstrations and ultimately to a call for a general strike. In turn, this resulted in open revolt, which quickly spread to other towns and cities.

In Tuscany, the May disturbances began in Figline Valdarno,[33] where the mob stormed a granary and opened fire on houses belonging to local dignitaries. The police intervened and a demonstrator was shot, while one of the officers of the law was seriously injured. The protest movement spread like wildfire. Everywhere there were calls for bread and work. In the Borgo San Lorenzo and Sesto Fiorentino, protesters clashed with the army, which resulted in four dead and many wounded. By 6 May the whole of the area between Florence and Prato was in a state of uproar. Disturbances were reported in Livorno, and here too there were fatalities.

The situation escalated in the centre of Florence, too, on 6 May, and it was these events that Mary Warburg described in the letter quoted earlier. During the afternoon, some three hundred individuals demonstrated in the Viale Regina Margherita, not far from the Warburgs' apartment, protesting against hunger, unemployment and low wages.[34] The following day the local senator Guglielmo Cambray-Digny, a former mayor of Florence and one of the leading moderates in Tuscany, telegraphed to Rome: 'Florence without a government. Prefect stripped of his powers. General Heusch absent. City in the hands of 300 scoundrels. Central government responsible.'[35] This was wildly exaggerated, its aim being to expose the Rudinì government and ensure that more repressive steps be taken to combat the Socialists. But Cambray-Digny's intervention and another one like it achieved the desired result,[36] and on 9 May a state of siege was declared in the provinces of Florence and Livorno. General Nicola Heusch assumed executive powers and lost no time in extending his command over the whole of Tuscany.

Catholics, Socialists and Republicans were regarded as conspirators against the liberal, laicist state of the Risorgimento. Chambers of trade, socialist and republican organizations, and finally even clerical circles, were disbanded. The press was subjected to strict censorship laws, and a whole wave of arrests ensued, a military tribunal sentencing socialist and republican activists to a total of 1156 years' imprisonment.[37] In other regions, too, the uprisings were put down with brutal force. In Milan alone there were a hundred dead and five hundred injured. Voices raised in favour of an authoritarian form of government based on the German model increased in stridency.[38]

When viewed retrospectively, the May Uprising of 1898 may be seen as ambivalent in character. On the one hand, it reveals criteria associated with an older type of crisis and, as such, can be interpreted by reference to models dating back to popular movements of the pre-modern period. According to such models, the masses are motivated by clearly circumscribed goals: they want bread, and they want work. But a novel feature of the May Uprising was the fact that the structural tensions ultimately underpinning the confrontations coincided with the radical upheavals caused by Italy's belated industrialization process and with the profound demographic changes which characterized the final decades of the nineteenth century. In a word, a dramatically increasing population found too little work in an insufficiently modernized economy. Between 1888 and 1896, the index of industrial production fell to 0.3 per cent from 4.6 per cent, as it had been during the first phase of expansion between 1882 and 1888.[39] At the same time, the old crafts and manufacturing industries came under increasing pressure from competitors – a problem which found particularly striking expression in the crisis of the Tuscan straw-weaving industry. And yet the state was both unwilling and for the most part unable to tackle the problems of unemployment, hunger and poverty by means of any efficient social policies. The country enjoyed no successes in its foreign policy that might have diverted the attention, from the problem with the result that only repression remained.

The social groupings responsible for the disturbances were deeply divided, as is only to be expected, given the complexity of the basic causes. Among the activists we can identify peasants, public employees, small businessmen, tradesmen, workers and a large number of women. In general, the existing social order was not called into question. Only rarely did the disturbances acquire a political thrust, notably in the case of the strikes at Pirelli's and Stiegler's.[40] Contemporaries thought that the events of May 1898 represented resistance to 'the state of Milan', to the cost of the army, to the country's colonial policies, to centralized government and to tax increases.[41] *Fieramosca* noted a general crisis of confidence between the common people and their politicians.[42]

The disturbances were followed by the government of General Luigi Pelloux who, like his predecessor, sought to master the situation by means of authoritarian measures. Civil liberties were further curtailed. But the widespread disquiet at this development ultimately had parliamentary consequences, the republican, radical and socialist opposition, together with left-wing Liberals, emerging from the elections in June 1900 with an increased share of the vote. Pelloux resigned, and the situation slowly became more liberal. If the road back to normality was a difficult one, the change to a more liberal, more democratic Italy was helped by favourable economic developments. The industrialization of the north of the country had begun to gain clear momentum as early as the mid-nineties, and it now became the solid basis of Giovanni Giolitti's reform policies.

This, then, was how the 'other' Florence and the 'other' Tuscany looked. One representative of the city's elite, Prince Tommaso Corsini, had only three words to say on the subject in his diary entry of 6 May: '*Disgraziati tumulti istigati*' – 'unfortunate riots instigated'. This was little better than the '*rien*' attributed to Louis XVI following the Storming of the Bastille.[43] For the most part, one looks in vain in the diaries and letters of visitors to Florence for signs of the bloody uprising of May 1898. Mary Warburg's résumé – if such we may call it – states merely that 'Social Democrats', whom she dismisses as 'adolescent youths' had got up to 'all manner of mischief', signalling in the clearest possible terms that many of the visitors to Arcadia felt utterly remote from all that was going on and had no understanding of the upheavals ushering in the modern period and of the social crises bound up with those upheavals.

Here one view of Florence once again overlaps with another. Mary Warburg had no difficulty answering the question why a line of demonstrators had snaked its way down the Viale Margherita: it was merely a hideous excrescence of a social democrat conspiracy. Rilke, too, happened to be passing through the inner city that same day and commented on events with the sense of distance that seemed to him befitting of an aesthete. Although the people of Florence were surrounded by high art, such art was infinitely remote from them:

> Some poor devil is sleeping off his hunger right beneath Cellini's *Perseus* in Andrea Orcagna's Loggia, and no chains encircle the fountains and statues that adorn the large piazzas. One is on the point of believing in a certain sympathy when one realizes that these common people are no different from the man who lived next to Schubert or Beethoven: the constant music begins by disturbing him, then it annoys him, until finally he no longer notices it.[44]

Of course, Rilke's 'Florence diary' is not a reflection of the world 'outside', but a record of his search for his own inner self. It is the blueprint for a life devoted solely to poetry, the manifesto of an artist's sense of identity defined by its distance from all lowly, vulgar existence. Art, Rilke goes on, 'passes from lonely individuals to lonely individuals, describing a high arc as it soars above the common people'. He spins a shimmering cocoon for himself and for beauty, which enables him to keep the things of this world at a safe distance. He adopts a psychological stance and sees the stones thrown at the Loggia dei Lanzi as attacks on the fetishes of luxury, and in doing so he touches on the interesting question of the logic of this iconoclasm: did the demonstrators know that they were striking at the 'humanistic middle classes' at the heart of Rilke's own intellectual existence? Whatever the answer, their actions were undoubtedly heavy with symbolism: the *populo minuto* – ordinary people – damaged the very things that the middle classes in the capital of Renaissance thought regarded as the essence of their glamour and the basis of their pride.

The events of May 1898 were like the resurgence of something that people had tried to forget, as they saw that, outside the iridescent purple and gold of the glass bubble of aestheticism and beyond the sensuous dreams of the historical Renaissance, there lay a complex reality, which included ugly facts. As a movement in art, naturalism seemed to subscribe to that reality, and for that very reason people hated it and treated it with suspicion, a hatred compounded by the fact that reality was also the setting for their own common lives. Such a malfunction had not been expected in Florence and was all the more unwanted in consequence. It spoilt the fantasies of a society which sought refuge in an artificial existence and was at pains to take seriously only the concerns of writers and scholars. Hugo von Hofmannsthal visited Florence in 1898 and noted that 'We have, as it were, no roots in life'.[45] He described what he saw in the city – Botticelli's paintings and Lorenzo de' Medici's *Trionfo*, for example – as the distilled nucleus of dreams, objects 'which to us are nothing but triumphal processions and pastoral plays about beauty, the beauty of dreams incarnate, transfigured by longing and distance, things that we conjure up when our thoughts are not powerful enough to find beauty in life and strive to discover the artificial beauty of our dreams'. It was a constant challenge to prevent 'freezing' life and 'shallow, desolate reality' from breaking into the Arcadian world of dreams, at least if one took seriously one's own vocation for beauty. Living in exile among the Tuscan peasants, the art historian and anarchist Jacques Mesnil was perhaps the only visitor to Florence who tried to embrace this tension between history, beauty and the present day.

During the late summer of 1902 there was a general strike in Florence, an event similar to the May disturbances of 1898, albeit much less dramatic, even though it, too, was accompanied by military cordons, *carabinieri* and lockouts. Significantly enough, the aesthetes of *Il Marzocco* attempted to incorporate these unedifying events into an idealized picture of the people of Florence. Their unruly behaviour could best be understood as a detail in a great history painting: 'It was logical that there was a wild animal there that had to be tamed as there were so many trainers present,' wrote the author of the article, Enrico Corradini:

> But the monster remained in its lair, hiding away and refusing to let itself be seen. In its place, the usual Florentine populace went on its way, having little to do, not very differently from any other days when it passes between rows of armed soldiers, a spectator adopting the mocking

attitude that befits it. . . . It seemed to me that the people of Florence had nothing to do with these events.

Of course, the people had always behaved like savages, the writer went on, as they were too lively a force, but their savagery and their scepticism had been tamed and were now expressed as irony. The strike was thus no more than a 'wretched profanation' of Florence's history. It must have been reassuring to be able to sum all this up by claiming that the strike had been 'the least aggressive' imaginable: 'An idyll, tedious, one might say.'[46]

And that was that. The creature that had raised its head during the critical years at the end of the century had been no more than a ghost, an unreal monster which lived hidden away in underground passages, where it could confidently be left. People imagined a beautiful, paradoxical Florence, in which there was a general strike and yet at the same time there was not. It was a place in which the Socialists and radicals of the present could be effortlessly incorporated into the overall aesthetic picture by being described as *ciompi*, the burghers and workers who had revolted in 1378. This was exactly the same attitude as the one adopted by the artist Jakobus von Halm in Heinrich Mann's *The Goddesses*: 'I dress up and disguise modern paltriness and perversities with such superior skill that they appear to share in the full-blown humanity of a golden age. Their wretchedness arouses no sense of contradiction but merely gives us a thrill.'[47]

From this perspective the common people could be ignored, the *populo minuto* being made up of the ignorant who allowed political life to pass them by dispassionately. They know nothing and were perfectly happy in their ignorance. In this way a synthetic 'eternal Florentine' was constructed with reference to the city's history. This character may have looked and behaved like old Gino Capponi, an aristocrat of republican stamp, cosmopolitan, cultured – in fact, basically an Englishman.[48] On other occasions he might appear to be a gentleman several hundred years old, someone who with the passage of time had grown more mellow, mocking and sceptical, a follower of Schopenhauer rather than a pupil of Nietzsche. Even the aesthetes of *Il Marzocco* could summon up a certain sympathy for such a creature, while foreigners were all the more able to use this construct for their airily idealized picture of Florence. According to the young Theodor Däubler, 'Archangels, elegant in eternal crystal, framed a precious stone that floated like a diamond between heaven and earth: this was the Florentine'.[49]

And Warburg? As far as we know, he failed even to notice the 'eternal Florentine' unexpectedly throwing stones at the Loggia dei Lanzi. At no point does he refer to the social upheavals taking place in turn-of-the-century Florence, and it is unlikely that he took any particular interest in the events which unfolded in the streets and squares of the city of the *ciompi* in May 1898. Social democracy, strikes and poverty were not his world, just as he was never a social historian, no matter what the received opinion may be. For a member of the upper classes like Warburg, the 'people' were not an object of any special interest. None the less, when he received news of the death of Bismarck, he wrote of his hopes that the united Reich would produce a new 'social ethics'.[50] But he knew nothing about the mental anguish suffered by the Florentines of his own day and thought he knew only about the Florentines of the past. And even then, he had enough to worry about with his own headaches. His 'eternal Florentine' was of a different stamp entirely.

Warburg's unpublished poem to 'The genius of old Florence' once again interprets the history of the city as a symbol of the eternal, the genius of Florence appearing as the diametrical opposite of modernity, strikes, insurrection and social and political change:

> I was no blasé dandy sipping vermouth
> As I ogled brightly painted women
> Driving in their coaches to the Cascine.
> No windbag I who, eaten up by malice,
> Raises his right hand against society
> And thrusts his left into his neighbour's pocket . . .
> Squarely I stood upon my patch of earth
> Which, stoutly fighting, I had won from princes,
> Robber knights and priests as my own city.
> Yes! There I ruled supreme where now I beg . . .
> But all our riches drifted on a skiff,
> Endangered goods to hostile foreign parts.
> You then could plough a straight-lined furrow through
> The waving fields, and winds that played with us
> Now heat as steam your patient kettles. Earth
> And dark and measureless expanses now
> Are tightly held by sterile wires. 'Space'
> Is all but lost to us: time's all that's left.
> Perdonci Bacco! You are far away.

The poem ends in a confession. History is praised as a source of consolation in a world without distances, a world in which there is no longer any space to think or contemplate. All that has been handed down from ancient Florence is compared to a 'thousand-piped organ of human hearts that has fallen silent in its torment':

Now try your skills upon this instrument.
Locate the note that purifies your soul.
And you who anxiously observe them, oh!
Do not fear that all the force and beauty
Of a foreign sound will subjugate
Your children with their incantation. No!
We spirits of the past are grateful souls.
The selfless man who seeks to lose himself
That we may live, we'll help unseen that he
May his own self apply to a new life.[51]

15   Harris Brown, *Herbert P. Horne*

'But when a belief vanishes, there survives it – more and more vigorously so as to cloak the absence of the power, now lost to us, of imparting reality to new things – a fetishistic attachment to the old things which it did once animate' (MARCEL PROUST)

10

In defence of history

T HE historical celebrations, the unveiling of monuments and the patriotic commemorations associated with *fin de siècle* Florence are all part of a wider picture involving the historicization of a world at pains to resist rapidly changing conditions. Even the new materials used in architecture – steel, iron and concrete – were hidden behind a historical façade, as if people were afraid of them.[1] The mountain of memorials continued to grow as the heroes of the Risorgimento and the great figures of literature and history were all commemorated with monuments. Marble and bronze were intended to preserve historical tradition in a present marked by rapid change. A social memory was being created. Relics of a bygone age became points of orientation in the search for a lost past and in educating the people.[2]

The Italian Dante Society was founded in Florence in 1888,[3] and two years later celebrations were held to mark the anniversary of the death of the poet's muse, Beatrice.[4] The result was a remarkable combination of an exhibition and a historical pageant. Local painters and sculptors exhibited works which were more or less closely related to the subject; manuscripts and other originals from Dante's day were on display, constituting a kind of 'theatre of memory' that increased the dignity of the relics and even sanctified them.[5] There were several aims which were meant to be achieved in this way, and council minutes show that even tourism was one such objective. At the same time, social elites were keen to demonstrate that the social order had a historical legitimacy to it, an order which the nationwide strikes and disturbances had shown to be under threat. None the less, they were keen to ensure that memories were 'correct', which meant that they were necessarily selective. It can hardly be an accident that in the wake of the May Uprising of 1898 the city authorities did not dare to mark the four-hundredth anniversary of the execution of Girolamo Savonarola – the popular man of God and reformer of Florentine politics – on 28 May 1498, the planned celebrations being postponed at the very last minute.[6]

In their place great pageants were held commemorating Amerigo Vespucci and Paolo Toscanelli.[7] A *calcio* tournament in Renaissance costumes was organized – *calcio* was a kind of football that had been popular in Florence as far back as the sixteenth century – and in the evening there were *tableaux vivants*. On the Piazza Indipendenza, monuments to the former mayor of Florence, Ubaldino Peruzzi, and to Cavour's successor as prime minister of Italy, Bettino Ricasoli, were unveiled.

Mary Warburg reports on these spectacles in a letter to her mother-in-law in Hamburg:

> Yesterday great unveiling ceremony of two highly patriotic but incredibly tedious-looking old bronze gentlemen on the Piazza Indipendenza, which gave us a chance to see the king and queen at close quarters. She still looks altogether ravishing, but we were all surprised by her auburn-blond hair, which we had thought was dark. Perhaps queens become blond, rather than grey, with age.[8]

The official speech was delivered by Prince Corsini, a former mayor of Florence, whose attitude to his fellow citizen, now condemned to a life of bronze, was every bit as reserved as Mary Warburg's. 'Poor me,' he noted as he contemplated the task of speaking at the unveiling ceremony, 'and poor Ricasoli, as if he was not really self-sufficient!'[9]

The official visit by King Umberto I ended with a great masked ball at the Sala dei Cinquecento to which the Warburgs too were invited. The event may be seen as a transition between the old and the new. *La Nazione* was impressed by the countless candelabra holding real candles, but no less impressive were the twenty-four electric lamps that lit the ball.[10] Wagner triumphed: the musicians played the Overture to *Die Meistersinger*, together with excerpts from *Parsifal* and *Tannhäuser* and pieces by Cherubini and Beethoven. Mary Warburg found the mood 'agreeably informal', failing to register the fact that Florence was on the brink of a bloody uprising and that dramatic events were in the offing.

The historicization of daily life went hand in hand with the destruction of history. Contact with real relics of the past and the changes brought about by the modern world, driving the past underground for ever, helped in their way to stimulate a sense of historical awareness. At the very time that the outlines of old Florence were being radically altered, Robert Davidsohn and

Cornel von Fabriczy were drawing up plans for the classical and medieval town whose impact can be seen to this day.

One of the fundamental experiences of the second half of the nineteenth century was that modernism was making its presence felt with overwhelming force in urban planning. Even before the turn of the century voices had been raised in Florence too, demanding an end to the destruction of the old city centre. Writing in *Arte e storia*, Guido Carocci, the inspector of antiquities and the arts, took a stand, movingly listing the buildings which were likely to fall victim to the workmen's pickaxes:

> The Brown Palace of the Giandonati from the fourteenth century . . . the Palazzo de' Canacci, decorated with amazing graffito frescos from the early sixteenth century, the *palazzo* of the *capitani* of the Guelph party . . . and the Tower of the Buondelmonti, the Palazzi of the de' Carducci and the impressive towers of the Amidei and de' Consorti – all these buildings have committed the error of disrupting the beautiful straight line of arbours and so they, too, must be sacrificed.[11]

A good ten years after the project for the '*riordinamento del centro di Firenze*' was approved on 8 March 1888, this major urban redevelopment had largely been completed. In 1897 the commune was still acquiring land for new buildings, and a large complex near the Piazza del Monte di Pietà was sold off to a private individual for 43,500 lire.[12] Here were the well-preserved Palazzi dei Consoli delle due Gilde and the headquarters of the old commercial court. One of the buildings still bore the Ghibelline coat of arms from 1542. Everything, however, was torn down and replaced by unattractive new buildings. The city laid new sewers, the streets were paved and pavements were provided for pedestrians. Among the final large-scale measures were the regulation of the Piazza del Duomo and the completion of a new road.

What the city fathers had described as a *riordinamento* amounted to nothing less than a revolution in urban planning, so that within a decade and a half one of the most famous city centres in the world had completely changed its appearance. Baudelaire's comment on the Paris of Baron Haussmann – that the shape of the city was changing more quickly than a man's heart – was no less true of Florence, where much of the old city had been cleared away in the name of hygiene, transport, amenities and modernity.

The outcome of the decision to 're-regulate' the old centre of Florence may be illustrated by a number of hard facts.[13] Twenty-six old streets were destroyed, together with twenty squares and twenty-one parks; 341 dwelling houses, 451 *botteghe* and 173 *magazzini* were torn down. And a total of 1,778 families numbering 5,822 individuals were forcibly resettled. Land speculation on a massive scale led to an enormous restructuring in terms of property ownership: previously there had been 1,091 property owners, but after the changes only six among the sixty-three landowners had property in the area which had been redeveloped. The new quarter of San Frediano, which was built by way of 'compensation', soon looked like the most wretched of slums and, as such, resembled the old heart of the city which had been cleared for that very reason.[14]

By 1897, people had had enough. Guido Carocci's article was read as far afield as Rome. The minister of culture, Emmanuele Gianturco, intervened and opposed all further demolition work, including plans to extend the area of redevelopment – plans which, yet to be approved, provided for the Via Pelliceria to be extended as far as the Ponte Vecchio. Feelings ran high on the Florence city council. Three of the councillors – Dino Uguccioni, Isidoro del Lungo and a Signor Gerini – drew attention to the importance of the historic town centre for local tourism and spearheaded the opposition to all further compulsory purchase orders and demolition work. The mayor, Pietro Torrigiani,[15] had to throw his whole weight into the scales in order to persuade the council to agree to the acquisition of further land on the Piazza San Biagio, arguing that the council could still afford to finance such a move. Their grandchildren could then be left to complete the restructuring of the city centre in fifty or sixty years' time. A tempestuous debate ensured, at the end of which Torrigiani's proposal was carried by eighteen votes to eight.

As a result, the opposition was left with no alternative but to pursue a course of action outside parliament. After all, it was not just the redevelopment of the whole area as far as the Arno and the famous Ponte Vecchio that was under discussion: the area around Santa Maria Novella and, above all, the quarters beyond the Arno were as yet barely affected by the redevelopment programme. Now the 'flood of modernization' so lamented by Carocci threatened these parts of the city too. It was, arguably, an initiative due first and foremost to 'foreigners' that was to prove of decisive importance in saving these remains of medieval Florence, especially the Borgo San Jacopo. This initiative involved the formation of a society 'to defend old Florence', the *Società per la difesa di Firenze antica*, which was founded in May 1898. The fact that it was established in the days following the strikes and disturbances which brought havoc to the city is of more than symbolic significance.

The society elected as its president Tommaso Corsini, Prince of Sismano and Laiatico, Duke of Castigliano, a grandee of Spain and a senator of the Kingdom of Italy. He represented a bygone age, a *gentiluomo* who owned vast

16   The old ghetto in Florence before it was torn down:
an oriental pageant during the 1886 carnival

estates and, as such, was the wealthiest man in Florence. His family had
produced a pope in Clement XII, while Corsini himself was married to
Anna Baberini, one of the queen's ladies-in-waiting. He had been mayor of
Florence from 1880 to 1886. Although he was no 'leopard', but sceptical and
melancholic by nature, there would have been a certain logic to his elevation to the head of the defenders of old Florence, had it not been for the
fact that his period in office coincided with the start of the city's major
rebuilding programme.

The *Società* held its inaugural meeting on 16 May at Corsini's rambling
palazzo between the Lungarno and the Via di Parione, a building that also
housed one of the great art collections of which we have already spoken.
The illustrious gathering included the historian Pasquale Villari, two city
councillors, Filippo Torrigiani and Isidoro del Lungo, the latter actively
engaged in cultural politics, and two foreigners, Adolf von Hildebrand and
Frederick Stibbert.[16] According to its statutes, the society was formed with

the aim of 'protecting the character and the historical and artistic legacy of Florence'.[17] In particular, it was hoped to mobilize public opinion against any further redevelopment of the city. The meeting more or less openly rejected the redevelopment programme, even though Corsini stressed that the society did not see itself as opposed to communal projects. In general the society adopted a moderate tone, seeking to present itself as a body keen to engage in dialogue with the commune rather than being its adversary.

It was around this time that Warburg met one of the protagonists in the struggle to preserve the old heart of Florence, and it was presumably in this way that the whole issue came to his attention. The man in question was the designer, art dealer and writer Herbert P. Horne. 'Heard yesterday about Herbert P. Horne from Casanova, visited him today at Berenson's,' Warburg noted in his diary on 4 May 1898. 'Dolichocephalic English skull, pale, thin moustache turned up at the ends, struggles with a stammer. Primavera said to have been painted for the other Lorenzo di Piero Francesco, in whose possession at Castello it was in 1478.' In other words, they discussed Botticelli, which is hardly surprising. Warburg, after all, was a known authority on the subject, and Horne was then working on a large-scale monograph on the artist.[18] Their friendly relations deepened with the passing years, and in 1902 Warburg wrote to his wife to say that Horne was his 'only really cultivated colleague'.[19]

Herbert Percy Horne was a remarkable man.[20] Two years older than Warburg, he had given early proof of his manifold artistic and artisanal talents and was not only a collector and an experienced art dealer but also one of the most creative minds of his day, writing poetry and editing seventeenth-century literary texts. He also produced a number of ornamental designs in the style of early *art nouveau* and was active as an architect. As early as 1882, Arthur H. Mackmurdo had welcomed him into the Century Guild, the first of the guilds associated with the Arts and Crafts Movement. Together with Selwyn Image, he was for a long time Mackmurdo's closest colleague. The three men also edited *The Hobby Horse*, which served as a link between the Pre-Raphaelites and the spirit of the 1890s.[21] Dedicated to Pater, Horne's book on Botticelli was designed by the author himself as a bibliophile edition, printed on handmade paper and the title on pale blue Ingres paper. The typeface was inspired by one used in the sixteenth century. Horne was at the very heart of his age, and his acquaintances numbered the Rossettis and their circle, Frederic James Shields, Oscar Wilde, William Morris and Pater. G. K. Chesterton's comment on Morris to the effect that the latter was 'vitally English and vitally Victorian' was also true of Horne.[22]

Horne had been living in Italy more or less permanently since 1894, the affluence of his lifestyle being supported by his art and by his dealings in antiquities of every description. He came from the same intellectual world as Ruskin, from which he increasingly distanced himself, and also from that of Pater. An aesthete and a connoisseur, he sought to reconcile within himself the extremes represented by his mentor Mackmurdo, extremes that included a relatively sentimental kind of Anglo-Catholicism, Pre-Raphaelite tendencies and, finally, a mystical Romanticism in the tradition of William Blake, with rigid rules of his own.

'Michael Field' – the pseudonym of Katharine Bradley and her niece Edith Cooper, two eccentric Victorian women also known as the 'double-headed nightingale' – maliciously described Horne as a decadent, 'not a milk-sop, but a tea-sop – mild, effeminate, with an art aroma, a choiceness'.[23] Another commentator, Ernest Dowson, noted the contrast between Horne, 'very erect & slim & aesthetic – & Image the most dignified man in London, a sort of cross in appearance between a secular abbé & Baudelaire, with a manner du 18me siècle – waiting in a back passage to be escort to ballet girls whom they don't even—!!!'[24]

In spite of the unfavourable impression left on him by Horne's appearance, Warburg eventually became friendly with the English writer, a friendship documented by a lengthy correspondence. During their years together in Florence, the two men met on a regular basis, being brought together by their shared interest in the early Renaissance. They sent each other essays, corresponded on research problems and helped each other with archival research. Horne was often in London, where he obtained material for Warburg from the British Museum, asking in turn about the meaning of currency descriptions in fifteenth-century manuscripts or about the owner of a particular tapestry: 'And now I am troubling you in this way – may I remind you of your kind promise to let me know who "de Baudreuil" was, for whom the Botticelli tapestry of "Pallas" reproduced in Müntz was made? Was he an abbot or a bishop? And who is the historian who mentions him?'[25] The correspondence between Warburg and Horne examines these and similar problems in great detail, often with an extensive array of evidence. On one occasion Warburg remarked that Horne was one of the few people he knew who were capable of appreciating the value of detailed work. 'I am sure that you too are convinced that as our immediate task, reading mountains of old paper is better than opening up far-ranging perspectives, with nothing concrete to show for it.'[26]

Horne had already produced some excellent results by the start of his acquaintance with Warburg. He had drawn Warburg's and Brockhaus's attention to a passage in Vasari which pointed to the existence of a fresco by Andrea del Castagno in the Montaguti Chapel in the Church of SS Annunziata.[27] Together with Warburg and other members of the German

Art Historical Institute, Horne duly applied to the authorities to remove a *Last Judgement* by Alessandro Allori, behind which the Castagno was thought to be located. The moment of truth came one day in June 1899,[28] when Castagno's account of the Trinity, with a representation of an ascetic Saint Jerome, was indeed revealed. The dramatic painting by a Cinquecento artist was obliged to give way to the austere beauty of a fresco which reflected the tastes of the Pre-Raphaelites. Florence's aestheticist art critics were duly ravished.[29] It is perhaps worth adding here that this discovery of the Castagno fresco had a sequel entirely worthy of 'old Florence', inasmuch as the family responsible for the chapel was by no means sympathetic to Pre-Raphaelite art and took steps to ensure that a curtain was placed in front of the fresco, eventually replacing the curtain by the original Allori.[30]

In 1912 Horne acquired a Renaissance palace on the Via de' Benci, which he carefully restored and filled with choice art works. Often plagued by cold and high temperatures, he himself lived in only a single small garret without hot water or electricity, evidently feeling that the rest of the building was worthy only of a 'great' race. Be that as it may, it is said that he regarded himself as the only unsuitable object in this whole seigneurial setting.

It is entirely understandable that a man like Horne – a Romantic, an aesthete, a moralist and and an artist – should have felt pain and indignation on seeing how the old city was being treated. He may also have been afraid of a future that seemed more unstable than ever. While Warburg sought refuge in books and archives, fleeing from the world and from himself, Horne sought his salvation in action, his entire life constituting a single protest at the developments taking place around him. He resisted the mass production of the industrial age by means of a craftsmanship based on ancient techniques, while his Romantic enthusiasm for the Renaissance and his reverence for the beauty of Botticelli's art was part of his stance against materialism and godlessness.

Although it was not until 1899 that Horne became a corresponding member of the *Società*, he took part in its activities from the very beginning.[31] Indeed, it seems to have been Horne and other 'Anglo-Florentines' who pulled the strings in the background and who made the problem of Florence the object of a campaign that came to a head at the end of 1898.[32] There was much talk of further plans for widespread redevelopment and of the threatened demolition of historic buildings of the first importance. 'Vandalism' and 'barbarism' were among the words used, and on one occasion the destruction of the Ponte Vecchio was even held up as a serious prospect.[33]

The whole matter acquired an explosive topicality for Florence's politicians not only as a result of all the readers' letters and articles which appeared in the local papers but also because of the names by which they were signed. An open letter to the mayor, Pietro Torrigiani, which appeared in *The Times* on 2 December 1898 and which was reproduced in *La Nazione,* bore the names of Edward Poynter, Lawrence Alma-Tadema, Walter Crane, William Blake Richmond, Holman Hunt and George Frederick Watts among others. With the support of the local press, Torrigiani, who was one of the leading shareholders of *La Nazione,* tried to appease his critics. But what power did he have to prevent the destruction of further parts of the historic city, no matter how much goodwill he might demonstrate?

This was precisely the question that the writer Violet Paget – 'Vernon Lee' – asked in a long letter to the editor of *The Times*.[34] Her attack was particularly damaging to the party of urban redevelopment as she was intimately familiar with the situation in Florence, quite apart from the fact that she was a brilliant stylist and knew how to argue her case. Henry James considered hers to be one of the keenest minds in the city, while Bernard Shaw once numbered her among 'the old guard of Victorian cosmopolitan intellectualism'.[35] And *The Times* was the leading newspaper in the world at this time.

Paget had conducted a lengthy interview with Torrigiani, and so she was well informed. In the course of the interview, a minor incident took place that reflects the uncertainty of the situation at this time. In answer to her question about plans for the area around the Borgo San Jacopo, Torrigiani had summoned the relevant official in order to be able to confirm that the planned redevelopment would barely encroach on this area, but the consultant was forced to admit that practically the whole area was to be redeveloped, including the medieval Torre dei Marsili, a replica of which would then be built elsewhere.

Paget questioned whether the authorities were actually in charge of the situation. Torrigiani insisted that they had the best intentions and were aware of the historical significance of the centre, to say nothing of their love of art, but he admitted that, even under the most enlightened of mayors, existing demolition work had shown that acts of extreme vandalism were still possible. Lectures and publications would have to educate ordinary people and workers so that they acquired a sense of taste and a 'spirit of history'. Above all, however, it was necessary to draw the attention of hotel owners, landlords and other businessmen and women to the damage that would result from such demolition work. After all, the medieval character of the city was one of Florence's main attractions. The people of Florence, Torrigiani went on, had already suffered enough from the exodus of tourists during the May disturbances. Paget demanded a 'crusade' to draw attention to the problem.

These various pieces in *The Times* gave rise to lively debates on the city council. At a specially convened meeting on 23 December 1898, the arguments for and against the redevelopment of the historic centre of Florence once again clashed head-on. Those responsible for the plans tried to dispel doubts and to demonstrate that their opponents' fears were unfounded. The claims made by the international press were dismissed as inaccurate reporting. There was also a nationalist note to the debate. Most people were in agreement in rejecting the involvement of the *inglesi* in local affairs, only Councillor Dino Uguccioni protesting that art had no boundaries and that foreigners, too, had the right to make their voices heard.

The result was a genuine debate on the need to preserve historical monuments – a discussion about the significance of tradition in the face of the demands of the modern world.[36] One of the building consultants, Silvio Berti, justified the measures by reference to the demands of hygiene, morals and public safety. It needed the pen of a Victor Hugo or an Emile Zola, said one speaker, to describe the filth in the older quarters of the city.

But there were also councillors who adopted a more nostalgic view of the situation, Isidoro del Lungo – the author of the inappropriate inscription in the Piazza Vittorio Emanuele – painting a particularly touching picture of the end of old Florence. He quoted the architect Camillo Boito, who, when the demolition work on the Mercato Vecchio was already underway, had written:

> The sun set. It felt as if I was attending the *post mortem* of a beloved person who was still alive; and meanwhile the moon began to light the dark and blood-stained ruins on the one hand and the perfectly new monuments from the nineteenth century on the other; the new ones appeared emotionless, without life. They seemed dead, frozen and glittering, like wax figures.[37]

The same stars shone down on the older period as they did on the new one. In their pale light, the harsh confrontation between the vanishing Italy of the classical period and the modern age found symbolic expression: the moon, as the indispensable source of light in the Romantics' picture of Italy, revealed not new life, but a corpse behind the ruins of the Mercato Vecchio.

The foreigners' fight to save the old city was ultimately successful – a development almost certainly helped by a petition organized by Horne, Violet Paget and other expatriates who had settled in Florence. In a series of printed letters, the *Società* informed the world about the threat to the old city, claiming in particular that the Ponte Vecchio was to fall victim to the demolition men's pickaxes. (None the less, it has to be admitted that this passage has been deleted in the copy in Horne's possession.[38]) The writers of these letters had certainly struck a nerve. As early as 1891, William Dean Howells, whose novel *Indian Summer* is set in Florence, had commented ironically that every so often the rumour that the Ponte Vecchio was about to be torn down unleashed a sense of panic in the city. He himself had hastened to see the famous sight as soon as he had arrived in Florence, in order to be able to observe it before the demolition men arrived that same afternoon.[39]

Reactions were not slow in coming. Some of the recipients of the *Società*'s letters tried to collect more signatures from their circle of acquaintances, in a kind of chain-letter campaign. And so we find a Miss Stillman of 12 Campden Hill Gardens, London SW, for example, writing to her female friends in order to persuade them to protest at the 'most recent act of vandalism, the destruction of the unique Ponte Vecchio'.[40]

By 1 March, Lady Paget, the wife of the former British ambassador in Rome, was able to present Prince Corsini with a list of more than ten thousand signatures.[41] The members of the *Società* crowded into the Great Hall of the Palazzo Corsini, where they were joined by a large number of expatriates. Under the heading of an expression of support for the *Società per la difesa di Firenze antica* lay concealed a warning to put a stop to the destruction of the old city centre once and for all.

Judged by the standards of other protests of the period, this was an enormous number of signatures, but it was not just their number that created such an impression, it was also the eminence of the men and women who had signed the petition: a list that reads like a who's who of international politics, literature and art, symbolizing the worldwide importance Florence enjoyed at the turn of the century as a preeminent *lieu de mémoire*. The long list of signatories ranged from Carducci to Verdi and from Swinburne, Shaw, Kipling and the actress Sarah Bernhardt to Auguste Rodin and painters such as John Singer Sargent, Léon Bonnat and Franz von Lenbach. Other names included those of Theodore Roosevelt, later president of the United States of America and at that date governor of New York, James Balfour and the Socialist Jean Jaurès. Academy presidents and museum directors such as Wilhelm Bode and Hugo von Tschudi, Cosima Wagner, Eugène Müntz and the explorer Henry Morton Stanley rubbed shoulders with bishops, princes and princesses. Even the governor of Tasmania added his name alongside those of other Australian statesmen, Florence evidently being capable of awakening strong feelings on the other side of the world. So impressive a show of support could not be ignored, even if the council demonstratively rallied around its mayor in the face of foreign pressure.[42] The demolition work came to a halt; and, if it is still possible to see the Torre dei Marsali and if the parts of the city on the other bank of the Arno have largely preserved their medieval character, this is largely thanks to foreign intervention.

In the course of the years that followed, the *Società* was transformed into a peaceful institution organizing lectures on art and history and modestly venturing its opinion on questions relating to urban aesthetics.[43] It took part, for example, in the debate surrounding the removal of the original of Michelangelo's *David* from its site outside the Palazzo Vecchio, and it also expressed its views on the now much more cautious attempts to redevelop the parts of the city on the other side of the Arno.

At the time when the battles over old Florence reached their height, between December 1898 and March 1899, the Warburgs had other worries, and also other pleasures in life. True, a number of brief entries in Aby Warburg's diary indicate that the arguments over the redevelopment of the old city played a role in his conversations with Heinrich Brockhaus,[44] but we may assume that the subject took second place to another concern: Mary Warburg was pregnant. But Warburg himself was once again plagued by sombre moods at this time. 'The claw of care is being stretched out towards me,' he noted in his diary in December 1898. In San Miniato he spoke darkly only of 'the open grave'. 'Disastrous mood', we read on another occasion, and the next day: 'It seems almost incredible that all should be well again; and yet I have neither a temperature nor a headache, nor am I in any pain! Grown soft? Why? Climate? I feel as if the cap has been raised only for a few moments before being put on once again.'[45] Mary's frame of mind was the exact opposite of her husband's: their daughter, Marietta, was born on 11 January 1899.

Immediately after the birth, Mary Warburg and her husband plunged back into their social round. They had lunch with Jessie Hillebrand, from whom they also received some concert tickets; they visited the Davidsohns, where they were introduced to the daughter of the history painter Gustav Spangenberg[46] and to the writer Renato Fucini. In turn, they received a visit from some Americans – 'Aby's American officer friends from Fort Wingate' – and on another occasion Mary reports on a dinner party for eleven, the 'tasty leftovers' providing the fare for the following morning's breakfast.

Winter pursued its course, and soon it was March. At least for Mary Warburg, Florence regained its old magic. 'Dearest Mama,' she wrote home at the beginning of March, 'I'm sitting here with the windows wide open; spring finally seems to want to be serious, we're having the most divine weather you can imagine & our little one is outside as much as possible.'

17   Leonardo da Vinci, *Mona Lisa* (1503–6)

'The liberating smile of the person rising above himself' (ABY WARBURG)

Neurasthenia and mental balance:
On Leonardo and Piero della Francesca

Oｎｅ of the least known facts in the history of *fin de siècle* Florence is that the city was then one of the world's leading centres of suicide. This is an aspect of municipal life which points to a deeper social and psychological malaise. The columns of *La Nazione* and *Fieramosca* were full of appalling accounts of the '*mania suicida*'.[1] An engineer suffocated himself and two women; the tramway conductor Gino Caldini ate an ice cream on the Piazza Vittorio Emanuele, then promptly shot himself on the public highway; an old man shot himself by St Joseph's altar in the Duomo, while another suicide shot himself no fewer than five times on the parapet of one of the bridges spanning the Arno before he plunged into the river below. Only months before, the bodies of two lovers had been recovered from the river, still clutching each other in death: 'It was a terrible sight,' reported *La Nazione* with little show of restraint. 'They were in a state of advanced putrefaction, distended by the water and covered in a layer of slime.' The deaths of lovers in the short stories set at the time of the Renaissance looked altogether different.

In comparison to other towns and cities in Europe, the suicide rate in Florence was high.[2] Even contemporaries were struck, not only by the fact that there were so many suicides in the city, but more especially by the dramatic increase in numbers as the century drew to an end.[3] Statisticians attempted to identify the reasons for this wave of self-inflicted deaths, terms such as 'world weariness', 'mental illness' and 'delusional behaviour' merely serving to cover up the commentators' helplessness. In the opinion of the statisticians, it was economic factors that were most likely to motivate suicides, a claim which receives some support from the fact that the suicide rate was abnormally high in those parts of the city inhabited by the lower classes and in the newer industrial quarters, where the discrepancy between desires and opportunities was painfully apparent.[4] Underdeveloped industry could not offer enough work, while the old economy was in decline – it is clear from the disturbances of May 1898 that the modernization crisis in Florence had complicated roots.

Suicide is an extreme form of behaviour, a radical reaction to problems to which there should be different answers. As a result, the suicide mania of the late nineteenth century must be seen in the context of a society which had lost its sense of certainty and no longer had any religious ties or other traditional ways of dealing with life. It must be numbered among the signs of the fundamental change in attitudes that was bound up with the radical upheavals associated with the dawn of modernism.

The Tuscan philosopher Alessandro Chiappelli speaks of the nineteenth century as a '*secolo nervoso*'.[5] In his view, increased mobility, better communications and greater needs – in short, a general over-stimulation – led to a loss of the 'meditative virtues' among all sections of society. In other words, there was no longer an ability to collect one's thoughts for any length of time. This, Chiappelli argued, was the price paid for the new communications media and scientific progress: 'The telegraph, the telephone, the railways . . . demand ever greater effort to think about them in every field; science deepens its secrets, and the mind immerses itself in them.'[6] Advances in civilization were taking place with extreme rapidity, making it correspondingly difficult to adapt to them. Paolo Mantegazza,[7] the author of the most popular Italian study of the problem of neurasthenia, adopted a similar view of his age. As late as 1887, he was still claiming – incorrectly – that neurasthenia did not affect Roman Catholic nations.[8] Many observers even thought it was possible to find signs of the psychological state of the age in art: the 'nervousness' of the Barbizon school and of the Impressionists, the bewilderingly telegraphic style that heralded modern art, seemed a perfect reflection of the restlessness which people felt in their inner lives. Freud's descent into the labyrinth of the ego was additionally motivated by the fact that he regarded existing interpretations of psychological conflicts as oversimplified.

According to this view, these acts of self-destruction were merely the tip of the iceberg and, as such, were spectacular signs of the existence of a psychological problem that affected far wider sections of the population. The striking increase in rates of suicide reflected the particular situation in a city where the process of modernization had been late to get underway. As a result, the destruction of traditional living conditions may have been regarded as all the more dramatic.

Fieramosca contained many an eye-catching advertisement for cures for the fashionable ailment of 'neurasthenia', an illness in which contemporaries saw the cause of suicides, nervousness and various other ill-defined evils. According to an advertisement detailing the symptoms of *nevrastenia*, it was a '*malattia speciale del nostro tempo*' – 'an illness specific to our own day':

> Tiredness, excitability, attacks of spleen, a tendency to change one's mind at every trivial incident, and a feeling of fear. Sometimes one has a kind of nightmare or is afraid of possible evils or of mixing with other people. Individuals suffering from this illness can be calmed through illusions, they complain about poor memory and an inability to concentrate, they think of suicide . . . and they suffer from headaches, stabbing pains in the chest and constipation.[9]

Warburg's torments seem, therefore, to fit into a wider context, and they can be paralleled by other famous cases such as that of Max Weber; Nietzsche's breakdown in Turin; and the psychological crises of great artists like van Gogh and Edvard Munch. Warburg's illness had not in fact made itself felt by the turn of the century, although there were already ominous signs of it. Time and again he tried to explain his own bouts of depression by seeing them as part of the 'normality' of a nervous and depressed age and by hoping in this way to relativize his own personal suffering: 'If our own *fin de siècle* didn't find it so attractive to hang its head like a weeping willow,' he wrote on one occasion, 'everything would be so much better.'[10]

Inner disquiet repeatedly drove him to wander aimlessly through the town, calling on friends and colleagues, including Edgar Kurz, who treated his haemorrhoids with tincture. On 3 March 1899, for example, we read in Warburg's diary:

> Felt depressed on getting up. Difficulty swallowing, pharyngitis. The carpet men arrive . . . common Hungarian Jews . . . Into town to see Horne, not at home, to Davidsohn at the archives to thank him for his notes. Chemist's, came home. Deep depression after lunch. To Kurz to get painted. Mary accompanied me to Brockhaus, both of them wanted to go to Arcetri. Kurz very preoccupied, is studying an old case history; paints me. Oh, what's the matter with me? Why can't I master these 'oriental states of anxiety'? There must be a physical reason. Might it be malaria?

The 'oriental states of anxiety' that tormented Warburg are closely related to the 'medieval, eastern' irrationality that he himself had once identified in a different context: the question of how to overcome them and the tension-laden process leading to enlightenment and reason had already exercised him during his work on Botticelli and was to resurface again and again in the course of his later research.

On one occasion he reflected on eye problems. The eyes, he writes in a letter to his mother, are old-fashioned and require of their owner 'the higher culture of rest', which 'in our century of mobility is easily lost, much to the detriment of our selves'. But he hopes that the new century will 'grant us a culture of constancy, or at least the principles thereto'.[11] This is one of the few passages in Aby Warburg's diary that gives particularly clear expression to his awareness of the rapid changes taking place in old Florence, which was then in the process of vanishing.

During this same difficult year of 1899 Warburg published a study of what, for him, was an unusual subject. In the September of that year, during the Warburgs' annual escape to northern Europe, he held a series of four lectures on Leonardo da Vinci in the Kunsthalle in Hamburg.[12] Behind the exercise may have lain the attempt to gain a professional foothold in Germany and to bring a certain steadiness to his life. He wrote to the director of the Hamburg Kunsthalle, Alfred Lichtwark, offering to catalogue a bequest of Italian drawings among the museum's holdings. He could no doubt have been given a permanent position but, as so often, he shied away from the regular duties that would have been associated with it. According to Ernst Gombrich, he wanted to prove to himself, to his family and to his in-laws that he had something to offer.[12] 'I am doing it all really as a kind of fulfilment of an obligation,' he noted, 'because I should like to digest the freedom that I enjoy in Florence.' The lectures were a great success, and the hall could barely hold the many people who turned up to hear Warburg speak.[13]

Hitherto Warburg had concerned himself almost exclusively with the Florence of the early Renaissance: with Botticelli and the inventories of the Medici. A glance at his published writings shows that his interest in the history of the Quattrocento dominates all other concerns. Indeed, it may even be regarded as a topos of the Warburg literature that he found the principal sources of his psycho-historical speculations in the lesser arts and in the craft industry, from wedding chests to tarot cards. Ultimately he saw himself not as an aesthete but as a scholar interested in the complex genesis of a new style. 'The most beautiful butterfly I have ever pinned down suddenly bursts through the glass and dances mockingly upwards into the blue sky,' he wrote to Jolles on one occasion:

> Now I should catch it again, but I am not equipped for this kind of loco-
> motion. Or, to be exact, I should like to, but my intellectual training does
> not permit me to do so. Also, I was born in Platonia and I should like,

in your company, to watch the circling flight of ideas from a high mountain peak . . . But it is given to me only to look backwards and to enjoy in the caterpillars the development of the butterfly.[14]

This time, however, Warburg was dealing with one of the truly great artists and with some of the legendary masterpieces of the Renaissance. He now approached the very mystery of beauty, something he had previously avoided doing.

Warburg's lectures helped him to clarify his ideas about the art of the Quattrocento by confronting them with one of the high points of the Renaissance. A deeper reason for his decision to undertake this exceptional study of Leonardo may perhaps be found in the distressing circumstances of 1899, when he was beset by a lack of direction, a fear of the future and increasing bouts of mental illness. There was no light at the end of the tunnel. He was now thirty-three and midway through his life. Did it not make sense to undertake the hazardous business of countering neurasthenia with beauty and escaping from the tormenting present? To Arcadia! On this occasion the journey took him also through Hamburg. The outlines of the unreachable land were projected on to the wall by means of slides.

No one reading Warburg's lecture notes will fail to see that, as so often, he was projecting his own inner tensions on to Leonardo and indeed on to the period as a whole, while at the same time interpreting the artist's work in a highly original way: 'Today', Warburg began his second lecture,

we must accompany Leonardo on the arduous paths that he pursued during the central section of his journey through life. We shall linger briefly with him in the inferno of his activities as a court engineer, before accompanying him at greater length through the purgatory of his purely experimental work as a draughtsman and finally glancing into the paradise of his impact as a painter, an area of his activity in which his most essential nature finds expression.[15]

The key word which Warburg uses to characterize Leonardo and which indicates an ideal Warburg himself spent his whole life striving to achieve, but which ultimately remained elusive, was 'balance'. In the balance of Leonardo's gifts lay a 'revelation of nature'; it indicated, 'much to our consolation', 'what one can be'.[16] A phrase like this makes clear the extent to which Warburg related his subject to his own physical and emotional state. He saw his historical studies in exactly the same light. In his work on memory – the essential quality of human beings – he was concerned to investigate the longed-for ontological state of calm and balance, a point he once explicitly stated. No less desirable were inner harmony towards creation and even the mere contemplation of beauty. To quote from Schiller's poem 'The Ideal and Life',

> But in yonder blissful realms afar,
> Where the forms unsullied are,
> Sorrow's mournful tempests cease to rave.

Warburg would hardly have denied that these lines of Schiller contain a grain of truth, but he would have argued that in beauty lurk dangers in the guise of emotions, 'Romantic' enthusiasm and ecstasy, all of which can drag the observer down into the whirlpool of the irrational. Apollo is glorious and at the same time terrible. He is like the night, and yet also a radiant sun-god; a helper and a destroyer in one and the selfsame person.

Warburg's second lecture is based on the same concept as that which had sustained his study of Botticelli, with its idea of progress from medieval ponderousness and restrictions to the 'freedom' of the Renaissance; from monsters to Olympian gods; from irrationality and superstition to reason; from the drolly fantastical to the real and the natural; and from the small-scale to the large-scale. In the figure of a 'mediating, transitional type' such as Leonardo, Warburg saw embodied the shift from the Middle Ages to the Renaissance.

The artist's milieu – the 'purgatory of reality'[17] – and tradition were described by Warburg as the artist's 'terrible adversaries'. Unlike Botticelli, Leonardo was not 'too flexible', nor did he submit to the influences on him but made creative use of all that they offered him, including the resistance they put up. Leonardo triumphed over 'petit-bourgeois craftsmanship', and also over the 'blinkered sentimentality' of an artist like Lorenzo di Credi and the courtly realism which came from the north.[18] In Warburg's view, the qualities that enabled Leonardo to meet the artistic challenges of his age were 'inner contemplation' and 'a sense of the theoretical and at the same time the ability to maintain a metaphysical seriousness of purpose'.[19]

The passages relating to Leonardo's principal works reveal the extent to which Warburg was in full command of the art of description, while the words he ultimately deleted indicate that, in approaching the mystery, he was struggling to find the right phrases while resisting the temptation to engage in bombast. Instead of referring to Leonardo's 'magic hand', he ended up speaking only of his 'hand'. In much the same spirit, the poetical formulation to the effect that Leonardo was in unique command of the art of 'lighting through shade . . . and shading translucently' fell victim to his own red pencil. What remained was: 'No one before or after him possessed that same capacity of using shadow as a silent colour, as a perfect means of conveying the inner life of human beings (the silent sounds of introverted people) and of letting them speak by means of their silence.'[20]

In Warburg's view, the artist's greatest achievement and an expression of Leonardo's 'astonishing' and 'God-given intellect' were the portraits painted during his later period in Florence and throughout his time in Milan, all of which revealed his ability to illustrate calm, harmonious states of mind and to come to terms, through painting, with the whole gamut of the passions without lapsing into 'mannerisms'.

Warburg reminded his listeners that the *Battle of Anghiari* and the *Mona Lisa* sprang from the same social world: 'As if his artist's soul was striving for a state of balance even in posing the problem, a miracle of lyric poetry came into being at precisely this time.'[21] This miracle was the *Mona Lisa*, a work emblematic of the 'art of beautiful, calm being' that Heinrich Wölfflin saw encapsulated in the masterpieces of the high Renaissance.

Warburg interpreted the Mona Lisa's smile as a way of coming to terms with a feeling of tension, a moment of calm in the upheaval caused by the clash between the Middle Ages and the modern period. Leonardo's art was seen as a humanistic art in the deeper sense of the term. In the light-hearted serenity of his figures lay a sense of kindness or politeness towards the observer, a quality that Leonardo was the first to introduce into art. He should remain in 'living and loving memory' precisely because of this humanity, rather than on account of his virtuosity.[22] Warburg regarded Leonardo's art as the antithesis of all the threats that may be posed by the world and by depictions of it. There is no trace here of Walter Pater's interpretation of the Mona Lisa as an erotic figure whose smile portends disaster.

Here, at the climax of Warburg's series of lectures, it becomes clear to what extent he derived his admiration of Leonardo's art from his own feeling of inadequacy in his dealings with the outside world. The *Gioconda* seemed to him to be an early example of a distanced, ironical, and yet open and friendly relationship with that world. The painting may be seen as an early high point in the process of civilization:

> Vasari reports that in order to rid the Mona Lisa of her peculiarly melancholic facial expression – an expression that one can easily acquire if one has to sit for a portrait for four years, even if one is not particularly melancholic by nature – Leonardo always sought to cheer her up by having people tell her jokes while he was painting her. But what we see is no smile of approval as might be produced by crude jokes, but the serene and somewhat ironical smile of a superior, elegant woman of the world, a smile that comes from within.

Warburg concedes that ultimately one stands helplessly before Leonardo's masterpieces as before a mystery, and he tells his listeners that not even his own journey has enabled him to achieve a state of total clarity. The elemental event as such must always remain a puzzle. It emerges from another of the passages he altered that, instead of 'a state of total clarity', he had originally considered referring to the observer as 'penetrating to the innermost holy of holies'. Time and again Warburg risked using this language of mysticism, only to delete almost all such phrases. The mystery, the puzzle, the inexplicable sentiment – these were none of his business. He was reluctant to admit that he too had encountered moments in art which defied rational analysis.

It seems likely that Pater's view of the *Mona Lisa* as an essentially Romantic work confirmed Warburg in his awe of Leonardo's art.[23] Moreover, even by this date the *Gioconda* was already the mythical masterpiece *par excellence*. D'Annunzio's play of the same name had had its première in 1899 and was soon staged in Florence. The principal role of the model, Gioconda Dianti, was played by Eleonora Duse, the '*donna dionisiaca*' being one of the author's symbols of womankind in general. And Dimitry Merezhkovsky's novel about Leonardo appeared in 1902. Before long it was a part of every private and public library, shelved only inches away from Burckhardt's *Cicerone*.

Warburg ended his series of lectures with an account of Leonardo as a scientist,[24] his final slide being the Turin drawing of a bearded old man that was then universally regarded as a self-portrait of the elderly Leonardo:

> Confronted by this wonderful old man's face, from which speaks the inner peace of someone who has experienced everything that human destiny can throw at him, a Frenchman[25] has suggested the following beautiful comparison: it is the head of an eagle used to flying up to the sun in its proud flight but which is now old and tired of having looked too often into the sun.

For Warburg, Leonardo was a Promethean figure, one of the heroes who stood on the brink of the modern world. His art and science were an expression of the new, while at the same time contributing to this development. In Warburg's eyes, this was a positive development inasmuch as it led to the liberation of mankind through enlightenment, reason and beauty and to a light-hearted joviality which also included a tinge of subtle irony and distance from the ego. A decisive pre-requirement was a 'scientific', logical and discursive approach to the world:

> We now know that as a scientific researcher, Leonardo was right to relegate the artist to the background. Anyone who, like him, suspected the

existence of laws that became the common property of us all only centuries later and who directly established those laws in all the areas of exact enquiry that he touched was no doubt bound to regard artistic activity per se as secondary.[26]

It is only against the background of the standards evident from his lectures on Leonardo that we can ultimately understand Warburg's 'discovery' of an artist who is now regarded as one of the truly great painters: Piero della Francesca. Around the turn of the century, a painter who, like Leonardo, was both an artist and a scientist was far from being part of the established canon.[27] Even Burckhardt had little to say about him and, indeed, was so unfamiliar with Piero's work that he even considered attributing to him the frescos in the Palazzo Schifanoia in Ferrara.[28] And if the art dealer and expert William Spence had had his way, Piero's *Baptism of Christ* would not now be hanging in London's National Gallery.[29] It was Spence, after all, who took John Charles Robinson to Sansepolcro, where the two of them were able to buy the masterpiece from the canons for the risible sum of four hundred pounds. In a letter to the London collector Gambier Parry, Spence spoke only of a 'painting in the cathedral at Borgo'. The price evidently seemed too high for him. Piero's painting initially ended up in the collection of Matthew Uzielli. But a number of Pre-Raphaelite painters, including Burne-Jones and Symonds, held Piero della Francesca in particularly high regard, while Lord Alexander Lindsay singled him out as an artist of international importance after he had seen his cycle of frescos in Arezzo in 1841.[30] The gradual breakthrough in Piero's fortunes may also be gathered from Roger Fry's correspondence.[31]

This neglect of Piero della Francesca had other, external causes, as few of his paintings have survived, his masterpieces being located in remote towns such as Sansepolcro, Monterchi and Rimini. Arezzo, with its famous cycle of frescos depicting the *Legend of the True Cross* in the town's Church of San Francesco, lay somewhat off the beaten track, even though the town had had a rail link with Florence since 1866.

Warburg travelled to Umbria at the end of April 1901, and there he met the 'graceful creature', as he called his old friend Alice Hallgarten Franchetti. She was proud to show him her enormous estates. His diary entry reads: 'Open-air impression in a symphony of gold-flashing green & light purple-blue mountain ridges and Piero della Francesca; her husband, Franchetti, in the prime of life, his will extending over valleys and hills: a patriarch's broadly flowing will lacking in a goal.'[32]

Warburg, too, seems to have been conscious of the close and instantly apparent links between Piero's art and the Umbrian countryside: 'The journey left a magical impression thanks to the beauty of the spring landscape and the profound artistic impression left on us by Piero della Francesca's paintings,' he wrote to Max Warburg.'His frescos in San Francesco in Arezzo, *plein air* painting in matt and yet colourful tones, may well be the grandest piece of fresco painting from the middle of the fifteenth century.These alone repay a visit to Italy.'[33]

During the years that followed, Warburg took a repeated interest in Piero's art, even though his scholarly endeavours never found expression in any major publication.[34] Not until 1914 did he give a public lecture in Florence on the subject, comparing Piero's *Battle of Constantine* with the representation of the same subject by pupils of Raphael in the Vatican. Here the 'pathos formulae', which were taken over from classical models and which Warburg called the 'superimposed Roman superlative', found uninhibited expression, whereas Piero imposed a sense of classical restraint on the dramatic events depicted.[35] The Vatican fresco seems strident and theatrical, a confused mass of bodies and movements; in Arezzo, by contrast, the battle is depicted as a soteriological event taking place with implacable inevitability and in silence.[36] In his notes Warburg stresses Piero's artistry in dispensing with all non-essential details while retaining a sense of realism. In Piero, the 'sense of liveliness' was always 'purified and satisfied'. Even the genre motif of the 'working man' – in the Arezzo cycle he is seen carrying the wood for the cross on his shoulder – acquires monumental grandeur. Every detail is subordinated to the whole: although 'the men are seen dragging the heavy wood for the cross, drawing water from the well and carrying out heavy manual work, their labours are idealized. There is an all-pervasive sound in which the individual note acquires meaning only through what it has in common with everything else'.

Above all, however, Warburg saw Piero as a master of capturing states of mind. 'In Piero della Francesca's hands a study in light executed with almost scientific coolness still retains its purely spiritual ability to provide a convincing symbol of a mental process. In Piero della Francesca's chiaroscuro we already see at work a force that again had to contend with the rhetoric of the Latinate language of gesture in late Rembrandt.'[37] In this way Warburg was able to admire Piero della Francesca also as a master of equilibrium, an artist who rose triumphantly above the pathos formula and hence over the 'Dionysian' Renaissance.

Judgements such as these make it particularly easy to see how constant Warburg's aesthetic criteria remained. In the case of Piero della Francesca, he praises the 'Umbrian superhuman composure of the eye' that renders one 'affect-less'; he admires the resistance of the 'solitary figure from Arezzo', as he calls Piero on one occasion, to foreign influences and to memories of the past. Faced by the 'threat' from the realism of the Flemish school, with its fondness for detail, Piero unerringly retained a 'conscience for the essential and the simple'. 'Almost like a northern miniaturist, this Italian artist can do everything, but he also had the ability to leave everything out and to stress the emotional expression at the expense of the prosaic detail; the button-holes are all there, but who thinks of them or does not forget them?'[38]

In this way Warburg sought to solve the mysteries of the art of the artist from Sansepolcro by examining the question of the importance of tradition and of the contemporary art of northern Europe; and yet even Warburg himself appears to have been plagued by doubts as to whether a genius like Piero could be decoded in this manner. Here, too, he ended up professing his belief in the significance of individual creative achievement: 'Who will risk identifying these visual abilities with emotional or anthropological boundaries?'

Almost uniquely among Warburg's writings, his notes on Leonardo and Piero grant us insights into his approach to works of art of the first order, and also into his own private aesthetics. He approached them with very clear standards, standards shaped by Wölfflin,[39] Pater and, above all, Jacob Burckhardt.[40] Terms such as 'harmony', 'higher reality', 'balance' and 'equilibrium' stand at the four corners of the system of aesthetic coordinates that was intimately associated in his thinking with reason and enlightenment. And if, in the case of Leonardo's art, he praises the 'liberating smile of the human being rising above himself',[41] then it is hard not to hear in such a phrase the longing of a man incapable of achieving the serenity which comes from this sense of self-discipline. In short, these are moving autobiographical texts, documenting a struggle for rationality and inner calm in what has been described as an 'age of nervous splendour'.

18   Bernard Berenson standing beside a sideboard in
his villa I Tatti (1900)

*'Berenson cold blue eyes, a pushy person and a snob, an affected
perspicacity'* (ABY WARBURG)

Dealers in beauty

THE masterpieces of Piero, Leonardo and other Renaissance painters, sculptors and architects were fixed stars on the firmament of art, offering points of orientation in the confusion of styles and theories of an age lacking in clear coordinates. And, in a secularized world, they provided the educated middle classes with a quasi-religious experience. The museums in which their epiphany was celebrated were the temples of a religion of art; for these buildings generally appeared as such from the outside. At the same time they represented self-contained worlds in an age rent by upheavals, places in which the worshippers could find consolation and could draw hope. 'True art', wrote the art patron and theorist Conrad Fiedler from Florence to Adolf von Hildebrand, 'always liberates us from everything that life can throw at us.' In defining art in this way, he was describing one of the essential functions of beauty in the final third of the nineteenth century.[1]

If Warburg was not entirely convinced that it was possible to find peace of mind by 'praying' to supreme beauty in the way a reading of Pater's *Renaissance* or Burckhardt's *Cicerone* might have suggested, there is no doubt that this scepticism stemmed from his fear of mysticism and Romanticism – even if, as his Leonardo lectures indicate, he occasionally inclined towards a 'Romantic' view of artistic creativity. To submit to the irrational aesthetic experience seemed to him to be dangerous, as it threatened level-headedness and meant abandoning a sense of distance. He tried to define his relationship with art as something scientific and sought in that way to maintain a sense of balance.

For Beauty's nothing
but beginning of terror we're still just able to bear,

and why we adore it so is because it serenely
disdains to destroy us.

Rilke's famous remark in the first of his *Duino Elegies* applies directly to
Warburg. But what can be said about the appropriation of art through the
acquisition of a work of art, an extreme method of destroying the distance
between the observer and the observed?

It comes as no surprise to find that the Warburgs rarely bought works of
art, as this would have been an irrational form of appropriation. On one
occasion Warburg compared the patronage that existed in the Florence of
Lorenzo the Magnificent with art collecting in his own day: in the earlier
period, he argued, creating and enjoying art had merely been 'different stages
in one and the same organic cycle', their function being to 'regard and use
all human qualities as a uniform tool in the art of enjoying life, an art that
delighted in extending its influence'. In this way, people's dealings with art
seemed to him to be a part of the difficult struggle to break free from
'medieval' ties. Enjoyment and creativity were active forces in the process of
western civilization. But this, he argued, was very different from 'culturally
educated individuals wearily picking themselves up to wander round an art
bazaar whose over-abundant riches are designed to stimulate passive attention and turn it into the desire to buy something or even force them to
make a purchase'.[2]

The acquisition of a work of art represents the most extreme form of
rapprochement. But, even with the true collector, for whom acquisition
means more than mere prestige, buying the work is no more than a substi-
tute act in the face of the impossibility of entering into a mystic union with
the beautiful object. At best, it offers the owner the ability to dispose of the
object fully and with impunity, to appropriate it through the legitimate
experience of 'tactile values', and even to destroy it. Its purchase is a self-
contradictory attempt to go beyond the unrequited love the work permits.
The sense of expectation provoked by the beautiful object is meant to be
resolved in a state of supreme satisfaction: the owner wants to salvage the
'disinterested pleasure' of a fleeting affair and to sanctify it as a form of
marriage in order to lend it permanence.

For serious collectors, collecting works of art can have a profoundly irrational side to it even in the modern world, at least if we ignore its social
functions. The artist is present in spirit in his artefact, the work of art. It thus
becomes a kind of relic that pilgrims are encouraged to touch, conveying
memories of its creator and of the age in which it was created – a function
of central significance in Warburg's iconography. In a rapidly changing
world, it achieves a permanence which is more than merely material.

Paradoxically, it is its very historicity that raises it above time. It is a special instance of those 'old things' of which Proust writes, these things being the fetishes in which the divine appears to exist in a godless world:

> But when a belief vanishes, there survives it – more and more vigorously so as to cloak the absence of the power, now lost to us, of imparting reality to new things – a fetishistic attachment to the old things which it did once animate, as if it was in them and not in ourselves that the divine spark resided, and as if our present incredulity had a contingent cause – the death of the gods.[3]

Warburg viewed the world of commercial art dealers with some suspicion, and yet in spite of this he was in contact with antique dealers in Florence, keeping in touch not only with Stefano Bardini and Bernard Berenson but also with the great museum curator Wilhelm Bode. The young private scholar was held in high regard as someone who knew about the early Florentine Renaissance, while in turn Warburg made use of his colleagues' knowledge of forms and styles. He himself took little interest in the business of 'attribution', one of the few exceptions being his plea – made during his lectures on Leonardo – that a drawing in the holdings of the Hamburg Kunsthalle should be ascribed to Leonardo.

In the years around 1900, antique dealers made up a large part of the physical map of Florence. The true 'dealers in beauty' appear in none of the travel guides of the period but belong in the context of the excesses of the Renaissance revival and of the aesthetic movement of the period. Piled up in their shops were objects that distilled the very essence of a florid imagination, and there were enough well-heeled foreigners wanting to possess the objects which it gave them such pleasure to behold.

James Jackson Jarves called Florence 'the world's capital of Bric-a-bracdom', claiming that its art market was as inexhaustible as the coal mines of England.[4] The Italian state had still made no attempt to prevent the export of its cultural assets. These were the years when the culture of the Etruscans was gradually being discovered by scholars such as George Dennis, who published his widely read *Cities and Cemeteries of Etruria* in 1848, and the afore-mentioned Charles Godfrey Leland, who sought to trace the old customs of Tuscany.[5] Etruscan vases, dressing-table mirrors formerly owned by Greek and Etruscan noblewomen, wedding chests, statuettes and medals could be picked up for next to nothing, as could altarpieces of the fourteenth and fifteenth centuries. The painter Francis Alexander from Boston bought up whole mountains of early art for a mere handful of dollars. His Pre-Raphaelite colleague Charles Fairfax Murray dealt in Renaissance paintings, using the profits to gratify his own passion for collecting,[6] while Walter Savage Landor was able to buy a number of panel paintings at a time when there was as yet no discernible enthusiasm for the art of the Quattrocento. If we may believe the legend, he managed in this way to stop them from ending up in carpenters' workshops and hearth fires.[7] Robert Browning, too, bought paintings hidden in attics and sacristies, finding no fewer than five among a pile of rubbish in a granary a mile from Florence.[8] The connoisseur, antiquary and spirit medium Seymour Kirkup had no qualms about attributing them to artists of the stature of Cimabue, Ghirlandaio and Giotto.

A golden age for gold-diggers, this heyday of art collecting reports many similar stories of a no less hair-raising nature. On one occasion a Titian was discovered in a pile of rotting linen, on another a Michelangelo was found in a junkshop and a Leonardo at a flea market.[9] Many of these tales belong in the realm of legend. The horror story to the effect that altarpieces with gold backgrounds were burnt in Tuscany for the sake of their precious metal must surely be an invention. None the less, it is undoubtedly true that Italy held a sort of end-of-summer sale of its ancient art treasures at this time. In 1863 members of the Arundel Society, including Ruskin, seem to have hatched the bizarre plan of buying the Arena Chapel in Padua and of transporting Giotto's cycle of frescos to England, much as had been done with the Parthenon frieze earlier in the century.[10]

Among the first to adopt a systematic approach to acquiring works from Florence's artistic past was James Jackson Jarves.[11] A native of Boston, he was one of those restless foreigners who ended up on the banks of the Arno only after protracted wanderings. For health reasons, he had lived for a time on Hawaii, where he had made a name for himself as a newspaper editor and as the author of a history of the Sandwich Islands. Later he wrote books on art and is still remembered for his *Italian Rambles*, its portraits of the smaller Tuscan towns being invaluable sources of a slice of bygone Italian life.

Jarves was an expert in early American cultures and also published on Japanese art. He first encountered great European art at the Louvre, an encounter that left him 'oppressed, confused, uncertain, and feverish'. From then on he wanted to own masterpieces of art, and in Florence he became one of the great collectors of early Tuscan and Umbrian painting, housing his treasures in the rambling Palazzo Guadagni, which forms the eastern end of the Piazza Santo Spirito. Later, much of his collection found its way into American museums. Jarves hoped to confront his own age with aesthetic models from the past, a consideration that inspired many a nineteenth-century arts-and-crafts collection.

The painter William Spence grew up in Florence and assembled an exquisite collection of paintings dominated by the Quattrocento, for all that he despised the work of Piero della Francesca. He refused to abandon his second career as an art dealer even though his father, fearing for his son's reputation as a painter, urged him to do so. He began this second career by acquiring a *Pietà* – possibly by Annibale Carracci – at Doney's for nine dollars, then selling it on almost immediately afterwards for forty pounds.[12] He even sold paintings to Queen Victoria and became one of the leading agents for English museums anxious to acquire Italian paintings and sculptures. In 1860 a legacy allowed him to buy the Villa Medici in Fiesole and to turn it into a hub of social activity. He even had a small theatre built not far away. But, as a classic *marchand-amateur*, he found it impossible to abandon his work as an art dealer. Few of the great English collectors of the period passed up the opportunity to visit him. His apotheosis as a connoisseur came when he discovered Botticelli's *Pallas and the Centaur*, long thought to be lost, in a remote apartment in the Palazzo Pitti, a discovery which proved little short of sensational. One of the first writers to publish details of the find was André Jolles,[13] who, appealing to the authority of Aby Warburg, floated the suggestion that the painting might originally have been used at a pageant.

The locals, too, acknowledged the enormous earning power of the art trade in an age of aestheticism, the Arts and Crafts Movement and the general enthusiasm for the Pre-Raphaelites. In 1873 we find Adolf von Hildebrand writing to Conrad Fiedler: 'Julius Meyer, the director of the Berlin Museum, has been buying old paintings here for quite dreadful sums, and, as people say, has been taken for a dreadful ride (some of them are completely over-painted!).'[14] Art came to life and passed from Florence to all the great capitals of Europe, from where it was often exported to North America. It was in this way that the dealer Joseph Duveen was able to acquire the collection of Oscar Hainauer, most of which had been bought in Florence, and to sell it on to John Pierpont Morgan and Henry Clay Frick.

This collecting mania may have been sustained by a spirit of romantic enthusiasm, but its importance for the history of art cannot be overemphasized. It was here that the holdings came together that created the basis for an empirical and critical discipline. How could a scholar like Warburg have worked with wedding chests and other objects and used them to produce his view of the Renaissance if there had not been dealers and fanatical collectors who bought up such items?

This was a time when first-rate collections were being assembled outside Italy, and not only by private individuals. The aesthetic categories to which their acquisitions belonged had been formulated by a mere handful of writers: Ruskin, Pater, Norton, Burckhardt and, finally, Berenson. The age of nationalism made itself felt in this area, too, works of art becoming weapons in a silent battle over cultural prestige. Most of the collections of major Renaissance paintings held by the national galleries in London and Washington and by the Metropolitan Museum of Art in New York were assembled at this time, largely as a result of gifts by wealthy patrons of the arts. Wilhelm Bode, soon to become the general director of all Berlin's royal museums, scoured Italy, and especially Florence, actively competing with others engaged in a similar quest. It was thanks to his skilful purchasing policy that the museums in the German capital were able to acquire Renaissance works of international importance.

In the wake of Italian unification, Florence was flooded with a vast number of bootied pieces and other works of art, a state of affairs which stemmed in part from the redevelopment of the city's historic centre and in part from the dissolution of religious houses. The city resembled a dead body which had been completely eviscerated. Many of its works of art found their way into the museum at San Marco's, but some of the debris from the old centre was scattered across the globe and can now be found in the neo-Renaissance *palazzi* of wealthy American collectors and in museums such as the Victoria and Albert in London, where they were intended to serve as models for local craftsmen. Other pieces, in turn, were incorporated into domestic interiors, becoming set pieces in an altered cultural environment. Contemporaries who felt uncomfortable at the thought of living inside steel-built modern houses which recalled nothing so much as cages hung their walls with old paintings, adding the occasional trophy or replica and concealing modernity and the harsh objectivity of the building's construction behind a nebulous aura of history.[15] A stone was more of a stone than it had been previously, which is why the old pieces of masonry bore all the greater magical substance within them.

This reverential attitude towards the relics of ancient Florence expresses at several removes a sense of historical awareness and a vestigial respect for the past. While on the one hand history was being destroyed on a grand scale, it was still being revered and preserved on a much smaller scale, what was left providing the material for historical studies. Here too, then, we find the old dialectics of modernization and historicism. The antiquary invariably gains in importance in times of radical upheaval.

Amateurs like Seymour Kirkup, Jarves and Spence dominated Florence's art market around the middle of the nineteenth century. Other names worth mentioning in this context are those of Alexander Barker, who was one of the first to rediscover Botticelli and who collected the paintings of François Boucher, Sir James Hudson,[16] Jean Paul Richter[17] and Karl Eduard von Liphart.[18] Warburg met Liphart,[19] and the two men appear to have discussed the identification of the backgrounds of Tuscan landscapes. By the final third of the century Florence's art market had gained a clearer profile thanks to the work of a handful of central figures. Trading became more professional: dealers and agents were not only astute businessmen but also genuine connoisseurs, in some cases building up significant collections of their own. It was these men who now came to prominence.[20] One of their number was Vincenzo Ciampolini, a follower of Garibaldi, who after 1866 had traded in weapons and tapestries in the orient and in that way had become very wealthy. He came into contact with Prince Anatoli Demidov and became 'artistic agent' for the city's Russian colony. The dealer Demetrio Tolosani and a number of his colleagues scoured Tuscany in search of spoils. Giovanni Palotti was the typical 'superior' antiques dealer, buying exclusively from other dealers and from junk dealers whom his distinguished clients were too refined to contact in person. Other leading dealers of the period included Giuseppe Salvadori and his partner Adolfo Mancini. Salvadori specialized in Gobelin tapestries and ran a large shop at 9 Via de' Fossi which was full of tapestries, items of furniture, smaller artworks, weapons, paintings and statues. In the years leading up to the First World War, his gallery on the Borgo San Frediano was one of the leading centres of the international art world. Another dealer who deserves at least a brief mention is Luigi Grassi, who did not start working in the profession until the turn of the century, but who was one of the antiques dealers used by D'Annunzio when furnishing his Villa della Capponcina.

And then there was Stefano Bardini, who at this date was the most important art dealer in Italy.[21] Like Ciampolini, Bardini was able to bask in the aura which came from having taken part in Garibaldi's expedition of the Thousand that liberated Sicily in 1860. After the war of 1870–1, he turned to antiques dealing and quickly became one among his profession's elite. Evincing exquisite taste and an enthusiasm for the chase that bordered on genuine fanaticism, he saw everything which came on the market in Italy as potential booty. He was able to make his fortune in this way because at a time when the old feudal agrarian economy was giving way to a modern industrial society many members of the Florentine and Tuscan nobility were obliged to sell their collections. He managed to gain access to country estates and *palazzi* owned by well-known families who hailed from Florence's legendary past: families such as the Strozzi, Rucellai and Capponi. Although these families were careful to retain their paintings and statues, they took less interest in older pieces of furniture and in tapestries, smaller bronzes, wedding chests, stucco reliefs and similar objects, allowing Bardini to acquire them for next to nothing. And the workmen engaged in tearing down the old centre of Florence were encouraged by means of tips to provide the dealer with many a bootied item.

In this way Bardini's *palazzo* on the Piazza dei Mozzi became one vast warehouse. Many of the items were sold on at an appropriate profit to collectors and curators such as the Prince of Liechtenstein, Louis Carrand, Wilhelm Bode and the Berlin collector Oscar Hainauer,[22] all of whom bought considerable numbers of statuettes and small bronze items from him. Even in his obituary of Bardini, Bode found it impossible not to criticize the dealer's egoism and lack of seriousness, contrasting these shortcomings with the consummate politeness of the grand seigneur whom Bardini otherwise physically resembled. Bardini's collection became a public museum in 1926, with Antonio Pollaiuolo's *Archangel Michael* as its uncontested centrepiece.

Relics of the collection of Bardini's long-time colleague, Elia Volpi, may also still be seen.[23] The two men worked together for a period of some fifteen years, during which time Volpi acquired a thorough knowledge of the subject, especially where restoration techniques were concerned. Bardini ran his own workshop for restoring the works that passed through his hands. In some cases new pieces were created from the fragments of several different items, so that it is hardly surprising to find that, as Bode recalled, Bardini was anxious to ensure that none of his customers ever saw into the storerooms at the Palazzo Mozzi.

Volpi finally set up in business on his own, but only under the most diffi-cult circumstances, retiring in 1893 to his home town of Città di Castello at the insistence of his former colleague, who was keen to avoid competition. Here Volpi importuned clerics, monks and private individuals in his quest for Umbrian paintings, pieces of furniture and all manner of craft objects. By 1900 he was once again able to set up in business in Florence, which was said to be his display window, while Città di Castello remained his inex-haustible warehouse. In 1904 he paid 62,500 lire for the fourteenth-century Palazzo Davanzati, which had been opened up after the redevelopment of the city centre. He then proceeded to restore the building, adding historical items of furniture and turning it into a veritable Casa museo. Its vast portals had once formed part of Città di Castello's town gates.

Volpi's experiences as an antiques dealer, and especially the insights he gleaned when furnishing the Palazzo Davanzati, provided him with the basis for an important study, *La casa fiorentina e i suoi arredi* (1908). The *palazzo* was formally opened to the public in 1910, in which year Volpi held his first important auction there. The building struck Arnold Bennett as the biggest exhibition hall he had ever encountered.[24]

Another sector of the market was overseen by the book dealer and publisher Leo S. Olschki,[25] who moved to Florence from Venice in 1897, when he became the unofficial antiquarian bookseller to high society, allowing the town's international visitors to gratify their love of the

Renaissance by acquiring valuable printed works and manuscripts from the period. In particular, he specialized in incunabula, which he advertised in magnificent catalogues. In 1899 he bought the library of Charles Fairfax Murray,[26] a student of Dante Gabriel Rossetti and a friend of Ruskin who lived at Galuzzo. Later he also acquired the choice collection assembled by Leonida Leonetti from Udine, some four thousand volumes which he sold to the city of Ravenna, where they now form the nucleus of the Sala Dantesca at the Biblioteca Classense.

Bibliophiles from all over the world frequented Olschki's 'Librairie ancienne' on the Lungarno Acciaiuoli, and in the years around the turn of the century it became the nub of a network of links with collectors throughout Europe and the United States. Berenson's teacher, Charles Eliot Norton, was one of his customers, as were John Pierpont Morgan, Willard Fiske,[27] who lived in Landor's villa at Fiesole, and, above all, Henry Walters, who in 1903 bought the whole contents of the catalogue headed *Monumenta typographica* for his collection in Baltimore. Olschki landed another *coup* when he bought up some of Paganini's original manuscripts, presenting these *trouvailles* within the framework of a concert featuring works by the 'devil's violinist'. The occasion must have been a magic moment in the encounter between music and written culture.

Olschki also maintained close, not to say friendly, dealings with Gabriele D'Annunzio, who lived in Florence from 1897 to 1910. When the writer fell into financial difficulties, Olschki did what he could to help by selling some of D'Annunzio's manuscripts to American collectors. In 1899 he established a new periodical, *La Bibliofila*, which became a forum for book lovers all over the world.

Warburg was a frequent visitor to Olschki's premises and placed a number of orders with him. Once his collection of books had begun to outgrow the dimensions of a private library, he sought to obtain a corresponding discount from the dealer: 'Please treat my library just as you would occasionally treat a public library.'[28] Even before this, Warburg had always generously made his holdings available to interested scholars.

With increasing competition in Florence's art market and with the ever greater sums of money involved, the local antiques dealers adopted the professionalism that we nowadays associate with the names of Bardini, Volpi and Olschki. By the turn of the century they had been joined by two other figures in the persons of Horne and Berenson, who, even more than Olschki and Volpi, backed up their business dealings with scholarly and literary endeavours. Both men, moreover, were convivial hosts, their houses providing the setting for elite public gatherings. Recalling the period around 1907, William Rothenstein remembered enemy camps and furious disputations in Florence, just as there had been in the past, but the battles, he went on, were now far less bloody than before, as they were concerned with questions of attribution rather than with ducal thrones: 'Berenson, Horne, Loeser, Vernon Lee, Maud Crutwell, all had their mercenaries – and their artillery.'[29]

We have already encountered Herbert P. Horne as a combatant in the battle to preserve the old heart of Florence. A man of many parts, he began his career as an art dealer on the strength of a number of advantageous purchases made during the early days of art dealing, when the Tuscan market was still dominated by 'gold-diggers'. His correspondence with Robert Ross – the director of London's Carfax Gallery and Oscar Wilde's literary executor – gives an indication of how much he sometimes earned. On one occasion he writes of a painting for which he paid one hundred francs and which he was able to sell on to an American collector for ten times that amount.[30] The same letter mentions three 'very beautiful' panels which were said to be the work of Pietro Lorenzetti and to have cost him twenty pounds each. He also enabled his friend Arnold Dolmetsch to gain access to the collection of the Marchese Torrigiani, from which the musician and instrument maker bought not only a violin by Nicolò Amati but also lute tablatures from the fifteenth and sixteenth centuries, paying an absurdly low price for them.[31]

Horne also sold works of art to John Pierpont Morgan, who was one of America's major collectors and Wilhelm Bode's keenest competitor on the Florentine market, and to Roger Fry, the editor of the *Burlington Magazine* and later the curator of the Metropolitan Museum of Art in New York. Fry was a man of great influence, who could be said to have laid the foundations of modern art. In Florence he was one of Horne's closest friends, alongside Robert Ross and Charles Loeser. It was through Loeser – one of the discoverers of the work of Paul Cézanne – that the Warburgs gained access to this circle. They joined him one day for breakfast and looked forward to the prospect of a visit to see 'the famous antiques dealer' Stefano Bardini.[32]

An artist in his own right, Horne was also extraordinarily gifted as a scholar. He was cautious in venturing attributions[33] and always keen to avoid risks as a businessman, which no doubt explains why he was so successful. His scornful laughter at auctions when paintings with over-optimistic attributions were called out was as proverbial as it was feared.[34] He was not really a typical connoisseur: indeed, Berenson once complained that Horne had an extraordinary inability to see things with his own eyes and that he went to extreme lengths to write down in his notebook everything that Horne had been able to squeeze out of him during their visits to galleries together.[35] Horne was an expert on artistic techniques, with a fanatical respect for archival sources. In short, he was a true art *historian*. This was very much the quality that formed the basis of his dealings with Warburg.

A good example of Horne's method is his essay on Paolo Uccello's famous battle scene in the Uffizi, detailed archival studies allowing him to throw light on the historical context in which the painting is to be placed. As a result of his demonstration that the piece alludes to the Battle of San Romano of 1432, when Florence defeated Siena, both the original and its two pendants in London and Paris now have their current titles.[36]

In his principal work, a monograph on Botticelli, Horne combined historical questions – on which he corresponded at length with Warburg – with the approach of a true expert. One aim of his study was to distinguish authentic works from those by imitators and pupils. The end product was to have been a *catalogue raisonné*, but in the event the second volume, which would have contained this catalogue, never appeared. Horne's approach was never less than extremely scrupulous. Roger Fry praised the book as a work of the Renaissance itself, monumental in its physical appearance and a product of 'dignity and style'. Above all, he praised the level of criticism: ' "What is it," he says . . . "that we really know about Simonetta?" "What is it that we really know?" is the question always in Mr. Horne's mind.'[37] In this way Horne set himself as far apart from Ruskin's view as from Pater's approach, for all that he remained indebted to the latter on many points, especially with regard to style. Whereas Pater had spoken of 'a sentiment of ineffable melancholy' in Botticelli's perception of his universe, Horne preferred a more sober observation, ascribing the cadaverous pallor of Venus that had so exercised Pater[38] to the decay of the tempera, which had been mixed with raw eggs, and to the fact that the painting had not been varnished. He drew attention to contemporary assessments of Botticelli's figures and to the fact that they were said to exude an '*aria virile*', a manly character. And he stressed the Florentine temperament, with its gloominess and cruelty, while also emphasizing the Florentines' 'keen sense of expressive beauty, the bizarre imagination, the amatorious sweetness and tenderness of the age in which he lived'.[39] It is very much these attempts to relate Botticelli's art to contemporary life that point particularly clearly to Warburg's influence.

Throughout all this, Horne's position – poised between art and commerce – remained ambivalent, and there were contemporary critics who described as offensive the contradiction between the airs of an aesthete and an interest in business. Arthur S. Mons, for example, cited a sentence from Pater's cynical review of Wilde's *Picture of Dorian Gray*: 'But his story is also a vivid, though carefully considered, exposure of the corruption of a soul, with a very plain moral pushed home, to the effect that vice and crime make people coarse and ugly.'[40]

Even more problematic, however, was – and is – the iconic figure of Bernard Berenson. Warburg did not have a particularly high opinion of the American dealer. The two men had met at Horne's villa in May 1898, and Warburg had noted afterwards in his diary: 'Berenson cold blue eyes, a pushy person and a snob, an affected perspicacity. Am to publish documents for him, no enthusiasm.'[41] His links with Berenson and the latter's circle were never particularly close, a state of affairs for which Warburg's youth and relative anonymity were largely to blame. Although Berenson later called on him in Hamburg in 1927,[42] Warburg never featured in the list that Berenson's partner, Mary Costelloe, drew up to categorize the Berensons' circle of friends in Florence, its headings including 'Common friends', 'B.B.'s', 'Those who count in every day life here', 'My world' and, finally, 'My real world'.[43] The list reveals the outlines of a network: Carlo Placci, who mediated between the different cultures, is included no fewer than three times, appearing in first and last position on the list of common friends and also on the list of those people who counted in everyday life in Florence. It was Vernon Lee who introduced Berenson to this polyglot, witty man of letters and journalist. Placci was also the link between the Berensons and the circle associated with Adolf von Hildebrand, with the result that Costelloe's list additionally includes the names of Hildebrand and Georg Gronau, the Berlin art historian who was later to become the director of the Cassel Gallery.

Like Spence, Berenson was the very epitome of the connoisseur. He was still only twenty-five when a fascinated female acquaintance wrote that he 'seems to know *everything* about *every* picture that has ever been painted'.[44] The son of Lithuanian Jews, he received his formative education on the east coast of America. At Harvard, he fell under the influence of Charles Eliot Norton, who was the supreme artistic arbiter of Boston[45] as well as being a friend of Ruskin, an acquaintance of Browning and the Pre-Raphaelites and a 'high priest' of beauty who inveighed against the materialism of his age and against the vulgarity and cheap superficiality that seemed to him to typify the American way of life. The intelligent and witty young man soon found himself accepted in Boston society and gained admittance to the legendary 'O. K.', a literary gathering made up of the town's patricians and *jeunesse dorée*. Among its more famous members were Theodore Roosevelt and the bibliophile John Fiske. During the 1880s the list included not only Berenson but also Charles Loeser.

This was also the period when the ambitious young student with the eccentric 'Pre-Raphaelite' mane of hair first came into contact with the *précieuse*, Isabella Stewart Gardner, or 'Boston's pre-cinema star', as Berenson later described her. 'Mrs Jack', as her friends called her, kept an open house, which as a disciple of Norton and an adherent of the aesthetic movement she saw it as her duty to fill with works of art on the grandest possible scale. It was no accident that Florence fell within her purview.

The links between New England and Florence could look back on a long tradition,[46] Americans having discovered their emotional affinities with the city on the banks of the Arno as early as the middle of the nineteenth century. Early enthusiasts included George Hillard, the author of an immensely influential book, *Six Months in Italy*, and George Ticknor, who likewise recorded his impressions of Italy. Also worth mentioning here are the publisher James Field and the poet James Russell Lowell. Senator Charles Sumner, an early advocate of the abolition of slavery in the United States, was another such visitor from New England, as were Nathaniel Hawthorne and the feminist writer Margaret Fuller. Beneath the foundation-stone of the monument to Dante on the Piazza San Croce a copy of Thomas William Parsons' translation of the *Inferno* was buried: the Bostonian poet being a pioneer of Dante research in the United States.[47] Other artists from Boston, including Francis Alexander, the composer Francis Boott and his daughter Elizabeth, likewise discovered Florence at an early date.[48]

'B.B.' was only twenty-one when he first contributed to *Harvard Monthly* in 1886, for the most part writing reviews and quickly gaining the reputation of a young genius with his exceptionally cultured background. Bursaries allowed him to travel to Europe, where he was introduced to William Morris and his 'god', Walter Pater. He also met Oscar Wilde, who was fascinated by the handsome young man. In the course of his travels throughout Italy, Berenson acquired the knowledge that was admired even by the elderly Giovanni Morelli, one of the nineteenth century's great art connoisseurs.

By 1888 Berenson had more or less settled in Florence, his studies finding expression in a steadily increasing stream of books and articles which appeared in well-respected periodicals on both sides of the Atlantic. A monk from Monte Oliveto recalled the young man returning to the monastery at sunset with one or two fourteenth- or fifteenth-century altar-pieces from Siena in his horse's saddlebag: he had bought them from impoverished priests and sacristans for a mere pittance.[49]

Berenson began to negotiate the sale of works of art in the spring of 1893, using his sense of taste to earn money – a lot of it. By 1899 the sum involved was some fifteen thousand dollars, or $885,000 at today's prices. He ran his business along inspired lines, his publications vouching for his reputation as an expert, while they formulated criteria that ultimately set the standards by which works of art could be judged – not only artistically but economically, too. At the same time Berenson cultivated the air of an aesthete, and his house became the meeting place of all manner of men of letters, art lovers, scholars and bohemians. A sketch written in the style of Anatole France by a female friend of Berenson and Mary Costelloe gives an idea of the ambiance there:

> Madame Costelloe, swathed in furs, was stretched out on her chaise longue, etc. Groups of young people broke away to discuss Italian politics. A young nobleman [Bertrand Russell] who had left the English embassy in Paris to marry an American female politician and to study German socialism – violently discussed the theories of Karl Marx with another person who had just concluded a romantic marriage, etc., etc., while in another room archaeologists heatedly argued over the question of the dates of the metopes, etc.; here and there one saw people amusing themselves leafing through albums of photographs selected by the celebrated connoisseur Mr. Berenson – and a group of adorable young girls leaned over the balcony admiring the valley of the Arno and Florence stretched out at their feet, etc., etc. From time to time all conversation stopped while a musician of rare talent evoked the melodies of Tristan on the grand piano, etc. etc.[50]

The reader may also imagine a certain erotic libertinage, this too being part of the picture of Florence as an 'island of the blessed'. England was a long way off, and a room with a view was easy to come by. This was the period when the whole of Florence was talking about the *fin de siècle*'s quintessential liaison between Gabriele D'Annunzio and Eleonora Duse. Both were frequent visitors to the Berensons' home after the turn of the century, D'Annunzio's legendary villa, La Capponcina, lying only a short distance away.

Berenson's clients included several wealthy Americans: William Randolph Hearst, Andrew W. Mellon, Samuel H. Kress, John Graver Johnson, Henry Clay Frick, John Pierpont Morgan and, finally, Joseph Duveen, who by the early twentieth century was the leading art dealer in the United States. But Berenson's first and most important customer was Isabella Stewart Gardner, his benefactress from his early days in Boston. She was an energetic and fanatical collector, fond of seeing herself as a latter-day Isabella d'Este. She transformed her Boston home, Fenway Court, into a *pasticcio*-like monument to her passion for the Renaissance, filling it with bootied items assembled from far and wide. One contemporary critic described it as a kind of petrified bulwark against the hectic bustle of modern life.[51]

Thanks to Berenson's efforts and its owner's wealth, Fenway Court was soon stocked with exquisite paintings. We can imagine Isabella Stewart Gardner's enthusiasm when Berenson negotiated the purchase of a

Botticelli, an acquisition that could hardly have been closer to her aesthete's heart. She paid seventeen thousand dollars – over one million dollars at today's prices – for *The Tragedy of Lucretia*, the highest sum that she had yet lavished on a work of art.[52] Other works in her collection included Titian's famous *Rape of Europa* and pieces by Bellini, Piero della Francesca and Tintoretto. The association between Berenson and Isabella Stewart Gardner lasted for three decades and is a tale of a choice collection that reads like a particularly exciting detective story. Berenson tracked down the paintings and haggled over the prices. Some of the pieces proved to be forgeries, and he may also have been offered stolen items. He described his finds to his client in glowing terms, hazarding the most sensational attributions. The two of them corresponded in code in order to avoid rousing suspicions: 'YELAQEZ' meant 'Velazquez yes', in other words, Berenson was instructed to buy the piece, whereas 'NOQEZ' indicated that he was not to do so. Prices were encrypted in Roman numerals, 'BENE, XVM, SUBITO', for example, meaning 'Send a cheque for £15,000 at once.'[53] Once the relevant cable had arrived, the agent of beauty could act. After that, it was a question of arranging for the work to be exported, obtaining authorization and bribing officials. If none of this worked, smuggling was a tried and tested alternative. It seems that throughout all this Berenson worked closely with Icilio Joni, a skilful forger based in Siena who is also known to have produced 'antique' Renaissance frames that included a patina and wormholes carefully bored into the wood.[54]

American collectors like Mrs Gardner were for the most part members of the east-coast aristocracy and had practically unlimited resources at their disposal. (Of course, not even they could afford the sum of more than a quarter of a million dollars, which was the asking price for Titian's *Divine and Human Love*.[55]) If Florence, as some people thought, was a kind of Italian Boston,[56] then Boston became the Florence of America thanks to Isabella Stewart Gardner's enthusiasm for the arts. Other cities such as New York, Baltimore, Philadelphia and Washington were soon home to other leading collectors.

As an agent and internationally acknowledged expert on matters of taste, Berenson soon enjoyed an exceptional standing in these circles. Much to the annoyance of rivals such as the director of Berlin's royal museums, Wilhelm Bode, the demands of Berenson's clients caused the Tuscan art market to overheat, and Italian art now began to be sold on a grand scale, albeit rarely to the detriment of the major masterpieces which, lavishly restored, remain to this day at the heart of America's great collections.

A letter from Berenson to his friend Herbert P. Horne reveals how the former proceeded when he was not acting on behalf of regular customers such as Isabella Stewart Gardner. He sent his English colleague *objets d'art* that the latter then sold on the English market. Horne had to bear the cost of shipping the items to England, while Berenson was responsible for any damage sustained during transport. In London these items were offered for sale by the dealer Charles H. Bessant, who received a commission of ten per cent, the profits being shared after this sum had been deducted.[57]

By 1906 Berenson was able to afford to buy the Villa I Tatti at Fiesole, a home worthy of the prince among Florence's art dealers.[58] It became his 'House of Life' – an allusion to a sonnet by Rossetti – and commanded a view of Florence from its terraces and pathways, the distance between them being covered with olive groves, pine trees and cypresses. Amid fourteenth-century altarpieces shimmering with gold and surrounded by Renaissance furniture and precious objects of every description, the 'passionate sight-seer' held court and wrote books on Italian art that were imbued with his profound knowledge of the subject, an aesthete's accompaniment to the contemptible antique shops that enabled their author to enjoy this magnif-icence, while at the same time setting the seal on his connoisseurship.

Berenson's attitude to the art of the Renaissance could not have been more different from Warburg's. His interest in the subject had been roused by Pater's *Studies in the History of the Renaissance* and, above all, by the same writer's *Marius the Epicurean* of 1885, in which Pater enthusiastically propounded a subjective, Romantic aesthetics: artistic objects, beautiful things and attractive scenes were here held up as objects of meditation that the observer should approach naïvely and with his eyes directed inwards. They were thus panaceas for the soul and a reflection of all that was most noble in the world. Writers are no doubt correct in seeing a link between this text and Berenson's conversion to Christianity in 1885, the year in which Pater's study first appeared. Certainly his conversion is known to have taken place in the wake of long conversations with the abbot of the monastery at Monte Oliveto and after his reading of *Marius the Epicurean*. In the circumstances it is hardly surprising that Berenson found himself in such profound disagreement with Russell over the latter's essay 'A free man's worship'.[59]

Berenson was schooled in Morelli's method of distinguishing between the hands of the different masters on the strength of the way in which they painted ears or hands or feet. In turn, this enabled him to suggest and ques-tion attributions with a particularly discerning eye, although this occasion-ally had unfortunate consequences for him: one time, he questioned the authenticity of a Leonardo in the collection of the elderly Lord Wemyss, causing the disappointed owner to throw him out of his Scottish castle in spite of a violent storm.[60] With time, Berenson built up the reputation of an uncontested authority, and a word from him could decide a painting's price, bringing delight or disappointment to its owner. His discerning eye was valued so highly not least because the age longed for men of genius and wanted works of art to have the aura of great names.

Warburg was in regular contact with at least one true connoisseur, namely Wilhelm Bode, the 'Bismarck' of Berlin's museums, a major player on the arts scene and a dictatorial influence of the taste of the age.[61] (Originally plain Wilhelm Bode, he acquired his patent of nobility in 1914.) Bode's policies towards the imperial museums lent dubious backing to the fatal international ambitions of the German Reich. Warburg had Jan Pieter Veth's lithograph of Bode hanging in his study in Hamburg, and he did all in his power to keep the famous privy councillor informed about the state of the art market in Florence:

> I just wanted to drop you a note to let you know that on 4 Jan. Rosa Piatti, the owner of a number of treasures in Florence, died. She lived on the Piazza Signoria. You know the apartment, it contains a number of highly remarkable pieces: a painted head (stucco?) of Leo X, simply stupendous & also a medusa mask by Benvenuto Cellini (?), also some smaller pieces of sculpture. I hope that your agent is on the case. I know the daughter (Countess di Nobili) well.[62]

But Warburg's correspondence with Bode was dominated by questions of a more scholarly nature. He shared his views on problems of attribution and helped to identify faces or coats of arms: 'I very much enjoy playing this kind of guessing game; it is also a kind of sport demonstrating one's ability to make logical connections.'[63]

Warburg numbered Bode among the group of 'enthusiastic art historians' which also included Berenson and other connoisseurs and scholars who had what he considered an obsessive interest in questions of attribution. 'These are hero-worshippers, but in their ultimate derivations they are only inspired by the temperament of a gourmand. The neutrally cool form of estimation happens to be the original form of enthusiasm peculiar to the propertied classes, the collector and his circle.'[64] In spite of this, Bode was, far more than Berenson, a man after Warburg's own heart. In particular, their intensive exchange of ideas indicates the solid historical foundations on which Bode's famous expertise was built.

Berenson, conversely, was someone whom Warburg, initially at least, found deeply unsympathetic, which prompted him to lump Berenson together with what he called 'snuffling riff-raff'. Warburg despised him as an upstart and profiteer and probably also as an eastern European Jew. And there were also professional differences between them. Warburg had little interest in questions of attribution. Instead, he represented a historical approach that was intended to integrate the findings of modern science and always to remain rationally controlled – his reluctance to concede that Leonardo's art was a 'secret' reveals this with particular, if indirect, clarity. More than that, he regarded works of art as source material which raised questions of a historical and anthropological nature. These problems were more central to his thinking than the formal qualities of the objects under discussion. In 1903 Berenson wrote that art 'can be, nay, should be studied as independently of all documents as is the world's fauna or the world's flora'.[65] This involved a purely aesthetic contemplation of works of art and was intended to take account of the fact that even the greatest expert could err in his attributions. At the same time, it branded detailed psychological and aesthetic discussions typically 'Teutonic', dismissing them as pedantic and unsuited to art. This attitude also emerges from Berenson's dismissal of Theodor Lipps, who was another of Warburg's most influential teachers;[66] and it may be inferred from the arguments that Berenson had with Vernon Lee and the latter's alter ego, Kit Anstruther-Thomson.[67]

Berenson's real significance lies in the fact that he was one of the founders of the modern history of Italian art. Through his tireless activities as a collector inspecting the works that passed through his hands and through his numerous publications, he prepared the way for a methodologically more circumspect and, above all, more subtly differentiated history of art, a process in which he was helped by other connoisseurs such as Bode, Morelli, Crowe and Cavalcaselle. The fame of painters such as Sassetta and the 'restless genius' Lorenzo Lotto is due to Berenson, for it was effectively he who discovered them. And, as a result of his attributions, he also helped, however unwittingly, to encourage representatives of a historical approach to art history such as Aby Warburg to adopt a greater degree of precision in considering the complex conditions in which works of art come into being, as well as the function of those works within a historical framework.

19   Edward Burne-Jones, *The Mirror of Venus* (1898)

'I mean by a picture a beautiful romantic dream of something that never was, never will be – in light better than any light ever shone – in a land no-one can define, or remember, only desire' (EDWARD BURNE-JONES)

The last Romantics

Bᴇʀɴᴀʀᴅ Berenson was not the only person whom Warburg found unsympathetic: he also had a low opinion of all the Americans in Florence, his bias being perhaps affected by more widespread prejudices against what Burckhardt called 'educated men and women lacking in a history of their own'. His contacts were limited to army officers and other people such as a certain Mrs Hall, a young teacher whom he described as lively and charming, 'with a carefully cultivated inner life but absolutely nothing behind it': 'The penguins' salon in which she received me was horribly full of American women; hellish faces, tufts of hair on their heads, either too thin or with hips as wide as ocean liners, jewellery on their paws, like a series of Hogarth caricatures.'[1] The reserve that Warburg maintained towards most Britons and Americans, especially towards the upper echelons of the expatriate community, with their villas on Bellosguardo and at Fiesole, reflected a more general attitude,[2] for the threads that bound the German colony to the Anglo-Americans were tenuous in the extreme. On the one hand, there were the scholars, who were members of the educated middle classes with a neo-humanist background and their eyes firmly fixed on university chairs or librarians' posts, while on the other there were sophisticated men of the world for whom education was not a means of advancing their careers but an attitude which could be nonchalantly activated at will: such an attainment was intended to shine, of course, and not just in dusty archives. There was no equivalent of the members of the German educated classes in Britain or America.[3]

None the less, the Florence of the Britons and Americans had many aspects to it, and indeed they left their mark on the city in far more ways than any other nationality.[4] 'Some *Inglesi* have arrived,' one hotel porter is quoted as telling his manager, 'but I haven't found out yet whether they are Russians or Germans.'[5] Of the 2,300 or so entries in the loan journal of the Gabinetto Vieusseux for 1897, some 1,100 are those of Britons or Americans. Writing in 1864, the American journalist Nathaniel Parker Willis reckoned that a third of all the foreigners in Florence were from England.[6]

In 1903 *La Nazione* calculated that there were around eight hundred English men and women who had settled in Tuscany,[7] where the world's first British Institute was established in 1917.[8] Florence was felt so strongly to be a city with an Anglo-Saxon quarter that the artistic and intellectual importance of the German and French communities was largely over-looked. It is significant in this context that in 1901 Thomas Mann found himself sharing a table with two English women at his guest house on the Via Cavour. One of them, Mary Smith, was described as looking 'as if she were by Botticelli' and appears to have had a brief liaison with the young writer. The short story 'Gladius Dei' is dedicated to this muse, 'in remem-brance of our days in Florence'.[9]

By the turn of the century, Florence, along with Rome and Naples, had long been one of the main destinations of visitors to Italy and had become an important centre of European tourism. 'If the level of conversation about a city may be taken as the decisive factor, then Florence is more European than many a metropolis,' recalled Sigmund Münz, who felt lucky at being invited to a ball at the Palazzo Riccardi. 'Society here has an international cachet. . . . Anglicized Italians and Italianized Britons are a frequent phenomenon.'[10] At five o'clock every afternoon, there was a regular clatter of tea cups in the city's guest houses, leading to the consumption of enough thinly sliced sandwiches to cover the entire roof of the Gabinetto Vieusseux.[11]

The English and Americans in Florence included some of the great men and women of their day:[12] John Ruskin, Elizabeth Barrett and Robert Browning, Frances and Thomas Adolphus Trollope, Charles Dickens, Harriet Beecher Stowe, Constance Fenimore Woolson and many more. Lady Walburga Paget waxed lyrical about a 'galaxy of spirits on this small plot of ground'.[13] In 1894, a year before his imprisonment, Oscar Wilde, too, visited the city[14] and met Berenson and André Gide, who remarked that the author of *The Picture of Dorian Gray* looked old and ugly, but was 'still an extraordi-nary raconteur, a little – I think – as Baudelaire must have been, only perhaps less shrill and more charming'. Wilde's decision to convert to Catholicism – a decision finally acted upon on his deathbed – is said to have been taken in Florence, a claim that Henri Ghéon likewise made for himself. Florence was evidently a metaphysical place well suited to inspiring feelings of religious devotion.[15]

It was above all through the writings of its English and American visitors that Florence was immortalized in the literature of the nineteenth century, inspiring them with its settings and providing them with their characters. Swinburne wrote 'Itylus' here, Mark Twain completed *The Tragedy of Pudd'nhead Wilson* and his *Personal Recollections of Joan of Arc* at the Villa Viviani in Settignano. Henry James was particularly closely associated with Florence, for it was here that he worked on *Roderick Hudson* and his *Transatlantic Sketches*, while *The Aspern Papers* was written at the Villa Brichieri in Bellosguardo in 1886–7. The Villa Castellani, which was the home of the artist Lizzie Boott, was his model for the home of Gilbert Osmond and his daughter Pansy in *The Portrait of a Lady*, while the Moreen family in *The Pupil* was based on the family of John Singer Sargent.[16] Arguably the most famous of E. M. Forster's novels, *A Room with a View*, begins in Florence, as does William Dean Howells' *Indian Summer*.[17] And what would the poetry of Landor, the Brownings, and so many other writers have been like without the city? It was above all to British and American authors that Florence owed its reputation as a literary city and now, as the century drew to a close, many 'old-time victims of Italy' returned there.[18] Henry James's brother, the psychologist and philosopher William James, thought that once *Gemütlichkeit* had been driven from the world, it would still survive in this dear, run-down old country.[19] Protocol requires us to head the list of British pilgrims to Florence with Queen Victoria, who stayed at Matteo Palmieri's villa near Fiesole in 1888 and who visited Florence on frequent occasions. (Among previous residents at Palmieri's villa were the novelist and historiographer George Payne Rainsford James and Alexandre Dumas *père*.) In 1897 a group of artists around Frederick Stibbert even devised a plan to erect a monument to Victoria to mark her diamond jubilee.[20]

Anglo-Americans evidently discovered Florence at an earlier date than other nations. Here one thinks of Sir Henry Enfield Roscoe, Nathaniel Hawthorne, Horace Walpole, John Boyle and Lady Sydney Morgan. Their head start may well reflect a Romantic need that developed as a way of countering the economic and technical modernization that was so advanced in Britain and America, as it was principally the sense that Florence was a 'Gothic' place that exercised so suggestive a sway on its visitors. Its tourists came to see Florence as the 'true' Italy, a microcosm of the promised land: the city was that 'Italy of Italy itself'.[21] 'How I long for Italy once more,' sighed one of them; 'Oh, Florence, Florence!'[22] Visitors knew that they were walking in the footsteps of the Guelphs and Ghibellines: here was the scene of bloody partisan fighting and dramas of jealousy that novelettes and novels painted in glowing colours. Puritans at least had Savonarola as their hero.

The Romantic enthusiasm for Florence on the part of the English and Americans could assume amusing forms. It is known, for example, that the painter and antiquary Seymour Kirkup, who together with Giovanni Aubrey Bezzi discovered the Bargello's famous portrait of Dante in 1840, employed an Italian peasant girl as a spirit medium, said to act as an intermediary between Kirkup and Dante as well as with medieval emperors and kings. Occasionally third parties such as Julian Hawthorne, Robert Browning and Adolphus Trollope were drawn into spiritualist conversation at Kirkup's apartment on the Ponte Vecchio.[23]

By the turn of the century such séances appear to have been fairly wide-spread among the English.[24] The Scottish spiritualist Daniel Home, for example, was a sensational attraction for all visitors to the city and was even said to celebrate black mass.[25] He later converted to Roman Catholicism, but was expelled from Rome as a sorcerer. Stories such as these are not simply curious tales of no more than farcical import. Rather, they show us the other side of the secularization process,[26] revealing as they do the longing for a metaphysical dimension to life and an attempt to discover mysteries in a world that had lost its mystique – an attempt which culminated in what Ernst Robert Curtius termed the 'twilight of the gods of rationalism' at the end of the nineteenth century.[27]

Gothic Florence offered the right ambiance for this. Writing to Hiram Powers, Nathaniel Hawthorne claimed that even the air in the city encouraged transcendental speculations, but now there was a more modern element inasmuch as the ritual designed to conjure up the ghosts of the past also involved psychological effort. There was now a sense in which the dead were conjured up from within and forced to take on a semblance of life in the outer world, the power of the imagination being complemented by means of natural magic. This went beyond those poets who, like Walter Savage Landor, conjured up the great Florentines of the past in imaginary 'conversations', ensuring that the eccentric poet became one of the most important figures in the creation of the myth of Florence: for many of his compatriots, Florence was above all 'the Florence of Landor'.

A slightly more rational counterpart to the spiritualists was Charles Godfrey Leland, to whom we referred in an earlier chapter.[28] With his white Viking's beard and velvet jacket and cap, Leland was one of the most colourful characters in the city he had chosen to make his home. He lived in a hotel not far from the Via Tornabuoni, where he surrounded himself with images of the Madonna, rolls of parchment, Roman lamps and picture frames. He had fought on the barricades in Paris in 1848 and for a time lived among the North American Indians in his home continent. Best known during his lifetime as the author of *Hans Breitmann's Ballads*, dialect poems in which he burlesqued the German Americans, he was also a serious student of folklore with a particular interest in the gypsies, whose ways he followed from Russia to Egypt and from Italy to Hungary. In Florence he busied himself with the myths and customs of the city itself and of the surrounding Tuscan countryside. His medium was a 'witch' named Maddalena, a peasant girl who came from a family of witches endowed with what her discoverer believed was an ancient tradition of witchcraft. For a fee of five francs a week, she told him everything about the secrets of the modern Etruscans. In his own words, he had taken a witch to catch witches, and she did indeed report in detail on occult arts transmitted from the pre-Christian era. 'Real folklorists', he once said, 'live in a hidden fairyland. We see elves and hear voices in the wind.'[29] Leland was convinced that Florence had a witch-like aura.

Maddalena was not the only person to take Leland for a ride: no doubt in return for a princely sum, wise women and sorcerers plied him with all manner of tales about fauns, woodland spirits and gods, including Jupiter, Mercury and Bacchus, all of whom were said to have survived from ancient times and to be worshipped in the modern world under different names. It was claimed that even the poet Virgil lived on in various reincarnations as a thaumaturge, a friend of the poor and a helper and healer. Sorcerers worked their magic spells in his name, resuscitating dead oxen, causing statues to sing and dance and performing all manner of other feats of magic.

Nor should we overlook the reasons – political in the wider sense – why most Britons and Americans preferred Florence to Rome: the picture of Florence which educated travellers formed was influenced by two writers above all, William Roscoe and Simonde de Sismondi. A self-taught dilet-tante, Roscoe owed his reputation to two books, his *Life of Lorenzo de' Medici* (1795) and *Life and Pontificate of Leo the Tenth* (1805). On the threshold of the nineteenth century he was arguably the most important authority on the Medici, painting a colourful portrait of Lorenzo the Magnificent, whom he held up as an enlightened ruler and patron of the arts and sciences. The Florence of the Medici seemed to him to be a latter-day Athens, wisely ruled and, as such, a model that the liberal historian regarded as the myth-ical prototype of his own political ideals.[30]

The writings of the Genevan historian Simonde de Sismondi similarly fuelled enthusiasm for the late medieval republic, but in a different way. For him, Lorenzo the Magnificent was a bloodthirsty tyrant. Sismondi's subject was republican Florence, which he saw as the model for a free political organism which encouraged the development of individual abilities. In this way, both writers helped to create a view of Florence which, however self-contradictory and however much they may have played on their readers' emotions, was none the less a myth. Those readers in search of a brilliant patron of the arts adopted Roscoe's approach, while those who wanted a liberal model state followed Sismondi's line.

Visitors to Florence thus felt close to the ideological roots of their own community. To enjoy Italy in Florence was more politically correct than to do so in Rome, a city which, although Romantic in its own fashion, was rotten to the core. For those travellers who were marked by the puritan upbringing of their homeland, the Eternal City seemed a place of darkness and the cause of all the evils that beset Italy, if not Europe. These visitors had greeted unification as an anti-papal crusade, Florence clearly functioning as a better symbol of the Risorgimento than Rome.[31] There was a regular Risorgimento tourist trail, travellers following in the footsteps of the heroes of the Italian unification movement. Jarves followed Mazzini and Garibaldi, while George Ticknor met the *carbonaro* Count Confalonieri and Silvio Pellico. Stibbert fought under Garibaldi, and Swinburne was fired by an ardent enthusiasm for Mazzini.

There were also aesthetic motives in addition to the political ones. The image of Florence maintained by the Victorians and by east-coast Americans stemmed from the tradition of Ruskin, who had seen the great art of the late Middle Ages arise in the shadow of monastery walls and church towers. This was a setting marked by simplicity, obedience and piety and reflected in the 'calm' beauty of the panel paintings and sculptures of the period.[32] This was the Florence that travellers sought, the enchanted garden of the Pre-Raphaelites. And here were to be found the aesthetic models for the school whose influence extended far beyond England and which owed its success, not least, to the writings of Ruskin. A whole series of Pre-Raphaelite artists spent time on the banks of the Arno, from Burne-Jones and Walter Crane to William and Marie Spartali Stillman and Charles Fairfax Murray.[33] Only hours before his death, Burne-Jones told his visitor Frieda Stanhope that 'Florence is everything and all the rest is nothing'.[34] And Robert Browning gave poetic expression to current Romantic clichés in 'Old pictures in Florence':

> But at any rate I have loved the season
>   Of Art's spring-birth so dim and dewy;
> My sculptor is Nicolo the Pisan,
>   My painter – who but Cimabue?
> Nor ever was man of them all indeed,
>   From these to Ghiberti and Ghirlandaio,
> Could say that he missed my critic-meed.
>   So, now to my special grievance – heigh ho!

The propagandists of the 'Primitives' believed that this art had an educative function – a view that also encompassed the aesthetic and political factors mentioned above. Sir Austen Henry Layard argued that the arts of the time were employed 'in the expression of earnest and political convictions, in the representation of deeply felt truths and in the advocacy of the principles of human freedom'.[35] He drew a parallel between artistic productivity and political developments, seeing in the former's alleged decline since the sixteenth century a consequence of Italian decadence. Like Ruskin and others, Layard was a founding member of the Arundel Society, an organization which was important in popularizing Italian paintings of the Middle Ages and early Renaissance. Another early member was Lord Alexander Lindsay, who settled in Florence in 1873, living until his death in 1880 at the Villa Palmieri, with a library comprising one hundred thousand volumes. He was numbered among the *crème de la crème* of the English expatriates in Florence, a group as socially diversified as English society in general.

Adolphus Trollope described three classes of Britons who travelled to Florence. The first group was that of 'the lost': itinerant young academics, determined old maids and small groups with modest demands who arrived by stage coach or train. Secondly, and above them in the social hierarchy, were those travellers who came by *vetturino*, one of the large carriages which served the whole of Italy: these travellers were for the most part made up of families who occupied all four seats in the vehicle itself, in addition to the two seats outside. The third group was drawn from the upper stratum of English society:

> But the real first-class prize, the arrival that is discussed that same night by the lodging-house owners, and touters of all kinds, is the fine large English family in its own travelling carriage, with papa and son and heir on the box, mamma with abundant daughters inside, and man-servant and maid-servant in the rumble, all complete. Great is the joy in Florence over the advent of such a prize as this. But still the anxious question has to be asked, 'Here for the winter, or going on to Rome?'[36]

Among the numerous guest houses in the immediate vicinity of the station, it comes as no surprise to learn that the most popular was the Anglo-American, but the Villino Trollope on the Piazza Indipendenza was also much frequented by English and American tourists. Mary Ann Evans – 'George Eliot' – is said to have copied out her notes for her novel *Romola* in the salon here in 1861; and a later guest was Thomas Hardy.[37]

And then there were the wealthiest visitors – people like the American who every lunchtime would drive round the Baptistery in a coach drawn by sixteen Isabella-coloured horses.[38] In the villas in Florence and at Bellosguardo and on the surrounding hillsides it was possible to encounter the social set described by William Dean Howells – the American consul in Venice and one of Florence's greatest admirers – in his novel *Indian Summer*: formal manners, reminiscent rather of a royal court; an avoidance of inappropriate words and actions; and an attempt to respect a complex ceremonial, which circumscribed certain gestures and behaviour to almost comical effect. William Spence informed one visitor, Richard Redgrave, that he never knew if he was going to have ten or twenty guests to supper. Redgrave offers a vivid account of the *palazzo* inhabited by the painter and art dealer, with its orangeries and terraces overlooking 'the garden of the world': 'In this villa I saw a little of Italian life, and of the easy, dreamy, lazy way in which people live here. . . . Of course, there was plenty of lounging on terraces, and love-making among the young people.'[39]

In her effusively written book on Florence, Lilian Whiting extols the charm and brilliance of the circle around Walter Savage Landor during the first half of the nineteenth century: she recalls excursions into the hills around the city and to the park at Pratolino with Giovanni da Bologna's colossal figure of Appennino. She also mentions nocturnal meetings on the terrace of an ancient *palazzo*, where the company discussed Italian politics and literature over tea and strawberries, beneath the light of the moon. There could be no more striking contrast than that between the scenes depicted here and those associated with the home cities of the Anglo-Saxon pilgrims who came to Florence from the 'most modern' parts of the world, namely Victorian England and east-coast America. In their lavish Florentine lifestyle we find the expression of an insatiable longing for an existence which was now threatened with extinction in old Europe; an existence whose forms sprang from historical models.

Think, for example, of the Romantic ambiance of the salon of the wife of the English ambassador, Walburga, Lady Paget née Hohenthal, a dreamy mystic, vegetarian and theosophist. It was a byword in eccentricity:[40] as one observer mockingly noted, her villa at Bellosguardo, which was surrounded by the old Torre dei Cavalcanti, was filled with pseudo-medieval furnishings, inauthentic paintings, false ceilings, *faux* chimneys and spurious coats of arms. When Queen Victoria commented on one of her visits that the house must have cost a lot to build, Lady Paget retorted, quick as a flash: 'Better than racing or gambling, your Majesty.' Gilbert Osmond's villa in Henry James's *Portrait of a Lady* was similarly notable for its gloomy ostentation, with its inevitable tapestries, damask, fifteenth-century paintings and neo-Renaissance furniture interspersed with innumerable bronzes and terracotta pieces.[41] In Florence, Lady Paget naturally knew the whole of the English community, and the reader of her memoirs is introduced to the

20   John Singer Sargent, *Vernon Lee (Violet Paget)* (1881)

chic villas in and around the city, gaining first-hand experience of high
society and its eccentric members. On one occasion we find her visiting
the writer Louise de la Ramée, who lived with a pack of uncontrollable,
barking dogs. It was said of her that she was so much in love with her
recently deceased mother that she refused to allow the body to be buried
but kept it embalmed in an upstairs room.[42]

In Lilian Whiting's view, even the Florence of the present day – in other words of the years immediately after the turn of the century, with their polyglot, international elite of visitors – differed considerably from the city familiar to tourists:

> The receptions given in Florence in these grand old palaces and historic villas might almost be stage scenes, set in perfection of beauty. The vast salons hung with tapestries, rich in sculpture; the paintings in the heavily carved Florentine frames; the great mirrors whose expanse in the past has reflected images and scenes long since vanished; with always a wealth of flowers; with rare books and bric-a-brac, – all the nameless objects and details that contribute to the artistic atmosphere of rooms, – in these vast salons the groups of people gather and seem almost like some pictures suddenly summoned by means of magic or necromancy out of the historic past. There is a resplendence of the golden atmosphere as of phantasmagoria, rather than the actual reality of to-day.[43]

One example among many was the Villa La Doccia on the hillside above Fiesole, owned from the early years of the twentieth century by the president of the New York Chase Manhattan Bank, Henry White Cannon. In 1906 he bought the entire collection of Italian masters from the holdings of Jean Paul Richter in order to furnish the place.[44]

Another particularly exquisite setting for elegant English visitors around the turn of the century was the villa at Poggio Gherardo below Settignano.[45] It had been bought in 1889 by Janet Ross, the daughter of Lady Duff Gordon, and her husband Henry James Ross, who had made his fortune as the governor of a British bank in Egypt. According to legend, Boccaccio had imagined the *palazzo*-like villa as a setting for his *Decameron*. The vermouth produced on the Rosses' estates is said to have been made to a Medici recipe. In her reminiscences Janet Ross describes the laborious work of restoring the property, but she also mentions the wonderful view of the Monte Nero and as far as Vallombrosa to the east. Above all, however, she was delighted to be surrounded by places filled with memories of former greatness: Settignano was the birthplace of Desiderio da Settignano, while the house of Michelangelo's father was said to lie not far away. The memory of Boccaccio gains an ironical dimension when we recall that it was here, during the winter of 1892/3, that Mark Twain read from *Jim Wolf* and *Huckleberry Finn* to a distinguished circle of listeners, while a mild outbreak of influenza raged in the valley below them.[46] On another occasion Bernard Berenson, who lived nearby, brought Lady Ottoline Bentinck to afternoon tea at Poggio Gherardo, where she cut an eccentric figure with her peacock-feather hat and crimson coat. As Lady Ottoline Morrell, she later acquired a somewhat ambivalent reputation as muse of the Bloomsbury Group, the leading group of English intellectuals and artists of the first quarter of the twentieth century.

We may finally mention those flamboyant salons in which discussion turned on the art and aesthetics of the present day. The writer Violet Paget – 'Vernon Lee', to whom we have already referred on more than one occasion – was something of an institution in intellectual circles in turn-of-the-century Florence.[47] She adopted her pen-name by way of homage to her brother, the poet and diplomat Eugene Lee-Hamilton. She was immortalized in one of his brilliant oil sketches by John Singer Sargent,[48] who was born in Florence and knew Violet Paget from her childhood: it shows an intellectual peering attentively through the round lenses of her spectacles, her short hair giving her an almost masculine appearance. She lived at the Villa Il Palmerino near San Domenico, a property surrounded by fields and vineyards that could be reached only along narrow winding pathways.

Vernon Lee was the most important of the aesthetes living in Florence around the turn of the century. A woman of international stature, she was born in Paris in 1856 but following the death of her parents she lived in Italy at the Villa Il Palmerino, the drawing room of which provided the setting for lively debates in which the young Bernard Berenson, among others, took part. In her memoirs, Dame Ethel Smyth, the resolute chronicler of turn-of-the-century Italy, has left an impression of the effusive manner in which Lee and her friend, Clementina ('Kit') Anstruther-Thomson, conducted their aesthetic 'analyses'.[49] All who knew her agreed that Lee could be brilliant, intelligent and sometimes arrogant and harsh, but that her dialectical reasoning enabled her to dismiss every counterargument out of hand.[50] On one occasion Berenson accused Lee and Anstruther-Thomson of stealing from him ideas for an essay on questions of psychological aesthetics, an accusation that led to a serious rift between them as well as to her calling Berenson an 'ill-tempered and egotistic *ass*'.[51]

Lee's essays on Tuscany and other parts of Italy, from *Genius Loci* to *The Golden Keys*, are among the most impressive travel writings of the period, and yet she too strives to conceal the more unattractive aspects of modern life, preferring to portray her own Italy with a sensitivity alien to present-day tourists and embracing genre scenes, landscapes and objects with which she associates memories of distant emotions and thoughts. In this way she emerges as the Romantic chronicler of a small old world then in the process of disappearing and as a 'sentimental traveller' who sought out beauty and the past. Aldous Huxley paid her the compliment of drawing a parallel between some of her essays and 'Wordsworth's natural pieties'.[52]

Warburg knew Vernon Lee's books and even studied some of her writings in detail. The underlinings in his copy of her essay on 'The imaginative art of the Renaissance' indicate that he was interested in her aesthetic approach and in her analyses of the psychological process by which art is created and observed.[53] The affinities between many of the questions she asked of the material and those that Warburg had been asking emerge not only from the fact that she was familiar with the aesthetics of Theodor Vischer, which she popularized in her writings, but also from her contribution of an introduction to the English edition of Richard Semon's *Mnemic Psychology*.[54] There were few books more important for Warburg's thinking. As far as we know, he never met Vernon Lee in person, even though the two of them were living in Florence at the same time. We can easily imagine what they would have argued over, notably Lee's interpretation of the art of Botticelli, which she viewed through the aesthetics of Pater and the Pre-Raphaelites. She compared the rose decoration in the background of some of Botticelli's Madonnas with the art of William Morris, even calling Botticelli a 'great decorator',[55] an assessment which Warburg is unlikely to have shared. Her own evaluation of Botticelli stemmed from a knowledge of what came next, namely, the decorative style of the English Arts and Crafts Movement, which meant ignoring the pre-conditions of Botticelli's art. What was important to her was not those elements of the *Zeitgeist* which could be identified in a work of art but the question of what goes on in the observer in the presence of that work. This problem was central to her 'psychological aesthetics'.

Lee's collection of essays, *Renaissance Fancies and Studies*, constitutes a summary of the Victorian view of the early Renaissance. By recalling the recently deceased Walter Pater in the final essay in the volume, 'Valedictory', Lee was in effect writing the epitaph of a whole era. She describes her mentor and friend as 'the natural exponent of the highest aesthetic doctrine – the search for harmony throughout all orders of existence'. He was, she writes, an interpreter of the beautiful, a man who did not see art subsumed within itself but as something that exercised a powerful, existential function.[56] At the same time, she acknowledges that she is now bidding farewell to the ambitions and plans of her youth, when she had been interested in the study of history and philosophy. During the years that followed, she turned away from a historical view of art to a psychological approach directly related to the present day, her work of this period reminding us that a psychological engagement with aesthetic problems was then in the air.[57] The form this approach could take has already been mentioned in the context of Warburg's attempts to explain the function of the ornament.

Unlike Warburg, who approached psychological questions chiefly from the standpoint of the extent to which he himself was personally affected by them, Lee's aesthetics had social implications, a state of affairs that was influenced not least by Kit Anstruther-Thomson. This reflects a more general aspect of her approach to art. Just as Morris and other representatives of the Pre-Raphaelite Brotherhood regarded their art and craftsmanship as a way of resisting the modern world with its mass production and cheap industrial products, so Lee's aestheticism was intended as a bulwark against Victorian England, regarded as a paragon of advanced modernity. She was appalled at the contradictions of the present day and at the juxtaposition of mass poverty with luxury, indolence and spiritual and intellectual deprivation.[58] Her fight to preserve the old centre of Florence and her later political activities – she championed women's rights, took part in the debate against vivisection and was a committed pacifist years before the outbreak of the First World War – were all part and parcel of this same aesthetic position, which involved placing the beautiful within an existential context and vehemently denying the principle of art for art's sake. For her, beauty had a function in life.

The art of the 'innocent' and 'pure' early Renaissance thus appeared to be in the starkest possible contrast with the present day. In the artists of the early Renaissance, Lee saw a fairytale imagination come to life and a 'Romantic, childlike charm'. For her too, the great age of Italian art was the period between Giotto, Cimabue and Leonardo – not the sultry 'red' Renaissance of the Renaissance Revival, but an age which produced contemplative masterpieces worthy of contemplation in return. On this point Lee and Berenson were agreed. Berenson admitted that he had sunk to his knees in veneration of Botticelli's *Pallas* after its rediscovery by Spence.[59] With *The Birth of Venus*, Florentine art, he went on, had come down to earth and produced something that invited no comparisons and demanded no explanation. Like the paintings of Degas or Hokusai, it was perfect unto itself.[60]

In the art of the painters of the Quattrocento, and especially in the masterpieces of Botticelli, the 'last Romantics' – and many of the English and American expatriates who settled in Florence were Romantics in terms of their whole manner and lifestyle – found what Yeats called 'traditional sanctity and loveliness'. The tremendous acclaim these artists enjoyed in late Victorian culture had various roots. They not only prefigured aesthetic patterns to which *fin de siècle* trends in art, from *japonaiserie* to *Jugendstil*, could effortlessly appeal; they also evoked religious feelings in a secularized world, without creating an unduly Catholic impression. They satisfied longings for transcendence and poetry. It was the metaphysical openness of this art that led to its extreme acceptance in the late nineteenth century.[61]

What could the present day offer that could stand comparison with the great art of the past? In one of his short stories set in Florence, Henry James writes about an artist who divines within himself the quintessential picture, the consummate work of art, but who doubts if he can ever express this ideal in real life. The narrative begins in Florence, at night, in the Loggia dei Lanzi, which is lit by the autumn moon and peopled by the spirits of the great artists of the past. Here the narrator encounters a painter. Together they walk through the city's churches and museums, sharing their admiration of the works of Raphael, Michelangelo and Mantegna. And they speak of the phantom of the painting that is to surpass all the others, the artist imagining a picture which exists outside history but is at the same time an expression of ideal beauty in an age which, like the present one, is hectic, full of bustle, grey and sombre. 'We live in the evening of time,' James has the artist say, and causes him to look back longingly to the light of the great Renaissance. And it is a work of art from that period that the author uses as a way of conveying to the reader an idea of what the imaginary masterpiece might look like: the *Madonna of the Future*, created by the artist's fevered imagination, is formed in the reader's head as an image from the remote past, a variant of Raphael's *Madonna of the Chair* of 1513/14, which was itself an early source of inspiration for Renaissance enthusiasts. In James's short story the ultimate masterpiece remains unpainted, its existence being restricted to the mind: at the end of the tale the narrator finds only a blank canvas in the artist's wretched atelier. It is even less clear than before what perfect beauty would have looked like.[62]

21   Giorgio Kienerk, *Il silenzio* (1900)

'We live in the evening of time' (HENRY JAMES)

Modern Florence

By the turn of the century Florence was not just a museum. True, the city on the Arno could not compete with the great centres of modern art such as Paris, Brussels, Berlin, Vienna and Munich. In Florence the road to modernity attracted only the more wary travellers. But the older forms of art it had to offer were so overwhelming that many painters, sculptors and architects sought out the city either to study these ancient models as the basis of their own art or to oppose tradition and maintain their own individuality and originality in the face of so tremendous a challenge. The painter and graphic artist Ernst Moritz Geyger called the city 'a treasure trove that was necessary to make me even smaller than I was. I shall reappear as a completely new man, without denying my individuality.'[1] Paul Klee left the Uffizi confused and yet deeply impressed, describing it as 'a gallery in which to lose yourself. But even the quality is unique. The *tribuna* with its masterpieces could not be more intellectually uplifting. I left after 2½ hours, profoundly moved, very small and with a certain amount of head-shaking.'[2]

Italy and its art were not just a source of inspiration but sometimes weighed heavily on people's thinking, like a layer of gilded lead. Of course, the painters and sculptors who had settled in Florence – in 1897 no fewer than 176 *pittori* and 96 *scultori* were listed in an official guide[3] – hoped to find customers among an international clientele. Some visitors obviously wanted to emulate the great merchants and statesmen of the Renaissance, at least on a smaller scale, and to acquire or commission art. Elvira Grifi's guidebook to Florence includes a long list of 'marble sculptors', 'wood carvers' and 'painters', most of whom have now been forgotten. The vast majority of them certainly did not produce avant-garde art but made replicas and worked in traditional styles: the neo-Renaissance or neo-Baroque. The result was art that comes under the heading of souvenirs.

Florence was also a treasury packed with specimens for the followers of the Arts and Crafts Movement. At the English churches in Florence – the Holy Trinity English Church on the Via Lamarmora and St Mark's English Church on the Via Maggio – congregations could admire examples of crafts-manship inspired by the Quattrocento, with the result that these places of worship became perfect enclaves of the British taste of the period. Much of this work was commissioned by George F. Bodley, around whom a group of capable Florentine craftsmen grew up working to Pre-Raphaelite and Symbolist criteria.[4]

Anyone wanting a marble relief of Dante's Beatrice or a portrait of Queen Victoria or Prime Minister William Gladstone would visit Dante Sodini's at 15 Viale Regina Vittoria. Elvira Grifi's guide mentions him as the holder of the gold medal at the 1889 Paris World Exhibition and, above all, as the creator of four statues on the cathedral's new façade. Sodini is still remembered as the perfect embodiment of Victorian aestheticism. Like him, many other artists and craftsmen tailored their work to suit the wishes of their English clientele. Among the products of this period are the sheets of paper illuminated with Quattrocento designs on which English ladies of the late nineteenth century wrote their finer thoughts and which are still sold to tourists today.

Mary Warburg was completely captivated by the skill of the firm of Bondi, which specialized in copies of Renaissance sculpture, and bought a replica of a head by Donatello. 'The man makes the most beautiful copies of classical & Renaissance sculptures in the most varied tones, also all manner of vessels and implements based on classical models. One would like to buy simply *everything*,' she wrote to her mother-in-law in 1898.[5]

There were two occasions during the final decades of the nineteenth century – in 1880 and, again, during the winter of 1896/7 – when Florence organized exhibitions to showcase the art of the present day.[6] At the first, the *Prima esposizione di quadri moderni*, Italian and Spanish painters were exhibited alongside works by Léon Bonnat, Edouard Manet and the Munich-based artist Franz von Lenbach, but this early exhibition was completely overshadowed by the legendary *Festa dell'arte e dei fiori* organized by the *Società di belle arti* in the inner city between December 1896 and the end of March 1897. This second exhibition was part of a trend that included the Milan Triennale, first held in 1891, the Venice Biennale (1895) and the Turin Triennale (1896).[7]

As the century drew to a close, contemporaries wanted to take stock, but there was also a desire to find a sense of direction amid a large number of different trends which defied a clear overview and had developed both with and in opposition to tradition. Ardengo Soffici recalled the exhibition as an event which was of 'capital importance' to him.[8] Some four hundred artists exhibited their work, and of these only a handful came from Florence. Among the artists to be admitted were the history painter Stefano Ussi, Francesco Vinea and, as the only famous foreigner to have settled in Florence, Arnold Böcklin. Those who had been turned down joined forces for a secessionist exhibition held at the gallery in the Palazzo Davanzati.[9]

One hundred thousand visitors are said to have attended the exhibition, which was accompanied by numerous spectacles and other cultural events. The monument to Donatello at San Lorenzo was unveiled in the presence of the king of Italy, while cinematograph shows by the Lumière brothers, parapsychological experiments and lectures – including some by Vittorio Pica on Japanese art and by Guido Carocci on the history of Florentine art – formed a remarkable mixture in which historical reminiscences played a major role. The exhibition poster and the invitations paraphrased the art of Botticelli. 'You have won back your lost consciousness, O Florence,' exclaimed *Il Marzocco*, the city's self-styled 'central organ' of aestheticism. 'Today you take up the idea of that great mission of beauty which is your own true calling.' In a series of articles headed 'European art in Florence', the paper dealt in detail with the exhibition, which successfully provided an overview of contemporary trends in art, even if some of the works were already somewhat antiquated and a number of leading artists were missing.[10] The prize for Italian artists was awarded to Giovanni Battista Quadrone for his canvas *Time Threatens*, the artist's surname – literally 'large picture' – inviting ironical comments. In carrying off the first prize, Quadrone triumphed over better-known artists such as Telemaco Signorini, Giovanni Fattori and Giovanni Segantini.

The exhibition was international in scope.[11] Claude Monet exhibited a landscape he had painted during his visit to the Antibes in 1888, Puvis de Chavannes his *Beheading of John the Baptist* of 1869. Benjamin Constant, Paul Albert Besnard and Léon Bonnat were also represented by examples of their work, as were Frank Dicksee, Lawrence Alma-Tadema and Edward Burne-Jones. Visitors saw Neoclassicists, *veristi*, Impressionists, Symbolists, representatives of *Jugendstil* and pointillism and painters whose art was not so easily reduced to one or another of these categories. John Singer Sargent – the chronicler *par excellence* of the Victorian age and a kind of *fin de siècle* Van Dyck – also exhibited one of his most famous portraits. He had been born in Florence, and it was there that he had received his early training.

Sargent was a virtuoso artist whose style represented a summation of the art of several centuries; some admired it while others condemned it root and branch. Be that as it may, the breathtaking perfection of his work suggests that a certain type of painting was drawing to an end – or, as other observers would have claimed, that it was then at its height. Nothing lay beyond such perfection except the need for something different. Paintings like Sargent's demonstrate the historical necessity of the work of Cézanne and Kandinsky and of Malevich's *Black Square*.

The question of aesthetic standards and hence of the nature of the work of art follows logically from the status enjoyed by the arts in the final years of the nineteenth century. A remark by Conrad Ferdinand Meyer which Warburg entered in his Florence diary goes to the heart of the matter: 'Art is really the only thing that raises us above the trivialities of this life; often, when I sit down at my desk, I feel I am crossing the threshold of a temple.'

The notion that art inhabited some numinous world may be illustrated by a curious argument.[12] Municipal workmen had taken the hazardous step of cleaning the statues beneath the Loggia dei Lanzi by throwing a bucket of water at them, an action that incensed *Il Marzocco*: as an 'Americanism' it was an extremely risible affair, but it reflected a lack of respect for great works of art. The story created quite a stir, and not just in Florence itself. Under banner headlines such as 'Le Doucheur de Florence', 'Singulière hydrothérapie' and 'Statues douchées', French and Belgian newspapers reported on the indignities suffered by these masterworks of the Florentine Renaissance.

The particular role played by art, and also by education,[13] becomes clear only when it is seen against the background of the loss of significance of religion at this time: religion forfeited its monopoly as an authority which gave meaning to the world and explained that world in a period of increasingly rapid change, when the old European order was being transformed into a new social and cultural reality. Art was worshipped as a ray of light in an infinite, dark and cold universe and as a trace of the divine after the death of God. In the eyes of its bourgeois panegyrists, beauty had an educative force and was a centre and goal of life. In the presence of the *Madonna of the Chair* in the Palazzo Pitti – the *nec plus ultra* of art in Henry James's short story – the audience should linger in awestruck silence, as though before an altar covered in candles.[14]

As a result, the arts saw themselves faced by a whole series of demands and expectations in the years around 1900. In the minds of the educated middle classes, some of these commonplaces included the belief that all art, including modern art, was a means of coming to terms with the present day by reflecting the tensions of modern life.[15] For Eugen Diederichs, who in 1896 chose Florence as the Italian base of his newly established publishing empire, 'living in a southern clime and immersing oneself in art and history' was not a source of enjoyment pure and simple but an opportunity to 'collect one's strength for the attempt to deal with life'.[16] Art, it was argued, contained something higher and more all-embracing. Here the contradictions of real life were resolved, and the individual, torn between nature and the spirit, regained his sense of unity.[17] Art was not concerned with banality but with the sublimation of earthly matters, a more intense expression of all that we associate with the term 'human'. If science was rational and positivistic, art paid tribute to the irrational, to feeling and the imagination. The view that art was a religion is likewise part of the 'revenge of the irrational' that modernism sought to subject to a thoroughgoing revision in the years around the turn of the century.[18]

Among other widespread views was the conviction that all that was fragmentary and imperfect in reality would appear whole and harmonious in art. During those moments when observers were able to lose themselves in the work of art, they would be able to overcome their sadness at being no more than temporarary guests in a transient present. Art was thus seen as valuable, and yet as something that could not be bought. It was not to be found in those areas of life colonized by business and commerce, technology and transport, all of which were aspects of the modern industrial world. Rather, the place of art was in the temples of the religion of art and in museums, salons and studios. Once this world of ours was reflected in art, it no longer appeared as hideous as before, but was covered in the gold-coloured varnish of beauty. The philistine, proud of his formal education, took it amiss when artists sought to depict that world in any other way.

Life was hectic and complicated, and so art should provide a sense of calm and silent simplicity. It should be non-threatening and exorcise the horrors of existence. It should aim to produce feelings of happiness and contentment, and even understanding. In short, it should console, for it was a 'rescuing, healing sorceress'. Some commentators even went so far as to ascribe a redemptive function to it,[19] and many artists assumed the air of seers capable of grasping the deepest essence of the world, while carrying on as if their actions were inspired by some higher power. Even the non-professional Mary Warburg believed this.[20]

It is clear, not least from Florence's example, that, economically and intellectually speaking, artists were toiling in a difficult market, as it was increasingly hard to find anyone able to lead the way in matters of taste. Who was to set the standards? And what were the rules governing beauty? Only a poet could permit himself the luxury of leaving the Madonna of the future unpainted. The exchange market for intellectual property where works of art were valued had grown in size since the disappearance of a class-based society in the eighteenth and nineteenth centuries, and it was now impossible for any

one person to gain an overview of it. Whereas the decisive figures had originally been a mere handful of patrons of the arts from the aristocracy and the
church, that group was now immeasurably greater in the newly expanded
middle-class society, as journalists and art critics – 'public opinion' – increased
in importance, and teachers at art colleges, gallery owners, art dealers and
officials of every description gained in power and influence. In turn, this
development was reflected in an increase in the number of artists and
consumers of art.[21] The tendency of buyers to see themselves as the natural
heirs of the great patrons of the Renaissance was exploited by many artists
who were certainly not among the leading representatives of their profession.

Many artists – and this applies not only to the visual arts – reacted to the
complex situation with what can only be called exotic marketing strategies.[22]
More than ever, originality was a criterion of quality. 'But previously everything was so much better,' Klee noted in his diary in May 1903. 'Art was then
much more accommodating. Now everyone wants to be a real individual.'[23]
Klee's own response to the heterogeneity of the modern world was to reject
the academic virtuosity which dominated the market at this time. True art, he
argued, was not a question of ability but of 'not being able to do otherwise'.
Only now, in the nineteenth century, did the 'myth of the artist' find its most
luxuriant expression in the form of brusqueness, of eccentric behaviour, of an
aestheticist demeanour and of a fondness for lonely isolation that involved an
extrovert lifestyle. The claim that the artist was producing 'original' art in
competition with other artists and in the face of tradition received support
from bizarre contingencies of a purely superficial nature, all of which played a
not insignificant part in the emergence of avant-garde art.[24]

In an essay about the artists working in Florence at the end of the
nineteenth century, the author Ugo Matini was tireless in listing the tics of
his subjects, in a manner reminiscent of Vasari's *Lives of the Artists*.[25] Italo
Nunes Vais always wore the same tie and hat; Domenico Trentacoste's black
poodle never left its owner's side; the portrait painter Vittorio Corcos would
sing operatic arias in a loud voice while working, to the dismay of all who
were present; and the *plein-air* artist Arturo Faldi would constantly whine to
himself. Some were serious and melancholic, others short-tempered and
liable to terrorize their models; many lived on their own and were nervous
and absent-minded, with a tendency to pluck at their beards, or else they
were so engrossed in their work that they would often forget to eat.

At the same time, however, there was signs that many artists were
becoming increasingly bourgeois in the years around 1900. They left their
work to speak for itself and, as Camillo Mauclair noted in the *Revue bleue*,
they could afford to dispense with eccentric clothing.[26] But in general the
lonely, self-reliant artist had to fulfil his mission in keeping with the myth

about him, flouting the society that created him, even if he were to be destroyed in the process. It was from this perspective that Hildebrand compared his friend Hans von Marées with Heinrich von Kleist, a man of high ideals who placed huge demands on himself: 'The need to develop a moral and artistic human being in the sense of fulfilling a task in life – the resultant impossibility of having any innocent, natural dealings with that person . . . the natural and profound instinct for everything that is art – the urge for "all or nothing" and so on. The terrible struggles, this constant desire to climb ever higher, followed by an all the greater plunge into the abyss.'[27] Before he became a celebrated member of the avant-garde, Paul Klee exclaimed: 'I am God. There is so much divinity heaped up inside me that I cannot die.'[28]

The *fin de siècle* novels which dealt with the lives of artists gave a tragic dimension to these tensions. Here one thinks, for example, of Zola's *L'Œuvre* or – to remain in Florence – of Hermann Sudermann's play *Sodoms Ende*, a drama inspired by the unhappy fate of the artist Karl Stauffer-Bern, who lived for a time by the Arno. Sudermann's hero allows himself to be seduced by the glamour and temptations of Berlin society and in doing so is distracted from his path in life, which leads to his ultimate destruction both as man and as artist.

There could be no better illustration of this development than the sensational 'Stauffer-Bern affair'.[29] The painter and sculptor Karl Stauffer-Bern was a gifted portrait artist with a brilliant technique. He toyed with a number of megalomaniac projects and was filled with a 'tempestuous drive for ever newer and loftier ideals', to quote Wilhelm Bode, who witnessed the unfolding of the drama.[30] In a word, Stauffer-Bern represented the typically modern artist torn between genius and delusion. The fact that, like his friend Max Klinger, he refused Bode's request to prepare etchings based on works by older artists for Bode's own publications is entirely consonant with our picture of the artist seeking to distance himself from all lowly craftsmanship.

The young artist won the heart of a woman from the cream of Zurich society, Lydia Escher, the wife of the Swiss industrialist Emil Welti. She lavished large sums of money on him, and they even considered buying a small villa in Florence. Stauffer-Bern's head was full of fantastical schemes, including a plan to build a temple at Paestum and to decorate it with statues. Klinger was to provide the frescos. Statues of the artists and their patrons were to be erected on a terrace overlooking the sea, the statues being those of Stauffer-Bern himself, Klinger and Emil Welti and his wife. In the end he eloped with Lydia to Rome, where her influential husband – he was the son of the most powerful Swiss politician of the time – had the couple arrested in the autumn of 1889. Stauffer-Bern was thrown into prison, his mistress

22   Karl Stauffer-Bern, *Self-Portrait*

placed in an asylum. The artist was accused of embezzling money and abducting a woman who was mentally ill. The truth of the matter is that Stauffer-Bern had been kept by his lover and even persuaded her to rewrite her will in his favour.

Together with galley slaves, thieves and murderers, he was taken to Florence's Murate Prison in a *vetturino*, but following an intervention by Adolf von Hildebrand he was released and placed in an asylum instead. Once again Hildebrand managed to rescue him, and Stauffer-Bern returned to Switzerland. He hoped to convert to Catholicism and to enrol at the art school attached to the Monastery of Beuron in Swabia, but nothing came of this plan. He tried to kill himself by shooting himself in the chest. A second attempt at suicide proved more successful, and Stauffer-Bern was found dead in a hotel room in Florence on 24 January 1891. He is thought to have poisoned himself. He was buried in the Cimitero degli Allori, his end apparently modelled on that of the painter Claude Lantier in Zola's *L'Œuvre*. Shortly afterwards Lydia Escher gassed herself.

Bode saw Stauffer-Bern as 'the victim of our modern society or, rather, pseudo-society', his Icarus-like flight being an expression of the dangers to which young and talented artists were exposed 'by the exaggerated cult of art and the artist which is so popular today'. In the disaster that befell

Stauffer-Bern Bode saw the social drama of a man destroyed in part by his own delusions of grandeur, but above all by his environment. He had been killed, Bode believed, by the implacable laws of a market which needed dramatic heroes. Stauffer-Bern appeared to be a star destroyed by the illusion of his own fame, a fame based on nothing but the clichés which an avid public entertained about the artist.

Stauffer-Bern was the genius in the proximity of death, and his suicide an act of self-liberation. Failure is now seen as an autonomous action; self-inflicted death as the ultimate form of the artist's work. *Fin de siècle* literature reformulated this drama on frequent occasions: by a terrible paradox, the deadly seriousness of life seemed close to all that was most extreme in the artist's work.[31] And the struggle for inspiration should be a battle with the angel.[32]

Warburg met one such artist in the sculptor Georg Roemer, a pupil of Hildebrand whom Isolde Kurz described as a man of choleric temperament, with a 'melancholic bronze head reminiscent of the ascetically ecstatic music-making monk in Giorgione's *Concert*'.[33] In short, he was difficult and moody. Warburg certainly took a disliking to Roemer, complaining that his 'envious boasting has already become an obsession. He really is one of the most conceited fellows that I know'.[34] Roemer provided Mary Warburg with a model she could work with. He was one of the army of artists who came to Florence in search of inspiration and, even more, in search of commissions and a source of income, but whose names are now known only to a handful of specialists. In spite of this, Roemer succeeded in assimilating the style of the Italian Renaissance so effectively that one of his bronzes, depicting a man putting on a pair of sandals, fooled even Bode.[35] Arrogant by nature, he may well have tried to arrogate the airs of a genius. 'He came from a narrow-minded Hanseatic background,' Isolde Kurz recalled, 'and it was in Italy that he first encountered the shade of Zarathustra. . . . During those times when his inner life was in turmoil, he would lose control, and anyone who was near him would be wounded and hurt.'

Other, more successful artists turned themselves into living art-works of Wagnerian comprehensiveness. Here one thinks of the courts held by the doyens among Florence's *fin de siècle* artists, of the elderly Böcklin's magnificent villa, of Hildebrand's monastic residence and of the interior of Francesco Vinea's home – with its tapestries, armour, bronze figures and other precious objects tastefully scattered around. Vinea is said to have been the first local artist to cultivate this style of living. Another was Edoardo Gelli, the portraitist of the European aristocracy.[36]

The way in which artists saw themselves gave legitimacy to the form of their works – a form which more than ever needed to be justified in an age

of confused standards and with a plethora of conflicting styles: the particular nature of the work of art reflected the mystification of the conditions
under which it was created. The extent to which such ideas were common
currency among the educated middle classes of the period is clear from
Mary Hertz's touching comments on her own artistry: she too thought that
she could sense a higher force working within her, compelling her art to
assume a necessary, and hence absolute, form.

Decent citizens strove in their own way to transcend their own secular
world, or at least to help a younger generation to peer into the numinous
realm of artistic existence. And so we find a certain Bernt Hansen asking
Warburg's advice on allowing his son to become an artist because he could
already draw 'very well'. He could 'live on the Mediterranean coast or
somewhere very close to it'. What was the climate like there? And would
his son find 'first-rate painters' to teach him?[37]

Among attempts to relocate artists within society was the construction
of a theoretical substructure. The nineteenth century was a time not only
for aesthetic theories but also of artists who theorized about their work.
Among the artists in Florence who come under this heading were Hans
von Marées, Adolf von Hildebrand, Telemaco Signorini and Giovanni
Segantini, all of whom justified their stylistic options by means of theoretical reflections, while at the same time seeking to substantiate their claims
to their eccentric social status.

With its sense of history, the nineteenth century had granted access to
every period in the history of art, from pharaonic Egypt to the Age of
Rococo, even if it simplified the question of artistic quality and 'correct'
style by reducing it to the level of middle-class home furnishings. If art
wanted to achieve its lofty, absolute goals, more thought would have to be
given to its basic philosophical principles. All the reviews and discussions
prompted by the great exhibition of 1896–7 turned on this fundamental
question of binding aesthetic standards. Commentators discussed the relationship between the world and the work of art and weighed up possible
arguments for naturalism, Symbolism and idealism.

The situation in Florence allows us to understand why the relationship
between modern art on the one hand and tradition, classical art and the art
of the Renaissance on the other played the role it did in these debates.
Writers drew comparisons and looked for standards but concluded by vehemently rejecting every historical approach to art in the sense of 'pure'
contemplation.[38] The aesthetes of *Il Marzocco* saw themselves as the protagonists of a 'purer and more beautiful art',[39] whatever that might be.
Certainly, it was not enough to draw attention to Tolstoy's view that, in order
to know what was beautiful, the observer needed merely to look at a

flower.[40] Critics, including the young Pirandello, drew inferences from the prizes generally awarded to the 'academic' art which was acceptable to the taste of a cultivated audience. The leading trend in Tuscan art in the second half of the nineteenth century, namely the Macchiaioli, who were related to the Barbizon school,[41] declared war on academic classical art, as one of their chief spokesmen, Giovanni Fattori, expressed it.[42] Fattori demanded a close study of nature; artists should not simply imitate other great artists, whether of the past or of the present day; for in doing so they would merely lapse into the most 'shameless mannerisms'. He himself had never bowed to the demands of art dealers.[43] Artists should follow their inner call and give expression to what they felt was the 'truth', a traditional topos which was now taken up once again. Art thus acquired a moral dimension.[44]

But how was it possible to retain a 'realistic' representation of the world in the age of the mechanical reproducibility of the work of art? What should be reproduced? And by what artistic means? 'The realm of what can be depicted looks increasingly abandoned,' Hans von Marées had complained in 1878. A visitor to the second Milan Triennale contemptuously criticized the sculptures which were on display, complaining that they were an example of applied socialism designed to give the educated audience a series of lectures on social criticism taking Marx's *Capital* as their starting point.[45] Artists evidently knew what they did *not* want – dull realism, aestheticism and Impressionism – but had yet to find a viable alternative. Following a visit to the Villa Marignolle studio of Ernst Moritz Geyger, who painted extremely lifelike pictures of animals, Warburg wrote dismissively in his diary: 'An expert but no artist.'[46]

But it was increasingly impossible to doubt that the traditional view of art, developing along straightforward lines and ending up in naturalism, was no longer tenable. Every attempt to locate art outside the course of history, and even to raise it to a metaphysical realm, was ultimately no more than a reaction to the theoretical problems and stylistic confusions that could no longer be ignored as the century drew to a close. The writer Enrico Panzacchi, who was an ardent admirer of Carducci, expressed a by no means isolated scepticism when, examining the Florence exhibition and its ramifications, he argued that the artistic creativity of the late nineteenth century was typified by a scatter-brained eclecticism.[47] The usual clichés were again trotted out, *decadenza*, feverish over-stimulation and a striving for empty effects all being held up as the root causes of the problem. Amid so much restlessness, these 'neurotic children' – Panzacchi's term for contemporary artists – were losing their creativity. In this way Panzacchi ended up by pleading for art for art's sake, an art that should strike out independently of market forces.[48]

From today's perspective, we have a clearer idea of what it was that turn-of-the-century Italians were prevented from seeing precisely because they were too close to the phenomenon in question: namely that contradictions were inevitable against the background of so many different styles and aesthetic theories, to say nothing of the deep-seated social changes which were taking place. First there was *art nouveau*, a consciously original and reflectively modern ornamental style, occasionally accompanied by a recourse to neo-classical positions. Then there was an equally conscious rejection of ornamental forms in architecture, a functionalist aesthetics which advocated 'organic' solutions. And, finally, in the visual arts there was a denial of all traditional rules. But these developments did not take place in Florence, and it was only after the period under discussion that they found full expression with the breakthrough of the avant-garde. Meanwhile the predominant impression was that of a general 'lack of direction', as Hans von Marées put it. Indeed, some of the foreign artists who elected to settle in Florence, including Marées himself, may even have been destroyed by this lack of direction inasmuch as they found themselves caught between two fronts: on the one hand there was an all-powerful tradition and, on the other, the challenge to create something new and original.

Although largely forgotten today, Ludolf Verworner is another example of this same trend. Verworner studied in Dresden and Paris before settling in Fiesole in 1894.[49] He spent his whole life looking for a solution to the aesthetic problems raised by the early years of the twentieth century. His work seems to be a summation of the tendencies of the age, his early period reflecting the virtuosity of Menzel and the art of the Impressionists as well as recalling his encounters with Munch and Böcklin and, above all, his study of Cézanne. The countryside around Fiesole and Settignano provided him with his subjects. He spent his years in Florence in circumstances that could hardly have been more favourable: from 1908 he was financially inde-pendent thanks to his well-to-do wife, which allowed him to occupy a villa near Fontelucente. In spite of this, he could not reconcile himself to his own art: obsessively self-critical, he refused to exhibit his work, and he even cut up and burnt one of his main pieces, a *Pietà*, when he discovered that Böcklin had been working on an identical subject. Repeatedly plagued by bouts of depression, he finally took his own life.

The architects who were active in Florence drew only the most cautious consequences from the confused situation at the end of the nineteenth century.[50] Now and again we find signs of the synthetic forms of the Liberty style – the Italian variant of *Jugendstil* – although they were never a prepon-derant influence. Overshadowing everything were the buildings designed by the great Renaissance architects, and it was the forms of a remarkably disciplined neo-Renaissance that dominated the picture of the newly designed city centre and the exclusive residential areas which sprang up around its periphery. On this point Florence was particularly old-fashioned.

Here, above all, it was no doubt inevitable that artists and critics alike should retreat to a safe neo-classicism in the face of so wide a range of available aesthetic positions. If they pleaded for closeness to nature, they were not thinking simply of the dull imitation of reality – photography, after all, could now assume that role.[51] Rather, they expected silent harmony, the communication of an idea, the hint of some 'higher' connection. And, with a certain aesthetic naïvety, they pleaded for a kind of 'beauty' corresponding to that of Tolstoy's flower.

The painter who came closest to fulfilling these criteria at the Florence exhibition and who additionally reflected the ideal of the solitary artist leading a withdrawn life and following his inner calling in a mountain village in the Engadine was Giovanni Segantini.[52] Although he did not receive a prize at the *Festa dell'arte e dei fiori*, he was fulsomely praised by the critics. This was the first time that he had exhibited his work, which was represented by several paintings. In particular, it was for a small but significant group of artists – which also included Ardengo Soffici – that the divisionist painters, centred around Segantini, proved a 'true revelation'.[53] It was perhaps because a number of the principal trends of the century culminated here that the latter's large-scale, radiant landscapes struck a chord with a generation of artists which was unsettled and confused. Segantini was a verist, but the nature he depicted had idealized features. At the same time it was mysterious and symbolic. Segantini combined an Impressionist view of the world with a 'scientific' pointillism *à la* Seurat, while avoiding the rigidity of the latter's style. Many of his paintings create a spectacular effect thanks to their luminous colours – in galleries they invariably draw attention to themselves from a distance – and yet they still fulfil the classical criterion of 'silent grandeur'. Segantini owed his success to the fact that he was no imitator but an artist capable of combining apparently contradictory elements to create a convincing synthesis. Eight months before his premature death on 28 September 1899 he expressed his views on the basic principles of his art in an article in *Il Marzocco*. It reveals the aesthetic standards of a regional avant-garde which was far from abandoning nineteenth-century traditions – this is also true of Hans von Marées – and which had enough to do to find a sustainable basis for its art in the 'direction-less' years of the *fin de siècle*.[54]

Although the Warburgs were not in Florence at the time of the 1896–7 exhibition, contemporary art continued to interest Warburg, a point already clear from his doctoral dissertation. Sometimes he would make fun of the lack of understanding of modern art on the part of the educated middle classes. Amiable compromise was preferred to the emotionally impressive, just as it had been during the Renaissance: 'The Lutteroths of this world have occupied the position that should have been taken by Segantini', he complained on more than one occasion,[55] and it was without regret that Max Klinger's *A Love* had been 'sent to the Kaffirs in Africa as a present for Dr Magin'. But the main front for him was undoubtedly provided by his engagement with the art and aesthetic beliefs of the Pre-Raphaelites.

The only Florentine artist of any importance whom the Warburgs got to know properly was the painter and sculptor Giorgio Kienerk,[56] a member of a group of young artists known, somewhat ironically, as the 'post-Macchiaioli', after the Tuscan Impressionists.[57] He had made a name for himself as a graphic artist and illustrator working in the ornamental Liberty style, and although he belongs to the second rank of Florentine artists, he none the less represents an international perspective.[58] Stylistically speaking, he followed in the footsteps of the Swiss-born painter Félix Vallotton, his elder by only a few years and a rigorous realist who was emphatically opposed to Impressionist fragmentation. A virtuoso colourist also known for his woodcuts, Vallotton had a notably formative influence as a graphic artist.

The Warburgs visited Kienerk in his studio on the Lungarno Serristori in the company of the Contessa Ginevra de' Nobili. He was a proper genius, Mary Warburg commented afterwards,[59] an impression she may have gleaned from her host's nervous demeanour – which, being typical of the artist, meant that he was never satisfied with his work.[60] Prone to biting his fingernails and to scratching his cheek or rubbing his chin, he would then turn round abruptly, exclaiming: 'I can't do it, I can't do it!' Warburg, too, was impressed by the thirty-two-year-old artist, describing him as very sympathetic, 'innocent of flattery, open and with a feeling for the artist's dignity in the face of philistines, but unhappy at his financial dependence'. He admired Kienerk's 'fine pastels', and even bought a portrait of a child in which he thought he could discern a 'conflict between a thinking pastel soul and a seeing clair-obscur'. He also mentions some 'masks in black and white', by which he meant woodcuts, and commissioned a portrait of himself.[61] Here too, Warburg demonstrated his openness to new trends, but only to those which were closely bound up with historical tradition.

Otherwise Warburg had virtually no contact with Florentine artists, the vast majority of whom were of only local significance. True, there were others such as Ardengo Soffici and Telemaco Signorini who were later to earn a place for themselves in the history of art. But the nineteenth century was not the fifteenth century, however unwilling contemporaries were to acknowledge that fact. No renaissance of the arts could be coerced by means of the sort of aesthetic manifestos that were then being published in the columns of *Il Marzocco*.

It was the foreign artists who settled in the city in the second half of the nineteenth century that were of importance for Florence's standing as a centre of modern art. We should at least mention the three visits that Degas paid to the city,[62] the presence of Maurice Denis during the winter of 1893/4 and the extended visit by the English Symbolist Frederick Cayley Robinson, who lived in Florence between 1898 and 1902, engaging chiefly with the work of Giotto, Mantegna and Michelangelo. The glamour of modernism came to Florence mainly from a handful of German and Swiss artists who worked in the city and the surrounding area for shorter or longer periods: Hans von Marées, Karl Stauffer-Bern, Albert Welti, Joseph Sattler and, above all, Max Klinger, who in 1905 established the Villa Romana,[63] the famous home of German artists on the Via Senese which would open its doors to many of the heroes of modern art, including Max Beckmann, Ernst Barlach, Käthe Kollwitz, Gustav Klimt, Max Pechstein and Emil Orlik. But in the years around the turn of the century by far the most important artists in Florence were Arnold Böcklin, who was a native of Basel, and the sculptor Adolf von Hildebrand, who hailed from Marburg in Germany.

Warburg was a not infrequent visitor to Hildebrand's home, and he also got to know Böcklin, although the latter lived a secluded life and, following a stroke, avoided large gatherings altogether. It was presumably Adolf Bayersdorfer who effected the introductions to both Hildebrand and Böcklin.

Böcklin lived in Florence for almost two decades, from 1895 at the Villa Bellagio in San Domenico near Fiesole.[64] There he still had the strength to decorate the local Loggetta with frescos in the Pompeian style, a task in which he was helped by his son Carlo. These years also saw the creation of works such as *Diana's Hunt, Melancholy, The Plague* and *War*. During his later years he was often bed-ridden, although on other occasions he might still be seen struggling to make his way along the streets of Florence. Almost up to the very end, however, he and his wife Angela were able to undertake excursions into the countryside around Florence, and he would invariably spend his summer holidays in Rimini.

By the end of the nineteenth century Böcklin was a celebrated 'painter-human being', to quote old Dubslav von Stechlin's description of him in Fontane's novel *Der Stechlin* of 1899. Composers as disparate as Brahms and Richard Strauss were inspired by Böcklin's art, the painter himself having by this date entered the consciousness of the educated middle classes.[65] He could ask practically whatever price he wanted for his mythological canvases, his gloomy islands and the depictions of Pan, tritons and

Nereids that peopled his paintings. Max Halbe recalls that no self-respecting middle-class home of the period was without its reproduction Böcklins.[66]

To buy examples of Böcklin's work meant assuming the air of a connoisseur of modern, if controversial, art. Such owners could feel that they were the legitimate successors of the great patrons of Renaissance art who had boldly opted for the new. 'But I have to laugh', wrote one client, who commissioned a second version of his *Centaurs Fighting*, 'when I think how strange such a picture will strike the philistines who know nothing about art.'[67] At the same time, however, Böcklin's paintings allowed observers to recognize the logic of the realist, no matter how exotic their subject matter might be. These 'mixtures of reality' were interesting and new,[68] without entirely losing their links with tradition. And they presented a poetic view of Italy and offered ideal formulas of Italian landscapes.[69]

In the confused situation which characterized art at the end of the nineteenth century, Böcklin's work functioned as a common denominator for several different trends. Commentators discovered parallels with the work of the even more famous Puvis de Chavannes, and Böcklin's admirers included Hugo von Hofmannsthal and Stefan George, both of whom had an equally high opinion of the English Pre-Raphaelites. Some of his paintings appeared to anticipate *Jugendstil* (here one thinks of a girl strewing flowers, which he painted in 1875), while others adumbrated Expressionism. Others again can be related to early examples of modernism. One such work is his *Centaurs Fighting* in Basel, a canvas that has been compared to Kandinsky's *Improvisation 14* in Paris.[70] One of the paintings which date from Böcklin's years in Florence, *Odysseus and Calypso* of 1883, also influenced the work of Alberto Savinio and Giorgio de Chirico.

Above all, however, it was Böcklin's themes that fascinated his contemporaries: Arcadia, myth, history and unfathomable states of mind were all combined to create a remarkable synthesis of often spectacular impact. His devoted public must have included the same people who devoured Isolde Kurz's symbolically laden short stories with a thrill of pleasure and who sat through Wagner's operas.

Many of Böcklin's paintings depict fantastic dream worlds painted with a spectacular eye for naturalistic detail, while seemingly being full of eerie puzzles: one thinks, for example, of *The Isle of the Dead*, an icon of the nineteenth century, and of the *Villa by the Sea*. 'Whenever people speak of psychological agitation in our own century, they will have to refer to this work,' Heinrich Wölfflin said of this last-named painting. And yet Böcklin consciously left things on a symbolic level and made no attempt to explain his work, but was happy for it to remain a riddle. In this way it could elicit moods: joy, grief, amazement, horror or, like *The Isle of the Dead*, it could invite the observer to dream. Brockhaus said that Böcklin's art prompted the viewer to follow him into his rich emotional world: 'He follows him to the *Villa by the Sea* in the evening twilight . . . He broods on the saying "*Vita somnium breve*" – "Life is but a brief dream" – and finds many points of contact with his own life.'[71] In this way Böcklin's paintings also take their place within the nineteenth-century discovery of the self. Such art inspired a journey into the inner life of the psyche, its mysteries reflecting the soul's unfathomability. Freud himself became lost in thought when looking at Böcklin's paintings.[72]

Böcklin was a modern artist following the pattern that Baudelaire proposed with Delacroix in mind. He took nature as his dictionary, an inexhaustible repository from which the imagination, the power of which Baudelaire defined as the essential element of modernism, could construct elaborate forms. This no longer had anything to do with 'imitating' nature. What emerged was rather a reality which was a law unto itself, an autonomous alternative world.

Even Böcklin's appearance conformed to the nineteenth century's quasi-mythical image of the artist,[73] his life seeming to be the novel of an artist's transfigured existence. He began his career as a misunderstood and penurious genius whose works were a source of controversy, and it was only at the end of his life that he came to be universally admired. An alcoholic, a craftsman with a virtuoso command of artistic techniques, an obsessive worker (his final word is said to have been: 'Work!') and, finally, an inventor, he was a nineteenth-century Leonardo, a man seeking his course in life in the face of manifold contractions.

Warburg had already begun to take a interest in Böcklin's art – an art on the cusp of two ages – even before he settled in Florence. He spent New Year's Eve in 1896 at home in Hamburg, and there he wrote a short play that takes as its subject matter the tension between an academic concept of art, appropriate to the educated middle classes, and a modern concept.[74] The text of his *Hamburger Kunstgespräche* – 'Hamburg conversations about art' – reflects this complex relationship, a relationship embodied in the exhibition held in Florence at that very time. It is clear from his play that Warburg was a mild 'bourgeoisophobe',[75] adopting an ironical tone to the bourgeoisie's pretensions to a loftier enjoyment of art without, however, availing himself of the caustic polemical wit that Zola and Flaubert could summon when railing against the philistines they so despised.

The main characters in his play are Alfred, a young Impressionist painter; his fiancée, who hails from a good family; her uncle Eduard, another representative of the nouveau riche merchant class in Hamburg; a certain Herr Merckendorff, who is in the import–export business; and the fiancée's aunt.

23   Arnold Böcklin, *Self-Portrait* (1893)

It is this last-named character who addresses the problem head-on. 'We old-fashioned people', she admits, 'judge works of art according to good, tried and tested principles which may be limited but which are at least *clear*. Naturally, we cannot understand that what is *ugly* can be *beautiful* and that what is *unclear* is capable of producing the greatest inner impressions.' This is evidently directed at the 'atmospheric paintings' of Böcklin, and also at the Impressionists. Uncle Eduard flatly admits that he hates all 'modern stuff' and inveighs against the 'scribblings' of artists such as the Danish engraver Anders Zorn, an exhibition of whose work was currently taking place in Hamburg. He refuses to accept the counterargument, namely that the telegraphic character of Zorn's work constitutes the progressive, novel nature of that style. And he claims that there is something morbid in the insistence of the moderns on moods and emotions: what he would prefer to see are pleasant and pretty things.

Alfred – who functions here as Warburg's alter ego – vehemently contradicts him. Non-essential details would merely destroy the mood of a landscape. He insists on the artist's autonomy and calling. Nothing can be learnt from small, dainty, pretty things, but only from those things which overwhelm us. Moreover, he tells the philistines, it is not the audience that should influence the artist with its wishes. Rather the opposite is true: 'The public has to be educated.' The rich merchants see the matter very differently. 'The public pays for the paintings, don't they?' asks Herr Merckendorff. 'When I return home, tired, from the office in the evening, I want to see something cheerful around me.' And the aunt says that she likes pictures with names such as *Maternal Bliss*. Alfred contradicts her and defends the work of Klinger and Böcklin 'instead of your *Sunset on Capri* by the obsequious Butterbrod or instead of your pale-faced *Melancholy* by Mabriel.'

Uncle Eduard attempts to placate Alfred: 'There are times when I find even Böcklin sympathetic in terms of his approach to landscape.' 'Well, that's fortunate,' Arthur responds sarcastically.

Uncle: 'But his brightly coloured and inappropriate sea spirits are disgusting, the excrescences of a morbid imagination, and Klinger is worst of all – he's the fellow who painted the girl in the blue grotto – it's simply insane and sometimes even indecent: I've seen his series of etchings *A Love* at the Commeter Gallery.'

The extent to which Warburg's comedy hit the mark emerges with particular clarity from the correspondence between Böcklin and a customer – a certain J. C. Schoen from Worms – who wrote to tell the artist that he had particularly liked the landscape element in Böcklin's paintings: 'And so I should like to ask you if you could not compose a picture in which the landscape is the main feature, either completely without staffage (if possible) or at least with the latter much reduced. . . . Florence, the garden of Tuscany, is particularly well suited to this, and I have always been tremendously enthusiastic about the landscape element in your paintings.'[76] The Italy that the foreigner longed for was in fact a land of paper, canvas, oil and ink, the Italy of Claude Lorraine, Jacob Philipp Hackert and Böcklin himself. On being shown a view of Florence from San Miniato, an 'art expert' of a very particular kind, Adolf Hitler, is said to have exclaimed: 'At last I understand Boecklin!'[77]

A further letter in which the buyer gives precise details of the size of a desired picture and of the way it should be hung introduces us to the real world of the artist's existence in the years following the establishment of the Reich in 1871. When we compare it with Böcklin's image of the artist as an inspired Titan, the whole affair becomes involuntarily comical:

> The picture – without a frame – should be between approximately one metre twenty and one metre fifty centimetres wide and therefore about a metre high, and is intended for the wall of my living room above my wife's sofa. It is meant to decorate this wall on its own and will immediately hold visitors in thrall, as soon as they enter the room. The room is lit only from the north, the walls are lined in brown and yellow leather, the woven woollen fabric of the furniture is red and black, with some yellow. The whole room is furnished in a pure Renaissance style. I think that a sunny landscape, a storm or an agitated sea would all suit the room equally well, as would an imaginary subject, which you are quite right not to wish to exclude.

Warburg was entirely familiar with this world of *nouveau riche* merchants, bankers and members of the educated middle classes. Even in his parents' house in Hamburg he saw modern art on the walls – paintings by Max Liebermann, Jozef Israëls and Valentin Ruths, for example. And Warburg himself bought a painting by Franz Marc at a time when Marc was still largely unknown.[78] Writing from Florence, conversely, he advised his father to buy only a copy of Giorgione's *Concert* for one thousand francs. He had seen it at the home of the painter Hans Krauss: 'Could you use it? For the music room? There are, of course, cheaper copies of the *Concert*, but it's unlikely that you'll find a better one.'[79]

While working on his comic play *Hamburg Conversations about Art*, Warburg was also trying to clarify, in his own mind, the historical context which produced the changing functions of art. 'Once art has abandoned its role as a pictographic writing system designed to interpret the ecclesiastical background,' he noted, 'conflict arises.' It was the process of secularization, therefore, that opened up art to a whole variety of themes and styles. The artist, he continued, wanted to reproduce unknown experiences in a more intense form and strove for 'concentrated impressions' – an assessment which related in particular to Impressionism, to the 'abbreviations' of present-day art and to the 'transience' that seemed to Warburg to be a defining feature of the modern world.

The artist's changing opportunities corresponded to changing demands on the part of the public at large. Once the work of art had broken free from its ecclesiastical context as an 'independent emotional substratum', it acquired a compensatory function for the emotional lives of its observers. 'Weary of life, the public wants to relax and demands to be distracted by detailed familiar milieus.'

It was the 'unfamiliar milieus' that occasionally puzzled Böcklin's public, although, in Warburg's eyes, it was this that constituted the artist's originality and modernity. He had made powerful use of the spaces that had opened up in a demystified world. These spaces were the worlds of the imagination and of libertinage. He had maintained his Romantic idealism amid all the confusions of the present day. 'Oh really!' Warburg defends Böcklin against criticism through the words spoken by Alfred in his play: 'art is for mature, vigorous individuals who want to understand life, not for old fogies and teenage girls'.[80]

Warburg later tried to place Böcklin's work – and that of the other central figure on Florence's art scene, Adolf von Hildebrand – in a wider context. In his 'Fragments', he noted that 'in Böcklin and Hildebrand antiquity lived on in the two accents of movement: Dionysian, enhancing, Böcklin outline in colour; Apollonian, restraining, Hildebrand, façade'.[81] The meaning of this somewhat cryptic passage emerges from the allusion to Nietzsche, who defined the spirit of ancient Greece in terms of the tension between the Dionysian and the Apollonian elements in life and art.[82] For him, the opposition was typical of classical antiquity, such basic 'archetypal' moods being handed down from one generation to the next over a period of many thousands of years.

Böcklin thus struck Warburg less as the 'pioneer of a new Renaissance'[83] than as a kind of 'organ' that helped the archetypes which slumber in the social memory to find expression – a process positively fostered by the turn of the century. The painter was seen as an agent of the *Zeitgeist*, which fuelled his imagination and provided him with the subject matter for his art.

Warburg sought to explain the variety of artistic trends in the years around 1900 as the reflex of a 'nervous' age, incapable of composure and concentration. Against this complex background, Böcklin's images seemed to him to be remarkable chiefly from a psychological point of view, but they also appealed to him aesthetically, by dint of their virtuoso technique.

And we may also assume that he was drawn to their subject matter, because here was an artist who had tamed the most terrible monsters and turned them into a thing of beauty.[84]

In spite of this, Warburg's openness to modern art had its limits. As far as we know, he never sought to engage with the avant-garde. The name of Picasso occurs in his correspondence only at a late date and in passing.[85] Although his *Hamburg Conversations* indicate a critical distance from, and even a contempt for, the members of the petty bourgeoisie who hung beautiful paintings in their neo-Renaissance salons as a form of 'relaxation', he believed that the decisive quality of a work of art was its ability to give 'harmonious' expression to a contemplative calm which could subjugate the world and its demons, and could do so, moreover, in the face of the challenges that every age presented to the artist, be he Botticelli, Leonardo, Böcklin or Marc.

Warburg soon came to see art as an attempt to impose order on the world. In his eyes, it could acquire a 'compensatory function' in one of two different ways: either as a result of the artist's creating a sense of order through his work, or as an object of sublimation in the face of the horrors of existence. This was a central theme in his correspondence with Mary Hertz at the time when he was working on Botticelli. Such considerations were also discussed by the circle of artists around Fiedler and Hildebrand in Florence. Hildebrand saw art as the expression of a basic human need, arguing that it brought together elements that were straining to move apart and placed them in an orderly arrangement before the observer's gaze; hence its agreeable, harmonious impact.[86]

It would be interesting to know whether Warburg's conversations with Hildebrand centred on similar questions, but unfortunately we have only fragmentary evidence of their contacts. That Warburg thought highly of Hildebrand's work is clear from the fact that he championed the latter's designs for the new Kunsthalle in Hamburg,[87] while his support for Hugo Lederer's planned memorial to Bismarck, also in Hamburg, allows us to appreciate the standards he expected when judging sculpture, standards that Hildebrand, too, upheld.[88] What Warburg admired was the refusal to indulge in empty effects or to make concessions to public taste. He preferred austere monumentality to superfluous details, for which reason he also thought highly of the art of Piero della Francesca.

For his part, Hildebrand had a relatively low opinion of the German art historians who flocked to Florence following the opening of the German Art Historical Institute. He dismissed the majority of them as 'insipid' and considered most of what they wrote to be 'pure nonsense': 'They have gained enough by being able to converse with us,' he commented on Schmarsow's request for financial support. 'I'm not paying extra for that.'[89]

Fortunately, Warburg did not know what Hildebrand thought of him and his kind. In January 1898, shortly after their arrival in Florence, he and Mary visited the sculptor at his home and studio at the Monastery of San Francesco di Paolo, in the shadow of Bellosguardo. This initial visit was to be followed by many more, and there resulted so close a relationship that Hildebrand helped Mary Warburg to alter her portrait bust of her daughter Marietta.[90] The atmosphere at San Francesco left visitors in no doubt that Hildebrand was now a Great Artist. They were received in the monastery gardens, where they were served by waiters dressed in white, while Hildebrand's studio, more open than that of the elderly Böcklin, was regarded as one of the sights of the city and drew genuinely distinguished visitors. These included Liszt and Clara Schumann, who reported on her visit to Johannes Brahms. On another occasion, Heinrich Homberger accompanied the elderly Theodor Mommsen on a springtime ramble along the Viale dei Colli to Hildebrand's monastery studio.[91]

The June evening in 1898, on which Mary Warburg reported enthusiastically in a letter to her mother-in-law, is bathed in a glow reminiscent of the 'old' San Francesco:

> On this occasion it was really quite ghostly there, as if in a fairytale. We found the family high on a hill in the *campi*, surrounded by buzzing & shimmering fireflies, beneath the nocturnally black trees where nothing but fairy-like figures in long flowing robes lay in the hay, their hair hanging loose, a really ghostly sight in the darkness & in the twinkling light of the fireflies.[92]

This was the life led by artists in Florence at the end of the nineteenth century. 'How Botticellian!' one is tempted to exclaim on reading Mary Warburg's account of the old monastery garden, with its evocation of the *fin de siècle* feeling of being alive. It is the picture of an Italian artist's existence as imagined by a visitor from the north, a play stage-managed by the major artist that Hildebrand was, for the edification of a bourgeois public. The Warburgs entered a dream-like world, poised between heaven and earth and caught between light and shade. In the popular belief of the south, glow-worms were unredeemed souls left to wander the earth. And yet the place described in Mary Warburg's report is real and can still be visited – a circular spot commanding a panoramic view of the whole city and surrounded by stone benches that are now overgrown with bushes and trees.

The former Monastery of San Francesco di Paola is a mythic place.[93] For a time, it was the scene of one of the most remarkable friendships between two of the nineteenth century's most eminent artists. In 1874, with the help of a loan from his father, Hildebrand bought the building, together with its extensive, park-like grounds, and for a year and a half Hans von Marées lived there as his house guest: as Hildebrand admitted, Marées was his most important teacher and the source of his greatest inspiration. The patron of the arts and theorist Conrad Fiedler also heeded his friend's invitation to move to Florence. But the experiment proved short-lived, and by the summer of 1875 the friendship between Hildebrand and Marées had broken down irretrievably, Marées moving out in September that year. In spite of this, San Francesco remained a meeting place for the foreign artists in Florence. In 1887, for example, Henry Thode's friend Hans Thoma painted a *veduta* of Florence from San Francesco di Paolo. But it is Isolde Kurz whom we have to thank for the most detailed accounts of San Francesco.

Her relations with the Hildebrands were close and friendly.[94] She helped the sculptor stylistically on his main theoretical work, *The Problem of Form*, while her brother Erwin, who was later to prove a successful sculptor in Munich, was a pupil of Hildebrand and spent some time under his roof:

> Whenever one went to San Francesco, it was like a glimpse into a Golden Age, because quite apart from the lofty culture everything had an original feel to it. A couple favoured by nature and still in the prime of life, surrounded by a host of *putti* that grew from year to year, a wonderful estate brought to life by poultry and quadrupeds and providing fruit and flowers for the simple but choice table, and a spirit which, not of this world or age, pervaded this refuge of happiness and peace. The monumental, almost empty rooms that the artist had decorated so richly over the years contained only a few pieces of furniture, but these too were powerful and monumental, as though they had grown up out of the room; here and there stood a Donatello bust on a plinth, between them the naïve *putto* of a Verrocchio; but the greatest impression of all was left by a copy by Hildebrand of a painting by Marées that was particularly powerfully moving.

It is the contrast between the old and the new that typifies the 'blessed isle' of San Francesco di Paola. In the copy of Marées' painting, an example of avant-garde art entered Hildebrand's Arcadian existence. But, if Isolde Kurz's account is to be believed, the atmosphere in his home was one of silent grandeur and bucolic simplicity: 'No newspaper ever found its way to San Francesco.' Initially the only books in the Hildebrands' library were the works of Shakespeare and Goethe, together with Rousseau's *Confessions* – a choice that could hardly have been more apt.

The artistic and temperamental differences between Böcklin and Hildebrand found symbolic expression in the situation of their respective residences, the former to the north of Florence, the latter directly to the south, with the town and river between them. Isolde Kurz describes Hildebrand as an Apollonian character, serenely calm, yet with a keen mind. As we know, the time he spent in Italy, especially his two decades in Florence, was of tremendous importance for his work, and even the earliest letters he wrote home allow us to appreciate the overwhelming impression that the country's art left on the twenty-year-old artist. His letters of the period are overflowing with ideas and the words tumble out, so barely is he able to control the images that jostle for attention in his memory.

Hildebrand's aesthetic position may be summed up as the wish to give conscious expression to a state of calm concentration, mere being and self-oblivion, together with the depiction of a universal concept of man. And yet this was never intended to end in a bloodless neo-classicism. Both Hildebrand and Marées were keen that their figures should 'have life'.[95] In January 1873, following a visit from the eccentric antiques dealer Karl Eduard von Liphart to see his *Sleeping Shepherd Boy*, Hildebrand wrote to Fiedler: 'Old Liphart called on me yesterday and, stretching out his arms, exclaimed in his original and outraged manner: "Flesh, flesh and yet more flesh!" '[96]

Hildebrand was eager to learn from tradition and to single out an elemental quality or, to be more exact, to create forms that were beautiful in a non-historical way.[97] Like every late nineteenth-century artist who reflected on aesthetic matters, Hildebrand fought a silent war on several fronts simultaneously. On the one hand he rejected the solutions proposed by the Pre-Raphaelites,[98] while on the other dismissing not only the neo-Baroque art of an artist like Reinhold Begas, who was a protégé of Wilhelm II, but also the work of the sensualist realists and of the Impressionists. His concerns emerge most clearly from his critique of Rodin,[99] a critique in which nationalist stereotypes play an all too obvious role. Here a French virtuoso hankering after superficial effects is contrasted with the honest, serious German, who is interested only in 'the whole'. It has been said that, in his subjectivity, Rodin was much more indebted to the sophistication of the *fin de siècle* than Hildebrand, while at the same time pointing the way ahead to modern art with his Expressionist vocabulary.[100] Like Marées, Hildebrand, by contrast, is said to have stood for a new rigour which laid the foundations for an abstraction based on a calm and clear form. But the world of sculpture, too, was soon to be turned upside down by the geometric pieces of Constantin Brancusi, Jacob Epstein, Alexander Archipenko and Jacques Lipchitz.

Warburg held both Rodin and Hildebrand in equally high regard. 'Yesterday I had my first experience of Rodin,' he wrote to his wife from Paris in 1899. 'No, it really is beautiful; I missed you (of course).'[101] Seeing things from a historical perspective, Warburg arguably lacked the ability to draw the distinctions that Hildebrand stressed so emphatically: the mere observer who accounts for the aesthetics of works of art was largely over-shadowed here by the historian who examines the conditions which produce works of art and asks questions about the way those works attest to the age that inspired them.

The mere fact that Rodin and Hildebrand were active at the same time, their works demonstrating a wide range of possible reactions to prevailing circumstances and, in particular, to the situation within the arts, shows how difficult it is to interpret works of art as an expression of the spirit of the age. Indeed, Heinrich Wölfflin once formulated this very idea in the context of both sculptors' work.[102]

Hildebrand himself expressed his thoughts on the *Zeitgeist* – that iridescent, indefinable entity that played so important a role in Warburg's research – in a letter to his stepson in which he draws on an especially fine metaphor, comparing prevailing circumstances to a glass dome which to a certain extent determines the growth and hence the form of the shrubs which grow under it and with which he likened the works of music, literature and the visual arts. And this was true, he argued, in spite of the autonomous laws that governed the way in which works developed within the 'glass dome' of prevailing conditions.[103]

The sculptor believed in the existence of 'eternal' aesthetic laws, which rested on natural principles. From this point of view, art can be explained and evaluated only on the basis of itself. History, social circumstances and conventions may define its outer limits, and may even encourage the most disparate outward forms, but something new always arises in the work of art – something which is independent of all this: the visible world should be transformed to appear as a universal, pure form divorced from all random and specific contingencies. The aim is to depict an ideal notion of nature which never changes. This comes very close to Cézanne's aim of reducing all natural laws to geometric forms such as spheres, cones and cylinders.

In his study on *The Problem of Form in Painting and Sculpture*, Hildebrand sought to develop these ideas and to couch them in a more precise language. His aim here was not to pass on his own 'views on art' but to demonstrate his notion that beauty was a consequence of the very nature of human perception.[104] His aesthetic ideal emerges from his belief that form can be derived from the logic of human sensory activity.[105] With this scientific basis for strict, classical beauty, Hildebrand sought to refute not only Rodin, but the whole of his 'nervous' age. The entire life he led may be interpreted as a refutation of the *fin de siècle*.

At the same time, there is no escaping the fact that the glass dome over Hildebrand's work is strikingly similar to the sky over Florence, and to that extent the sculptor from San Francesco di Paola may be said to embody Florentine modernity twice over – not only through his presence in the city as the representative of an internationally relevant response to the challenges of his age, but also through his recourse to local traditions in a form which he himself felt to be timeless. His neo-classicism appears as an acceptable alternative in an age of upheavals, be they aesthetic or part of a more general shift in the modernization process. And yet here too a limit was reached, for this was, arguably, the last time when this option could be seen as a plausible way out of the problems caused by an all-too-powerful tradition, which could now be viewed as a whole. The neo-classical revivals that were to be associated with the dictatorships of the twentieth century belong in a different context.

For its part, Florence made no attempt to deny Hildebrand the recognition which was his due, although it has to be admitted – and this indicates the vagueness of the battlefronts in turn-of-the-century debates – that he received his loudest applause from that enigmatic man of letters, Carlo Placci – a supporter of D'Annunzio and a cosmopolitan aesthete.

Did this really indicate the end of art, an art that seemed to amount to little more than a confused mass of styles, or a timid escape into the world of neo-classicism? As we know, it was emphatically not in Florence that modernity achieved its breakthrough. And yet in spite of this the city was of decisive importance for the new. After all, it was no accident that many contemporary observers felt that in Florence art had run its course. Here, in this mythical centre of universal art, a standard had been set once and for all. 'But you wanted to paint,' says the Duchess of Assy to her lover, Nino, in Heinrich Mann's novel, but he replies: 'Last year – yes, but then we went on holiday to Florence, together with my whole class. I saw the Uffizi: Yolla, my heart was filled with grief. I have decided once and for all that I'll never paint, never. There is nothing left to do, it has all been done.'[106] But was it not possible to survey the situation from this vantage point and to calculate from a historical perspective how things might develop in the future? After all, a critic and Pre-Raphaelite apologist like Ruskin had been able to discover a breathtakingly modern painter like Turner in spite of – or precisely because of? – his understanding of history.

Ultimately, none of the heroes of modern art could ignore the painters of the Florentine Renaissance, the creative force of tradition demonstrating its potency even through contradiction. It comes as no surprise, therefore, to discover that many of the 'agents of change' struggled to understand Florence and its art and stayed in the city for some time: one thinks in particular of Charles Loeser and Roger Fry, who admired Cézanne and who triggered the 'Post-Impressionist earthquake' in London in 1910.[107] Far from despising the old, they used their knowledge of tradition to come to far-reaching conclusions. In Maurice Denis, who admired both Piero della Francesca and Paul Gauguin, we find a symbolic marriage between the great art of a much earlier period and the art of the modern age. His 1901 group portrait of young artists was conceived as a homage to Cézanne.

When one examines the tentative attempts by the great exponents of modern art in Florence to return to the past and to bolster those attempts by engaging in theoretical discourse, it becomes clear that there was a compelling logic to their desire to throw open the existing canon. It was a logic that stemmed from the very problems created by the stylistic developments of the time but which does not have to be derived from social conditions such as electricity, transport and speed.[108] And yet its dynamics were very much bound up with the market structures that had been changing so dramatically in the course of the nineteenth century. The modern world provided new subjects, asking questions and encouraging new techniques. The new art's aesthetic outlook drew its impact from a twofold opposition: first, from the wish to be 'different' from all previous, older art; and, second, from the belief that the work of art should represent an alternative to the real world and create a reality all of its own. Finally, and of particular importance, the increasing number of ways in which people communicated, although bitterly resented by Warburg, led to a fascinating process of cultural exchange: African, Asiatic and American art could now be apprehended more intensely than before and, as such, they found their way into modern aesthetics.[109] A handful of forlorn traces of this process may be identified in the oriental accessories in the apartments occupied both by Isolde Kurz and by the Warburgs in Florence.

Not until 1908 are there any real signs that modern art had been discovered in Tuscany. This was the year in which Vittorio Pica published his book on the French Impressionists, including an assessment of the work of Cézanne; Ardengo Soffici's essay on this leading artist of early modernism appeared later that same year. Berenson is said to have been the first writer to draw Leo Stein's attention to Cézanne, and in a letter to the editor of the New York *Nation* he also came out in support of Matisse, even though the avant-garde ultimately remained a closed book to him. His enthusiasm for a drawing depicting dancing nudes that he saw in Matisse's studio and that was presumably a sketch for the painting *Joy of Life*, which is now in Merion, is significant for the links between tradition and the foreign artists who elected to live in Florence.[110] The sketch appears to have struck Berenson as the closest that Matisse ever came to producing a masterpiece, reminding him as it did of the naked dancers in the Villa Galletti ascribed to Pollaiuolo. He rejected Picasso's work on the grounds that the search for innovation had previously begun in the classical past, never in conscious opposition to it.

None the less, there were more paintings by Cézanne than by Botticelli in Florence in the years around 1900. Most were to be found in the collections of Gustavo Sforni and Egisto Fabbri,[111] who by 1899 had acquired no fewer than sixteen of Cézanne's canvases. Others found their way to Charles Loeser's Villa Gattaia. Here, as Lord Acton reports, memorable soirées were held under the artist's very eyes, as it were. At a later date, the Léner Quartet played works by Schubert, Mozart and Brahms in the room containing these paintings, while outside the sun set over the Tuscan countryside, blurring the outlines of the hills and the shapes of the cypresses and pines. One of the violinists played a Stradivarius, which Loeser had given him as an expression of his enthusiasm for the player's virtuosity. A remarkable encounter between the old world and modernity thus took place in the presence of objects associated with particular memories – an encounter expressed in forms, colours and musical sounds.

24   Domenico Ghirlandaio, *The Birth of John the Baptist* (1486–90)

'A fantastic figure – should I call her a servant girl, or rather a classical nymph? – enters the room, bearing on her head a bowl of glorious citrus and tropical fruits and wearing a billowing veil' (ANDRÉ JOLLES)

'Ninfa fiorentina'

For two of the participants in the New Year's Eve celebrations at the Warburgs with which our narrative began, there was a particular glamour to the final night of the year. The main actor in the little piece about Merlin was the young Dutch writer André Jolles, who in the course of the play encountered Fortuna, the goddess of good fortune. The following week he asked for – and received – the hand of the woman who had played the part of Fortuna, Tilli Mönckeberg. The happy couple spent some time in the Warburgs' circle, renting the Villa delle Palazzine in San Domenico, not far from Böcklin's villa. 'It would be hard to imagine a more poetic little spot for a young couple,' Tilli Mönckeberg wrote home. There they led a carefree, somewhat bohemian life, with plays and other celebrations providing the high points of their stay. Jolles and Warburg staged an opera in no fewer than ten acts. 'Aby and André are singing a duet that's enough to make you die laughing. Even if everyone else finds it insanely silly, we shall certainly be amused by it.'[1]

The production reflected the participants' interest in the art of the Quattrocento. 'Aby wore a Lucco, Mary a Domenico Veneziano costume and André the costume of a Dutch planter.'[2] The local carnival made it impossible to obtain any Quattrocento costumes, the Renaissance revival having had certain consequences for the foreigners living in Florence. Tilli Mönckeberg herself wore a costume based on paintings by Ghirlandaio. 'I had done my own hair in a Ghirlandaio style, and several experts congratulated me on my brilliant success.'

Warburg and Jolles had met by 1895 at the latest,[3] and by the time they were working together in Florence they were bound by ties of what can only be described as friendship. In a letter of recommendation, Warburg described his colleague as undoubtedly made of the stuff of which important men are made: 'He has an inspired understanding of art and science alike and is acknowledged to be a good poet and a very skilful and feared critic.' But he had 'fairly squandered' his gifts as a journalist. Warburg hinted that he considered his friend a little unsettled.[4]

In many respects Jolles was the exact opposite of Warburg.[5] The son of a naval officer, he saw himself as an atheist and Social Democrat. Specialists know his name as that of a poet working in the tradition of the French Symbolists, while others remember him writing for the Dutch weekly *De Kroniek* from the mid-nineties.[6] This heterogeneous circle of writers was held together by its shared conviction that the present day was decadent and in need of both literary and moral renewal. Unlike those of many aesthetic movements of the day, the literary aspirations of this particular circle were sustained by an interest in history, including that of the Renaissance. Johan Huizinga, who for a long time was friendly with Jolles, has left a vivid account of its mood.[7] Authors such as Rémy de Gourmont, Edgar Allan Poe and Robert Louis Stevenson were held in high regard, as were Dante Gabriel Rossetti and hence the Pre-Raphaelites. Scientific aspirations, by contrast, were dismissed in favour of the aesthetic experience and artistic impulse. According to the group's watchword, the soul should come before the intellect, the inner life of the individual before all outward concerns. It is said that, as a result, Huizinga did not read a single newspaper throughout his studies. He himself claimed to have been an 'incorrigible fantast and daydreamer' until his late twenties.

'Jolles makes fun of my tendency to see the black side of things,' Warburg wrote on one occasion, 'but he is an indispensable critic in literary matters, and I feel that he is enormously valuable to me.' He felt close to Jolles in terms of his 'intellectual development', but not on a practical level:

> Yes, and against that, André! The limits of humanity! And yet I have the feeling that in the main, André too is probably powerfully stimulating and keeps the great goals of life in sight, but he disturbs me more by calmly getting on in life through his annoying craving for status. I now realize that it is only with small steps that we can gain a proper overview of the great field before us. Everything else is an amateurish, greedy, coquettish swindle or the sort of gourmandizing lust associated with a new red wine. I pray only that I have the strength ruthlessly to implement these principles; it is difficult to leaf through around 1,000 pages in two to three hours in the dank archives and take in the contents of these notebooks.[8]

There is no doubt that the Dutch writer confronted the archive-digging Warburg with an awareness of his own artistic aspirations. Jolles wrote and thought in the tradition of Ruskin, his subject being the discussion of formal and aesthetic problems. On his arrival in Florence, he set out to study the development from the 'Gothic' Trecento and the mysticism of Cimabue to the individualism of the Renaissance and the paintings of Lippi and Botticelli.[9] Written sources seemed to him to be dispensable. His fiancée has left an account of his sight-seeing habits in Florence:

> He finds running around with a Baedeker terrible and wants to provide us with a guide to the most intimate developments in art. . . . I've already seen a lot, and it has given me great pleasure, but when I am at Santa Croce, for example, I look at the whole church, of course, not just at Giotto, and then I leave. But that is what Jolles wants: one shouldn't see older and newer art in no particular order, one shouldn't shy away from travelling great distances to see the next Giotto, the next Orcagna. It will be a beautiful introduction.[10]

The tone that Jolles adopted in conversation with Warburg was not always an agreeable one. On one occasion they must have discussed Böcklin. Jolles peremptorily refused to grant that his friend was competent to speak on the subject as he was not an artist: 'Your language is art, and at present you know nothing but the most pitiful generalities. When you speak about Böcklin in this way, you put yourself on the level of someone writing about Dante in the sort of Italian that is spoken by waiters.'[11] In his dealings with Warburg, he saw himself in a teacher–pupil relationship, even though Warburg was his elder by eight years. If Warburg found it difficult to accept this, Jolles concluded, then 'all artistic contact' between them should cease forthwith, although this need not harm their friendship. 'You are no less of a friend and thinker, even if you never learn to understand this,' Jolles went on, 'but as an artist I know that in this case only your bones will survive your death, and as a Social Democrat I try in my own small way to ensure that the individual is useful to the community. But, however arrogant this may sound, I can only repeat that as an untrained person from a country which in this regard is barbaric you still have everything to learn.' Far too many people – and Jolles included the recipient of these lines in his strictures – saw the discomfort which was commonplace in art as birth-pangs. Only a few years earlier, Jolles had appealed to Warburg as an unquestionable authority in the matter of the rediscovered painting by Botticelli in the Palazzo Pitti.

Given Warburg's constitutional instability and the fundamental differences between him and the not exactly easy Jolles, it is remarkable that the friendship between the two men lasted as long as it did. The high point of their exchange of intellectual ideas was a fictitious correspondence which centred on a 'classically' clothed servant in one of Domenico Ghirlandaio's frescos in Santa Maria Novella, an early example of Quattrocento art.[12] Problems of aesthetics and art history are dealt with in a playful manner. Written in a Romantic style that seems to have been inspired by Joseph von Eichendorff, this fragmentary correspondence is an important source of views on turn-of-the-century aesthetics.

For Warburg, the text marked a turning point; for, although it was never published, it proved to be the beginning of his pioneering studies on Florence in general and of the essays he was to write during the first decade of the new century. This was also the period at which Warburg decided to build up a library that would provide him with a tool in his research into the psychological and social conditions of art. Ernst Gombrich has spoken in this context of 'what, in retrospect, must be counted the most important decision of his life'.[13] It was a decision that presupposed a fundamental reappraisal of his attitude to the sort of unscientific aestheticism to which Jolles subscribed and to an art history which, conducted with the eye alone, mindlessly echoed such effusive literary movements as the Pre-Raphaelites and the Renaissance revival of the turn of the century.

By the end of the nineteenth century the picture of the Renaissance had changed. Countless novels and short stories, most of which have now been forgotten, painted a picture of an age of bloody dramas inspired by jealousy, infamous heroes and magnificent courtesans. Greatness was revealed through crime as much as through art,[14] while red was now the colour which was increasingly associated with the Renaissance.[15] The backdrops were lit by firelight and by the rays of the setting sun, the stage was awash with blood, and the actors were aflame with feverish passion. It was the sixteenth century that became the true symbol of the age, Nietzsche's picture of the Renaissance now being joined by that of Houston Stewart Chamberlain, for whom the period was one of breathless, rank efflorescence, like the *fin de siècle*, rather than its antithesis, as it had been for Nietzsche.

As it died away in its sultry beauty, the autumn of the Renaissance was felt to bear many of the features of the late nineteenth century: not only was it 'new', but it was also seen as decadent. Members of the educated middle classes projected themselves on to the people of the Renaissance and, if the opportunity arose, they even wore Renaissance costumes. Tilli Mönckeberg's theatrical costumes are paralleled in the literature of the period. In Thomas Mann's *Blood of the Wälsungs*, for example, Sieglinde wears a Bordeaux-red velvet dress, 'its cut coming close to the Florentine fashion of the fifteenth century'.[16] Contemporaries adopted a historical air, elevating the style of the earlier period to a symbol of their own uncertain sense of identity.[17] Mabel Dodge, a friend of Gertrude Stein, commented ironically that Florence was a fancy-dress party at which everyone tried to look like someone from the past, be it Savonarola, a figure from *Primavera* or a Bronzino portrait, the general idea being to combine the *pittoresque* with the *chic*.[18]

The process was complex and contradictory. In the empire of Wilhelm II, there was a middle-class variant of the Renaissance revival which was known as *altdeutsch*, but which derived its forms from Italy, either through copies or through originals bought from antiques dealers. Writing in the mid-1880s, Georg Hirth claimed that the proud beauty of Italian art had acquired a 'comfortably middle-class character well suited to German craftsmen'.[19] According to a ministerial directive, post offices in towns of up to fifty thousand inhabitants had to be built in the style of the German Renaissance, otherwise a Romanesque style should be preferred, as it created a more monumental impression.[20] Renaissance interiors implied solid middle-class values, while Rococo was the preserve of the aristocracy. 'Studies' were seen as the studios of businessmen, counterparts to the office and the meeting room that were associated with commerce and politics. Writing in 1880, Otto Mothes suggested in his instructions for decorating the home that the master of the house could read his favourite poets here, test the antiques he had been offered or even create his own art 'in order that, having in this way cast aside the serious concerns of the profession to which he is obliged to devote the day and regained the inner equilibrium that these cares have destroyed, he may abandon himself entirely to the happiness of his home among his nearest and dearest'. It was a question of recreating an idealized setting, the picture that Machiavelli paints in a famous letter in which he describes himself retiring to a room in his country house near Florence after the day's business is completed and, festively attired, communing with the great figures of the past.

In this way people tried to assimilate themselves with the period they longed to recreate, the whole reason for their desire lying in the remoteness and exoticism of that age. 'The cult of the Renaissance appears in a tragic dichotomy of past and present, the expression of an attitude that cannot embrace life and that must experience it like a book.'[21] People were repelled by all that lay around them and reminded them of home. With an agreeable thrill, they read of a time over which lay a sweetly oriental, yet challenging and dangerous, breath of sin and death. And they noted with satisfaction that they resembled a figure by Raphael or Titian.[22]

This world seemed to offer all that they themselves lacked or were not allowed to have, but which they none the less coveted: freedom, wealth and measureless power. It was of these things that they dreamt, and these things that they pursued in secret: sex without taboos, and the eroticism accompanied by death at the moment of climax, or for which the 'little death' was the supreme sensual experience. In a scene in *The Goddesses*, Heinrich Mann combines Botticelli's foam-born Venus with Böcklin's Nereids and with Franz Stuck's *Sin*:

> When they climbed back on land, they were sparkling with the foam and still panting with the pleasure that had climaxed again and again. Like algae, long and wet, the Duchess's dark hair flapped in the tempest around her lover's body. Red blossoms lashed against their brows in the storm, they knew not whence they came. Others clung to the tops of their heads, red. And meanwhile the whole sky arched, fiery red . . . glittering and dripping with droplets, his companion shone, her arms outstretched, her breasts exposed to the wind, her brow wreathed by the sun as it broke forth from behind the clouds – her thighs, long and sinewy, were resplendent, as were her hips, which writhed like Sirens. He knelt and raised his hands towards her: she was the goddess who had emerged from the sea.[23]

In this way, the Renaissance became weighed down with meanings which had nothing to do with historical reality.[24] It was inevitable that voices would be raised in protest, not least from the side of the naturalists. Burckhardt's classical view gained a new topicality, and the aesthetic outlook of his *Cicerone*, which looks back to the time of Goethe, must have found widespread acceptance, with its belief that the harmonious forms and restful colours of the high Renaissance represented a peak in the history of art. Afterwards there had been only mannerism, Baroque degeneration and decadence. People thought they knew how difficult it must have been to achieve a 'golden mean'. Certainly, it is no accident that Burckhardt's writings had never been more widely read than in the years around the turn of the century, which was a time of discontinuity and disharmony; for they seemed to offer relief from the feverishness not only of the hysterical Renaissance, but also of an overheated present.

Others returned to the 'primitives', an attitude summed up by Marcel Reymond's polemic against the decadence that overtook Italy in the wake of Raphael and Michelangelo.[25] The 'hysterical Renaissance' was to be offset by contemplation of pure ascetic beauty, Savonarola being pitted against Titian. This tension finds expression in the most famous turn-of-the-century drama to be set in Florence, Thomas Mann's *Fiorenza*, a work which seeks to combat the aesthetics of vice and to put in its place a renaissance of human values.[26]

The recourse to the art of the Quattrocento was equally ambiguous, of course. Warburg disapproved of its Romantic approach: to sit down one fine day, like Ruskin and Gide, in the chancel of Santa Maria Novella and worship the art of a painter like Ghirlandaio as if it were something 'pure' and even 'naïve' struck him as risible and as an inappropriate response to the art of the fifteenth century. His plea for a historico-critical perspective was at odds with Jolles' effusive aestheticism. 'Dear friend, do you recall our conversation of about a year ago that moonlit night on the terrace of your villa at San Domenico?' This is how they started their exchange of views, some time during the late autumn of 1900. 'The orange trees were as fragrant as in a fairytale. Far away in the cold clearness of the blue moonlight lay the city like a sleeping woman dreaming of her past. It was as if one could see her breath in the wonderfully white trembling mist. All around, the hills kept watch, their shapes stretching out towards each other like giants shaking hands. The leaves hung above us, black and motionless.'[27]

The two men argued over the true course of art, and it required the beauty of the nocturnal landscape to reduce them both to silence. All logic failed in the face of such a spectacle, Jolles maintained. His text sounds like a parody of an aesthete's position, its author pulling out all the stops and conjuring up associative images: flowers made from gemstones, a woman who rouses the most dangerous desires spirited away to a Platonic world as an archetypal symbol of beauty. One thinks of Botticelli and Fra Angelico, but also of the gloomy eroticism of Salome.

'*Cherchez la femme*, my dear,' Jolles continues, before announcing that he has begun an 'intellectual flirtation', having fallen in love with a girl in Ghirlandaio's fresco in Santa Maria Novella, the '*Ninfa fiorentina*' from which the correspondence takes its name.[28] We can now understand the 'Ghirlandaio hairstyle' of Jolles' fiancée: was she not also a revenant of the Florentine nymph? Jolles describes honest Florentine matrons visiting Elizabeth in childbed in Ghirlandaio's fresco:

Behind them, close to the open door, there runs – no, that is not the word, there flies, or rather there hovers – the object of my dreams, which slowly assumes the proportions of a charming nightmare. A fantastic figure – should I call her a servant girl, or rather a classical nymph? – enters the room, bearing on her head a bowl of glorious citrus and tropical fruits and wearing a billowing veil. . . . Perhaps I am making her more poetical than she really is – but what lover does not do this? – and yet from the very first moment that I saw her I had the strange feeling that I had seen her somewhere before. . . . It is as if an earlier acquaintanceship had bound us together from the outset, something (do not smile) that is mystical, as if we suddenly recognized a dear friend or a favourite place from an earlier existence. . . . Enough, I lost my heart to her. . . . My condition varied between a bad dream and a fairytale. When I picked up my genie's lamp and spoke the magic word, what appeared was not fifty Circassian slaves bearing on their heads gold bowls that were filled with flowers made from nothing but precious stones (you no doubt remember: tulips from rubies, with calyxes of dull amber, dark irises of lapis lazuli from which diamantine drops of dew are suspended, lilies of opal, with leaves of jasper, violets of transparent amethyst and so on), but this time it was only the running serving girl with her veil who appeared. Sometimes she was Salome dancing with her fatal charms in front of the lecherous[29] tetrarch; sometimes she was Judith proudly and triumphantly returning to the city with a light step and bearing the head of the murdered general. . . . I tried to see her again as I saw her that first time in the chancel of the Dominicans' church, but she had multiplied ten times over. I lost my reason.

Jolles hoped that Warburg – the 'high priest of official science' – would be able to tell him something about the girl's origins. 'Above all, however, will letters addressed poste restante to "The Running Nymph" reach their destination?'

Warburg replied to Jolles' factitious letter by striking a humorous note which reflected the relaxed tone that his friend had adopted. 'I once saw her [the *ninfa*] in Settignano and took a photograph of her,' he claimed, before adding that he was 'no authority on erotic questions'. The photograph attached to the letter may well depict Tilli Mönckeberg: 'She was walking past a hay wain in the tiny market square in the late autumn – it was only by chance that I was able to snap her with my Kodak.'

It is no accident that Warburg applied his historical scalpel to a number of icons of the Renaissance revival and the Pre-Raphaelite brotherhood, namely to works by Botticelli, Leonardo and Ghirlandaio. Among the characters in Thomas Mann's *Fiorenza* is Lucrezia Tornabuoni, the mother of Lorenzo the Magnificent and the sister of Giovanni Tornabuoni, who commissioned the cycle of frescos in Santa Maria Novella. In this way, Ghirlandaio's work was introduced into turn-of-the-century literature. Warburg saw himself as an orator inveighing against the hysterics of the Renaissance revival and against the effusive enthusiasms of the Pre-Raphaelites. His motto may well have been: 'Back to history and away from *décadence*.' But far from returning to a false and fictional construct, he wanted to go back to the fifteenth century as it 'really was': its beauty was certainly not as straightforward as visitors, weary of the present day, imagined. There is a note of unmistakable irony to his response to Jolles' letter:

The modern languid art lover who has gone to Italy to refresh himself feels greatly superior to so much trivial realism and turns away with a discreet smile. Ruskin's word of command sends him to the cloisters, to a mediocre Giottesque fresco, where he must discover his own primitive mentality in the charming, unspoiled and uncomplicated Trecento work. Ghirlandaio is not that kind of rural, bubbling brook for the refreshment of Pre-Raphaelites, nor is he a Romantic waterfall which inspires that other type of tourist, the superman on his Easter holiday with *Zarathustra* in the pocket of his tweed cape, seeking fresh courage from its mad cascadings for his struggle for life, even against political authority.[30]

Warburg attempts to persuade Jolles to accompany him on the somewhat tortuous path of historical analysis: 'Abandon for a moment the standpoint of purely artistic enjoyment. The colossal walls of the choir of the new church dedicated to the Virgin Mary are not an angelic dancing floor for Easter holidays, nor a Romantic ruin for tired exquisites, with murky corners to hide in.' Still less were they built for 'all-consuming primary school teachers drunk on beauty'. Rather, it was a question of regaining a historical perspective and interpreting the frescos against the background of the age that produced them. 'What they mean to the modern man and artist is initially a matter of indifference to us.' Ghirlandaio's figures ignored the observer or reacted calmly to his gaze: 'They are not for a moment thinking of the *forestieri* inspecting them, men who may look elsewhere to refresh themselves bucolically or talk themselves up into a state of Romantic effusiveness. Life weighs heavily on the Tornabuoni, but they are too proud to tell this immediately to every tourist who is pressed for time.' Only when the visitor lingers in silence and does not tire of enquiring after their fate will they allow him to share in their sufferings – sufferings that stiff brocades and heavy folds of Lucca cloth conceal so magnificently.

'No, my friend,' Warburg goes on,

I cannot introduce you to the girl without further ado; even without having been introduced to her, you have thrown yourself at the estates of a Florentine patrician family that have been closed in their absence, and in doing so you have acted just as impetuously as your fleet-footed girl. One cannot adopt such a cavalier attitude in seeking to make the intimate acquaintance of someone who is a member of the Tornabuoni household, even if only as a willing hand.

With a reference to Ruskin, he continues:

Let us sit down in the choir stall and don't let us make a noise, so as not to disturb them: for the Tornabuoni are here performing a miracle play in honour of the Virgin Mary and of the Baptist. . . . The fact that your pagan stormy petrel is permitted to rush into this slow-moving respectability of subdued Christianity reveals to me the enigmatic and illogical aspects of the Tornabuoni in their primitive humanity, which attracts me no less than you are attracted by the flighty charm of your unknown apparition.

You feel prompted to follow her like a winged idea through all the spheres, in a Platonic frenzy of love; I feel compelled to turn my philologian's gaze to the ground from which she rose and to ask with surprise: 'Is this strangely delicate plant really rooted in the sober Florentine soil?' Was it perhaps a cunning gardener (with a secret *penchant* for the higher reaches of Renaissance culture) who insinuated the idea to the reluctant worshipful Tornabuoni that everyone must now have such a fashionable flower, such a joyfully fantastic point of attraction, in the centre of his sober domestic garden? Or was it rather both the merchant and his gardener who, imbued with the same elemental will-to-life, wrested a place in the dark soil of the churchyard for their luxuriant exotic plant from the sombre rigour of fanatical Dominicans?

Warburg was convinced that only written sources would reveal how the high Renaissance emerged from its 'chrysalis' and explain why the exotic bloom appeared at all. 'Until now I have been searching for documents in an icy, airless archive while suffering from a cold; in vain,' he wrote, with reference to his archival work on Ghirlandaio's art,

> but when those documents turn up,
> Wintry days become dear and beautiful,
> A blessed life warms all my limbs (vorrei, va!),
> And, ah, when you unroll his worthy Pergamon,
> The whole of heaven descends on you.

For Warburg, the central question revolved around the conflict between the Christian Middle Ages and the 'pagan' Renaissance, and the relationship between the church and the world. The series of frescos struck him as ambiguous evidence of a transition from a profoundly religious period to one that would later achieve an aesthetic, secular view of art. Warburg saw modern aspects above all in the artist's recourse to classical forms represented chiefly by the 'nymph', who seemed to him rather out of place in this setting. Warburg was convinced that the new had to be implemented in situations of conflict, and he was sure that it was possible to make out one of the principal obstacles to this development in the stubborn fanaticism of the

25   Isadora Duncan (1900)

'medieval' Dominicans who ran Santa Maria Novella. (As we now know, this view is untenable.) Against this background, however, a phrase he uses to describe Tornabuoni and his artist – 'fighters in the battle over Renaissance culture' – is highly revealing, indicating as it does the parallels that struck a historian who hailed from the enlightened world of Hamburg.

Giovanni Tornabuoni seemed to Warburg to be a 'fast-living philistine', the 'saturated sponge of prosperity' bearing within him all the characteristics of a member of the nouveau riche *fin de siècle* educated middle classes, while Ghirlandaio was torn between his own artistic conscience and the demands of his employer, unable to stand up to the world around him and to resist the images which crowded upon him from the past. Indeed, he himself emerges as a philistine open to the demands of his employers precisely because they reflected his own mentality. In spite of all this, the painter took an interest in classical antiquity and used 'pathos formulae' in the process. These were modern features, which appeared to justify the label 'fighter in the battle over Renaissance culture'.

And what of the *ninfa* that the painter conjured up and introduced into the lying-in room in early Renaissance Florence? What role did she play in the historical drama which Warburg recounted for his friend's delectation? 'In her true essence,' he explained the mystery, 'she is an elemental sprite, a pagan goddess in exile. If you want to see her ancestors, look at the relief beneath her feet.' He saw in the nymph a kind of revenant from classical antiquity, a symbol of energy rising up from the darkness of history as a 'function of organized matter'.[31]

Once again we touch on a curious and even questionable aspect to this psycho-history, for it emerges from all this – and it is an element which invests the matter with a more general interest – that even thinkers like Warburg, who could never be suspected of a militant racism, were not immune to the darker side of the science of their day. It is clear from the present text, as it is from Warburg's whole attitude to Böcklin's art, that certain forms of expression were stored in the cultural memory, in a kind of biological chip that the physiologist Ewald Hering had called 'engrams' as early as 1870. According to this theory, events that impact on living matter are encrypted in the brain in the form of these engrams. The energy potential which is stored in this way can be activated and discharged under certain conditions; but this is conceived of as a biological, not a social entity, hence the notion of the existence of a 'racial memory'.

A passage in a book by Arthur Moeller van den Bruck shows what this theory might look like in practice. Here this relatively obscure racial theorist examines Berenson's question of how it is that Botticelli's works contain elements which are non-classical, exotic and in some ways reminiscent of

Japanese art. His reply is that an 'Asiatic racial karma' has come to the surface here and 'reactivated' the 'archetypal Italian forms'.[32] In Moeller van den Bruck's view, the burial chambers of the Etruscans already contained examples of the light-footed steps of the dancers, examples which prefigured the 'Salome-like cruelty' that resurfaced in the art of Botticelli. Warburg saw in the image of the mysterious *ninfa* a 'discharge of energy' in which the early Renaissance's tempestuous desire for progress, suppressed by the Middle Ages, had broken through, an eruption of 'Dionysian antiquity' at a whole unexpected juncture, namely at a time of 'oppressive' and traditional respectability and Christian allegiance to existing rules – an eruption culminating in a passion typical of the modern age.

Passion and eroticism were thus embodied in the *ninfa fiorentina* in the choir of Santa Maria Novella. In the eyes of *fin de siècle* observers, Ghirlandaio had included in his fresco a 'line of vice'. Observers such as Jolles must certainly have seen her as a woman of a sensual bent, a symbol of the 'eternal feminine'. Warburg, too, ascribed an 'erotic physiognomy' to her. Gombrich saw a parallel between this image of the fleet-footed *ninfa* and the movement for women's emancipation in the years around 1900 – a battle which included resistance to whalebone corsets and stiff collars and advocated light, free-flowing garments in general. He also recalls the dancer Isadora Duncan, who floated barefoot over the stage, striking 'classical' attitudes, entirely at odds with convention: here was a turn-of-the-century nymph.

Warburg was evidently more attracted to the eroticism of Ghirlandaio's *ninfa* than to that of her modern counterpart. After attending a performance by the dancer, he commented ironically:

> She really gets into her stride when she is pleased and hops around like a happy bunny rabbit: in serious pieces she still officially repudiates her bare legs below by means of a painful expression on her face above. Also, she should really mime her roles with several other dancers, all this rushing around on her own between cardboard sets is too stupid for words.[33]

26   Max Klinger, *The Isle of the Dead* (after Arnold Böcklin) (1890)

*'What chance has Vulcan against Roberts & Co., Jupiter against the
lightning-rod and Hermes against the Crédit mobilier?'* (KARL MARX)

A farewell to Florence

T HE Italy that tourists visited in the nineteenth century seemed to enjoy one long radiant summer: here was a remote land dotted with towns and cities shimmering in the midday haze; roofs on whose burning tiles snakes could be heard rustling; dusty roads lined with sharp-edged grass lit by the sun which, high in the sky, was lost in flickering specks beneath the trees of ancient gardens; trattorie with their vine bowers and verandas, cool Frascati, fountains whose water evaporated over mossy river gods, turning to gold glitter and rainbows, and, drowning all other sounds, the perpetual concert of the cicadas.

In winter, by contrast, the days were short and could vanish beneath a blanket of clouds, and sometimes it would rain for weeks on end. Dampness and cold would seep through the walls, and the *tramontana* would sweep along avenues lined by plane trees, tearing from their branches the leaves turned grey under the summer brightness. Among the smells which make up the memories of a real Italy there has always been that of wood burning in a grate. 'Even in Florence it was difficult to heat the rooms,' Max Klinger reported in February 1893. 'But such an Italian winter is nothing.'[1]

Warburg, too, often complained about the gloomy weather, the leaden wintry sky weighing heavily on his mind. 'Dull and overcast. When will there be any sun? When will things get better? . . . Oh, my head!'[2] He also thought of death: 'The child of Dr Ostermeyer, who came here to study Botticelli, is becoming more and more unwell, I imagine he'll have difficulty pulling through: almost every winter is associated in my memory with a life slowly snuffed out.'[3] The bewitchingly beautiful, cold days which transfigure the winter in Italy brought relief. These were the days when the sun, low in the sky, etched deep shadows into the façades of churches and *palazzi* and formed crystalline sculptures from hills and valleys. Writing from her tower overlooking Bellosguardo, Walburga Paget noted: 'The country in Italy is always, I think, particularly attractive in January. The town feels cold and cellary, but the sunny land, with here and there some white frost under the trees, or on the shady side of a hill, is to me delightful. The peace and joyousness of it is so great.'[4]

It was on just such a cold winter's day that Arnold Böcklin died, on 16 January 1901.[5] The following day his body was taken to the Cimitero degli Allori – the 'Cemetery of laurels' – while the *Società filarmonica* from Fiesole accompanied the procession, playing funeral marches. The graveyard had opened as recently as 1878 and was situated on the Via Senese, at the point where the road reaches the top of the hill between the valleys of the Arno and Ema. The old English cemetery, where other non-Catholic foreigners had been buried, was now completely full. Following the destruction of the Porta Pinti, Poggi had surrounded it with a square, the Piazza Donatello, and declared it to be an '*isola dei morti*', an 'isle of the dead' – an expression no doubt suggested by Böcklin's famous painting. Among other actors of the present narrative who found their final resting place in the *Cimitero degli allori* were Karl and Jessie Hillebrand, Heinrich Homberger and Karl Stauffer-Bern.

The procession reached the cemetery in the late afternoon, just as the sun was sinking below the horizon. Almost the whole of the German and Swiss community gathered around the grave: not only Warburg, but also Adolf von Hildebrand, the dead man's colleague and friend; Isolde Kurz and her brother Edgar, who had treated Böcklin right up to the end; the Swiss consul, Karl Steinhäuslin; Böcklin's pupil Gerhard Fieseler; and Heinrich Brockhaus. Warburg described the scene in a text he wrote down immediately after the burial:[6]

> White marble funerary monuments, piled up on top of each other in semicircles, are fingered by the cold blue winter sun. Shivering with the cold, we walk up and down the rows, in this amphitheatre of silence, past hundreds of fallen visitors to Italy, to whom the decorative and hospitable country has offered places as if to an audience of curious onlookers beyond their wretched death. We are waiting for Arnold Böcklin to join them.[7] In the twilight they place him before the open grave, in a polished walnut coffin with a plain cross upon the lid. The earth will reclaim this son of hers, just as she has reclaimed all the others.

Eugen Lessing, the city's Protestant pastor, spoke 'clearly, but' – Warburg felt – 'in a tone lacking in any heartfelt sincerity'.[8] The large wreaths were laid on the ground, and the various academies and the Secession paid their final respects.

Warburg was profoundly affected by the event. As always, he kept tinkering with his account, changing odd words and carefully weighing up each phrase: there are no fewer than ten different versions of the opening sentence alone. His little piece was not without literary ambitions: Warburg submitted it to Isolde Kurz for her approval, and it appears that she was unstinting in her criticisms.[9] The text ends with a melancholic valediction to the old world that Böcklin had embodied in his life and art. The result is a reflection on the foreigners – including Warburg himself – who had gone into voluntary exile:

> Will no mysterious pirates suddenly appear on the hills around San Domenico, pale, black-bearded and wearing tattered red cloaks and carrying weapons that flash with white, and carry him off on their shoulders at lightning speed to their ghost ship and on to the dark blue raging sea? Are there no priests, walking on dark green meadows, no women, singing quietly to themselves, to bear him to the burning pyre? The cart carries him past, in a shining brown wooden coffin, just as it does with the others.

There was no miracle, and Böcklin's burial was staged with the same banal ritual as the interments of all other mortals. The incantatory power of art is emasculated in the face of death.

Warburg treats the scene of Böcklin's burial as an allegory of the present day, in which the machinery of modernism is implacably destroying all the myths of the past. 'What chance has Vulcan against Roberts & Co., Jupiter against the lightning-rod and Hermes against the *Crédit mobilier*?' had asked Karl Marx. 'All mythology overcomes and dominates and shapes the forces of nature in the imagination and by the imagination; it therefore vanishes with the advent of real mastery over them.'[10] The very gods that Böcklin had conjured up in his paintings were now being threatened. He had sought to maintain their Romantic idealism 'in our age of traffic and of distance-destroying chaos'. It almost looks as if Warburg were already opposing the ideas of the Futurists:

> No inquisitive faun gazes out from behind the cypresses in search of the magician who is his master. Before the open grave is the foolish one-eyed machine, the impertinent staring cyclops of the technical age, the photographic camera.[11] With his black goatee beard and a confident hyena's laugh on his lips,[12] the requisite camera-clicking contemporary

prances around nearby. Otherwise all that still surrounds the spot are cool inquisitive travellers and old maids in red capes.

Böcklin's friend, Karl Stauffer-Bern, who was buried only a few paces away from his colleague's open grave, had railed against the 'parliamentarians of the photographic age' in a delusional piece of writing setting out his politico-artistic programme.[13] It would seem that all the foreigners who elected to live in Florence were at one in their anti-modernist stance, while in the city itself the first panegyrists of the age of technology were celebrating the automobile, the aeroplane and speed in general. Filippo Tommaso Marinetti's *Manifesto of Futurism* contains expressions which seem to treat Böcklin as a symbol of the art of old Europe: 'Let's go! . . . Friends, away! Let's go! Mythology and the Mystic Ideal are defeated at last. We're about to see the Centaur's birth and, soon after, the first flight of Angels!'[14] Traditional images seem to be turned on their head: the legendary centaur is now a hybrid creature, part man, part machine, a cyborg, and the heavenly angel is a symbol of those types of apparatus that triumph over time and space: the car and the aeroplane. In the eyes of the Futurists, it is in them that the old mythic dream of humanity will finally come true.

With the death of the mythopoeic artist, all that remained for his survivors was a desolate present:

> We feel Böcklin's proximity only when his coffin gathers together his scattered admirers, the voluntary exiles,[15] the searchers. They stand in a wide circle, not like bodies aware of the central point around which they revolve, but like timid children at the edge of a frighteningly deep lake. They seek and feel only despair; he trusted and found – silent Arnold, who collected the barbs of criticism in your breast and then with the divine breath of your myth-forming power blew all these pen-wielding philistines away. Ave!'

Warburg felt acutely that Böcklin's death marked the end of the old world, a world which impudent and uninhibited modernism was even then invading. There was still an 'older' type of death: people died of smallpox and other epidemics, and it was still by no means the exception for young people to die, any more than it was normal for them to reach a ripe old age. The consolation of religion was now joined by the aestheticization of death and its transfiguration as a Romantic event, symbolized by the Pre-Raphaelites' classic image of death: Millais' *Ophelia* of 1852, its rosy-cheeked heroine floating gently down the river, her body strewn with flowers.

Among their literary pretensions, many of the short stories written around the turn of the century reveal a closeness to death which was to be lost during the later period.[16] Prior to that time, life and death had been interpreted more clearly as serving the will of God; but, as the nineteenth century pursued its course, there was an increasing tendency to protest at the very idea of death, as new strategies were sought to deal with the experience of dying. Among these strategies were sentimentality, literary kitsch and an appeal to the supernatural. Even as doubts in the truth of religion grew, the existence of an intermediary realm between life and death continued to be posited, and not just in art. Finally, there was eroticism. Thanatos was invited to share a bed with Eros, vouchsafing a moment of happiness even in horror and thus reflecting a threatened feeling of being alive and a death which may not have been followed by Heaven but was certainly preceded by life, with all its fleeting opportunities. From the couch she shares with Dechartre in Anatole France's *Lys rouge,* Thérèse can see the pines in the English Cemetery, while in Isolde Kurz's *Anno pestis* the beautiful, plague-infected Bianca avenges herself on her former admirer by allowing him to sleep with her.

By the end of Böcklin's funeral service there was no longer the faintest glimmer of Romanticism. 'The clergyman is still speaking beneath the evening sky as it slowly drains of colour,' and Warburg ended his report thus:

> It was some time since he had known Böcklin as a man, but he was unwilling simply to add the artist's name to his register of deaths, as he too had admired Böcklin with genuine awe. The speech was over, the sons had disappeared at once – two men stand at the graveside, the stone masons who place broad granite slabs on the coffin. The huge wreaths from the academies and Secession will see if they will fit on the coffin; old Böcklin sets no store by them, nor by the fact that we throw a handful of yellow earth after him. The community of expatriates disperses, the cold damp night wind driving them hurriedly home.

The Swiss and the Germans organized a memorial service for Böcklin on the afternoon of Sunday 27 January.[17] Isolde Kurz hymned the dead man from the black-draped podium, and Brockhaus offered an appraisal of Böcklin's art.[18]

On the very day of Böcklin's burial, Warburg wrote down his instructions on how he himself wanted to be buried: it was to be with Mary, not in an Orthodox Jewish cemetery but at the *Cimitero degli allori*. If Jews were not allowed to be buried there, then he would settle for Ohlsdorf in

Hamburg: 'But in no circumstances in an Orthodox nose-squasher. As man lives and breathes, so he clings to the wish, even in death, to have his head resting freely.' Warburg's diary contains notes which attest to his fatalistic mood at this time. He recorded the news of Queen Victoria's death with a cross: an era had come to an end. 'Böcklin's legacy is said to be a horrific image of the plague,' he noted on 20 January:

> Looking at the newspapers is like reading a pseudo-archaic prophecy. In Hall pulmonary consumption has been brought from Alexandria. In Constantinople a sailor has died of bubonic plague, his body half eaten by rats!!! In Hamburg a large number (15) of dead rats was found on the *Pergamon* coming from Smyrna; they'll have to be bacteriologically examined.

And he closes on a prophetic note: 'This twentieth century will see the great hangover of communications.'

This apocalyptic mood was compounded by private problems. A female visitor offers a depressing picture of life in the Warburg household. It shows scenes of a marriage held together only by Mary Warburg's forbearance and understanding:

> Aby studied while Mary painted, drew, embroidered. Then the high-strung Aby worked himself into a state of nervous exhaustion and grew distraught. Mary read to him and took dictation, and this cheered and tranquillized him for a time. Then he plunged into even deeper despondency. Finally, like some wandering, restless apparition, he approached his startled visitors and said that, if he were institutionalized, he hoped they would care for Mary.[19]

Warburg was a representative of the 'nervous age' by his own right, as it were. His gloomy mental state was a case for the psychiatrist rather than the historian or sociologist. Even so, the mood of the age cast its shadow over his thoughts and increased his sense of gloom. He had now passed his critical thirtieth year, allowing inner ghosts to haunt him and to take increasing possession of his brain, as in a fever or in the oppressive daydreams of which he writes.[20] 'The whole grotesque and horrific world threatened to draw me down into its whirlpool, just like Klinger's head.'[21]

He was tormented by the question of where his dark thoughts came from. In his despair he looked for physical explanations of his sufferings and became Edgar Kurz's long-term patient. Kurz regarded Warburg as a hypochondriac and tried to make him see reason, presumably demonstrating

27 Aby Warburg working in the archives: caricature, presumably drawn by
Warburg himself

a crude provincial insensitivity that took no account of Warburg's mental
illness. 'What are you afraid of, then?' he asked Warburg. 'Do you want things
to be better for you than they are for other people?'[22] Like so many others,
he ended up incurring the wrath of his patient, who spoke only contemptuously of the 'clique . . . Kurz-Vanzetti' and of 'intelligent asses'.[23]

Warburg confided his inner distress to his diary, jotting down his thoughts
in disjointed notes. He writes of his life 'in a tunnel' and feels to be wearing
a 'cap of mist' – a reference to the cap, often worn by dwarves in medieval
narratives, which allows them to become invisible. He would anxiously scan
the newspapers for reports of epidemics, making fun of the sanitary provi-
sions in Florence and at least on one occasion leaving for Switzerland or
Germany on the strength of a mere rumour. On another occasion he had
to spend three hours at the town hall, trying to persuade the authorities to
send a man with smallpox symptoms to the hospital at Macelli. 'We've only
just scraped through again! If German resolve chances to intervene . . . .'[24]
Genuine illness – the hay fever, for example, that afflicted Warburg during
the summer months, and a mild form of diabetes – left him more depressed
than ever. He awaited the results of medical tests with positively neurotic

tension, consulting 'oracles', for instance by pulling out the petals of flowers. It is striking that Warburg analysed his own mental condition with the same concern for detail that he applied to the field of art history: mind and matter were linked together, and so he sought external reasons for his inner moods in an attempt to rid himself of the pressure. And, consciously or unconsciously, he repeatedly drew parallels between his own situation and the psychology of the historical characters who were the subject of his research. Turning Nietzsche's famous remark on its head, he sought to interpret his own suffering as a universal. 'Dear God!' he wrote on one occasion to his mother. 'In this world of despair, of uncertainty, grey mists and sore throats (I've just got over my sixth this winter), mutual love is the only thing left to us as a refreshing, inexplicable (praise be to God!) gift from heaven.'[25] He was particularly dismayed by the fact that it was in Florence, where he had imagined an 'ordering cosmic force' to function, he was so overwhelmed by a pervasive sense of chaos.

Anyone examining Warburg's research in Florence needs to be aware of this background. Although he resisted them with all his powers of reason, the figures from the past who formed the object of his research and included monsters, grotesques, gods and demons must sometimes have come threateningly to life for him. He preferred to think of them as banished to the land of grisailles or, even better, defeated by the gods of Olympus and trampled into dust. Warburg's affinity for the psychologizing aesthetics of his day must be attributed not least to his own anxieties. During his years in Florence he struggled as best he could to regain his concentration, but his diaries make it clear how hard that struggle was. We find him hurrying through the city's streets, calling in at the state archives and paying the odd call. Back home, he would then sit at his desk for hours on end, leafing through books and articles and wrestling for the right phrase. By the end of the afternoon the page was still blank, or else it contained only a few words, a handful of fragmentary thoughts which were then rethought and rewritten the very next day, providing the starting point for a new train of thought. By his own admission, the course of Warburg's whole scholarly career was marked out by 'mutilated or unfinished milestones', as he once told Bode.[26]

And yet it is clear that his interest in history and his scholarly work provided the neurotic, ailing man with a sense of support. Reading calmed him down. In libraries and archives he came out of himself, even though he believed that − like every 'act of conjuration' − historical work brought its own dangers. Towards members of his own family he was always at pains to see the inevitable difficulties and inconveniences of his archival work in the right light. In the summer it was hot and stuffy, while in winter it was freezing cold: 'You get used to working in the archives when it's 9.5°,' he wrote to his brother, Max. 'I have now donated a thermometer to this intellectual convenience.'[27] 'Put a paper sole in your boots,' his mother advised him; 'that should protect you against cold feet, use grey, soft blotting paper.'[28] At the same time he admitted to finding his work on historical subjects sometimes tiring, and even oppressive. 'Today I began to read Guidetti-Ricordi in an entirely mechanical way; some of it was undoubtedly interesting, but on the whole I felt like an automaton hypnotized by some sorcerer into eating the dust of the archives, while the sirocco continues to blow.'[29]

Warburg's personal fate is, of course, an extreme case even in a 'nervous age', but it reflects the more universal conditions of historicism. For most intellectuals, history is more of a life force than a science. It functions as a comfort and offers support and calm in a hectic world. People observe and collect its relics, they read historical novels and scientific studies. The professionalization of the relevant subject areas is as much a part of this development as the institutionalization of the various disciplines bound up with history – disciplines which entered the universities and encouraged the establishment of historical societies and scholarly congresses and the setting up of institutes such as the German Art Historical Institute in Florence.

With the passing years, Florence lost its magic for Warburg. The 'Florentine setting' made him 'salad-like', he wrote home on one occasion.[30] He would get worked up about the commune's inadequate sanitary arrangements, and in a letter to the mayor, Pietro Torrigiani, he wrote to complain about a dead donkey that had been found in a channel normally used for drinking water.[31] On another occasion he told Prince von Bülow that the reason why the Italians of his own day had no interest in the 'original Latin' element of organization was that modern Italy had come into being by virtue of a revolution against 'the country's remaining princes'. As a result, there was a rampant 'cult of the revolutionary gesture' that 'made a hero of every secondary school pupil who accused his teacher of something'.[32]

Warburg's reflections on Italian life in his letters and diary jottings never rise above the level of everyday clichés. Italy is a country of servants, badly organized, dirty and gone to seed. He once complained to Jolles about his longing for the 'nordic countryside', adding: 'We're all exiles here, self-exiles; we've come here because we first want to complete our moral doctorate; anyone who goes back earlier has failed to achieve what he set out to do.'[33] So sorely was Warburg's patience tried that in his anger he once committed to paper the words 'I hate Italy'.[34] Italy was a form of self-purgation, and that is certainly how Thomas Mann saw it in *Tonio Kröger*.

A less literary interpretation is found in a letter from Alice Hallgarten to Aby Warburg. The sirocco, she told him, was enough 'to make us *fin de siècle* people incapable of achieving anything at all'.[35]

At the same time, there was a discernible gulf opening up between Warburg and his wife. Only with difficulty could he cope with his psychological problems, and it seems as if she repeatedly tried to avoid being with her difficult husband, their alienation acquiring a spatial dimension, too. On one occasion Warburg visited a sanatorium in Lucerne in his search for solace. The treatment included a course of atropine drops, in addition to which Warburg had to wear dark glasses and was not allowed to read or write. Hay fever, asthma and insomnia tormented him. From this period dates a letter that illustrates the tempestuous atmosphere that had built up during the couple's early years of marriage. Mary offered to visit her husband, prompting the latter to explode with long pent-up anger:

> You'd 'really like' to come here? Really! You never change! You're still the same person that you were before, the daughter of a Hamburg family, easily satisfied, lacking in temperament. . . . All right: I expect you here on around 10 June; get your father to transfer 500 marks travelling expenses to reach your account by 1 July. Otherwise you can sell your figures . . . you need come here only when I'm about to kick the bucket . . . You've an above-average amount of dim-wittedness about you. . . . There are times when you remind me of a Watteau shepherdess who attempts to maintain her airs and graces even in Dante's *Inferno*. . . . If one really lives together, damn it, this is a moment when one belongs together.[36]

Needless to add, the good-hearted Mary hurried off to join her husband without a moment's delay. In fact she seems to have spent little of the forthcoming period in Florence: her second child, Max Adolph, was born in Hamburg on 10 July 1902. Meanwhile Warburg was left to enjoy his works of art and archives on his own, but he also had to endure long evenings, when his anxieties returned and 'the claw of care' stretched out towards him. In his lucid moments he succeeded in 'copying out the old furniture inventories of people who have been dead for 500 years', an activity he described as 'macabre'.[37] Everything, he went on, was infinitely difficult: 'It is my misfortune to work so slowly and that the mountain brings forth such tiny mice,' he wrote to Bode in Berlin. 'As a result my entire summer has been one long sultry day of examinations.'[38] The letters from this period are full of bitter reproaches and of more or less veiled accusations. And on a scrap of paper inserted in his diary, he entreats himself: 'If it can be defeated, I shall change my life.'[39]

During the month of November a ray of light unexpectedly entered the gloom of Warburg's life.[40] He was on the point of leaving for a meeting at the Savoy Hotel when his eye was caught by a bound notebook: it was his wife's diary. He opened it, started to leaf through it, and then read it in detail. Here he found a young girl torn to and fro by her feelings and recalling their first tentative approaches and the beginnings of their lost time in Florence. 'My dearest, dearest wife,' he wrote to her, his pen flying over the paper, 'as I was lying awake last night, it occurred to me that you had left your diary here, and what did I do, indiscreet man that I am? I am now making the acquaintance of the queen of my heart from the days of her maidenly inner life. How wonderful to find something like this of yours! You really are the most cuddlable woman!' Mary was not at all indignant but replied thought- fully and sadly.[41] Half pitifully, half enviously, she expected that she would see her own former self coming alive before her. Had she made any progress in the meantime, she wondered. No, she was by no certain that she had. Quite the opposite. But was that her fault? 'Dearest old man, I do not think that you found in me what you were looking for.' Finally she recalled their first meeting in Florence on 4 December 1888 – 'fourteen years ago yesterday . . . then came the fourteen days that are still surrounded by a golden glow in the calendar of my life. In yours too? . . . Do you know . . . it would do us no harm to recall this period from time to time.'[42]

Mary Warburg longed to 'find composure and clear things up' in her mind, as she wrote. They must be more purposeful and less aimless in their wanderings. 'We have already frittered away five years, and we are no longer as young as we once were.'[43] This is her sober summing up of their time together in Florence. Slowly the two of them came to realize that it was time to move on. 'Break with Florence?! Yes!' Warburg had written in his diary as early as November 1902.[44] The following year he spent only a few months in the city, and by the spring of 1904 his bags had been packed, including a library of some four thousand volumes.[45] Odd words in his diary provide an impressionistic picture of the final scenes in Florence on 1 May 1904:

> Departure and clearing out of the Via Paolo Toscanelli; hot day, Fritz the removal man here by eight. Brockhaus . . . Slight show of affection between the two of us, mendacious really. A certain Pietro creeps around, intimating that he wants a tip . . . Fräulein Becker helps with the packing, lunch, old meat in an omelette. . . . Mary somewhat pale beneath the Loggiata . . . At seven the Baroccio man is due . . . once again up to the Loggia, evening mood. 'Adieu, house' . . . To the station in plenty of time, more or less where we met in 1888, when Mary said: 'I think I could tell you everything.'

28   View of Florence (*c*.1900)

'*The sun was just going down over the city on the banks of the Arno,
the sky was clear, the corona was on fire, towers, domes and palazzi stood
in a sea of flames. . . . We were sitting in a room which opened on to
the garden*' (ISOLDE KURZ)

17

In the new century

GRIEF at the time they had lost is something felt by many visitors to Italy, the underlying tone of sadness also stemming from the fact that in Italy the world of the present day contains more of the past than is true of any other country, a situation that is almost troublingly striking. Italy is the very essence of a historical place. History has everywhere left its traces, and even its countryside is a 'historical countryside', as Johann Jacob Bachofen once observed: the south, Apulia, Sicily; the Roman Campagna; Lombardy and Veneto, Etruria, Tuscany. It was enough to speak the magic words, and images from the past would be stirred into life, taking shape in the form of figures and great narratives. Even more concretely, the large number of *palazzi* and ruins, municipal organisms, churches, monuments, frescos and graves – these objects and places were all bound up with memories of a reality which had disappeared for good. All that the historian sought to reanimate through his 'necromantic art'[1] could never be more than a pale reflection of the original, never a resurrected Lazarus, a figure of flesh and blood, but at best a torso, which was felt to be 'indescribably' beautiful only because what was missing allowed the imagination the freedom to construct its perfect beauty. This elegiac grief in the presence of history was also the expression of a sense of suffering at the inability to assimilate it completely. It was like the feeling of a final unbridgeable distance that separates the work of art from even the most absorbed observer.

The grief of visitors to Italy also had a paradoxical aspect to it, inasmuch as Arcadia struck the foreign visitor as being closer to them here than anywhere else, while the contemplation of works of art and the Italian countryside allowed travellers momentarily to share in a mode of existence in which there no longer seemed to be any dislocation between the present and a past that was irretrievably lost. Goethe, Stendhal, Burckhardt and many others had felt this for themselves. And yet death was present even here: even here, the ancient walls, the marble reliefs and the statues were transitory, revealing their frailty in the moonlight. The world was changing, time was taking its toll, its work being seen as dramatic and disastrous. For the disappearance of objects brought with it the disappearance of other enclaves of this fantasy land, in which it was possible to escape from the present while still living in the present.

Each generation of visitors to Italy has its own concrete experience of the changes that are taking place, encouraging them to see the past in a Romantically transfigured light. (This attitude is additionally fostered by the fact that this experience is bound up with their own lives and with their realization that they, too, are growing old.) Burckhardt was reduced to tears when seeing the Roman Campagna lit by the evening sun, while Ferdinand Gregorovius was dismayed to watch 'his' Rome disappear. Isolde Kurz suffered as she stood by helplessly while old Europe, with its sociable ways, vanished from Florence. As she sadly looked back on the past, new arrivals in the city such as Aby and Mary Warburg continued to think of it as a beautiful old world, and yet even they were unable in the longer term to rid themselves of feelings of sentimentality and nostalgia and, finally, of nostalgia's ailing sister, melancholy. Like others before them, they tried to construct their own Florence, a Florence that existed only in works of art, in the city's old walls and in its archives. One did not even need to be in the modern city in order to find it, with the result that Aby Warburg's departure did not really mark a break in his relationship with Florence and Italy.

In reality, the change from the old *Italietta* to a modern industrial state was gaining in momentum as the century drew to a close. The *Gemütlichkeit* so valued by William James was disappearing, a point that the country's visitors gradually noticed as a result of the rising prices.[2] In 1897 a German visitor to Italy would still receive 141 lire for one hundred gold marks, whereas by 1907 the figure was only 123. But the structural change which was taking place in the country's economy and the upturn in its fortunes which finally began to make itself felt at the end of the century helped to stabilize society, a development fostered by the reform policies of the governments associated with the 'Giolitti era', which set store by liberalization, social reforms and the integration of the workers' movement. There would be no repetition of the events of May 1898. The right to strike was guaranteed. In 1901 alone, wage increases of some two hundred million lire are said to have been won by means of walkouts.

The mortality rate, especially among children, continued to fall, and by 1902 it was 22.39 per cent of the population against 27.66 per cent in

1882. The eradication of 'old European' illnesses found a potent symbol in the cultivation of the Roman Campagna, the sublime sight of which had caused old Jacob Burckhardt to burst into tears only a few years earlier. 'Picturesque malaria has step by step had to yield to unaesthetic sanitation in the picturesque Campagna Romana,' one observer noted dryly. 'A crying shame for the aesthete, but a cause for jubilation for the economist.'[3]

There was work, and Italy gained access to international markets. Between 1890 and 1907 exports rose by 118 per cent, while farm production increased from five thousand million lire in 1896 to seven in 1910. Equally impressive was the growth in the textile industry: in 1876 there had been 27,000 looms in the country, while in 1906 there were 110,000. Between 1896 and 1907 the industrial index rose from 0.3 to 6.7 per cent.

By the beginning of the new century the car industry was operating more than sixty factories, car production contributing some one hundred million lire to the national economy.[4] Founded in 1899, Fiat of Turin was soon the market leader, with more than 50 per cent of national production. For the present, the figures were still quite modest: in 1904 there were only 1,800 cars in the whole of the country, the price of each of them – eight million lire – being beyond the means of the average Italian. Carlo Placci was able to afford one, and he would often taken Berenson on extended tours of Tuscany, much to his friend's delight.

Only rarely were voices raised in Florence against the *pazza gioia di automobilizzare* – 'the mad joy of driving'.[5] Indeed, a number of the writers living in the city, including Vernon Lee, were enthusiastic advocates of the new technology, having discovered for themselves the elegance of speed, the beauty of locomotives and the aesthetics of the automobile. Maurice Maeterlinck's praise of the car was soon being repeated on the banks of the Arno, and *Il Marzocco* wrote approvingly of an essay by Lothar von Konowski which had appeared in *Die Zeit*. As symbols of power and work, these machines could be the basis of new artistic concepts and a great source of beauty. In 1902, the art critic and Nietzschean, imperialist and blinkered representative of anti-democratic views, Mario Morasso,[6] published an article on the aesthetics of speed in the same journal: 'With their jaws of steel and iron, they are bound to crush the old forms and all the old dogmas and prejudices.'[7]

It was very much the circle of writers associated with *Il Marzocco* that, years before the 'heroic phase' of Futurism, formulated ideas which articulate some of the positions of the 'historical avant-garde'.[8] These were the champions of the 'passionate art of speed' of which Filippo Tommaso Marinetti was later to speak. Morasso argued that legitimate reactions to the changes taking place in the world were not flight, nostalgia and sentimentality. Rather, contemporaries should allow themselves to be swept along by the feverish tempo and should leap aboard the rapidly accelerating train. Dionysus' carnival procession pursued its course with increasing speed, its carriages being made of iron and steel. Zarathustra returned, now in the form of a centaur fuelled by fire, hatred and speed.[9] In a secularized world, space shrank to nothing, time was suspended, and people were happy to affirm this. The fatally injured motorcyclist was hailed as a warrior of space, an athlete of speed and a gladiator fighting against the infinite forces of nature. A new Muse on Olympus, Energia, was challenging the giants.[10]

The ultimate consequence of this conscious acceptance of modernity was the urgent and even hysterical desire to negate all historical links. The *Manifesto of Futurism* of 1909 – a key text of the early twentieth century – seeks to get even with the old world:

> It is from Italy that we launch through the world this violently upsetting, incendiary manifesto of ours. With it, today, we establish *Futurism* because we want to free this land from its smelly gangrene of professors, archaeologists, ciceroni, and antiquarians. We mean to free her from the numberless museums that cover her like so many graveyards.[11]

It was with an appropriately grand gesture that the 'steam-engine intellectuals' – as Carlyle had called such people decades earlier – triumphantly affirmed the will to power over men and objects. 'We stand on the last promontory of the centuries! Why should we look back, when what we want is to break down the mysterious door of the Impossible? Time and Space died yesterday. We already live in the absolute, because we have created eternal, omnipresent speed.' Here, once again, we hear the voice of the 'blond beast' which boldly, rashly and ruthlessly seeks to build its world on a tabula rasa. It is impossible to overlook the fact that its brother is the man of violence of the Renaissance revival. The historicist golem sets out to destroy the world that created it. The end of history is announced and war – 'the only cure for the world' – is glorified, militarism and patriotism praised in the same breath as 'the destructive gesture of freedom-bringers, beautiful ideas worth dying for'.

As we know only too well, these confused ideas were not only of theoretical significance: on the eve of the First World War, modernism showed its ugly and at best risible face. It is perhaps easiest to come to terms with the *Manifesto of Futurism* if we are aware of its unwitting humour.

It can scarcely be an accident that Futurism as a movement began in a country overflowing with beautiful old objects and bewitching *vedute*, and it is likewise no accident that its cause was championed by Italians rather

than by foreigners. And yet its early stirrings in Florence and its environs –
one thinks of Morasso, and then of Soffici – were grounded in ancient
bellezza and in history inasmuch as Futurism presupposed voices raised in
protest at traditional art and history – and how could such a protest be
expected from cultured holiday-makers from north of the Alps who were
weary of modernism? The Futurists bombarded Italy's cultural towns and
cities with fusillades of verbal abuse: Venice was 'a magnet for snobbery and
universal imbecility, a bed broken in by entire caravans of lovers, a bejew-
elled hipbath for cosmopolitan courtesans, a supreme sewer of passéism',[12]
while Rome and, finally, Florence were no less roundly reviled.

In this way voices were increasingly raised in protest at the 'passéism' of
foreigners and their fondness for the past. The preface to Mark Twain's
Pudd'nhead Wilson contains an echo of this mentality on the part of these
visitors to Arcadia, a mentality which was philosophical in the wider sense
of the term. Here the author rhapsodizes about the view from his villa at
Settignano, from which he could see 'the most dreamlike and enchanting
sunsets to be found in any planet or even in any solar system'. Florence
becomes the centre of the universe: it is 'the most beautiful place', in
contemplation of which the observer forgets time and space – but in a
different way from the one demanded by the Futurists. Things no longer
have to be located in history but acquire their reality in that ecstatic
moment of heightened awareness which even as grumpy a writer as Wolf
Dieter Brinkmann once felt, a moment in which he claimed eternity was
condensed. In the absolute beauty of Florence there no longer seemed to
be any questions worth asking about the meaning of life in a God-forsaken
universe: fears over man's pitiful condition appeared to have been fully
exorcized. Bertrand Russell had been struck by a similar thought on the
terrace at I Tatti, and even Jolles had put forward an identical argument.
Arcadia had been achieved, if only for a fleeting moment.

But Warburg never achieved this epiphany. For him the matter was more
difficult, and yet his attitude, too, represents an extreme position that could
hardly have been further removed from that of the Futurists. Developments
he saw as threatening – the loss of distance, the growth in communications
and the destruction of the space in which one could collect one's thoughts –
were hailed by Morasso, Marinetti and their fellow combatants as positive
achievements. Of course, Warburg too had no time for the effusive response
of many tourists to the object of their infatuation: he abhorred the 'false',
Romantic and hysterical approach to the Renaissance and he could not have
been further removed from the mysticism of writers like Theodor Däubler.
Nor, finally, did he reject history as such. Quite the opposite. Like Burckhardt,
he regarded himself as someone striving to demonstrate the continuity of the

mind or spirit. In a hectic world careering towards an unstable future, he was an archaeologist studying western thought. His famous library, it has been said, was designed to explain 'the phenomenology of the mind'.[13] Ultimately he would attempt to compile a monumental picture atlas with the title *Mnemosyne* – 'Memory'.[14] Its line of argument was to be based on the evidence of the links between the works reproduced. On seeing these collages, the observer would become aware of the process by which civilization had evolved. Warburg himself saw this as a process of 'the conscious creation of distance between the self and the external world' and, as such, of the 'fundamental act of civilization'.[15] His desire to come to terms with the history of the early Florentine Renaissance drew its inspiration from this all-important question.

Warburg found no cure in Florence, but he wrested from his progressive mental illness a number of important studies, for which he prepared the groundwork in the city by examining the relevant sources: *Portrait Art and the Middle Classes of Florence* (1902), 'The art of Flanders and the early Florentine Renaissance' (1902) and 'Francesco Sassetti's testamentary disposition' (1907) – a study on what might have been subtitled 'The bipolarity of early Renaissance man' which bears particularly close affinities with its author's own situation, depicting as it does an inwardly torn individual at the dawn of the modern age whose characteristics are indistinguishable from those of his biographer.

Warburg's correspondence with Bode is filled with complaints at the difficulty of writing but also mentions numerous projects that he already had in mind. At the end of 1904 he sketched the outlines of a study on the exchange of cultural ideas between North and South in the shape of Flanders and Florence, adding: 'Unless I die or go mad first, I shall throw light on a dark and decisive phase in the history of Florentine art. The material has already been assembled.'[16] In the event, however, Warburg got no further than a lecture on the subject, a summary of which he published in 1905.[17]

It was in 1912, at an international conference of art historians in Rome, that Warburg delivered his famous paper on the astronomical cycle of frescos in the Palazzo Schifanoia in Ferrara.[18] This was only superficially about the genesis of the art of the high Renaissance, which seemed to Warburg – as it had since his early days in Florence – the expression and hence one of the preconditions of the humanism of the later period. Basing his argument on the cycle of frescos in Ferrara, he believed it was possible to uncover the traces of a transfer process in world history: the preconditions of a modern world that was interpreted as enlightened and steeped in humanity. In the course of his paper he spoke of his beginnings in Florence and of his first attempt to grapple with the problem of the emergence of a 'pseudo-classical idealizing style'. Everything he said seemed to be a summing up of the scientific findings of the years when he had worked on Botticelli, Leonardo and Piero della Francesca. Now, in Rome, he was at the very peak of his powers and he pulled out all the stops in a virtuoso display of eloquence and scholarship. He interpreted the cycle as evidence of the whole process of western civilization and as an expression of the struggle between the praxis of magic and calm humanity, which seemed capable of awakening to new life the beautiful gods of Olympus from the depths of the social memory and of helping them to triumph over the demons coming from the sultry and dangerous orient.

In his work on the mysterious cycle from Ferrara, Warburg also gained a perspective on the past which allowed him to locate more accurately the artist who had been the subject of his early research in Florence, namely Botticelli:

In the present context it now becomes clear that Botticelli's images of Venus – a goddess whom the Middle Ages shackled twice over, both mythographically and astrologically – are an attempt to restore her to her Olympian freedom. Venus appears surrounded by roses, an unshelled Aphrodite Anadyomene, on the water in her sea-shell. Her companions, the Three Graces, are also part of her retinue in the other painting, which many years ago I called 'The Realm of Venus'. Today I should like to propose a slightly different nuance to this same explanation, a nuance that allowed the astrologically aware observer of the fifteenth century to understand the very nature of the goddess of beauty and mistress of reawakened nature without further ado: 'Venere pianeta', Venus the goddess of the planet appearing in the month of April over which she presided.

Although the older tradition had provided Botticelli with the elements he needed for his depiction of Venus, the artist had achieved this 'most quintessential and idealizing human creation' above all 'because classical sculpture had itself allowed him to see how, following Plato, the world of Greek gods performs its round dance in higher spheres'.

Warburg ended his lecture with a passage which, more clearly than any other in his writings, throws light on his whole approach to the theory of civilization and at the same time reveals how closely beauty and reason seemed to him to be:

The great new style that the artistic genius of Italy has given us was rooted in the social will to free Greek humanism from medieval, oriental–Latin 'praxis'. With this desire to restore antiquity, the 'good

European' began his struggle for enlightenment in an age when painting was already setting out on its international migrations, an age which somewhat too mystically we call the Renaissance.

In 1912, on the eve of the First World War, Warburg still believed that the process of civilization was irreversible and that the 'good' European would ultimately triumph. He saw a parallel between the latter's struggle to achieve enlightenment and reason and his own inner struggle for stability and calm, a battle he spent his whole life fighting. The war shattered once and for all his confident belief that man's road to humanity, on which he had set out at the time of the Renaissance, would lead constantly and irrevocably to all that was good.

It was at this time that Warburg revised his view of history. During the war years he wrote a study on 'Classical pagan prophecy in word and image in Luther's day', in which the individual's ability to lead a civilized life no longer appears to be the result of a linear process but is a state that must be achieved by dint of constant struggle. This view of the world likewise had an autobiographical element to it.[19] 'Athens demands to be constantly won back from Alexandria,' as he summarized his new position. This was not so much an insight vouchsafed by his study of the sixteenth century as a bitter realization gleaned from his own experience in the here and now. Warburg dedicated his study to Mary 'in memory of the winter of 1888 in Florence'.

With mounting despair, Warburg struggled to come to terms with the experience of war. His colleagues, wife and children were made to read every available publication, including newspapers, periodicals and propaganda tracts, in order to collect cuttings on the war. In this way the danger was reduced to scraps of paper and chaos was catalogued. In an attempt to master the phobias conjured up by the war, Warburg plunged into a round of hectic activity, including founding a newspaper intended to explain the German attitude to the Italians. When Italy entered the war in May 1915 on the side of the entente, he tried to find a military post as a translator or as a propagandist in camps holding Italians prisoners of war.[20] Like most German intellectuals, he toed the official line in his dealings with the outside world, making direct contact with the special German ambassador in Rome, the former chancellor, Bernhard von Bülow, and advocating a settlement between Austro-Hungary and Italy. Bülow valued Warburg's knowledge of the Italian mentality and received him for dinner at the Villa Malta, where they recalled old times:

The prince rather pale, but otherwise uncommonly composed, caustic and friendly, showing off his peculiarly broad education and quick-wittedness in the course of the evening. . . . After supper we sat in a most comfortable corner of the courtyard, and the princess told us about Nietzsche, Lou Salomé, Rée and Maysenburg [*recte* Malwida von Meysenbug].[21]

Shortly before Italy entered the war, Warburg returned to Florence, as if wanting to bid farewell to the old world. The now seventy-year-old Bode took the opportunity to ask him if he would consider taking over the running of the German Art Historical Institute, as Brockhaus had enlisted. Noting the threatening political situation, he added: 'We need Italy for our spiritual sustenance, this country and its art, a country that has been the object of our yearning and of our love for almost 1,500 years.'[22] Warburg called on his friend Herbert Horne, whose country was now at war with Germany. Horne, who seemed close to death, created a 'noble' impression, as though being already raised above all material concerns.[23]

'Germany's war represents a degeneration of the instinct for inhumanity and of the rampant will to power,' wrote Warburg in mid-August 1918. 'We shall still have a great deal of suffering to endure while we remain at war this year.' And he added: 'May I not lose heart – but I really cannot abide myself.'[24] During this time he also read Fontane's *Frau Jenny Treibel*, a book which took him back to the familiar world of the nouveau riche bourgeoisie, with its contradictions between money and spirit. One could learn from Fontane's concentrated irony, he wrote, with an envious glance at Fontane's ability to distance himself from things – an ability he himself lacked. He was still convinced that Germany would win the war 'because' – in Max Warburg's words – 'he believed in the strength of Germany's superior culture'.[25]

Germany's defeat left him deeply shocked. Mastered with effort hitherto, his psychological crisis now grew worse, and in October 1918, shortly after the country had sought a brokered peace, he suffered a nervous breakdown. He seized a pistol, screaming that he would shoot his wife and children in order to prevent them from being captured by enemy soldiers. As one eyewitness recalled, he also shouted that he was not a Jew but a Christian. He was restrained and taken to a Hamburg sanatorium, then to the University Clinic at Jena. In 1921 he was transferred to the Bellevue Sanatorium at Kreuzlingen on Lake Constance, which was run by a pupil of Freud, Ludwig Binswanger, who diagnosed schizophrenia and 'manic depression'.[26]

The illness that Warburg had struggled so long to identify in Florence had at least been given a name. Freud, who had read some of Warburg's writings and may have been reminded of the holiday he spent at Galileo's villa in 1896, enquired after the patient's health. Was there any chance that he would be able to work again, he asked Binswanger.[27] The psychiatrist was sceptical. 'It is a crying shame, but it looks as if he will not be able to draw any more on his vast store of knowledge and on his huge library.'

Aby Warburg seems to be a prime example of the type of person who is destroyed by modern life and, as such, serves as a literary metaphor. In the profound crisis he suffered in 1918, it appears that Warburg was dimly aware of his metaphysical sense of abandonment: familiar as he was with the writings of Feuerbach, who invariably distanced himself from all matters of faith, he now asked himself the question of his own religious identity, and he fell back on the faith of the 'enlightened' figure of Luther. In the face of the present catastrophe, art, Italy and Florence were all meaningless, and certainly of no use any longer in coming to terms with the excessive strain under which he was suffering. But the matter was more complicated than that. There must also have been medical reasons for Warburg's mental illness, reasons that defy any mysticization. Warburg's case history is not simply a symbolic process emblematic of the pathology of the modern world.[28]

Warburg remained on his magic mountain until 1924, when, in spite of Binswanger's prognosis, he was released after having proved that he had recovered his mental stability by delivering a lecture – his legendary paper on the serpent ritual of the Hopi Indians. In the event, however, it was not so much the strength of his own reason that helped Warburg to escape from the inferno of his illness as a course of opium treatment which calmed him down.[29] It gained him another five years, a period filled with travel and scholarly work. He also revisited Florence, as if a repetition of his dream would bring him fulfilment. But had he really become a '*Fiorentino . . . d'anima*', as he wanted it emblazoned on his tombstone?[30] To us, he seems closer to the type of person whom Klaus Mann categorized as 'essentially German in character, with his Hamlet-like psychology', a German counterpart to the Latin type: 'The constant hesitation, the neurotic inability to act, the split consciousness, the profound insecurity, the doubts in oneself, the incurable problems . . . . .'[31]

Warburg suffered a fatal heart attack at his home in Hamburg on 26 October 1929. Mary had been worn down by decades of living on the edge of a volcano – this is how their son Max Adolph once described life with his father – and survived him by only five years.

Robert Davidsohn was one of the few Germans to remain in Florence in spite of all the upheavals. He was now the doyen of the German colony. Following the war he once again sat on the committee of the German Art Historical Institute. With the National Socialists' seizure of power, the town became a place of exile for him, as it did for many others. The confused situation at this time is clear, not least, from the fact that Davidsohn, a Prussian Jew, not only hoped for Germany's national resurgence but proclaimed himself a supporter of Mussolini.[32] Following Italy's victory in Abyssinia, he seriously thought that the *duce* would find a pretext to attack the German Reich and put an end to the incubus of Nazism. The historian of old Florence died in 1937 and was buried in the Protestant Cemetery at the Porta a Pinti.

In a letter of condolence that he wrote to Heinrich Brockhaus on the death of his wife in 1926, Davidsohn claimed that the Florence which Else had loved no longer existed, but had been replaced by a terrible mass of people. The petty bourgeois character of the city was revealing itself and obscuring the charm of the past.[33] Certainly, *la belle époque* of the brilliant elite gatherings of the period when Florence had been the country's capital and hosted a community of sophisticated foreigners was now gone for ever. Even so, Berenson continued to live at I Tatti and would eventually become a legend in his own lifetime, even surviving the Second World War. Together with its inhabitants, his villa in the hills overlooking Fiesole enjoyed special protection under the terms of an order personally signed by Mussolini.[34] Vernon Lee, too, had many years ahead of her, a period during which she retained a hearty loathing of her neighbour.

Others followed Warburg's lead and sought northern climes. Hildebrand went to Munich, where his brilliant career reached a fitting climax and where he died in 1921. A few years later, Brockhaus wistfully recalled the sculptor visiting him at Forte dei Marmi and drawing in the sand the ground plan of the Hubertus Fountain which he was planning for Munich, a symbol of the transience of all moments of human happiness.[35]

André Jolles moved initially to Germany, earning a reputation for himself as a man of letters and critic, before taking up an appointment as Professor of Dutch Language and Literature in post-war Leipzig. He joined the National Socialist Party in 1933, a move that led to an immediate break with Johan Huizinga, his friend of many years' standing. Jolles ended his own life in 1946.

Mesnil remained in Tuscany for several years, writing effusive letters to Warburg, who remained friendly with him until the end.[36] More and more he regarded Florence as his true home, he told Warburg, which made it more and more difficult for him to break free. And yet he too had to return to the North. His great monograph on Botticelli appeared in 1938, portraying its subject not as the melancholy dreamer envisaged by Pater but as sprung from the same powerful stock as the Tuscan peasants with whom Mesnil had lived for so many years. The grief of Botticelli's beautiful Madonnas was interpreted theologically as a reference to the fate awaiting the Son of Man. The result is a book in which the humanism of the political creature that Mesnil was goes hand in hand with a simple love of beauty, vaguely reflecting the view adopted by Warburg. It is to Warburg – the 'companion of those beautiful years in Tuscany' – that the study is dedicated.[37] Not long after the book was published the Second World War broke out, and the Germans occupied Belgium. Mesnil fled to France, where he died in the summer of 1940, on a pitiful straw bed in a monastery at Montmaur-en-Diois.[38]

Like most other long-term visitors to Florence, Isolde Kurz, too, was finally drawn back to Germany, her brother Edgar having died in 1904. Following the death of her mother, who survived Edgar by seven years, she went to Munich to be near Heyse and Hildebrand. During the First World War she enjoyed a new kind of celebrity thanks to her patriotic poems. Following the German defeat, she sought comfort in short stories which take the reader back to summer days by the Italian sea and to the hills of Tuscany and Latium. She, too, welcomed Mussolini with open arms. Although her attitude was far too influenced by the self-awareness of an elitist middle class for her to accept the National Socialist movement unreservedly, she was dazzled by Hitler's early successes. And she was even willing to respond to a request from her publisher to remove the names of her Jewish friends, including Davidsohn's, from the 1937 reissue of her reminiscences of Florence and also from her memoirs.[39] In general, however, she distanced herself from the anti-Semitic witch-hunt of the National Socialists and remained in correspondence with Robert Davidsohn and his wife.[40]

The cosmopolitan atmosphere in the Florence of her youth became a transfigured memory for Isolde Kurz. 'Perhaps we were a trial run for the Europeans of tomorrow,' she wrote retrospectively of the city's expatriate community, which had led a utopian existence in Florence.[41] But was she right? True, urbane forms of social intercourse and the compelling power of art had helped them to overcome any national misgivings they may have had, conversations on the subject of beauty creating a sense of community among Britons and Americans, French, Russians and Germans that is symbolized by the circle around Ludmilla Assing, who had continued the salon of her aunt Rahel Varnhagen in late Biedermeier Berlin and who now kept an open house in Florence, offering a meeting place for visitors from all four corners of the earth.

But on the eve of the First World War, this was far from providing the model for a beautiful European future. Rather, Florence's expatriate community gave a final glimpse of a world that was fast disappearing, a world that could look forward to no tomorrow. Instead, travellers from the present day wanted to stop the wheel of time from turning, seeking an artificial past and in the process inventing a city beyond the oppressive burden of history. The result was a land of the imagination which lay far beyond the reach of mere mortals. The ultimate spiritual impression of life at that time could not be depicted or captured in words. Isolde Kurz addresses us – the coming generations – once more: 'No researcher who examines the history of this community at a later date will really be able to sense it.'[42]

By the turn of the century, modernism had reached even Florence. Contemporaries were left to seek out an even more remote Arcadia in the Tuscan countryside, in the valleys of the Chianti and in the hills surrounding the city. In the dying light of an autumn evening, Florence still appeared from here to be the artificial construct that Henry James had described in 1874: 'The domes and towers were washed over with a faint blue mist. The scattered columns of smoke, interfused with the sinking sunlight, hung over them like streamers and pennons of silver gauze; and the Arno, twisting and curling and glittering here and there, was a serpent cross-striped with silver.'[43] Seen from the distance, the Arno was not the muddy yellow river which it is when viewed at close quarters.

The sun then sank beneath the hills, their contours being obscured by the twilight.

The leave-taking was not only melancholic. For many, Warburg among them, it was tantamount to an act of liberation from the shadows of the past, with their tormenting riddles and menacing demons, and from the ghosts of the present, who were now engaged in a life-and-death struggle with the ancient spirits:

> Was this claustrophobic Florence never to end? He suddenly felt a violent desire for the air from its hills, the air filled with the shimmering leaves of the olive trees and spiced with the laurel, air that kissed him bitterly and gently on the lips. The narrow alleys still resounded with their night-time echo. The shadow of horse and coachman rose up and down the walls. Then the suburban houses began to thin out. The first gardens were bathed in moonlight.[44]

Notes

Chapter 1 The mirror of Florence

1. *La Nazione*, lxi/365 (31 Dec. 1899); see also *Fieramosca: Giornale del Popolo*, xxi/1 (1/2 Jan. 1901), which gives the picture for 1900/1, when, in the opinion of the majority of the inhabitants of Florence, the twentieth century actually began.

2. The following details are taken from AWI, FC (letter from Mary Warburg to her mother, 9 Jan. 1900) and Diaries 10.1.

3. R[obert] D[avidson], 'Zum Jahre 1900', Diaries 10.1 (31 Dec. 1899).

4. See Antoine Bodar, 'Aby Warburg en André Jolles: Een Florentijnse vriendschap', *Nexus*, i (1991), 5–18.

5. See E. H. Gombrich, *Aby Warburg: An Intellectual Biography* (Oxford 1986), 22.

6. See Bernd Roeck, *Der junge Aby Warburg* (Munich 1997); and Gombrich, *Warburg* (note 5).

7. Gertrud Bing, *Aby M. Warburg: Vortrag anläßlich der feierlichen Aufstellung von Aby Warburgs Büste in der Hamburger Kunsthalle am 31. Oktober 1958* (Hamburg 1958), 9–32.

8. Robert Musil, *Tagebücher* (Reinbek bei Hamburg 1983), 12.

9. Roger Willemsen, *Der Selbstmord in Berichten, Briefen, Manifesten, Dokumenten und literarischen Texten* (Cologne 1986), 30–40.

10. See Thomas Rietzschel, *Theodor Däubler: Eine Collage seiner Biographie* (Leipzig 1988).

11. See Rietzschel, *Däubler* (note 10), 66; and Theodor Däubler, *Das Nordlicht* (Munich and Leipzig 1910), 273 and 295.

12. Bertrand Russell, 'A free man's worship', *Contemplation and Action 1902–14* (London 1985), 66–7.

13. Quoted by Ronald W. Clark, *The Life of Bertrand Russell* (London 1975), 94.

14. Russell, 'A free man's worship' (note 12), 68.

15. Arthur Schopenhauer, *Die Welt als Wille und Vorstellung* (Stuttgart and Frankfurt am Main 1968), i.280 (III § 38); trans. E. F. J. Payne as *The World as Will and Representation* (New York 1969), i.196.

16. See Alfred Kantorowicz's introduction and afterword to Heinrich Mann, *Die Göttinnen oder Die drei Romane der Herzogin von Assy* (Berlin 1969), 714.

17. Clark, *Life of Bertrand Russell* (note 13), 93; see also Michael Naumann, 'Bildung und Gehorsam: Zur ästhetischen Ideologie des Bildungsbürgertums', *Das wilhelminische Bildungsbürgertum: Zur Sozialgeschichte seiner Ideen*, ed. Klaus Vondung (Göttingen 1976), 34–52, esp. 44.

18. Ruth Z. Temple, 'Truth in labelling: Pre-Raphaelitism, aestheticism, decadence, fin de siècle', *English Literature in Transition*, xvii/4 (1974), 201–22; and Ian Fletcher, 'Some aspects of aestheticism', in *Twilight of Dawn: Studies in English Literature in Transition*, ed. O. M. Brack Jr (Tucson 1987), 1–31.

Chapter 2 Trials and tribulations

1. FC (letter from Aby Warburg to Charlotte Warburg, 29 Dec. 1888).
2. Diaries 9 (25 Oct. 1886); see also Isolde Kurz, *Florentinische Erinnerungen* (Stuttgart and Berlin 1920), 16–17.
3. Diaries 9 (28 Oct. 1888).
4. Bernd Roeck, *Der junge Aby Warburg* (Munich 1997), 60 (also the following quotation).
5. See Siegfried Käss, *Der heimliche Kaiser der Kunst: Adolf Bayersdorfer, seine Freunde und seine Zeit* (Munich 1987) and *Adolf Bayersdorfers Leben und Schriften: Aus seinem Nachlaß*, eds Hans Mackowsky, August Pauly and Wilhelm Weigand (Munich 1902).
6. See Lutz Tittel, *Arnold Böcklin: Leben und Werk in Daten und Bildern* (Frankfurt am Main 1977), 70; Anna Maria von Winterfeld, 'Arnold Böcklin und Florenz', *Storia dell'arte e politica culturale intorno al 1900: La fondazione dell'Istituto Germanico di Storia dell'Arte a Firenze*, ed. Max Seidel (Venice 1999), 143–77, esp. 154–6.
7. See Oskar Bätschmann and Pascal Griener, *Hans Holbein d. J.: Die Darmstädter Madonna. Original gegen Fälschung* (Frankfurt am Main 1998).
8. Diaries 10.1 (31 March 1900).
9. See Anna Maria Szylin, *Henry Thode (1875–1920): Leben und Werk* (Frankfurt am Main 1993); see also Roeck, *Der junge Aby Warburg* (note 4), 46–8.
10. AWI, 33.2, 1–2; and GC (letter from Aby Warburg to Henry Thode, 31 Jan. 1889).
11. AWI, 50 (Box of notes, Modern art).
12. Warburg collected newspaper reports on the subject; see AWI (Zettelkästen 50, Böcklin; Thode/Liebermann).
13. See Max J. Friedländer, *Erinnerungen und Aufzeichnungen: Aus dem Nachlaß*, ed. Rudolf Moritz Heilbrunn (Mainz and Berlin 1967).
14. See Hans W. Hubert, *Das Kunsthistorische Institut in Florenz: Von der Gründung bis zum hundertjährigen Jubiläum (1897–1997)* (Florence 1997), 13–16; for a visit to Prince Corsini's Gallery, see Diaries 9 (12 Jan. 1889).
15. See Roeck, *Der junge Aby Warburg* (note 4), 62.
16. Diaries 10.1 (15 Dec. 1888).
17. FC (Family recollections, recollections of Max Warburg, with corrections in his hand, 5).
18. Ron Chernow, *The Warburgs: The Twentieth-Century Odyssey of a Remarkable Jewish Family* (New York 1993), 67.
19. GC (letter from Alice Hallgarten to Aby Warburg, 27 Dec. 1897).
20. AWI (Mary Hertz's diary entry, 16 June 1893).
21. AWI (Mary Hertz's diary entry, 2 June 1891).
22. See Roeck, *Der junge Aby Warburg* (note 4), 81–2.
23. Ibid. 71–5.
24. Ibid. 81.
25. FC (letter from Aby Warburg to Mary Hertz, 21 May 1891).
26. FC (letter from Aby Warburg to Mary Hertz, 16 June 1894).
27. Walther Rehm, 'Der Renaissancekult um 1900 und seine Überwindung', *Zeitschrift für deutsche Philologie*, liv (1929), 296–328, reprinted in Rehm, *Der Dichter und die neue Einsamkeit: Aufsätze zur Literatur um 1900* (Göttingen 1969), 34–77; and Peter Gay, *The Bourgeois Experience: Victoria to Freud*, iv: *The Naked Heart* (London 1996), 13–14.
28. AWI (Mary Hertz's diary entry, 24 Oct. 1890).
29. AWI (Mary Hertz's diary entry, 3 Sept. 1890).

30. AWI (Mary Hertz's diary entry, 19 Sept. 1890).
31. FC (letter from Mary Hertz to Aby Warburg, 23 Dec. 1890).
32. AWI (Mary Hertz's diary entry, 31 May 1892).
33. Bram Djikstra, *Idols of Perversity: Fantasies of Feminine Evil in fin-de-siècle Culture* (New York and Oxford 1986).
34. Lea Ritter-Santini, 'Maniera Grande: Über italienische Renaissance und deutsche Jahrhundertwende', *Deutsche Literatur der Jahrhundertwende*, ed.Viktor Zmegac (Königstein 1981), 242–72.
35. E. H. Gombrich, *Aby Warburg: An Intellectual Biography* (Oxford 1986), 85.
36. FC (letter from Aby Warburg to Mary Hertz, 16 June 1894).
37. FC (letter from Mary Hertz to Aby Warburg, 8 June 1894).
38. FC (letter from Aby Warburg to Mary Hertz, 19 July 1894).
39. FC (letter from Aby Warburg to Mary Hertz, 9 July 1894).
40. FC (letter from Aby Warburg to Mary Hertz, 2 Oct. 1894).
41. Ibid.
42. Ibid.
43. Alan Gauld, *A History of Hypnotism* (Cambridge 1992), 344 and 352–3. Grossmann edited the *Zeitschrift für Hypnotismus* from 1892 and in 1894 published a study on the importance of hypnotic suggestion as a form of therapy.
44. FC (letter from Aby Warburg to Mary Hertz, 2 Oct. 1894).
45. Gombrich, *Warburg* (note 35), 109, n. 1.
46. FC (letter from Aby Warburg to Mary Hertz, 28 Sept. 1894).
47. FC (letter from Mary Hertz to Aby Warburg, 1894).

Chapter 3 In the realm of Venus

1. Edgar Jepson, *Memories of a Victorian* (London 1933), 102.
2. See Lillian B. Miller, 'Celebrating Botticelli: The taste for the Italian Renaissance in the United States, 1870–1920', *The Italian Presence in American Art, 1860–1920*, ed. Irma B. Jaffe (New York and Rome 1992), 3–22.
3. Carolyn Williams, *Transfigured World: Walter Pater's Aesthetic Historicism* (Ithaca, NY, 1989); William E. Buckler, *Walter Pater: The Critic as Artist of Ideas* (New York and London 1987), 62–7; and J. B. Bullen, *The Myth of the Renaissance in Nineteenth-Century Writing* (Oxford 1994), 273–98; on the question of whether Ruskin or Pater was the first to rediscover Botticelli, see Gail S.Weinberg, 'Ruskin, Pater, and the rediscovery of Botticelli', *The Burlington Magazine* ccxix/1006 (1987), 25–7.
4. John Ruskin, *The Works* (London 1903–12), xxiii.255.
5. Hilary Fraser, *The Victorians and Renaissance Italy* (Cambridge, MA and Oxford 1992), 126.
6. Walter Pater, *The Renaissance: Studies in Art and Poetry*, ed.Adam Phillips (Oxford 1986), 36 and 40; see also Weinberg, 'Ruskin, Pater, and the rediscovery of Botticelli' (note 3), 27.
7. Bernd Roeck, 'Psychohistorie im Zeichen Saturns: Aby Warburgs Denksystem und die moderne Kulturgeschichte', *Kulturgeschichte Heute*, eds Wolfgang Hardtwig and Hans-Ulrich Wehler (Göttingen 1996), 231–54.
8. See also E. H. Gombrich, *Aby Warburg: An Intellectual Biography* (Oxford 1986), 43–66.
9. Aby Warburg, 'Sandro Botticelli', *Das Museum*, iii (1898), 37–40, esp. 40.
10. AWI, 75.2 (Hamburg lectures, 1909, iv; Botticelli p. 47 (fol.462)).
11. See also Henry James' reflections in 'The autumn of Florence' (1874), in *Travelling in Italy with Henry James*, ed. Fred Kaplan (New York 1994), 231.
12. See Francis Haskell, *Rediscoveries in Art: Some Aspects of Taste, Fashion and Collecting in England and France* (Ithaca, NY 1976), 114; Miller, 'Celebrating Botticelli' (note 2); and *Letters of Roger Fry*, ed. Denys Sutton (London 1972), 141.
13. GC (Correspondence with Mesnil, 20 Sept. 1896); see also Warburg, 'Sandro Botticelli' (note 9), 38: 'It was left to modern sentimental aesthetes to offer the general public

Sandro's innermost nature as "charming naïveté" or "delightful melancholy" for them to enjoy. Botticelli does not flaunt his temperament like some delicate garment for all to see. Rather, it is a chafing shell which it was the conscious aim of his life's work to enlarge by the inadequate means of the thinking artist.'

14. See Irving Wohlfarth,' "Construction has the role of the subconscious": Phantasmagorias of the master builder (with constant reference to Giedion, Weber, Nietzsche, Ibsen and Benjamin', *Nietzsche and 'An Architecture of Our Minds'*, eds Alexandre Kostka and Irving Wohlfarth (Los Angeles 1999), 141–98, esp. 155.

15. Aby Warburg, 'Amerikanische Chap-books', *Pan*, ii/4 (April 1897), reprinted in *Gesammelte Schriften* (Leipzig and Berlin 1932), ii.577; see also Gombrich, *Warburg* (note 8), 92.

16. Gombrich, *Warburg* (note 8), 155–6. Ascan Lutteroth (1842–1923) and his cousin Emma (1854–94) were landscape painters active in the Hamburg area.

17. Ian Fletcher, *Rediscovering Herbert Horne: Poet, Architect, Typographer, Art Historian* (Greensboro 1990), 72.

18. AWI, 43.1, Grundlegende Bruchstücke zu einer monistischen Kunstpsychologie I (seit 1888), p. 4.

19. But see Gombrich, *Warburg* (note 8), 58; and Miller, 'Celebrating Botticelli' (note 2), 6.

20. AWI, 43.1. For more on this problem, see E. H. Gombrich, *Ornament und Kunst: Schmucktrieb und Ordnungssinn in der Psychologie des dekorativen Schaffens* (Stuttgart 1982).

21. AWI, 43.1, fol. 19 (2 June 1889).

22. Ibid., fol. 14.

23. Ibid., fol. 33.

24. Ibid., fol. 47.

25. Ibid., fol. 15.

26. Giovanni Landucci, *Darwinismo a Firenze: Tra scienza e ideologia* (Florence 1977), 107–27; see also Isolde Kurz, *Pilgerfahrt nach dem Unerreichlichen: Lebensrückschau* (Tübingen 1938), 171–2; and Eugenio Garin, 'Note sulla cultura a Firenze alla fine dell'Ottocento', *Giornale critico della Filosofia Italiana*, 6th series, v/1 (1985), 1–15.

27. For evidence of Warburg's depressed state of mind while he was writing down his thoughts on the psychology of art, see for example AWI, 43.1, fol. 22. After reading Darwin's book *The Expression of Emotion in Animals and Men*, Warburg noted in his diary: 'At last a book which helps me.' Presumably he was expressing his belief that he now thought he was close to solving a problem that had been greatly troubling him personally; see Gombrich, *Warburg* (note 8), 72.

28. FC (letter from Aby Warburg to Mary Hertz, 15 Dec. 1890; letter from Mary Hertz to Aby Warburg, 23 Dec. 1890; letter from Aby Warburg to Mary Hertz, 31 Dec. 1890 [copy in the hand of Max Adolph Warburg]); see Gombrich, *Warburg* (note 8), 81–2, where Gombrich's transcription differs from my own, which is based on Max Adolph Warburg's copy of the letter.

29. This is how Warburg formulated this idea in his fragmentary jottings: 'The artistic recreation of an object is the work of reaction in a man who, delighting in battle and thirsting for action, reacts against the unattainability of what is visible to him. An object can be unattainable, 1st, as a result of obstacles that seem unalterable, and, 2nd, as a result of temporal obstacles that may be thought of as alterable (human laws, our picture of history, etc.' See AWI, 43.1, fol. 6.

30. Diaries 10.1 (31 March 1900).

31. See M. da Siena, 'La "Primavera di Sandro" ', *Il Marzocco*, iv/9 (2 April 1899) and vi/11 (16 April 1899).

32. Jacob Burckhardt, *Briefe*, ed. Max Burckhardt, 10 vols (Basel 1949–86), x.65–6.

33. Gombrich, *Warburg* (note 8), 85–7.

34. Diaries 9 (25 Feb. 1894 and 22 March 1894).

35. Diaries 9 (29 Oct. 1894).

Chapter 4 Judaeo-Christian *divan*

1. For more on Moritz M. Warburg, see Ron Chernow, *The Warburgs: The Twentieth-Century Odyssey of a Remarkable Jewish Family* (New York 1993).
2. See Morten Reitmayer, *Bankiers im Kaiserreich: Sozialprofil und Habitus der deutschen Hochfinanz* (Göttingen 1999).
3. See Chernow, *The Warburgs* (note 1), 17.
4. See Helga Krohn, *Die Juden in Hamburg: Die politische, soziale und kulturelle Entwicklung einer Großstadtgemeinde nach der Emanzipation 1848–1918*, 2 vols (Hamburg 1974), i. 65–6 and 79. The Jewish population of Hamburg numbered some 14,000 individuals at this period, about 4% of the total. The average for the rest of the country was 1.25%.
5. Chernow, *The Warburgs* (note 1), 18.
6. Ibid., 27.
7. Bernd Roeck, *Der junge Aby Warburg* (Munich 1997), 75.
8. Chaim Weizmann, *Trial and Error: The Autobiography of Chaim Weizmann*, 2 vols (Philadelphia 1949), i.31.
9. Weizmann, *Trial and Error* (note 8), i.18. For a detailed analysis of the questions raised here, see Michael A. Meyer, *Response to Modernity: A History of the Reform Movement in Judaism* (Oxford and New York 1988).
10. See Weizmann, *Trial and Error* (note 8), i.19; see also Julius von Eckardt, *Lebenserinnerungen*, 2 vols (Leipzig 1910), i.202–4.
11. FC (letter from Aby Warburg to Charlotte Warburg, 2 April 1897).
12. Roeck, *Der junge Aby Warburg* (note 7), 84; for a similar view, see Eckardt, *Lebenserinnerungen* (note 10), i.204.
13. For more on this whole problem, see Shulamit Volkov, 'The dynamics of dissimulation: Ostjuden and German Jews', *The Jewish Response to German Culture*, eds Jehuda Reinharz and Walter Schatzberg (Hanover, NH and London 1985), 192–211 and 'Selbstgefälligkeit und Selbsthaß', *Antisemitismus als kultureller Code*, 2nd edn (Munich 2000), 181–96; see also Charlotte Schoell-Glass, *Aby Warburg und der Antisemitismus: Kulturwissenschaft als Geistespolitik* (Frankfurt am Main 1998).
14. FC (letter from Aby Warburg to Charlotte Warburg, 24 Nov. 1898).
15. Roeck, *Der junge Aby Warburg* (note 7), 74.
16. On this whole nexus of ideas, see E. H. Gombrich, 'Aby Warburg und der Evolutionismus des 19. Jahrhunderts', *'Ekstatische Nymphe, trauernder Flußgott': Portrait eines Gelehrten*, eds Robert Galitz and Brita Reimers (Hamburg 1995), 52–73.
17. FC (letter from Aby Warburg to Mary Hertz, 8 May 1891).
18. Diaries 10.3 (25 May 1904).
19. Diaries 10.1 (31 Jan. 1901).
20. Diaries 10.1 (19 July 1894).
21. FC (letter from Mary Hertz to Aby Warburg, 15 May 1897).
22. AWI (Mary Hertz's diary, 26 Oct. 1890).
23. AWI (letter from Mary Hertz to Aby Warburg, 26 July 1894).
24. FC (letter from Mary Hertz to Aby Warburg, 11 June 1891).
25. AWI (Mary Hertz's diary, 26 Oct. 1890).
26. Chernow, *The Warburgs* (note 1), 67.
27. Björn Biester, *Der innere Beruf zur Wissenschaft: Paul Ruben (1866–1943). Studien zur deutsch-jüdischen Wissenschaftsgeschichte* (Hamburg 2001), 89.
28. See Biester, *Der innere Beruf zur Wissenschaft* (note 27).
29. GC (letter from Paul Ruben to Aby Warburg, 24 April 1897).
30. Diaries 10.3 (30 Jan. 1910).
31. FC (letter to Moritz Warburg to Aby Warburg, 16 April 1897). The first quotation comes from Goethe's *Faust*, the second is attributed to Martin Luther.
32. FC (letter from Aby Warburg to Charlotte Warburg, 21 June 1897).

33. FC (letter from Aby Warburg to Charlotte Warburg, 13 June 1897).
34. FC (letter from Mary Hertz to Moritz and Charlotte Warburg, 11 July 1897).
35. FC (letter from Aby Warburg to Charlotte Warburg, 3 July 1897).
36. FC (letter from Aby Warburg to Moritz Warburg, 7 July 1897).
37. FC (letter from Moritz Warburg to Aby Warburg, 9 Sept. 1897).
38. FC (letter from Moritz Warburg to Aby Warburg, 7 Oct. 1897).

Chapter 5 Wonderful light: A city at the dawn of the modern age

1. Isolde Kurz, *Florentinische Erinnerungen* (Stuttgart and Berlin 1920), 70–2; see also Anna Maria von Winterfeld, 'Arnold Böcklin und Florenz', *Storia dell'arte e politica culturale intorno al 1900: La fondazione dell'Istituto Germanico di Storia dell'Arte a Firenze*, ed. Max Seidel (Venice 1999), 143–77, esp. 158–9.

2. Charles Godfrey Leland, *Etruscan Magic and Occult Remedies* (New York 1963).

3. See for example the advertisement by the faith healer Anna d'Amico in *Fieramosca: Giornale del Popolo*, xviii/5 (5/6 Jan. 1898).

4. See 'Censimento del 10.2.1901', *Nuova Antologia*, iv (1902), 765. The literacy level was 84.1%, compared with 34.7% in Caltanisetta, 82% in Rome and 93.6% in Turin. In the surrounding area it was 60%. These figures should be treated with some caution, however, as it is unclear on what basis they were compiled. In 1888/9 only 48% of Italian children aged between six and ten attended school, a figure which rises to 54% in the north of the country; see Rudolf Lill, *Geschichte Italiens in der Neuzeit*, 4th edn (Darmstadt 1988), 210; see also *La Nazione* xl (1 Nov. 1898).

5. For a comprehensive account, see Marco Meriggi, 'Italienisches und deutsches Bürgertum im Vergleich', *Bürgertum im 19. Jahrhundert*, i: *Einheit und Vielfalt Europas*, ed. Jürgen Kocka (Göttingen 1995), 147–65; and Ernesto Sestan, 'La destra toscana', *Rassegna storica toscana*, vii/2–4 (1961), 227.

6. C. Pazzagli, 'La vita sociale', *Firenze 1815–1945: Un bilancio storiografico*, eds Giorgio Mori and Piero Roggi (Florence 1990), 181; on life among the upper classes in Florence, see Arnaldo Nesti, *Vita di palazzo: Vita quotidiana, riti e passioni nell'aristocrazia fiorentina tra Otto e Novecento* (Florence 1994).

7. C. Romby, 'Immagine urbana, presenze industriali, divenire della città', *Arte e industria a Firenze* (Florence 1983), 17–18.

8. Kurz, *Florentinische Erinnerungen* (note 1), 27–9, esp. 27.

9. Theodor Fontane, *Werke, Schriften und Briefe*, eds Walter Keitel and Helmuth Nürnberger, 20 vols (Munich 1994), vol. iii/3: 976 ('Erinnerungen, ausgewählte Schriften und Kritiken').

10. See Carlo A. Corsini, 'La demografia', *Firenze 1815–1945* (note 6); according to *La popolazione fiorentina: Archivio comunale di Firenze* (p.30), there were 114,000 inhabitants in the city in 1861; the official statistics for 1890 numbers 187,075 men, women and children.

11. Between 1810 and 1936 the number of nuclear family households rose from 42.9% to 43.1%, while the percentage of large families declined from 12.9% in 1810 to 10.2% in 1936. Only one other statistic for 1951 indicates that conditions in Florence were approaching those of any other modern industrial city: by this date, the number of small households with up to three persons had increased to 59.9% of the total, while the number of large households with more than six persons had dropped to 8.9%.

12. Corsini, 'La demografia' (note 10), 16.

13. Typhoid fever struck in 1801 and 1817, while in 1833 an influenza epidemic caused the mortality rate to peak again. This was followed in 1855 by a severe outbreak of cholera resulting in 800 deaths per 10,000 of the population – more than double the normal rate. A further increase was recorded in 1862.

14. See L. Castelli, *La popolazione e la mortalità del centennio 1791–1890: Studi e raffronti con la salute pubblica nel biennio 1891–92* (Florence 1893), Table 2: 'Curva della mortalità di Firenze'; see also Davis Ottati, *L'acquedotto di Firenze dal 1860 ad oggi* (Florence 1992) and *Firenze pulita: Il problema dei rifiuti urbani dal medioevo ad oggi* (Florence 1990).
15. Isolde Kurz, *Pilgerfahrt nach dem Unerreichlichen: Lebensrückschau* (Tübingen 1938), 316.
16. GC (25 Feb. 1898).
17. See for example *Il Marzocco*, vii/17 (27 April 1902).
18. *Il Marzocco*, ii/41 (14 Nov. 1897), 2.
19. See Chapter 10 below; see also Carlo Cresti and Silvano Fei, 'Le vicende del "risanamento" di Mercato Vecchio a Firenze', *Storia urbana*, i/2 (1977), 99–126; Silvano Fei, *Firenze 1881–1898: La grande operazione urbanistica* (Rome 1977); and *Firenze 1815–1945* (note 10), 169–84 (Bibliography).
20. Luciano Artusi and Vincenzo Giannetti, '*A vita nuova*': *Ricordi e vicende della grande operazione urbanistica che distrusse il centro storico di Firenze* (Florence 1997).
21. Marie-José Cambieri Tosi, *Carlo Placci: Maestro di cosmopoli nella Firenze fra Otto e Novecento* (Florence 1894), 31.
22. Kurz, *Florentinische Erinnerungen* (note 1), 21–5; see also Lea Nissim Rossi, 'Vita fiorentina', *Rassegna storica toscana*, xii (1966), 71–90, esp. 71–2.
23. BCF, 64 D 1/32 (17 Nov. 1897), 184; Davis Ottati, *Storia dell'illuminazione pubblica a Firenze* (Florence 1988); and Lionello Giorgio Boccia, *Firenze: Illuminazione pubblica e ambiente urbano* (Florence 1983).
24. For more on Rosadi, see Cosimo Ceccuti, 'Un parlamentare fiorentino in età giolittiana: Giovanni Rosadi', *Rassegna storica toscana*, xxvii/1 (1981), 73–96.
25. Kurz, *Pilgerfahrt nach dem Unerreichlichen* (note 15), 150; Ferdinand Runkel, *Böcklin-Memoiren: Tagebuchblätter von Böcklins Gattin Angela* (Berlin 1910), vi.
26. See BCF, 64 D 1/31 (15 Feb. 1897), 1189–90.
27. See also BCF, 64 D 1/37, p. 2252; and 64 D 1/38, pp. 952–4.
28. For more on Puvis de Chavannes, see Stefan Germer, *Historizität und Autonomie: Studien zu Wandbildern des 19. Jahrhunderts im Frankreich des 19. Jahrhunderts. Ingres, Chassériau, Chenavard und Puvis de Chavannes* (Hildesheim, Zurich and New York 1988).
29. See *Fieramosca: Giornale del Popolo*, xxi/14 (14/15 Jan. 1901) and xxi/15 (15/16 Jan. 1901); *La Nazione*, xlv/5 (5 Jan. 1903), lxiii/91 (1 April 1901); xlv/320 (16 Nov. 1903).
30. Luigi Rava, 'Il telefono in Italia', *Nuova Antologia*, iv/93 (1901), 705–12, esp. 708.
31. In Germany there was on average a telegraph office for every 2,360 inhabitants, whereas in Italy the figure was one for every 5,509.
32. Elvira Grifi, *Saunterings in Florence: A New Artistic and Practical Hand-Book for English and American Tourists* (Florence 1896), xiv–xv.
33. BCF, 64 D 1/34 (18 Dec. 1899), also 4 Jan. 1900, p. 1034 and 64 D 1/35, p. 1560; see also Francesco Ogliari and Franco Sapi, *Segmenti di lavoro: Storia dei trasporti italiani* (Milan 1971), vi.47 and 102; and Albert Schram, *Railways and the Formation of the Italian State in the Nineteenth Century* (Cambridge 1997).
34. See BCF, 64 D 1/38 (3 Jan. 1902), 36–7.
35. See Giovanni Rosadi's contribution to the discussion at the council meeting on 20 July 1900 in BCF, 64 D 1/35, pp. 2084–5. A bicycle for the local police force cost 275 lire a year in 1900 (p. 2087). A commandant in the *Guardie comunali* earned 2,400 lire a year, a brigadier 1,500 lire. It would have cost a female cemetery attendant more than ten months' salary to buy a bicycle; see BCF 64 D 1/32, pp. 206 and 626. In Germany there was 'a great leap forward in the history of the bicycle' in the years around 1890; see Joachim Radkau, *Das Zeitalter der Nervosität: Deutschland zwischen Bismarck und Hitler* (Munich and Vienna 1998), 203.
36. See Grifi, *Saunterings in Florence* (note 32), xiv.
37. Cesare Lombroso, 'Il ciclismo nel diletto', *Nuova Antologia*, iv/86 (1900), 5–14.

38. BCF, 64 D 1/38 (3 Feb. 1902), 270; more generally, see Fabio Tomasetti, 'Trasporti pubblici nella città e nel territorio di Firenze 1860–1915', *Storia urbana*, iii/7 (1979), 115–62.
39. *La Nazione*, xvl/111 (21 April 1903).
40. See, in particular, BCF, 64 D 1/37, p. 2252.
41. BCF, 64 D 1/32 (21 March 1898), 751.
42. Ibid., 759.
43. Ibid., 758.
44. DLA, A: Isolde Kurz, 'Rede in der Deutschen Akademie', fol. 1.
45. Kurz, *Florentinische Erinnerungen* (note 1), 18.
46. On this section, see Diaries 10.1 (31 Dec. 1900), 50v. Among 'great feats' he numbered Carlyle's *Sartor Resartus* and the fact that Emperor Wilhelm listened to his advisors, this being a precondition for the establishment of a German national state. Warburg also expressed his admiration for Gottfried Keller's *Die Leute von Seldwyla*, for Heinrich Heine's *Der Rabbi von Bacharach* and for Ludwig Feuerbach's *Theogony* (see above, p. 38). In his diary Warburg refers to 'Feuerbach's *Antigone*', but he must have meant the philosopher's *Theogony*, the similarities between the ideas formulated here and what we otherwise know about Warburg's religious feelings being too striking to ignore. Warburg must have become familiar with Feuerbach's philosophy of religion during his years of study in Bonn, presumably through Hermann Usener. The painter Anselm Feuerbach is known to have produced a drawing of Antigone, but Warburg cannot have been aware of its existence.
47. Aby Warburg, *Schlangenritual: Ein Reisebericht*, ed. Ulrich Raulff (Berlin 1995), 56.
48. Hermann Hesse, *Italien: Schilderungen, Tagebücher, Gedichte, Aufsätze, Buchbesprechungen und Erzählungen* (Frankfurt am Main 1996), 110.
49. Stephan Oettermann, *Das Panorama: Die Geschichte eines Massenmediums* (Frankfurt am Main 1980).
50. *La Nazione*, xxxix/31 (31 Jan. 1897); see also Louis Lumière, 'The Lumière cinématographe', *Journal of the Society of Movie Pictures*, xxvii/1 (1936), reproduced in *Technological History of Motion Pictures and Television: An Anthology from the Pages of The Journal of the Society of Motion Picture and Television Engineers*, ed. Raymond Fielding (Berkeley, CA 1967), 49–51.
51. *La Nazione*, xlii/144–5 (24/5 May 1900).
52. Iacopo Gelli, 'Il duello in Italia nell'ultimo ventennio (1897–1899)', *Nuova Antologia*, iv/91 (1901), 151–60.
53. BCF, 64 D 1/33, pp. 294–5.
54. Giulio Bizzozero, 'Le macchine da scrivere dal punto di vista dell'igiene', *Nuova Antologia*, iv/72 (1897), 45–68.
55. BCF, 64 D 1/32 (2 Feb. 1898), 664.
56. *La Nazione*, xxxix/184 (3 July 1897).
57. Vernon Lee, 'Charcoal and ice', *Genius Loci and The Enchanted Woods* (Leipzig 1906), 73–8, esp. 77–8.
58. C[harles] J[oseph] Singer, E[ric] J[ohn] Holmyard, A[lfred] R[upert] Hall and Trevor I[lltyd] Williams, *A History of Technology* (Oxford 1982), v.45–51.
59. Ouida [Louise de la Ramée], 'Pescarel', *Nuovo Osservatore Fiorentino* (Florence 1885).
60. Arnold Bennett, *The Journals*, ed. Frank Swinnerton (Harmondsworth 1971), 288 (1 April 1910), 294 (5 April 1910), 307 (19 April 1910) and 314 (5 May 1910); see also Bennett's 'Night and morning in Florence', *English Review*, v (1910), 442–55.
61. Marcel Proust, *In Search of Lost Time*, trans. C. K. Scott Moncrieff and Terence Kilmartin, rev. D. J. Enright, 6 vols (London 2000), i.384.
62. Paul Klee, *Tagebücher 1898–1918*, ed. Wolfgang Kersten (Stuttgart 1988), 138.
63. Alan Sheridan, *André Gide: A Life in the Present* (London 1998), 100.
64. Lilian Whiting, *The Florence of Landor* (Boston 1905), 309.

65. Thomas Mann, *Briefe an Otto Grautoff 1894–1901 und Ida Boy-Ed 1903–1928*, ed. Peter De Mendelssohn (Frankfurt am Main 1975), 137; see also Egon Eilers, 'Perspektiven und Montage: Studien zu Thomas Manns Schauspiel "Fiorenza" ' (diss., University of Marburg 1967).
66. Fred Kaplan (ed.), *Travelling in Italy with Henry James* (New York 1994), 226.
67. FC (letter from Aby Warburg to Charlotte Warburg, 8 Feb. 1901).
68. Adolf von Hildebrand, *Briefwechsel mit Conrad Fiedler*, ed. Günther Jachmann (Dresden 1927), 28 (letter of 16 May 1872).
69. Rainer Maria Rilke, *Das Florenzer Tagebuch*, eds Ruth Sieber-Rilke and Carl Sieber (Frankfurt am Main and Leipzig 1994), 13.
70. Rilke, *Das Florenzer Tagebuch* (note 69), 26.
71. Kurz, 'Rede in der Deutschen Akademie' (note 44), fol. 2.

Chapter 6 Florentine circles

1. Thus Jacob Burckhardt on Rome.
2. AWI (Mary Hertz's diary entry, 10 Dec. 1891).
3. FC (letter from Mary Warburg to Charlotte Warburg, 22 Nov. 1897).
4. FC (letter from Aby Warburg to Charlotte Warburg, 28 Oct. 1897).
5. FC (letter from Mary Warburg to Charlotte Warburg, 6 Dec. 1897).
6. Now the Viale Spartaco Lavagnini. The house was torn down in the 1960s. The relevant documents are in the Ufficio Toponomastica in Florence.
7. See AGV, Benutzerbücher (22 Oct. 1896): Miß Hallgarten, 42 Viale Margherita; for a note on Alice Hallgarten, see Ron Chernow, *The Warburgs: The Twentieth-Century Odyssey of a Remarkable Jewish Family* (New York in 1993), 79.
8. BCF, 64 D 1/33 (12 June 1899), 1071–2, 1078; and 64 D 1/37 (4 July 1901), 1444–5.
9. See Fred Kaplan (ed.), *Travelling in Italy with Henry James* (New York 1994), 226.
10. FC (letter from Mary Warburg to Charlotte Warburg, 3 Nov. 1897).
11. FC (letter from Aby Warburg to Charlotte Warburg, 28 Oct. 1897).
12. FC (letter from Mary Warburg to Charlotte and Moritz Warburg, 4 March 1898): 'The letter's vignette is cut out of a photograph that we took last Sunday with Fritz's camera along with several others.'
13. FC (letter from Mary Warburg to Charlotte Warburg, 28 Dec. 1897).
14. See Mario Praz, *La filosofia dell'arredamento: I mutamenti nel gusto della decorazione interna attraverso i secoli dell'antica Roma ai nostri tempi* (Milan 1993), 68–9; on Florence, see Claudio Paolini, 'Oggetti come specchio dell'anima: Per una rilettura dell'artigianato artistico fiorentino nelle dimore degli anglo-americani', *Gli anglo-americani a Firenze: Idea e costruzione del Rinascimento*, ed. Marcello Fantoni (Rome 2000), 143–64.
15. AWI, 20.3 (Expenses for flat in Florence). In the years around 1897, 100 Italian lire were the equivalent of about 77 reichsmarks, or a little over £200 at today's prices (2008).
16. AWI, 20.3 (Expenses for flat in Florence); see also Diaries 10.1 (23 Oct. 1899). Here Warburg lists his annual outgoings, which between 1896/7 and 1899 dropped from 22,400 to 15,330 marks (= £66,000 to £45,000 at today's prices).
17. See Peter Gay, *The Bourgeois Experience: Victoria to Freud*, v: *Pleasure Wars* (London 1998), 50.
18. FC (letter from Charlotte Warburg to Mary and Aby Warburg, 26 May 1898).
19. Diaries 10.1 (19–23 May 1898); for more on Umbria, see Chapter 11 below.
20. BCF, 64 D 1/33, p.1078; 64 D 1/37 (4 July 1901), 1444–5.
21. FC (letter from Mary Warburg to Charlotte Warburg, 30 May 1898). The house in which the Warburgs lived was torn down in 1963. The building that now occupies the site is 27 Viale Giovanni Milton. The relevant documents are in the Ufficio Toponomastica in Florence.

22. According to the land register in the Ufficio Toponomastica in Florence.
23. Diaries 10.1 (19 Oct. 1900) and AWI, 23 (Address Books). The property is still 1 Via Paolo Toscanelli.
24. FC (letter from Aby Warburg to Charlotte and Moritz Warburg, 17 Jan. 1900): 'You can barely get a decent red wine here, even though you sometimes need it.'
25. FC (letter from Mary Warburg to Charlotte Warburg, 20 Feb. 1901); for more on the *Circolo degli artisti*, see *La Nazione*, xxxix/29 (29 Jan. 1897).
26. FC (letter from Aby Warburg to Charlotte Warburg, 28 Jan. 1900); for more on the founding of the Naval Association, see *Fieramosca: Giornale del Popolo*, xx/29 (29/30 Jan. 1900).
27. See *La Nazione*, xli/29 (29 Jan. 1899) and xlv/28 (28 Jan. 1903).
28. Diaries, 10.1 (15 Nov. 1903).
29. FC (letter from Mary Warburg to Moritz and Charlotte Warburg, 4 March 1898).
30. Isolde Kurz, *Pilgerfahrt nach dem Unerreichlichen: Lebensrückschau* (Tübingen 1938), 404.
31. GC (letter from Alice Hallgarten to Mary and Aby Warburg, 22 Jan. 1898).
32. *Il Marzocco*, iii/5 (6 March 1898), 3; for a further performance in 1899, see *Il Marzocco*, iv/16 (21 May 1899).
33. FC (letter from Aby Warburg to Charlotte Warburg, 25 Jan. 1898).
34. See AWI, GC (20 Sept. 1897) for a comment on a meeting at the Villa Prevost with Oskar Bulle, Dove's successor as correspondent of the *Allgemeine Zeitung*.
35. Hans W. Hubert, *Das Kunsthistorische Institut in Florenz: Von der Gründung bis zum hundertjährigen Jubiläum (1897–1997)* (Florence 1997).
36. NL Bode 5251/1, 9.3 (letter from Aby Warburg to Wilhelm Bode, 2 Aug. 1902).
37. For Warburg's comments on Schmarsow, see NL Bode, 5251/1, 1.1; for his comments on Gronau, see NL Bode, 5251/1, 20.1. On Gronau, see also Diaries 10.1 (5 April 1904) and Ernest Samuels, *Bernard Berenson: The Making of a Connoisseur* (Cambridge, MA and London 1979), 322.
38. NL Bode, 5251/1, 11.1–2 (letter from Aby Warburg to Wilhelm Bode). For more on Steinmann, see Hubert, *Das Kunsthistorische Institut in Florenz* (note 35), 28; see also Arnold Esch, 'L'esordio degli istituti di ricerca tedeschi in Italia: I primi passi verso l'istituzionalizzazione della ricerca nel campo delle scienze umanistiche all'estero 1870–1914', *Storia dell'arte e politica culturale intorno al 1900: La fondazione dell'Istituto Germanico di Storia dell'Arte a Firenze*, ed. Max Seidel (Venice 1999), 223–48, esp. 235–7; and Christof Thoenes, 'Geschichte des Instituts', *Max-Planck-Gesellschaft: Berichte und Mitteilungen*, iii (1991), 9–35.
39. NDB, iii (Berlin 1957), 538; Gino Luzzatto, 'Necrologio Roberto Davidsohn', *Nuova Rivista Storica*, xxi (1937); Friedrich Schneider, 'Robert Davidsohn als der Geschichtsschreiber von Florenz', *Deutsches Dante-Jahrbuch*, xxviii (New Series xix) (1949), 165–72; and Steffi Roettgen, 'Dal "Börsencourier" di Berlino al "Genio" di Firenze: Lo storico Robert Davidsohn (1835–1937) e il suo inedito lascito fiorentino', *Storia dell'arte e politica culturale intorno al 1900* (note 38), 312–58. A number of letters and postcards from Robert and Fili Davidsohn to Isolde Kurz are preserved in DLA (A: Nachlaß Isolde Kurz).
40. NL Bode, 5251/1, 13.1 (letter from Aby Warburg to Wilhelm Bode, 4 March 1903).
41. Firenze, Biblioteca Ricciardiana, Carteggio Fucini, Cass. 4/7 (29 Nov. 1908).
42. Namely the *Accademia dei Lincei* and the widely respected *Deputazione toscana di storia patria*. In 1906 he was appointed to a commission set up to see into the restoration of Ghirlandaio's frescos in Santa Maria Novella; see *La Nazione*, xl/58 (27 Feb. 1898) and BNF, Fondo Chiappelli, Cass. 3, N. 81 (21 Jan. 1906).
43. See *La Nazione*, xl/216 (4 Aug. 1898) and Roettgen, 'Dal "Börsencourier" di Berlino' (note 39), 314.
44. Roettgen, 'Dal "Börsencourier" di Berlino' (note 39), 318.
45. Diaries 10.1 (14 April 1904).

46. BNF, Fondo Chiappelli, Cass. 3, N. 81.
47. FC (letter from Aby Warburg to Mary Warburg, 30 Nov. 1902).
48. FC (letter from Aby Warburg to Mary Warburg, 24 Oct. 1902).
49. Jacques Mesnil, *En Italie: G. d'Annunzio* (Brussels 1894); *Le Parti socialiste italien* (Brussels 1896); and *Les Mouvements anarchistes* (Brussels 1897). An important source, albeit one that does not cover the period discussed here, is the archives of the Casa Buonarotti in Florence. I am grateful to David Bianco, who is currently preparing a longer study of Dwelshauvers, for drawing these references to my attention. For earlier writings, see Fritz Saxl, 'Three "Florentines": Herbert Horne, Aby Warburg, Jacques Mesnil', *Lectures* (London 1957), i.331–48.
50. See Max Nettlau, *Elisée Reclus: Anarchist und Gelehrter 1830–1905* (Berlin 1928).
51. Saxl, 'Three "Florentines" ' (note 49), i.343; see also Mesnil's foreword to *Botticelli* (Paris 1938).
52. E. H. Gombrich, *Aby Warburg: An Intellectual Biography* (Oxford 1986), 321–2.
53. GC (letter from Aby Warburg to Jacques Mesnil, 2 Nov. 1897).
54. GC (letter from Alfred Doren to Aby Warburg, 30 May 1901).
55. GC (letter from Alfred Doren to Aby Warburg, 22 Dec. 1900).
56. Diaries 10.1 (23 Oct. 1902).
57. Diaries 10.1 (31 March 1900).
58. Diaries 10.1 (1 Nov. 1902); see also Adolph Goldschmidt, *Lebenserinnerungen 1863–1944*, ed. Marie Roosen-Runge-Mollwo (Berlin 1989), 103–4, n. 106.
59. For more on Ludmilla Assing (1821–80), see Isolde Kurz, *Florentinische Erinnerungen* (Stuttgart and Berlin 1920), 105–8.
60. Kurz, *Florentinische Erinnerungen* (note 59), 102–3.
61. On the increasingly professional approach to art history in Italy, see Giovanni Agosti, *La nascita della storia dell'arte in Italia. Adolfo Venturi: Dal museo all'università* (Venice 1996).
62. Diaries 10.1 (14 April 1904).
63. FC (Mary Warburg to Charlotte Warburg, 6 Jan. 1898 and 31 Jan. 1898).
64. BNF, Fosc. XIII, 17e (1 April 1884).
65. See Martin Gregor-Dellin, *Richard Wagner: Sein Leben, sein Werk, sein Jahrhundert* (Munich and Zurich 1980), 298–309; trans. by J. Maxwell Brownjohn as *Richard Wagner: His Life, His Work, His Century* (London 1983), 194–205.
66. Wolfram Mauser, *Karl Hillebrand: Leben, Werk, Wirkung* (Dornbirn 1960); R. Vierhaus, 'Zeitgeschichte und Zeitkritik im essayistischen Werk Karl Hillebrands', *Historische Zeitschrift*, ccxxi (1975), 304–25; Jean Nurdin, *L'Idée d'Europe dans la pensée allemande à l'époque Bismarckienne* (Metz 1977); *Karl Hillebrand: Eretico d'Europa, Atti del Seminario*, ed. Lucia Borghese (Florence 1984); and Alfred von Reumont, *Charakterbilder aus der neueren Geschichte Italiens* (Leipzig 1886).
67. *Karl Hillebrand: Mostra di documenti*, ed. Lucia Borghese (Florence 1984), 23. The 'bel ovile' or 'beautiful sheepfold' is presumably a reference to Dante's *Paradiso*, Canto xxv, line 4.
68. Adolf von Hildebrand, *Briefwechsel mit Conrad Fiedler*, ed. Günther Jachmann (Dresden 1927), 57 (letter of 11 Feb. 1876).
69. Kurz, *Pilgerfahrt nach dem Unerreichlichen* (note 30), 212–13.
70. Angela Koller, 'Südsehnsucht und Süderlebnis bei Isolde Kurz' (diss. University of Zurich, 1963).
71. Kurz, *Pilgerfahrt nach dem Unerreichlichen* (note 30), 259.
72. See Georg Karo, *Selbstgespräche: Aus Heinrich Hombergers Nachlaß* (Munich 1928).
73. Kurz, *Pilgerfahrt nach dem Unerreichlichen* (note 30), 258.
74. BStBM, Heyse-Nachlaß (letter from Isolde Kurz to Paul Heyse, 9 Nov. 1904): 'Dear Friend, in my heart I have always said "du" to you from the moment when you shed the final, brightest light on my father's joyless life. That I was now able to say it openly often robbed me of speech or made it seem different from the way it sounded in my soul.'

75. FC (letter from Mary Warburg to Charlotte Warburg, 15 Feb. 1898).
76. Isolde Kurz, *Meine Mutter* (Tübingen 1926). The remnants of her estate, including a letter from Jessie Hillebrand, are now in the Marbach Literary Archives.
77. Kurz, *Florentinische Erinnerungen* (note 59), 121.
78. Kurz, *Pilgerfahrt nach dem Unerreichlichen* (note 30), 250–51. The episode probably took place in the autumn of 1883; see John C. G. Röhl, *Wilhelm II.: Die Jugend des Kaisers 1859–1888* (Munich 1993), 432.
79. Adolf von Hildebrand, 'Edgar Kurz'.
80. NL Bode 5251/1, 23.2 (letter from Aby Warburg to Wilhelm Bode, 4 June 1904).
81. Eva Walter, *Isolde Kurz und ihre Familie: Eine Biographie* (Mühlacker/Irdning 1996), 198–200.
82. See the obituary in Diaries 10.1.
83. For more on Vanzetti, see Isolde Kurz's beautiful characterization in her 'Rede in der Deutschen Akademie', DLA, A, fol.7: 'Italianissimo in the older sense, half a mad condottiere from the Quattrocento, half a life-loving Venetian cavalier from the age of Goldoni.'
84. For more on the following, see Walter, *Isolde Kurz und ihre Familie* (note 81); and Kurz, *Florentinische Erinnerungen* (note 59) and *Pilgerfahrt nach dem Unerreichlichen* (note 30).
85. BStBM, Heyse-Nachlaß (letter from Isolde Kurz to Paul Heyse, no.7, *c*.1878).
86. See the correspondence in BStBM, Heyse-Nachlaß (21 Dec. 1878).
87. BStBM, Heyse-Nachlaß (letter from Isolde Kurz to Paul Heyse, no.13, 13 Feb. [1882]).
88. Kurz, *Pilgerfahrt nach dem Unerreichlichen* (note 30), 211.
89. BStBM, Heyse-Nachlaß (letter from Isolde Kurz to Paul Heyse, no.17, 10 July 1882).
90. Diaries 10.1 (15 March 1900).
91. Charlotte Nittke, 'Isolde Kurz und ihre Verleger: Geschichte der Buchveröffentlichungen einer Erfolgsautorin zwischen 1888 und 1944', *Archiv für Geschichte des Buchwesens*, xxxiv (1990); for an overview of her fees, see pp. 110–12. The following quotation is taken from p. 75.
92. Nittke, 'Isolde Kurz und ihre Verleger' (note 91), 78.
93. See the appendix to the eighth reprinting of Kurz's *Florentinische Erinnerungen* (note 59).
94. DLA, A (Kurz, Manuscript 'Menschenleugner').
95. Kurz, *Pilgerfahrt nach dem Unerreichlichen* (note 30), 325.
96. BStBM, Heyse-Nachlaß (letter from Isolde Kurz to Paul Heyse, 14 March 1874): 'Mörike, whom to my immense delight I recently got to know in Stuttgart, gave me the enclosed poems, the love songs strike me as very familiar, but I don't know if they are in the anthology. He asked me to give you his very best wishes'; see also Kurz, *Meine Mutter* (note 76), 29.
97. On Maria Janitschek (1859–1927), see Isolde Wernbacher, 'Maria Janitscheks Persönlichkeit und dichterisches Werk' (diss., University of Vienna, 1950).
98. DLA, A: Kurz (letter from Aby Warburg to Isolde Kurz, 11 Feb. 1901). Warburg gives his correspondent bibliographical information about Napoleon.
99. Koller, 'Südsehnsucht und Süderlebnis' (note 70), 35–7.
100. Warburg was presumably annoyed that Kurz used images from his essay 'Bildniskunst und florentinisches Bürgertum' in the first edition of her *Stadt des Lebens* (Stuttgart 1902) without acknowledging a source for them; see FC (letter from Isolde Kurz to Aby Warburg, 1 Nov. 1902); see also FC (letter from Aby Warburg to Mary Warburg, 7 Nov. 1902: 'Business with Isolde superficially settled.')
101. GC (Isolde Kurz to Mary Warburg, *c*.1900).
102. Isolde Kurz, *Die Nacht im Teppichsaal: Erlebnisse eines Wanderers* (Tübingen 1933).

Chapter 7 The Florence of foreigners

1. Sigmund Freud, *Unser Herz zeigt nach dem Süden: Reisebriefe 1895–1923*, ed. Christfried Tögel (Berlin 2002) (letter from Sigmund Freud to Martha Freud, 7 Sept. 1896).

2. Christfried Tögel, *Berggasse – Pompeji und zurück: Sigmund Freuds Reisen in die Vergangenheit* (Tübingen 1989), 88–93.

3. On the Gabinetto Vieusseux, see Maurizio Bossi, 'Cultura tedesca al Gabinetto Vieusseux tra Otto e Novecento', *Storia dell'arte e politica culturale intorno al 1900: La fondazione dell'Istituto Germanico di Storia dell'Arte a Firenze*, ed. Max Seidel (Venice 1999), 381–90.

4. French nationals and people with German names – there may be some Swiss and Austrians among them – make up only around 4% of all users. Even Italians constitute a greater percentage, with 19% of the total. The remainder comprises individuals whose nationality is unclear.

5. Isolde Kurz, *Pilgerfahrt nach dem Unerreichlichen: Lebensrückschau* (Tübingen 1938), 162; the users' books contain between 25 and 30 identifiable references.

6. Alan Sheridan, *André Gide: A Life in the Present* (London 1998), 100.

7. It seems that, as far as possible, visitors avoided the left bank of the Arno and the quarters around San Spirito and the Church of Santa Maria del Carmine, although an exception was the Via Maggio, which appears as an address in eleven entries. On the parts of the city inhabited by English and American visitors, see Daniela Lamberini, 'Residenti anglo-americani e genius loci: Ricostruzioni e restauri delle dimore fiorentine', *Gli anglo-americani a Firenze: Idea e costruzione dell' Rinascimento*, ed. Marcello Fantoni (Rome 2000), 125–42, esp. 133–4.

8. Charles Loeser, AGV, p. 144 (21 Dec, 1897); see also Marcello Vannucci, *L'avventura degli stranieri in Toscana: Ottocento e novecento: Fra cronaca e storia* (Aosta 1981), 103–4; and Ernest Samuels, *Bernard Berenson: The Making of a Connoisseur* (Cambridge, MA and London 1979), *passim*.

9. AGV, p. 140; see also the entry for 9 Feb. 1894 (p. 16), where Warburg (11 Via del Presto) has entered his name as a user alongside that of Alfred Doren.

10. William D. Howells, *Tuscan Cities* (Leipzig 1891), 21.

11. Cristina Tagliaferri, *Olschki: Un secolo di editoria 1886–1986: La libreria antiquaria editrice Leo S. Olschki (1886–1945)* (Florence 1986), 67: 'An American town built in the style of the Italian Renaissance.'

12. Paul Klee, *Tagebücher 1898–1918*, ed. Wolfgang Kersten (Stuttgart 1988), 135.

13. Howells, *Tuscan Cities* (note 10), 22.

14. *Firenze d'oggi* (Florence 1896), 55; see also Hans Barth, *Osteria: Kulturgeschichtlicher Führer durch Italiens Schenken vom Gardasee bis Capri* (Stuttgart 1911), 134–6.

15. Giuliana Artom Treves, *The Golden Ring: The Anglo-Florentines 1847–1862* (London, New York and Toronto 1956), 10–11; and John William De Forest, *European Acquaintance: Being Sketches of People in Europe* (New York 1858), 192–3.

16. *La Nazione*, xxxix/29 (29 Jan. 1897).

17. Theodor Fontane, *Werke, Schriften und Briefe*, eds Walter Keitel and Helmuth Nürnberger, 20 vols (Munich 1994), vol. iii/3: 969 ('Erinnerungen, ausgewählte Schriften und Kritiken').

18. Ardengo Soffici, *Il salto vitale*, iii: *Giovinezza* (Florence 1954), 85.

19. Hans Barth, *Est! Est! Est! Italienischer Schenkenführer* (Oldenburg and Leipzig 1902), 27.

20. Thomas Rietzschel, *Theodor Däubler: Eine Collage seiner Biographie* (Leipzig 1988), 123.

21. Fred Robert von Klement, *Bei Lapi in Florenz* (Salo 1911) (copy in the Villa Romana Archives, Florence); see also Arnold Bennett, *The Journals*, ed. Frank Swinnerton (Harmondsworth 1971), 318–19 (15 May 1910); and Barth, *Osteria* (note 14), 140–41.

22. For a number of anecdotes about Otto Erich Hartleben, see Selma Hartleben, *'Mei Erich': Aus Otto Erichs Leben* (Berlin 1910).

23. Hanover, Stadtbibliothek, Hartlebeniana (4.4105).

24. Carol M. Osborne, 'Lizzie Boott at Bellosguardo', *The Italian Presence in American Art 1860–1920*, ed. Irma B. Jaffe (New York and Rome 1992), 188–99, esp. 194.

25. Carlo Placci, *Un furto* (1892); see Marie-José Cambieri Tosi, *Carlo Placci: Maestro di cosmopoli nella Firenze fra Otto e Novecento* (Florence 1894), 31.

26. Elvira Grifi, *Saunterings in Florence: A New Artistic and Practical Hand-Book for English and American Tourists* (Florence 1896), ix; see also Giuseppe Conti, 'Feste e usanze tradizionali', *Firenze Ottocento: Dalla dominazione 'illuminata' dei Lorena all'elezione a capitale d'Italia, fino agli ultimi anni del secolo, in un clima di generale rinnovamento: Cento anni di storia rivistati anche alla luce delle dirette testimonianze degli scrittori del tempo*, ed. Marcello Vannucci (Florence 1992), 266–83, esp. 266–9; on this point and the following, see Luciano Artusi and Silvano Gabrielli, *Le feste di Firenze* (Florence 1991). The festival of the 'scoppio del carro' continues to be celebrated to the present day.

27. AWI, FC (Mary Warburg to Charlotte Warburg, letter of 13 April 1898).

28. Anatole France, *Œuvres* (Paris 1923), xvi/2: 462–5.

29. On the council debates, see BCF, 64 D 1/32, pp. 870–71; 64 D 1/33, pp. 93–8; and *Il Marzocco*, iii (10 Oct. 1898).

30. G. Gabardi, 'Un teatro *sui generis*', *Firenze Ottocento* (note 26), 136–43, esp. 139.

31. Gabardi, 'Un teatro *sui generis*' (note 30), 142.

32. Thomas Kuchenbuch, *Die Welt um 1900: Unterhaltungs- und Technikkultur* (Stuttgart and Weimar 1992), 76.

33. Klee, *Tagebücher* (note 12), 135.

34. Ibid., 138.

35. *Il Marzocco*, iv/45 (10 Dec. 1899), 4.

36. A. Manzi, 'I teatri di musica', *Firenze Ottocento* (note 26), 119–28, esp. 120–1.

37. Eugenio Checchi, 'La popolarità del teatro in Italia', *Nuova Antologia*, iv (1897), 341–3.

38. See also Leo Charney and Vanessa R. Schwartz, *Cinema and the Invention of Modern Life* (Berkeley and Los Angeles 1995).

39. Vannucci, *L'avventura degli stranieri in Toscana* (note 8), 90–1.

40. Ibid., 88–90.

41. On the way in which Florence's galleries were 'stocked' following the dissolution of the monasteries, see Fiorenza Scalia, 'Il patrimonio artistico del Comune', *La città degli Uffizi* (Florence 1982), 43–51, esp. 44–5.

42. John Fleming, 'Art dealing in the Risorgimento III', *The Burlington Magazine*, cxxi/918 (1979), 568–80, esp. 575–6.

43. Lilian Whiting, *The Florence of Landor* (Boston 1905), 289–94.

44. Grifi, *Saunterings in Florence* (note 26), xxxi; on a Botticelli in the last-named Galleria Corsini, see Rainer Maria Rilke, *Das Florenzer Tagebuch*, eds Ruth Sieber-Rilke and Carl Sieber (Frankfurt am Main and Leipzig 1994), 89–90. A further description may be found in Bennett, *The Journals* (note 21), 304–5 (16 April 1910).

45. See Archivio Corsini, Diari (20 April 1898).

46. Bennett, *The Journals* (note 21), 305 (16 April 1910).

47. See Dominique Charles Fuchs, 'Il museo di Frederick Stibbert', *La città degli Uffizi* (note 41), 121–30; Fuchs, 'Acquisti dalle collezioni Demidoff e Favard nelle raccolte del Museo Stibbert', *L'idea di Firenze: Temi e interpretazioni dell'arte straniera dell'Ottocento*, eds Maurizio Bossi and Lucia Tonini (Florence 1989), 147–51; for the most recent study, see Susanne E. L. Probst, 'La fortuna del museo "inglese" a Firenze: Il Museo Stibbert', *Gli anglo-americani a Firenze: Idea e costruzione del Rinascimento*, ed. Marcello Fantoni (Rome 2000), 223–34. On Stibbert's death in 1906, his collection passed into the possession of the commune.

48. Diaries 10.1 (20 March 1901).

49. Sheridan, *Gide* (note 6), 257 and 133.

Chapter 8 North and South: Germans and Florentines

1. Wilhelm Waetzold, *Das klassische Land: Wandlungen der Italiensehnsucht* (Leipzig 1927). Burckhardt's *Der Cicerone* first appeared in 1855 and had been translated into English, at least in part, by 1873 and into French by 1885.
2. GC (letter from Alice Hallgarten to Aby and Mary Warburg, 23 Nov. 1897).
3. Isolde Kurz, *Deutsche und Italiener* (Stuttgart and Berlin 1919), 9–10.
4. See Alfred Kantorowicz's introduction and afterword to Heinrich Mann, *Die Göttinnen oder Die drei Romane der Herzogin von Assy* (Berlin 1969), 713.
5. *Max and Will: Max Beerbohm and William Rothenstein. Their Friendship and Letters 1893–1945*, eds Mary M. Lago and Karl Beckson (London 1975), 63 n. 2.
6. Arnold Bennett, *The Journals*, ed. Frank Swinnerton (Harmondsworth 1971), 300 (12 April 1910).
7. Fred Kaplan, *Henry James: The Imagination of a Genius* (London 1994), 191.
8. BStBM, Heyse-Nachlaß, I, 22 (23 Nov. 1896).
9. Sigmund Münz, *Italienische Reminiszenzen und Profile* (Vienna 1898), 218.
10. Robert Michels, *Italien von heute: Politik, Kultur, Wirtschaft* (Zurich and Leipzig 1930), 13; and Christof Dipper, 'Helden überkreuz oder das Kreuz mit den Helden: Wie Deutsche und Italiener die Heroen der nationalen Einigung (der anderen) wahrnahmen', *Jahrbuch des Historischen Kollegs 1999* (Munich 1999), 91–130, esp. 98.
11. Karl Hillebrand, obituary of Gino Capponi, *Zeiten, Völker, Menschen* (Strasbourg 1873–85), iv.266–90, esp. 278–9.
12. Georg Karo, *Selbstgespräche: Aus Heinrich Hombergers Nachlaß* (Munich 1928). The quotation 'standing on freedom's soil, a people free' is taken from Part II of Goethe's *Faust*.
13. Michels, *Italien von heute* (note 10), 14. Among the Germans who fought under Garibaldi was Ludwig Meyer, a friend of Heinrich Homberger. Wilhelm Rüstow was the chief of his general staff in Sicily.
14. Titus Heydenreich, 'Politische Dimensionen im literarischen Italienbild: Die zweite Hälfte des 19. Jahrunderts', *Immagini a confronto: Italia e Germania dal 1830 all'unificazione nazionale*, eds Angelo Ara and Rudolf Lill (Bologna and Berlin 1991), 283–303, esp. 294–5.
15. Jens Petersen, 'Risorgimento und italienischer Einheitsstaat im Urteil Deutschlands nach 1860', *Historische Zeitschrift*, ccxxxiv (1982), 63–99.
16. Published in St Petersburg in 1867; see also Paul David Fischer, *Italien und die Italiener am Schlusse des neunzehnten Jahrhunderts: Betrachtungen und Studien über die politischen, wirtschaftlichen und sozialen Zustände Italiens* (Berlin 1899).
17. Klaus von See, *Deutsche Germanen-Ideologie* (Frankfurt am Main 1970), 59–62. For a corresponding phenomenon in Italy, see Otto Weiss, 'Deutschland, Dreibund und öffentliche Meinung in Italien (1876–1883)', *Quellen und Forschungen aus italienischen Archiven und Bibliotheken*, lxxi (1991), 548–624, esp. 561.
18. Hillebrand, obituary of Capponi (note 11), iv.284.
19. Kurz, *Deutsche und Italiener* (note 3), 18.
20. Isolde Kurz, *Pilgerfahrt nach dem Unerreichlichen: Lebensrückschau* (Tübingen 1938), 347.
21. Isolde Kurz, 'Unsere Carlotta', *Der Ruf des Pan: Zwei Geschichten von Liebe und Tod*, 2nd edn (Tübingen n.d.), 85.
22. *La Nazione*, xl/321 (17 Nov. 1898).
23. *Il Marzocco*, vi (7 July 1901), 3.
24. Klaus Werner Jonas and Helmut Koopmann, *Die Thomas Mann-Literatur: Bibliographie der Kritik*, 3 vols (Berlin 1972–80, R/1997), iii.26–7.
25. Thomas Mann, 'Betrachtungen eines Unpolitischen', *Gesammelte Werke*, 13 vols (Frankfurt am Main 1974), xii.96; see also Jonas and Koopmann, *Die Thomas Mann-Literatur* (note 24), iii.51–3; and Walther Rehm, 'Der Renaissancekult um 1900 und

seine Überwindung', *Zeitschrift für deutsche Philologie*, liv (1929), 296–328, reprinted in Rehm, *Der Dichter und die neue Einsamkeit: Aufsätze zur Literatur um 1900* (Göttingen 1969), 74.

26. Thomas Mann, 'Der Willen zum Glück (1896)', *Gesammelte Werke* (note 25), viii.56.
27. Lea Ritter-Santini, 'Maniera Grande: Über italienische Renaissance und deutsche Jahrhundertwende', *Deutsche Literatur der Jahrhundertwende*, ed.Viktor Zmegac (Königstein 1981), 242–72, esp. 252–5.
28. Few German authors painted a realistic portrait of Italy; see Franz von Löher, *Das neue Italien* (Berlin 1883).
29. Thomas Mann, 'Tonio Kröger', *Gesammelte Werke* (note 25), viii.305–6; translated by David Luke in *Death in Venice, Tonio Kröger, and Other Writings*, ed. Frederick A. Lubich (New York 1999), 29.
30. Adolf von Hildebrand, *Briefwechsel mit Conrad Fiedler*, ed. Günther Jachmann (Dresden 1927), 223 (22 Jan. 1885).
31. Enrico Nencioni, *Impressioni e ricordi* (Florence 1923), 171; more generally, see Weiss, 'Deutschland, Dreibund und öffentliche Meinung' (note 17), 612.
32. AWI, 52.4, Gedichte und Dramatisches. It is more likely that the author was Robert Davidsohn. The poem may have been written for Jolles' wedding or for the arrival of the Warburgs in Florence. The first volume of Davidsohn's main work is famously dedicated to the 'Genius of Florence'.
33. FC (letter from Aby Warburg to Mary Warburg, 11 Oct. 1902).
34. On one occasion Hildebrand was able to write home to the effect that he was to be introduced to the Peruzzis' salon by Karl Hillebrand. (Among the Germans living in Florence, Heinrich Homberger similarly enjoyed this privilege.) See Bernhard Sattler, *Adolf von Hildebrand und seine Welt* (Munich 1962), 128 (13 April 1872); Karo, *Selbstgespräche* (note 12), xiii; on Placci, see Marie-José Cambieri Tosi, *Carlo Placci: Maestro di cosmopoli nella Firenze fra Otto e Novecento* (Florence 1984).
35. See Clara Louise Dentler, *Famous Foreigners in Florence 1400–1900* (Florence 1964), 140–41.
36. On Angelo de Gubernatis (1840–1913), see Lucia Strappini's article in the *Dizionario biografico degli italiani* (Rome 1988), xxxvi.227–35.
37. BNF, De Gub., C.V., 457, 25; Cass. 70, 64.
38. Weiss, 'Deutschland, Dreibund und öffentliche Meinung' (note 17), 601–2.
39. On Bakunin's visits to Florence and Tuscany, see Elio Conti, *Le origini del socialismo a Firenze (1860–1880)* (Rome 1950); and Max Nettlau, *Bakunin e l'Internazionale in Italia dal 1864 al 1872* (Geneva 1902), 45–7.
40. BNF, De Gub., 133,6 (Richard Wagner to Angelo de Gubernatis, 19 Feb. 1872 and 24 Feb. 1872); see also 133, 3.
41. BNF, De Gub., 133,3.
42. Cosima Wagner, *Die Tagebücher*, eds Martin Gregor-Dellin and Dietrich Mack, 2 vols (Munich and Zurich 1976–7), i.1017–19 (entries of 3–17 Dec. 1876).
43. AWI, GC (letter from Alice Hallgarten to Aby Warburg, 20 Nov. 1898).
44. BNF, Cass. 68, no. 81 (letter from Paul Heyse to Angelo de Gubernatis, 8 Feb. 1874).
45. BNF, Cass. 68, no. 81 (letter from Paul Heyse to Angelo de Gubernatis, 11 March 1892).
46. BNF, Cass. 68, no. 81 (letters of 9 May 1902 and 10 Sept. 1902).
47. Rosario Romeo, 'La Germania e la vita intellettuale dall'Unità alla prima guerra mondiale', *Momenti e problemi di storia contemporanea* (Assisi and Rome 1971), 153–84.
48. The reception of Schopenhauer's writings in Italy would also need to take account of the work of Helen Zimmern, who, although born in Germany, took English nationality and later moved to Fiesole, She wrote a monograph on Schopenhauer in 1876 and later translated Nietzsche's *Beyond Good and Evil* and *Human, All Too Human*; see

Eugenio Garin, 'Note sulla cultura a Firenze alla fine dell'Ottocento', *Giornale critico della Filosofia Italiana*, 6th series, v/1 (1985), 1–15, esp. 8–9.

49. Carlo Cantoni, 'Le università tedesche: Descritte e giudicate da professori tedeschi', *Nuova Antologia*, iv/75 (1898), 417–42; Giovanni Boglietti, 'L'evoluzione della democrazia socialista in Germania', *Nuova Antologia*, iv/78 (1898), 612–37; and Giovanni Franciosi, 'Il "misterio della passione" di Oberammergau', *Nuova Antologia*, iv/89 (1900), 300–11.

50. *Il Marzocco*, vii/48 (1902).

51. This can also be seen from the relevant figures. In 1900 the library of the Gabinetto Vieusseux contained almost 32,000 volumes, of which a mere 4.1% were by German-language authors, whereas 46% were by French writers and 34% by English writers. Italians managed to make up less than 16% of the total. These figures not only reflect the predominance of English-speaking tourists in Florence, they are also indicative of a Romance, Italo-French culture group.

52. See Alessandro Chiappelli, 'I poeti paesisti nel nostro secolo', *Nuova Antologia*, iv/74 (1899), 78–99, esp. 80.

53. *Il Marzocco*, viii/5 (2 Feb. 1902).

54. See, for example, Karo, *Selbstgespräche* (note 12), xvi; more generally, see Wilhelm Altgeld, 'Das Deutsche Reich im italienischen Urteil 1871–1945', *Das Deutsche Reich im Urteil der Großen Mächte und europäischen Nachbarn*, ed. Klaus Hildebrand (Munich 1995), 107–21, esp. 109–13; Weiss, 'Deutschland, Dreibund und öffentliche Meinung' (note 17), 557–8; Umberto Corsini, 'Il problema tedesco nell'immagine italiana tra il 1848 e il 1870', *Immagini a confronto* (note 14), 161–4.

55. See Weiss, 'Deutschland, Dreibund und öffentliche Meinung' (note 17), 610–11; see also Neal's obituary of Bismarck in *Il Marzocco*, iii/27 (27 Aug. 1898).

56. B. di San Giorgio, 'Lettere di Berlino', *La Nazione*, xli/45 (14 Feb. 1899); see also Karl-Egon Lönne, 'Relazioni tra la vita culturale della Germania e dell'Italia', *Annali della Facoltà di Lettere dell'Università di Napoli*, xxv (1982/3), 231–43; and Weiss, 'Deutschland, Dreibund und öffentliche Meinung' (note 17), 602–4.

57. On the following, see Marco Meriggi, 'Italienisches und deutsches Bürgertum im Vergleich', *Bürgertum im 19. Jahrhundert*, i: *Einheit und Vielfalt Europas*, ed. Jürgen Kocka (Göttingen 1995), 147–65.

58. In 1882 the figure stood at 62%.

59. In Italy there were 0.74 lawyers for every 1000 inhabitants, whereas the figure north of the Alps was only 0.12.

60. See Romeo, 'La Germania' (note 47), 162; the reader may recall Sidney Sonnino's 'Torniamo allo statuto' and the council debates on the subject; see Otto Weiss, 'Staat, Regierung und Parlament im norddeutschen Bund und im Kaiserreich im Urteil der Italiener', *Quellen und Forschungen aus italienischen Archiven und Bibliotheken*, lxvi (1986), 310–77, esp. 350–51, 354–5 and 365.

61. See, for example, the descriptions of Berlin in Ferdinando Fontana, *In Tedescheria* (Milan 1883), 25–8; see also Weiss, 'Deutschland, Dreibund und öffentliche Meinung' (note 17), 612–13.

62. Giuseppe Antonio Borgese, *La nuova Germania* (Turin 1909), 453.

63. Münz, *Italienische Reminiszenzen* (note 9), 217.

64. See *Nuova Antologia*, iv/85 (1900), 184: 'As the century draws to a close, Germany appears to us to be in the best possible health thanks to the lofty talents of its Kaiser, the abilities of his statesmen and the energy of the entire nation which, with positively extravagant verve, is working to acquire wealth'; see also Mario Morasso, 'L'arte moderna alla III esposizione di Venezia', *Nuova Antologia*, iv/83 (1899), 123–53, esp. 139; and *Il Marzocco*, ix/1 (3 Jan. 1904).

65. *Il Marzocco*, vi/14 (7 April 1901).

66. Weiss, 'Staat, Regierung und Parlament' (note 60), 311; but see also Diego Garoglio, 'Il metodo storico e la specializzazzione', *Il Marzocco*, i/50 (10 Jan. 1897).

67. See the overview by Claudio Visentin, *Nel paese delle selve e delle idee: I viaggiatori italiani in Germania 1866–1914* (Milan 1995).
68. See Cambieri Tosi, *Carlo Placci* (note 34), 161–5.
69. Kurz, *Pilgerfahrt nach dem Unerreichlichen* (note 20), 347.
70. Isolde Kurz, 'Neue deutsch-florentiner Erinnerungen: Abdruck eines Vortrags vor den "Freunden der Deutschen Akademie in Florenz" ', *Münchner Neueste Nachrichten* (2/3 May 1927).
71. DLA, A: Isolde Kurz, 'Rede in der Deutschen Akademie', fol. 1.
72. Quoted in Marion Ónodi, *Isolde Kurz: Leben und Prosawerk als Ausdruck zeitgenössischer und menschlich–individueller Situation von der Mitte des 19. bis zur Mitte des 20. Jahrhunderts* (Frankfurt am Main 1989), 268–70.

Chapter 9 May 1898

1. Steffi Roettgen, 'Dal "Börsencourier" di Berlino al "Genio" di Firenze: Lo storico Robert Davidsohn (1835–1937) e il suo inedito lascito fiorentino', *Storia dell'arte e politica culturale intorno al 1900: La fondazione dell'Istituto Germanico di Storia dell'Arte a Firenze*, ed. Max Seidel (Venice 1999), 312–58, esp. 319.
2. Rainer Maria Rilke, *Das Florenzer Tagebuch*, eds Ruth Sieber-Rilke and Carl Sieber (Frankfurt am Main and Leipzig 1994), 39–40.
3. FC (letter from Mary Warburg to Charlotte Warburg, 7 May 1898).
4. Giorgio Mori, *La Toscana* (Storia d'Italia: Le regioni dall'Unità a oggi) (Turin 1986), 132 n.17; and Giannino Parravicini, *La politica fiscale e le entrate effettive del Regno d'Italia (1860–1890)* (Turin 1958), 613.
5. James Whiteside, *Italy in the Nineteenth Century* (London 1848), 98; and C. Pazzagli, 'La vita sociale', *Firenze 1815–1945: Un bilancio storiografico*, eds Giorgio Mori and Piero Roggi (Florence 1990), 55–75, esp. 60.
6. Luigi Tommassini, 'Firenze operaia all'inizio del XX secolo', *Il socialismo in Firenze e Provincia (1871–1961)*, eds Stefano Caretti and Maurizio Degl'Innocenti (Pisa 1987), 76–83.
7. Almost 109,000 individuals emigrated to the south between 1876 and 1880, the numbers continuing to grow from then on: between 1891 and 1895 the figure reached 256,500, and in the last five years of the century it was over 315,000. The figures for Tuscany alone are 6,545 in 1876 and 21,971 in 1900; see Mori, *La Toscana* (note 4), 129.
8. Gab. Vieusseux, Fondo Orvieto, Carte Cantoni Orvieto Laura Can. 300 (unpaginated).
9. Gino Luzzatto, *L'economia italiana dal 1861 al 1914*, i: *1861–1894* (Milan 1963), 231–3.
10. Janet Ross, *The Fourth Generation: Reminiscences* (London 1912), 286–7.
11. C. F. Ferraris, 'La disoccupazione e l'assicurazione degli operai', *Nuova Antologia*, ii/126 (1897), 73–103 and 322–47, esp. 327.
12. Mori, *La Toscana* (note 4), 142; the figure for 1898 is in BCF, 64 D 1/33, p. 282.
13. Ibid., 141.
14. Ibid., 187 n.19.
15. Pier Carlo Masini, *Storia degli anarchici italiani da Bakunin a Malatesta* (Milan 1969), 129–31.
16. Mori, *La Toscana* (note 4), 179–80; Alfredo Angiolini, *Socialismo e socialisti in Italia* (Florence 1900), 275 and 340; and Giorgio Galli, *I partiti politici* (Turin 1974), 457.
17. Carlo Pinzani, *La crisi politica di fine secolo in Toscana* (Florence 1963), 56; and Mori, *La Toscana* (note 4), 180.
18. *La Nazione*, xxxix/36 (5 Feb. 1897) and xxxix/80 (21 March 1897) (on the student gathering and on Frilli).
19. *La Nazione*, xxxix/292 (19 Oct. 1897).
20. Mori, *La Toscana* (note 4), 186; see also Nicla Capitini Maccabruni, 'Gli scioperi delle trecciaiole toscane del 1896–97 e l'azione della Camera del Lavoro di Firenze', *Movimento operaio e socialista*, x (1964), 121–36.

21. Mori, *La Toscana* (note 4), 228–9.
22. Ercole Vidari, 'Gli scioperi in Italia nel 1897', *Nuova Antologia*, iv/86 (1900), 103–13, esp. 104.
23. Vidari, 'Gli scioperi in Italia' (note 22), 108.
24. BCF, 64 D 1/32, p.654 and passim.
25. *La Nazione*, xl/18 (18 Jan. 1898); xl/24 (24 Jan. 1898) and xl/29 (29 Jan. 1898).
26. Silvano Fei, *Firenze 1881–1898: La grande operazione urbanistica* (Rome 1977), 224–5. For a time the authorities considered locating the library *oltr'Arno*. Not until 1911 did they begin to build it on its present site.
27. Vidari, 'Gli scioperi in Italia' (note 22), 109.
28. *La Nazione*, xlii/9 (10 Jan. 1900).
29. *La Nazione*, xl/70 (11 March 1898).
30. Prices reached 30–38 *centesimi*; see Giovanni Spadolini, *Firenze fra Ottocento e Novecento: Da porta pia all'età giolittiano* (Florence 1983), 242; in addition to the reports in *La Nazione*, see also *Fieramosca*, xviii/121–2 (22/23 May 1898) and especially xviii/127 (7/8 May 1898).
31. Napoleone Colajanni, *L'Italia nel 1898: Tumulti e reazione* (Milan 1898, R/1953).
32. Raffaele Colapietra, *Il Novantotto: La crisi di fine secolo (1896–1900)* (Milan 1959); and Alfredo Canavero, *Milano e la crisi di fine secolo (1896–1900)* (Milan 1976).
33. On the following, see Mori, *La Toscana* (note 4), 187–8.
34. *Fieramosca*, xviii/128 (8/9 May 1898).
35. Mori, *La Toscana* (note 4), 189.
36. Spadolini, *Firenze fra Ottocento e Novecento* (note 30), 243; see also *Fieramosca*, xviii/128 (8/9 May 1898).
37. Colajanni, *L'Italia nel 1898* (note 31), 98.
38. Otto Weiss, 'Staat, Regierung und Parlament im norddeutschen Bund und im Kaiserreich im Urteil des Italiener', *Quellen und Forschungen aus italienischen Archiven und Bibliotheken*, lxvi (1986), 310–77, esp. 355–6.
39. For a summary, see Rudolf Lill, *Geschichte Italiens der Neuzeit*, 4th edn (Darmstadt 1988), 242.
40. For an analysis of the crisis, see Ernesto Ragionieri, *La storia politica e sociale* (Storia d'Italia iv/3) (Turin 1976), 1842–66.
41. Thus Antonio de Viti de Marco, quoted in Ragioneri, *La storia politica* (note 40), 1844.
42. *Fieramosca*, xviii/129 (9/10 May 1898).
43. Archivio Corsini, Stanza V, Tommaso Corsini 1896–1901, Diari (6 May 1898).
44. Rilke, *Das Florenzer Tagebuch* (note 2), 39.
45. Walther Rehm, 'Der Renaissancekult um 1900 und seine Überwindung', *Zeitschrift für deutsche Philologie*, liv (1929), 296–328, reprinted in Rehm, *Der Dichter und die neue Einsamkeit: Aufsätze zur Literatur um 1900* (Göttingen 1969), 34–77, esp. 56.
46. Enrico Corradini, 'Lo sciopero nella città dei Ciompi', *Il Marzocco*, vii/36 (7 Sept. 1902).
47. Heinrich Mann, *Gesammelte Werke in Einzelausgaben*, vol. ix (Berlin 1969) ('Die Göttinnen oder die Romanze der Herzogin von Assy'), 137.
48. Karl Hillebrand, obituary of Gino Capponi, *Zeiten, Völker, Menschen* (Strasbourg 1873–85), iv. 266–90, esp. 269–70.
49. Thomas Rietzschel, *Theodor Däubler: Eine Collage seiner Biographie* (Leipzig 1988), 66.
50. Diar. 10.1 (31 July 1898): 'Bismarck dead! Our best card, which we'd been keeping up our sleeve. In him the German soul was roused to a life of activity: but through him a contrast between receptivity and expansion has been introduced to the German Empire that he himself created. [. . .] The balance that I hope Germany will produce must also lead to a new social ethics.'
51. AWI, 52.4, Gedichte und Dramatisches.

Chapter 10 In defence of history

1. Siegfried Giedion, *Bauen in Frankreich, Bauen in Eisen, Bauen in Eisenbeton* (Leipzig 1928), i.5.
2. *Il Marzocco*, vii/21 (25 Feb. 1902).
3. Francesco Adorno (ed.), *Accademie e istituzioni culturali a Firenze* (Florence 1983), 256.
4. See the account in Sigmund Münz, *Italienische Reminiszenzen und Profile* (Vienna 1898), 264–81.
5. Patrick H. Hutton, *History as an Art of Memory* (Hanover and London 1993), 75–84.
6. *Fieramosca*, xviii/139 (19/20 May 1898).
7. See the reports in *La Nazione* and *Fieramosca* xviii/118 (28/29 April 1898).
8. FC (letters from Mary Warburg to Charlotte Warburg, 9 March 1898 and 28 April 1898).
9. Firenze, Archivio Corsini, Diari (18 March 1898).
10. *La Nazione*, xl/111 (21 April 1898).
11. Quoted in Silvano Fei, *Firenze 1881–1898: La grande operazione urbanistica* (Rome 1977), 226.
12. Fei, *Firenze 1881–1898* (note 11), 221.
13. Ibid., 235; for the following, see 226–9.
14. *The Times* (15 Dec. 1898), 8.
15. For more on Pietro Torrigiani, see Fei, *Firenze 1881–1898* (note 11), 266–7.
16. On the inaugural meeting of the *Società*, see *Fieramosca* xviii/136 (16/17 May 1898).
17. Florence, Archivio Horne, H X II: 'Fine dell'Associazione è la tutela del carattere e dell' patrimmonio storico di Firenze'; see also Fei, *Firenze 1881–1898* (note 11), 230.
18. Herbert P. Horne, *Alessandro Filipepi Commonly Called Sandro Botticelli: Painter of Florence* (London 1907).
19. FC (letter from Aby Warburg to Mary Warburg, 16 Oct. 1902).
20. On the following, see Ian Fletcher, *Rediscovering Herbert Horne: Poet, Architect, Typographer, Art Historian* (Greensboro 1990); and Brenda Preyer, 'Renaissance "Art and Life" in the Scholarship and Palace of Herbert P. Horne', *Gli anglo-americani a Firenze: Idea e costruzione del Rinascimento*, ed. Marcello Fantoni (Rome 2000), 225–47.
21. Edgar Jepson, *Memories of a Victorian* (London 1933), 210.
22. Fritz Saxl, 'Three "Florentines": Herbert Horne, Aby Warburg, Jacques Mesnil', *Lectures* (London 1957), i.331–48, esp. 333; the following information is taken from Saxl's essay.
23. T. Sturge Moore and D. C. Sturge Moore, *Works and Days: From the Journal of Michael Field* (London 1933), 118.
24. Fletcher, *Rediscovering Herbert Horne* (note 20), 18.
25. GC (letter from Herbert P. Horne to Aby Warburg, 24 July 1903); on Warburg's 'commercia litteraria', see Michael Diers, *Warburg aus Briefen: Kommentare zu den Kopierbüchern der Jahre 1905–1918* (Weinheim 1991), 37–40.
26. GC (letter from Aby Warburg to Herbert P. Horne, 15 Nov. 1902).
27. Giorgio Vasari, *Le vite de' più eccellenti pittori, scultori ed architettori*, ed. Gaetano Milanesi (Florence 1906), ii.671.
28. For a report on the unveiling, see *La Nazione* (4 June 1899); an excerpt may be found in Notebook 1897–1902 (3 June 1899).
29. A. Conti, 'L'affresco di Andrea del Castagno', *Il Marzocco*, iv/21 (25 June 1899).
30. 'La commedia dello scoprimento', *Il Marzocco*, vii/24 (15 June 1902). This is presumably the reason why Vasari's editor, Gaetano Milanesi, writes that none of Andrea del Castagno's works is to be seen in the Church of SS Annunziata 'today'.
31. Florence, Archivio Horne (letter from Corsini, 31 May 1899).
32. The most important press reactions may be found in the Archivio Horne, Carte Horne, X II, Articoli estratti.

33. *La Nazione*, xli/137 (17 May 1899). The fears of opponents of the plan were not entirely unjustified, as two architects recommended that a *linea di communicazione* be opened up between the Mercato Nuovo and the Palazzo Pitti, a plan that would have resulted in the destruction of the goldsmiths' shops on the bridge.

34. *The Times* (15 Dec. 1898).

35. Peter Gunn, *Vernon Lee: Violet Paget 1856–1935* (London 1964), 2 (quoting from a review published in *The Nation* on 18 Sept. 1920).

36. BCF, 64 D 1/33, pp. 691–3.

37. Ibid., pp. 711–12.

38. Florence, Archivio Horne, Carte Horne, H X II.

39. William D. Howells, *Tuscan Cities* (Leipzig 1891), 15.

40. Florence, Archivio Horne, Carte Horne H X II.

41. *La Nazione*, xli/70 (11 March 1899); see also Archivio Horne, Carte Horne, H X I.

42. Fei, *Firenze 1881–1898* (note 11), 232–3.

43. BCF, 64 D 1/38, pp. 769–70; *Il Marzocco*, vi/19 (12 May 1901), 3.

44. Diar. 10.1 (6 Dec. 1898).

45. Ibid. (27 Dec. 1898 and 28 Dec. 1898).

46. It is not entirely certain that the individual mentioned here is Gustav Spangenberg, as Gustav had a brother, Louis (1824–93), who produced architectural landscapes in Italy and Greece. For more on the Warburgs' social contacts, see FC (letter from Mary Warburg to Charlotte Warburg, 5 Feb. 1899).

Chapter 11 Neurasthenia and mental balance: On Leonardo and Piero della Francesca

1. The term is quoted in *Fieramosca*, xviii/11 (11/12 Jan. 1898); for examples, see *La Nazione*, xliii/216 (4 Aug. 1901); xxxix/222 (10 Aug. 1897); xli/27 (27 Jan. 1899); xl/236 (24 Aug. 1898); and *Fieramosca*, xviii/5 (5/6 Jan. 1898).

2. See *The British Medical Journal*, i (1898), 1424. In 1904 the figure for the United States of America was 19.5 per 100,000 inhabitants. In San Francisco the figure rose from 23.7 in 1890 to 49.9 in 1900 and to 72.6 in 1904, whereas in Chicago it fell back to 30.6. In 1894 the figure for Paris was 42.5, falling to 26.7 by 1903. In Berlin the rate was 27.5 in 1904 and in London 10.8, also in 1904. See *Ärztlicher Ratgeber* (1904), 143–4; and the *Journal of the American Medical Association*, xlv (1905), 469. Figures for Italy are taken from Georg von Mayr, *Allgemeines Statistisches Archiv* (Tübingen 1896), iv.716–23, esp. 721. (In 1881, the rate had been 13.43, in 1894, 17.32.) Far more cases were reported in the newspapers, and, if we also include attempted suicides, we end up with a figure of more than 170 cases a year, although here the figures relate only to the later period. By the end of the nineteenth century, the average suicide rate in Italy was 17.3 per 100,000 inhabitants. In Rome there were 11.4 cases, in Calabria 2.39. In Lombardy, too, the rate – 7.17 – was far lower than that in Florence. We have to turn to the Protestant world, the German Reich (20.0) and the larger conurbations of North America and western Europe to find comparably high figures; see G. Styles, 'Suicide and its increase', *American Journal of Insanity*, lvii (1900), 97–102; and, as an example of a contemporary interpretation, L. Fuld, 'Die Zunahme des Selbstmordes', *Über Land und Meer*, lxiii (1890), 148.

3. In 1897 the sociologist Emile Durkheim observed that the suicide rate in Prussia had risen by 411% between 1826 and 1890, while the figure in France had risen by 318% during the same period. In Italy the rate increased by around 50% between 1886 and 1896.

4. C. Pazzagli, 'La vita sociale', *Firenze 1815–1945: Un bilancio storiografico*, eds Giorgio Mori and Piero Roggi (Florence 1990), 55–75, esp. 68.

5. Alessandro Chiappelli, 'Sul confine dei due secoli', *Nuova Antologia*, iv/86 (1900), 620–39, esp. 627.

6. *Il Marzocco*, ix/42 (16 Oct. 1904); for an interpretation of suicide as a consequence of changes in society, see *Fieramosca*, xviii/93 (3/4 April 1898).

7. Isolde Kurz, *Pilgerfahrt nach dem Unerreichlichen: Lebensrückschau* (Tübingen 1938), 171–2.

8. Joachim Radkau, *Das Zeitalter der Nervosität: Deutschland zwischen Bismarck und Hitler* (Munich and Vienna 1998), 121–2; for a critique of Radkau's concept, see Volker Roelcke, *Krankheit und Kulturkritik: Psychiatrische Gesellschaftsdeutungen im bürgerlichen Zeitalter (1790–1914)* (Frankfurt am Main and New York 1999).

9. See, for example, *Fieramosca*, xviii/97 (7/8 April 1898).

10. Diaries 10.1 (after 11 Jan. 1899).

11. FC (letter from Aby Warburg to Charlotte Warburg, 28 Dec. 1899).

12. E. H. Gombrich, *Aby Warburg: An Intellectual Biography* (Oxford 1986), 99–105. Warburg had no intention of publishing this text, although he did consider reworking it as the basis for a lecture designed to further his academic career; see GC (letter from Aby Warburg to Heinrich Brockhaus, 25 Sept. 1899).

13. GC (letter from Alice Hallgarten to Aby Warburg, 28 Sept. 1899): 'Dear Aby, everyone has been telling me how you succeeded through the sheer seriousness of your lectures in raising people to the best they are capable of: to a feeling of the true significance of art!'

14. Quoted from Gombrich, *Aby Warburg* (note 12), 110.

15. AWI, after 5.2.1, Leonardo Lectures, ii.7.

16. AWI, 50.11, p. 15.

17. Leonardo Lectures, ii.61.

18. AWI, 50.11, p. 9.

19. AWI, 50.11, p. 2.

20. AWI, 5.2.1, Leonardo Lectures, ii.75–7.

21. AWI, after 50.3.1, Leonardo Lectures, iii.9–10.

22. AWI, 50.1.1, Leonardo Lectures, i.14.

23. J. B. Bullen, *The Myth of the Renaissance in Nineteenth-Century Writing* (Oxford 1994), 293; see also William E. Buckler, *Walter Pater: The Critic as Artist of Ideas* (New York and London 1987).

24. Leonardo Lectures, i.8. The following quotation is taken from AWI, 50.3.1, Leonardo Lectures, iii.73–4. The words 'thinking' (before 'man') and 'to a certain extent' (after 'it is') have been struck out.

25. The 'Frenchman' mentioned here is presumably Gabriel Séailles, whose monograph on Leonardo, *Leonardo de Vinci: L'Artiste et le savant*, was published in Paris in 1892.

26. AWI, 50.3.1, Leonardo Lectures, iii.50 and 69–70.

27. Ian Fletcher, *Rediscovering Herbert Horne: Poet, Architect, Typographer, Art Historian* (Greensboro 1990), 119; see also the dismissive attitude expressed by Carl Friedrich von Rumohr in his *Italienische Forschungen*, 3 vols (Berlin and Stettin 1827–31), ii.336.

28. Jacob Burckhardt, *Der Cicerone: Eine Anleitung zum Genuß der Kunstwerke Italiens* (1855, R/1986), 768.

29. John Fleming, 'Art dealing in the Risorgimento II', *The Burlington Magazine*, cxxxi/917 (1979), 492–508, esp. 492 and 507.

30. Bullen, *The Myth of the Renaissance* (note 23), 118; Nicolas Barker, *Bibliotheca Lindesiana: The Lives and Collections of Alexander William, 25th Earl of Crawford and 8th Earl of Balcarres and James Ludovic, 26th Earl of Crawford and 9th Earl of Balcarres* (London 1977), 111–12: 'like the Elgin Marbles . . . masterly . . . I know no other word'. See also Fleming, 'Art dealing in the Risorgimento II' (note 29), 500 n. 58; for more on Layard as a further 'discoverer' of Piero, see Robyn Cooper, 'The popularization of Renaissance art in Victorian England', *Art History*, i/1 (1978), 263–93, esp. 273.

31. *Letters of Roger Fry*, ed. Denys Sutton (London 1972), 170 (letter from Roger Fry to Sir Edward Fry, 24 May 1897): 'They [i.e. the cycle of frescos at Arezzo] are extraordinarily beautiful frescoes [sic] and the only ones by this painter in existence, and as we both admire them almost more than any other early Italian painter (he certainly comes

nearer to the Greeks than any other Italian painter) we enjoyed seeing them very much.'

32. Diaries 10.1 (28 April 1901); see also FC (letter from Aby Warburg to Max Warburg, 1 May 1901).

33. FC (letter from Aby Warburg to Max Warburg, 1 May 1901).

34. See Aby Warburg, 'Piero della Francescas Constantinsschlacht in der Aquarellkopie des Johann Anton Ramboux', *L'Italia e l'arte straniera: Atti del X Congresso Internazionale di Storia dell'Arte* (Rome 1922), 326–7; see Gombrich, *Aby Warburg* (note 12), 182–3; also NL Bode 5251/1, 32.2 (letter from Aby Warburg to Wilhelm Bode, 12 Jan. 1906).

35. AWI, 88.2: 'The entry of the classizizing [*sic*] ideal style in the painting of the early Italian Renaissance.' The following notes may be found in AWI, 72.1.3, fols 2–5, 7 and 14.

36. Gombrich, *Aby Warburg* (note 12), 182–4.

37. AWI, 88.2: 'The entry' (note 35), fol. 19.

38. AWI, 88.2: 'The entry' (note 35), fol. 20.

39. Heinrich Wölfflin, *Renaissance und Barock* (1888, R 1970), 22–3.

40. Warburg's interpretation of *The Last Supper* is almost completely independent of Burckhardt's account in *Der Cicerone*; see Burckhardt, *Der Cicerone* (note 28), 819: 'But what is so divine about this work is that what is in every way conditional appears to be entirely unconditional and necessary. An altogether tremendous mind has revealed all its treasures to us here and combined every degree of expression and physical formation in wonderful principles to create a very real sense of harmony.' For Pater's interpretation, see William E. Buckler, *Walter Pater: The Critic as Artist of Ideas* (New York and London 1987), 58–63. It may be added at this juncture that Warburg's aesthetic outlook is rooted in the theories of the Renaissance Platonists and of the German idealists.

41. AWI, 50.1.2: Leonardo Lectures, ii.41.

Chapter 12 Dealers in beauty

1. Adolf von Hildebrand, *Briefwechsel mit Conrad Fiedler*, ed. Günther Jachmann (Dresden 1927), 48 (23 Jan. 1875).

2. AWI, 51.1: Untitled. Ghirlandaio in S. Trinità', fol. 39–40.

3. Marcel Proust, *In Search of Lost Time*, trans. C. K. Scott Moncrieff and Terence Kilmartin, rev. D. J. Enright, 6 vols (London 2000), i.419–20.

4. Van Wyck Brooks, *The Dream of Arcadia: American Writers and Artists in Italy 1760–1915* (New York 1958), 79; see also 80–4.

5. Cristina Tagliaferri, *Olschki: Un secolo di editoria 1886–1986*, i: *La libreria antiquaria editrice Leo S. Olschki (1886–1945)* (Florence 1986), 161–3.

6. Sandra Berresford, 'Preraffaellismo ed estetismo a Firenze negli ultimi decenni del XIX secolo', *L'idea di Firenze: Temi e interpretazioni dell'arte straniera dell'Ottocento*, eds Maurizio Bossi and Lucia Tonini (Florence 1989), 191–210, esp. 202.

7. Sylvia Sprigge, *Berenson: A Biography* (London 1960), 97.

8. *The Letters of Elizabeth Barrett Browning*, ed. Frederic C. Kenyon, 2 vols (London 1898), i.448.

9. Wyck Brooks, *The Dream of Arcadia* (note 4), 80.

10. Robyn Cooper, 'The popularization of Renaissance art in Victorian England', *Art History*, i/1 (1978), 263–93, esp. 279.

11. For more on Jarves, see Francis Steegmuller, *The Two Lives of James Jackson Jarves* (New Haven 1951); and, more recently, Flaminia Gennari Santori, 'James Jackson Jarves and the diffusion of Tuscan painting in the United States', *Gli anglo-americani a Firenze: Idea e costruzione del Rinascimento*, ed. Marcello Fantoni (Rome 2000), 177–206.

12. John Fleming, 'Art dealing in the Risorgimento II', *The Burlington Magazine*, cxxi/917 (1979), 492–508, esp. 498.

13. Silvia Contarini,' "Botticelli ritrovato": Frammenti di dialogo tra Aby Warburg e André Jolles', *Prospettiva*, lxviii (1993), 87–93, esp. 92; and Enrico Ridolfi,'Un grande scoperta artistica: Ritrovamento della "Pallade" di Sando Botticelli', *La Nazione*, xxxvii/61 (2 March 1895).

14. Hildebrand, *Briefwechsel mit Fiedler* (note 1), 35 (19 Jan. 1873).

15. Irving Wohlfarth,' "Construction has the role of the subconscious": Phantasmagorias of the master builder (with Constant Reference to Giedion, Weber, Nietzsche, Ibsen and Benjamin', *Nietzsche and 'An Architecture of Our Minds'*, eds Alexandre Kostka and Irving Wohlfarth (Los Angeles 1999), 141–98, esp. 147.

16. John Fleming, 'Art dealing in the Risorgimento I', *The Burlington Magazine*, cxv (1973), 4–17.

17. Irma Richter and Gisela Richter, *Italienische Malerei der Renaissance im Briefwechsel von Giovanni Morelli und Jean Paul Richter 1876–1891* (Baden-Baden 1960).

18. Isolde Kurz, *Florentinische Erinnerungen* (Stuttgart and Berlin 1920), 103–5; Wilhelm von Bode, *Mein Leben*, eds Thomas W. Gaehtgens and Barbara Paul (Berlin 1997), 43–4; Adolf Bayersdorfer, obituary of Karl Eduard von Liphart, *Münchner Neueste Nachrichten* (20 Feb. 1891); Cosima Wagner, *Die Tagebücher*, eds Martin Gregor-Dellin and Dietrich Mack, 2 vols (Munich and Zurich 1976–7), i.1017–19 (entries of 3–17 Dec. 1876); Hans W. Hubert, *Das Kunsthistorische Institut in Florenz: Von der Gründung bis zum hundertjährigen Jubiläum (1897–1997)* (Florence 1997), 8–10; and Siegfried Käss, *Der heimliche Kaiser der Kunst: Adolf Bayersdorfer, seine Freunde und seine Zeit* (Munich 1987), 165–77.

19. AWI, 50.11: Notizen Leonardo. Pencil note II and III, p. 13.

20. For an overview, see Simone Bargellini, *Antiquari di ieri* (Florence 1981).

21. Wilhelm von Bode, 'Stefano Bardini', *L'antiquario*, x (1923), 1–2; also Bode, *Mein Leben* (note 18), i.206. Volpi's collection passed into the hands of the commune in 1922; see Roberto Ferrazza, 'Elia Volpi e il commercio dell'arte nel primo trentennio del Novecento', *Studi e ricerche di collezionismo e museografia a Firenze 1820–1920* (Quaderni del Seminario di Storia della Critica d'Arte 2) (Pisa 1985), 397.

22. Volker Krahn, 'Ein ziemlich kühnes Unterfangen . . .': Wilhelm von Bode als Wegbereiter der Bronzeforschung, seine Erwerbungen für die Berliner Museen und seine Beziehungen zu Sammlern', *Von allen Seiten schön: Bronzen der Renaissance und des Barock*, ed. Volker Krahn (Berlin 1995), 34–55.

23. See Ferrazza, 'Elia Volpi' (note 21).

24. Arnold Bennett, *The Journals*, ed. Frank Swinnerton (Harmondsworth 1971), 313 (4 May 1910).

25. Cristina Tagliaferri, *Olschki: Un secolo di editoria 1886–1986*, i: *La libreria antiquaria editrice Leo S. Olschki (1886–1945)* (Florence 1986).

26. Tagliaferri, *Olschki* (note 25), 76–7; on the following, see also 84–7 and 91–8.

27. Horatio Stevens White, *Willard Fiske: Life and Correspondence. A Biographical Study* (New York and Oxford 1925).

28. Dorothea McEwan, *Ausreiten der Ecken: Die Aby Warburg–Fritz Saxl-Korrespondenz 1901–1919* (Hamburg 1998), 14.

29. William Rothenstein, *Men and Memories: Recollections of William Rothenstein 1900–1922* (London 1932), ii.122.

30. Margery Ross (ed.), *Robert Ross: Friend of Friends. Letters to Robert Ross, Art Critic and Writer, together with Extracts from his Published Articles* (London 1932), 137 (10 Nov. 1906).

31. Margaret Campbell, *Dolmetsch: The Man and His Work* (Seattle 1975), 110.

32. FC (letter from Mary Warburg to Charlotte Warburg, 31 Jan. 1898).

33. Ian Fletcher, *Rediscovering Herbert Horne: Poet, Architect, Typographer, Art Historian* (Greensboro 1990), 120.

34. Ibid., 145.

35. *The Selected Letters of Bernard Berenson*, ed. A[rthur] K[ilgore] McComb (Boston 1964), 65.
36. Herbert P. Horne, 'The Battle-Piece by Paolo Uccello in the National Gallery', *The Monthly Review*, v (1901), 114–38.
37. Roger Fry, 'Mr. Horne's Book on Botticelli', *The Burlington Magazine*, xiii (1908), 83–7, esp. 84.
38. Michael Levey, 'Botticelli and Nineteenth-Century England', *Journal of the Warburg and Courtauld Institutes*, xxiii (1960), 291–306, esp. 303.
39. Herbert P. Horne, *Alessandro Filipepi Commonly Called Sandro Botticelli: Painter of Florence* (London 1907), 334.
40. Fletcher, *Rediscovering Herbert Horne* (note 33), 13.
41. Diaries 8.1 (4 May 1898).
42. Nicky Mariano, *Forty Years with Berenson* (New York 1966), 165.
43. Ernest Samuels, *Bernard Berenson: The Making of a Connoisseur* (Cambridge, MA and London 1979), 324.
44. Samuels, *Bernard Berenson* (note 43), 108.
45. Ibid., 32–3.
46. Giuliana Artom Treves, *The Golden Ring: The Anglo-Florentines 1847–1862* (London, New York and Toronto 1956), 160–62; and Van Wyck Brooks, *The Dream of Arcadia: American Writers and Artists in Italy 1760–1915* (New York 1958), 110–21 and *passim*.
47. Wyck Books, *The Dream of Arcadia* (note 46), 71 n. 3.
48. Carol M. Osborne, 'Lizzie Boott at Bellosguardo', *The Italian Presence in American Art 1860–1920*, ed. Irma B. Jaffe (New York and Rome 1992), 188–99.
49. Sylvia Sprigge, *Berenson: A Biography* (London 1960), 111.
50. Quoted by Samuels, *Bernard Berenson* (note 43), 270.
51. Lillian B. Miller, 'Celebrating Botticelli: The taste for the Italian Renaissance in the United States, 1870–1920', *The Italian Presence in American Art, 1860–1920*, ed. Irma B. Jaffe (New York and Rome 1992), 3–22, esp. 13.
52. Miller, 'Celebrating Botticelli' (note 51), 11.
53. McComb, *The Selected Letters of Bernard Berenson* (note 35), 52–3 (letters to Mrs Jack Gardner, 9 Nov. 1896, 29 Nov. 1896 and 6 Dec. 1896).
54. Sprigge, *Berenson: A Biography* (note 49), 185–7.
55. Samuels, *Bernard Berenson* (note 43), 306–7.
56. Margaret Fuller, *Memoirs* (Boston 1852), 216: 'Florence is a kind of Boston with the same good and the same ill – and I have had enough of both. I do not like it . . . because it seems like home.' W. W. Story said the same when he described Florence as a 'continental Boston', a description which he no doubt intended to be even more negative than Margaret Fuller's.
57. Florence, Archivio Horne, K I 6, Carteggio Horne, 7 Bernard Berenson (9 Jan. 1899); see also Samuels, *Bernard Berenson* (note 43), 311.
58. William William, *A Legacy of Excellence: The Story of Villa I Tatti* (New York 1997).
59. Samuels, *Bernard Berenson* (note 43), 38.
60. Ibid., 155.
61. See Manfred Ohlsen, *Wilhelm von Bode: Zwischen Kaisermacht und Kunsttempel. Biographie* (Berlin 1995).
62. NL Bode 5251/1, 32.1 (letter from Aby Warburg to Wilhelm Bode, 12 Jan. 1906); see also Michael Diers, *Warburg aus Briefen: Kommentare zu den Kopierbüchern der Jahre 1905–1918* (Weinheim 1991).
63. NL Bode 5251/1, 17.2 (letter from Aby Warburg to Wilhelm Bode, 7 July 1903).
64. E. H. Gombrich, *Aby Warburg: An Intellectual Biography* (Oxford 1986), 143.
65. Samuels, *Bernard Berenson* (note 43), 230.
66. AWI, 111.1, fol.8: Fritz Saxl, 'Biography of Warburg' (1939/40) (see Unpublished Sources).
67. Samuels, *Bernard Berenson* (note 43), 152–3.

Chapter 13   The last Romantics

1. FC (letter from Aby Warburg to Mary Warburg, 24 Nov. 1902).
2. Daniela Lamberini, 'Residenti anglo-americani e genius loci: Ricostruzioni e restauri delle dimore fiorentine', *Gli anglo-americani a Firenze: Idea e costruzione dell Rinascimento*, ed. Marcello Fantoni (Rome 2000), 125–42.
3. Hans-Ulrich Wehler, 'Deutsches Bildungsbürgertum in vergleichender Perspektive – Elemente eines "Sonderwegs"?', *Bildungsbürgertum im 19. Jahrhundert*, iv: *Politischer Einfluß und gesellschaftliche Formation*, ed. Jürgen Kocka (Stuttgart 1989), 215–37, esp. 223.
4. Luigi Mascilli Migliorini, 'Stranieri a Firenze', *Firenze 1815–1945: Un bilancio stori-ografico*, eds Giorgio Mori and Piero Roggi (Florence 1990), 465–85; Clara Louise Dentler, *Famous Foreigners in Florence 1400–1900* (Florence 1964); Olive Hamilton, *Paradise of Exiles: Tuscany and the British* (London 1974); Luigi Mascilli Migliorini, *L'Italia dell'Italia: Coscienza e mito della Toscana da Montesquieu a Berenson* (Florence 1995); and, most recently, *Gli anglo-americani a Firenze: Idea e costruzione del Rinascimento*, ed. Marcello Fantoni (Rome 2000).
5. Giuliana Artom Treves, *The Golden Ring: The Anglo-Florentines 1847–1862* (London, New York and Toronto 1956), 6.
6. Nathaniel Parker Willis, *Pencillings by the Way* (London 1864), 17.
7. *La Nazione*, xlv/327 (23 Nov. 1903).
8. Francesco Adorno (ed.), *Accademie e istituzioni culturali a Firenze* (Florence 1983), 79.
9. Thomas Mann, *Notizbücher*, eds Hans Wysling and Yvonne Schmidlin, i: *Notizbücher i–vi* (Frankfurt 1991), iv.201; see also Hermann Kurzke, *Thomas Mann: Das Leben als Kunstwerk. Eine Biographie* (Munich 1999), 154–6.
10. Sigmund Münz, *Italienische Reminiszenzen und Profile* (Vienna 1898), 223.
11. Laurence Hutton, *Literary Landmarks of Florence* (New York 1897), 67.
12. Van Wyck Brooks, *The Dream of Arcadia: American Writers and Artists in Italy 1760–1915* (New York 1958); see also Oreste Del Buono, Gherardo Frassa and Luigi Settembrini, *Gli anglo-fiorentini: Una storia d'amore* (Florence 1987); and Giuliana Artom Treves, *Anglo-fiorentini di cento anni fa* (Florence 1953).
13. Walburga, Lady Paget, *In My Tower*, 2 vols (London 1924), i.67.
14. Jean Delay, *La Jeunesse d'André Gide*, 2 vols (Paris 1956–7), ii.326; see also H. Montgomery Hyde, *Oscar Wilde* (New York 1975), 169.
15. Alan Sheridan, *André Gide: A Life in the Present* (London 1998), 255–6.
16. Wyck Brooks, *The Dream of Arcadia* (note 12), 173.
17. James Leslie Woodress, *Howells and Italy* (New York 1952), 183–5.
18. Henry James quoted by Wyck Brooks, *The Dream of Arcadia* (note 12), 227.
19. Wyck Brooks, *The Dream of Arcadia* (note 12), 227.
20. BCF, 64 D 1/35 (1900), 2082–4 (20 July 1900). The affair was by no means uncontroversial, one of the town councillors – a certain Signor Minuti – objecting that Victoria represented a government which was combating the *italianità* of Malta and suppressing Italian language on the island. On Queen Victoria's visits to Florence, see Paget, *In My Tower* (note 13), i.59–60.
21. Artom Treves, *The Golden Ring* (note 5), 2.
22. Lady Betty Balfour, *Personal and Literary Letters of Robert First Earl of Lytton*, 2 vols (London 1906), i.37.
23. Lilian Whiting, *The Florence of Landor* (Boston 1905), 108–12; and Artom Treves, *The Golden Ring* (note 5) 56–61.
24. Frances Eleanor Trollope, *Frances Trollope: Her Life and Literary Work from George III to Victoria* (London 1895), 266–70; Dentler, *Famous Foreigners* (note 4), 138; and Isolde Kurz, *Florentinische Erinnerungen* (Stuttgart and Berlin 1920), 209–10.
25. Wyck Brooks, *The Dream of Arcadia* (note 12), 130–32.

26. Robert Stockhammer, *Zaubertexte: Die Wiederkehr der Magie und die Literatur 1880–1945* (Berlin 1999).

27. Ernst Robert Curtius, *Maurice Barrès und die geistigen Grundlagen des französischen Nationalismus* (Bonn 1921), 39.

28. See Charles Godfrey Leland, *Etruscan Magic and Occult Remedies* (New York 1963), xix (Margery Silver); see also John William De Forest, *European Acquaintance: Being Sketches of People in Europe* (New York 1858), 235–50; and Wyck Brooks, *The Dreams of Arcadia* (note 12), 227–36.

29. Quoted by Wyck Brooks, *The Dream of Arcadia* (note 12), 231.

30. J. B. Bullen, *The Myth of the Renaissance in Nineteenth-Century Writing* (Oxford 1994), 38–58.

31. Artom Treves, *The Golden Ring* (note 5), 160–61.

32. John Ruskin, *Val d'Arno: Ten Lectures on the Tuscan Art Directly Antecedent to the Florentine Year of Victories* (London 1873); see also Wilton and Upstone, *The Age of Rossetti, Burne-Jones and Watts: Symbolism in Britain 1860–1910* (London 1997).

33. Sandra Berresford, 'Preraffaellismo ed esteticismo a Firenze negli ultimi decenni del XIX secolo', *L'idea di Firenze: Temi e interpretazioni dell'arte straniera dell'Ottocento*, eds Maurizio Bossi and Lucia Tonini (Florence 1989), 191–210.

34. Dentler, *Famous Foreigners* (note 4), 36.

35. Robyn Cooper, 'The popularization of Renaissance art in Victorian England', *Art History*, i/1 (1978), 263–93, esp. 280.

36. T. Adolphus Trollope, *La Beata*, 2 vols (London 1861), i.127–8.

37. Whiting, *The Florence of Landor* (note 23), 84–5; and Hutton, *Literary Landmarks* (note 11), 69.

38. DLA, A: Isolde Kurz, 'Rede vor der Deutschen Akademie', fol. 1.

39. Richard Redgrave, *A Memoir*, ed. Frances Margaret Redgrave (London 1891), 238.

40. Walburga, Lady Paget, *Scenes and Memoirs* (London 1912); *In My Tower* (note 13), i.60; and Albert Spalding, *Rise to Follow: An Autobiography* (New York 1943), 85–6.

41. Henry James, *Autobiography*, ed. Frederick W. Dupee (Princeton 1983), 518–22.

42. Paget, *In My Tower* (note 13), i.16; on Ouida, see Monica Stirling, *The Fine and the Wicked: The Life and Times of Ouida* (London 1957).

43. Whiting, *The Florence of Landor* (note 23), 104–5.

44. Ernest Samuels, *Bernard Berenson: The Making of a Connoisseur* (Cambridge, MA and London 1979), 377–8.

45. Janet Ross, *The Fourth Generation: Reminiscences* (London 1912), 287–9; and Samuels, *Bernard Berenson* (note 44), 216–17.

46. Hutton, *Literary Landmarks* (note 11), 15–16.

47. See Peter Gunn, *Vernon Lee: Violet Paget 1856–1935* (London 1964); and *Vernon Lee's Letters*, ed. Irene Cooper Willis (London 1937).

48. *John Singer Sargent* (exhibition catalogue), eds Elaine Kilmurray and Richard Ormond (London 1998), 94–5.

49. Samuels, *Bernard Berenson* (note 44), 152–3; Ethel Smyth, *What Happened Next* (London 1940); and Gunn, *Vernon Lee* (note 47), 157.

50. Percy Lubbock, *Portrait of Edith Wharton* (London 1949), 113; and Samuels, *Bernard Berenson* (note 44), 169–71.

51. For the argument between Berenson and Violet Paget, see Gunn, *Vernon Lee* (note 47), 151–7, esp. 155.

52. Gunn, *Vernon Lee* (note 47), 184; see also R. Cary, 'Aldous Huxley, Vernon Lee and the "Genius loci" ', *Colby Library Quarterly* (June 1960).

53. See the copy of Lee's *Imaginative Art of the Renaissance* in Warburg's library, AWI 75, 68–70 and *passim*.

54. See AWI, Library, DAD 650.

55. Vernon Lee, 'The Imaginative Art of the Renaissance', *Renaissance Fancies and Studies* (London 1895; reprinted 1977), 67–133, esp. 99.

56. Vernon Lee, 'Valedictory', *Renaissance Fancies and Studies* (London 1895; reprinted 1977), 235–60, esp. 258: 'Standing as he did, as all the greatest artists or thinkers (and he was both) do, in a definite, inevitable relation to the universe . . . his conception of art, being the outcome of his whole personal mode of existence, was inevitably one of art, not for art's sake, but of art for the sake of life – art as one of the harmonious functions of existence.'

57. Gunn, *Vernon Lee* (note 47), 142. In the context of her interest in questions of the aesthetics of a work's impact on its audience, she made a detailed study of contemporary psychology, especially of William James' work on a theory of the emotions and of Giuseppe Sergi's book on the preconditions for feeling pain and pleasure, *Dolore e piacere*, of 1894.

58. Gunn, *Vernon Lee* (note 47), 149.

59. Samuels, *Bernard Berenson* (note 44), 218.

60. *The Selected Letters of Bernard Berenson*, ed. A[rthur] K[ilgore] McComb (Boston 1964), 13 (letter to Mary Costelloe, Jan. 1892).

61. John La Farge, quoted in Lillian B. Miller, 'Celebrating Botticelli: The taste for the Italian Renaissance in the United States, 1870–1920', *The Italian Presence in American Art, 1860–1920*, ed. Irma B. Jaffe (New York and Rome 1992), 3–22, esp. 7.

62. Henry James, 'The madonna of the future', *Complete Stories 1864–1874*, Vol. i (New York 1999), 730–66; James himself had considerable reservations about Raphael's art; see Lynne P. Shackelford, 'The significance of the Raphael references in Henry James's "The madonna of the future" ', *Studies in Short Fiction*, xxvii (1990), 101–4.

Chapter 14   Modern Florence

1. NL Bode 1543/1 (letter from Ernst Moritz Geyger to Wilhelm Bode); see also Philipp Kuhn, 'Villa Romana: Geschichte eines Künstlerhauses in Florenz 1904–2000' (typescript).

2. Paul Klee, *Tagebücher 1898–1918*, ed. Wolfgang Kersten (Stuttgart 1988), 135 (17 April 1902) and p. 184 (no. 556).

3. Mauro Pratesi and Giovanna Uzzani, *L'arte italiana del Novecento: La Toscana* (Venice 1991), 5–36, esp. 12.

4. Giancarlo Gentilini, 'Arti applicate, tradizione artistica fiorentina e committenti stranieri', *L'idea di Firenze: Temi e interpretazioni dell'arte straniera dell'Ottocento*, eds Maurizio Bossi and Lucia Tonini (Florence 1989), 155–76, esp. 165–6.

5. FC (letter from Mary Warburg to Charlotte Warburg, 19 March 1898); see also Lucia Bassignana, 'La manifattura di Signa: Dai frammenti di una storia', *La manifattura di Signa*, eds Andrea Baldinotti and others (Florence 1986), 3–4.

6. See Pratesi and Uzzani, *L'arte italiana* (note 3).

7. See *Le grandi esposizioni in Italia 1861–1911*, ed. Mariantonietta Picone Petrusa (Naples 1988); and Elizabeth Basye Gilmore Holt, *The Expanding World of Art 1874–1902*, i: *Universal Expositions and State-Sponsored Fine Arts Exhibitions* (New Haven and London 1988), 335–59.

8. Ardengo Soffici, *Passi tra le rovine: Autobiografia d'artista italiano nel quadro del suo tempo*, ii: *Adolescenza* (Florence 1952), 374; see also Pratesi and Uzzani, *L'arte italiana* (note 3), 5.

9. Pratesi and Uzzani, *L'arte italiana* (note 3), 11–12.

10. *Il Marzocco*, i/47 (20 Dec. 1896), 1. On the aesthetic movement in Florence, see Gianni Oliva, *I nobili spiriti: Pascoli, D'Annunzio e le reviste dell'estetismo fiorentino* (2002).

11. Vittorio Pica, 'L'arte europea a Firenze, i: I pittori inglesi', *Il Marzocco*, ii/4 (28 Feb. 1897); for more on Pica, see Holt, *The Expanding World of Art* (note 7), 357.

12. See *Il Marzocco*, iv/31 (3 Sept. 1899), 4; iv/33 (17 Sept. 1899), 4.

13. Hans Weil, *Die Entstehung des deutschen Bildungsprinzips* (Bonn 1930), ix–x and *passim*.

14. Henry James, 'Florentine Notes', *Transatlantic Sketches* (Freeport, ND 1972), 293.
15. Thomas Nipperdey, *Deutsche Geschichte 1800–1866: Bürgerwelt und starker Staat*, 2nd edn (Munich 1984), 539–40.
16. See A. Beyer, 'Blicke auf die Kunst und Kultur der Renaissance: Der Eugen Diederichs-Verlag im kunsthistorischen Diskurs des Jahrhundertbeginns' (unpublished typescript).
17. Friedrich Theodor Vischer, *Das Schöne und die Kunst* (Stuttgart 1898), 2–3.
18. Pierre Milza, *Les Fascismes* (Paris 1985), 13.
19. See *Il Marzocco*, v/6 (11 Feb. 1900), 4; see also Ugo Ojetti, 'Diritti e doveri del critico d'arte moderna', *Nuova Antologia*, iv/96 (1901), 734–42, esp. 742; and Isolde Kurz, *Pilgerfahrt nach dem Unerreichlichen: Lebensrückschau* (Tübingen 1938), 296.
20. See M. Gioli, 'A proposito dell'arte moderna', *Festa dell'Arte* (10 Feb. 1897).
21. In Germany the number of painters and sculptors rose from 8890 to 14,000 between 1895 and 1907; see Robin Lenmann, *Die Kunst, die Macht und das Geld: Zur Kulturgeschichte des kaiserlichen Deutschland 1871–1918* (Frankfurt and Paris 1994), 81.
22. *Il Marzocco*, vii/16 (20 April 1902), 3; for generally, see Franz Roh, *Der verkannte Künstler* (Munich 1948).
23. Paul Klee, *Tagebücher 1898–1918*, ed. Wolfgang Kersten (Stuttgart 1988), 174 (May 1903).
24. See *Die literarische Moderne: Dokumente zum Selbstverständnis der Moderne um die Jahrhundertwende*, eds Gotthard Wunberg and Stephan Dietrich, 2nd edn (Frankfurt 2002); on the distinction between modernism and avant-garde, see Heinrich Klotz, *Neuzeit und Moderne* (Munich 2000) (= Geschichte der deutschen Kunst 3).
25. See Ugo Matini, 'Gli artisti (impressioni del vero)', *Firenze Ottocento: Dalla dominazione 'illuminata' dei Lorena all'elezione a capitale d'Italia, fino agli ultimi anni del secolo, in un clima di generale rinnovamento: Cento anni di storia rivisitati anche alla luce delle dirette testimonianze degli scrittori del tempo*, ed. Marcello Vannucci (Florence 1992), 241–65.
26. *Il Marzocco*, vii/16 (20 April 1902), 3.
27. Adolf von Hildebrand, *Briefwechsel mit Conrad Fiedler*, ed. Günther Jachmann (Dresden 1927), 282–3 (letter of 7 July 1889).
28. Klee, *Tagebücher* (note 23), 65; see also Paul Klee, *Briefe an die Familie 1893–1940*, ed. Felix Klee (Cologne 1976), i.338.
29. See Otto Brahm, *Karl Stauffer-Bern: Sein Leben, seine Briefe, seine Gedichte* (Berlin 1911); Joachim Burmeister, 'Turismo in Arcadia: Un "panoptikum" delle presenze tedesche a Firenze nell'Ottocento, per il 75° anniversario di Villa Romana (1905–1980)', *Arnold Böcklin e la cultura in Toscana* (Rome 1980), 66–82, esp. 79–80; Burmeister, 'Überlegungen zu den Ursprüngen des deutschen Künstlerhauses Villa Romana in Florenz: Eine schriftliche Geisterbeschwörung', *Storia dell'arte e politica culturale intorno al 1900: La fondazione dell'Istituto Germanico di Storia dell'Arte a Firenze*, ed. Max Seidel (Venice 1999), 391–413; and Kuhn, 'Villa Romana' (note 1).
30. Wilhelm von Bode, *Mein Leben*, eds Thomas W. Gaehtgens and Barbara Paul (Berlin 1997), i.241; on the following section, see i.239–41.
31. Roger Willemsen, *Der Selbstmord in Berichten, Briefen, Manifesten, Dokumenten und literarischen Texten* (Cologne 1986), 34 and 37.
32. A good example from Florence may be found in Gabinetto Vieusseux, Fondo Orvieto, Carte Cantoni, Orvieto Laura. Cass. 300 (11 Nov. 1899), 5.
33. Kurz, *Pilgerfahrt nach dem Unerreichlichen* (note 19), 359 and 362.
34. FC (letter from Mary Warburg to Charlotte Warburg, 19 March 1898).
35. Volker Krahn, 'Ein ziemlich kühnes Unterfangen . . .': Wilhelm von Bode als Wegbereiter der Bronzeforschung, seine Erwerbungen für die Berliner Museen und seine Beziehungen zu Sammlern', *Von allen Seiten schön: Bronzen der Renaissance und des Barock*, ed. Volker Krahn (Berlin 1995), 34–55, esp. 42.
36. Marcello Vannucci, *Firenze Ottocento: Dalla dominazione 'illuminata' dei Lorena all'elezione a capitale d'Italia, fino agli ultimi anni del secolo, in un clima di generale rinnovamento: Cento*

anni di storia rivistati anche alla luce delle dirette testimonianze degli scrittori del tempo (Florence 1992), 246 and 250.

37. GC (letter from Bernt Hansen to Aby Warburg, 28 Feb. 1901).
38. A. Conti, 'L'educazione artistica', *Il Marzocco*, iv/21 (25 June 1899).
39. 'Multa renascentur', *Il Marzocco*, i (2 Feb. 1896), 1.
40. *Il Marzocco*, iv/3 (19 Feb. 1899), 3.
41. Raffaele Monti, *I Macchiaioli* (Florence 1987); and A. Del Soldato, *Luoghi e ricordi dei Macchiaioli* (Florence 1985).
42. Giovanni Fattori, *Scritti autobiografici editi e inediti*, ed. Francesca Errico (Rome 1980), 32.
43. Ibid., 36.
44. T. Neal, 'Morale e arte', *Il Marzocco*, i/50 (10 Jan. 1897).
45. Pratesi and Uzzani, *L'arte italiana del Novecento* (note 3), 14.
46. Diaries 10.1 (10 March 1898); on Geyger, see *Allgemeines Lexikon der bildenden Künstler von der Antike bis zur Gegenwart*, 36 vols, eds Ulrich Thieme and Felix Becker (Leipzig 1907–47, R1999), xiii.510–12; and Kuhn, 'Villa Romana' (note 1).
47. Enrico Panzacchi, 'L'arte e il progresso', *Nuova Antologia*, iv/70 (1897), 393–404.
48. Panzacchi, 'L'arte e il progresso' (note 47), 403–4; see also Pratesi and Uzzani, *L'arte italiana del Novecento* (note 3), 15 n. 34.
49. *Heinrich Ludolf Verworner: Il colore del dubbio*, ed. Stefano de Rosa (Milan 1997).
50. See Carlo Cresti, *Firenze 1896–1915: La stagione del Liberty* (Florence 1978).
51. F. Chiappelli, *Il Marzocco*, iii/6 (13 March 1898), 4 (after *Nuova Antologia*); and Conti, 'L'educazione artistica' (note 38).
52. See Segantini's letter to the editor, *Il Marzocco*, iii/52 (29 Jan. 1899), 1.
53. See Pratesi and Uzzani, *L'arte italiana del Novecento* (note 3), 18.
54. *Il Marzocco*, iii/52 (29 Jan. 1899).
55. GB (letter from Aby Warburg to Paul Ruben, 4 Jan. 1904); for a note on Ascan and Emma Lutteroth, see ch. 3, note 16. Dr Magin remains unidentified.
56. On Giorgio Kienerk (1869–1948), see Thieme and Becker, *Allgemeines Lexikon* (note 46), xx.268–9; see also *Fieramosca*, xviii/100–101 (11/12 April 1898) on a piece by Kienerk in the Municipal Cemetery at Bologna.
57. Pratesi and Uzzani, *L'arte italiana del Novecento* (note 3), 16; and Alessandro Parronchi, *Momenti della pittura toscana dal neoclassicismo ai postmacchiaioli* (exhibition catalogue) (Florence 1977).
58. Cresti, *Firenze 1896–1915* (note 50), 264–5.
59. FC (letter from Mary Warburg to Charlotte Warburg, 18 March 1901).
60. Ugo Matini in *Firenze d'oggi* (Florence 1896), 321–2.
61. Diaries 10.1 (17 March 1901): Warburg described the portrait of himself as 'tall and slim, yellow, colourless face, eyes concealed by projecting eyebones, cheek bones broader than brow, hair tête carrée, forehead deeply furrowed.'
62. Beatrice Paolozzi Strozzi, 'Degas e Firenze', *L'idea di Firenze: Temi e interpretazioni dell'arte straniera dell'Ottocento*, ed. Maurizio Bossi and Lucia Tonini (Florence 1989), 85–92.
63. See Kuhn, 'Villa Romana' (note 1); Burmeister, 'Turismo in Arcadia' (note 29); and Burmeister, 'Überlegungen zu den Ursprüngen des deutschen Künstlerhauses Villa Romana in Florenz' (note 29), 391–413.
64. Ferdinand Runkel, *Böcklin-Memoiren: Tagebuchblätter von Böcklins Gattin Angela* (Berlin 1910), 310–36; Bernhard Wyß, *Erinnerungen an Böcklin* (Basel 1921), 148–9; Anna Maria von Winterfeld, 'Arnold Böcklin und Florenz', *Storia dell'arte* (note 6), 143–77; Raffaele Monti, 'Böcklin e la pittura in Toscana', *Arnold Böcklin e la cultura artistica in Toscana: Hans von Marées, Adolf von Hildebrand, Max Klinger, Albert Welti* (Fiesole and Rome 1980), 56–60 (exhibition catalogue); and *L'Arcadia di Böcklin: Omaggio fiorentino*, ed. Joachim Burmeister (Livorno 2001).

65. Jürgen Wissmann, *Arnold Böcklin und das Nachleben seiner Malerei: Studien zur Kunst der Jahrhundertwende* (Münster 1968).

66. Wissmann, *Arnold Böcklin* (note 65), 64.

67. Letter from J. C. Schoen to Arnold Böcklin quoted by Runkel, *Böcklin-Memoiren* (note 64), 269.

68. This concept is discussed by Werner Hofmann, *Die Moderne im Rückspiegel: Hauptwege der Kunstgeschichte* (Munich 1998), 291.

69. Winterfeld, 'Arnold Böcklin und Florenz' (note 64), 169–72.

70. Johannes Langner, ' "Gegensätze und Widersprüche – Das ist unsere Harmonie": Zu Kandinskys expressionistischer Abstraktion', *Kandinsky und München: Begegnungen und Wandlungen 1896–1914*, ed. Armin Zweite (Munich 1982), 107–32, esp. 127.

71. Heinrich Brockhaus, *Arnold Böcklin: Rede der Gedächtnisfeier zu Florenz im Palazzo Medici-Riccardi am 27. Januar 1901* (Leipzig 1901), 12–13.

72. Sigmund Freud, *The Interpretation of Dreams*, trans. Joyce Crick (Oxford 1999), 128.

73. Georg M. Blochmann, *Zeitgeist und Künstlermythos: Untersuchungen zur Selbstdarstellung deutscher Maler der Gründerzeit, Marées – Lenbach – Böcklin – Makart – Feuerbach* (Münster 1991), esp. 202.

74. AWI, 62/5; see also E. H. Gombrich, *Aby Warburg: An Intellectual Biography* (Oxford 1986), 93–5.

75. Peter Gay, *The Bourgeois Experience: Victoria to Freud*, v: *Pleasure Wars* (London 1998), 24–45.

76. Runkel, *Böcklin-Memoiren* (note 64), 269–71; see also Klee, *Tagebücher* (note 2), 174.

77. Bernard Berenson, *The Passionate Sightseer* (London 1960), 186 and 188.

78. Gombrich, *Aby Warburg* (note 74), 317.

79. FC (letter from Aby Warburg to Moritz Warburg, 27 March 1898); for more on Hans Krauss, see Thieme and Becker, *Allgemeines Künstlerlexikon* (note 46), xxi.452.

80. AWI, 52, IV.

81. AWI, W 43.1, fol. 161 (26 Feb. 1900).

82. Ewald Hering, *Über das Gedächtnis als eine allgemeine Funktion der organisierten Materie*, 3rd edn (Leipzig 1921), 24–5 and 30–31.

83. Gombrich, *Aby Warburg* (note 74), 153.

84. See Diaries 8.1 (4 Aug. 1897), where Warburg notes having seen some 'wonderful Böcklins' in the art gallery at Basel.

85. GC (letter from Aby Warburg to Frank Bittner, 25 Sept. 1929). As Warburg is unsure if he can afford to buy some original lithographs by Picasso, he asks after the price of colour reproductions.

86. Sigrid Esche-Braunfels, *Adolf von Hildebrand (1847–1921)* (Berlin 1993), 30.

87. Warburg also championed Hildebrand's plans to widen the Jungfernstieg; see AWI, GC (letter from Aby Warburg to Alfred Lichtwark, 2 Feb. 1898); and FC (letter from Aby Warburg to Moritz Warburg, 15 Feb. 1898).

88. AWI, 52.6. If Lederer's statue were to be erected, 'an idea that Adolf Hildebrand has illustrated so convincingly to only a small circle, namely, that only through the felici-tous interpenetration of architectural and plastic elements can a monument with the power of inner conviction be created, will become a popular idea'. On Warburg's atti-tude to modern art, see Mark A. Russell, 'Aby Warburg and art in Hamburg's public realm 1896–1918' (diss., University of Cambridge 2000).

89. Bernhard Sattler, *Adolf von Hildebrand und seine Welt* (Munich 1962), 421 (letter from Adolf Hildebrand to his wife, 5 Feb. 1894).

90. FC (letters from Mary Warburg to Charlotte Warburg, 6 Jan. 1898 and 20 April 1901).

91. See Burmeister, 'Turismo in Arcadia' (note 29), 79; Sattler, *Hildebrand und seine Welt* (note 89), 284 and 322; and Georg Karo, *Selbstgespräche: Aus Heinrich Hombergers Nachlaß* (Munich 1928), 178–9.

92. FC (letter from Mary Warburg to Charlotte Warburg, 9 June 1898); the reading 'Feen Gestalten' (= 'fairy figures') is uncertain.

93. For more on San Francesco di Paolo, see Sattler, *Hildebrand und seine Welt* (note 89); Isolde Kurz, *Florentinische Erinnerungen* (Stuttgart and Berlin 1920); Esche-Braunfels, *Adolf von Hildebrand* (note 86); and Harry Brewster, *The Cosmopolites: A Nineteenth-Century Family Drama* (Wilby 1994), 132–55.

94. See Isolde Kurz, 'Adolf Hildebrand: Zu seinem 60. Geburtstag', *Florentinische Erinnerungen* (note 93), 176–219, esp. 178–9; see also Isolde Kurz, *Der Meister von San Francesco* (Tübingen 1931). The most important sources on Hildebrand are listed in Esche-Braunfels, *Adolf von Hildebrand* (note 86), 620–23.

95. Christa Lichtenstern, 'Der "Bildhauer" Hans von Marées und seine verborgene Aktualität in der Plastik des 20. Jahrhunderts', *Hans von Marées*, ed. Christian Lenz (Munich 1987), 163–78, esp. 168 (exhibition catalogue).

96. Esche-Braunfels, *Adolf von Hildebrand* (note 86), 41; for a note on Liphart, see p. 154 above.

97. Gottfried Boehm, 'Hildebrand und Fiedler im Florentiner Kontext', *Storia dell'arte e politica culturale intorno al 1900* (note 29), 131–41, esp. 138; see also Carolyn Williams, *Transfigured World: Walter Pater's Aesthetic Historicism* (Ithaca, NY, 1989); and Bernard Smith, *Modernism's History: A Study in Twentieth-Century Art and Ideas* (New Haven and London 1998).

98. Sattler, *Hildebrand und seine Welt* (note 89), 242–3 (letter from Adolf Hildebrand to Irene Hildebrand, 2 July 1877). Of all the Pre-Raphaelites, only Burne-Jones escaped his strictures, whereas he had little to say in favour of the other members of the group, whose work he saw in London in 1877.

99. Esche-Braunfels, *Adolf von Hildebrand* (note 86), 38 and 84; see Adolf von Hildebrand, 'Auguste Rodin', *Gesammelte Schriften zur Kunst*, ed. Henning Bock (Cologne and Opladen 1969), 425–30.

100. Esche-Braunfels, *Adolf von Hildebrand* (note 86), 84.

101. FC (letter from Aby Warburg to Mary Warburg, 2 July 1899: 'I was at the exhibitions [in Berlin] yesterday. The "Große" is repulsively flat . . . the Secession, by contrast, has produced some very fine work, Liebermann . . . Böcklin, Leibl and Hildebrand'). For Warburg's note on Rodin, see FC (letter from Aby Warburg to Mary Warburg, 15 Oct. 1900).

102. See Hildebrand, *Gesammelte Schriften* (note 99), 593, n. 279; see also Sattler, *Hildebrand und seine Welt* (note 89), 670–72.

103. Sattler, *Hildebrand und seine Welt* (note 89), 294–5.

104. Ibid., 410–11 (letter from Adolf von Hildebrand to Heinrich Wölfflin, 15 July 1893); see also p. 517 for Hildebrand's letter to his son Dietrich; and p. 469 for his admiration of Eduard Mörike, whom he compared – favourably – to the detested figure of Wagner.

105. Boehm, 'Hildebrand und Fiedler' (note 97), 18.

106. Heinrich Mann, *Die Göttinnen oder Die drei Romane der Herzogin von Assy* (Berlin 1969), 612.

107. Roger Fry, 'French Post-Impressionism', *Vision and Design* (London and New York 1981), 166–70; and *Max and Will: Max Beerbohm and William Rothenstein. Their Friendship and Letters 1893–1945*, eds Mary M. Lago and Karl Beckson (London 1975), 67–9.

108. On the relationship between art and the modern world, see Harold Osborne, 'Expressionism', *The Oxford Companion to Twentieth-Century Art* (Oxford 1981), 179–82; and Smith, *Modernism's History* (note 97).

109. Smith, *Modernism's History* (note 97), 98.

110. Sylvia Sprigge, *Berenson: A Biography* (London 1960), 241, n. 2 and 243.

111. Egisto P. Fabbri (1866–1933) was a painter, amateur architect and collector who moved to Florence with his family in 1884. In Paris he came into contact with the art

of the Impressionists. He was also in touch with Mary Cassatt, Loeser and Berenson; see William Rothenstein, *Men and Memories: Recollections of William Rothenstein 1900–1922* (London 1932), i.132. On Loeser's concert evenings, see Harold Acton, 'Stranieri a Firenze all'alba del Novecento', *Nuova Antologia*, cxii/532, 64–72.

Chapter 15 'Ninfa fiorentina'

1. Silvia Contarini, ' "Botticelli ritrovato": Frammenti di dialogo tra Aby Warburg e André Jolles', *Prospettiva*, lxviii (1993), 87–93.
2. This was the 'middle-class state costume' worn in Florence; see AWI, 51.1, Untitled, Ghirlandaio, fol. 15.
3. On the relations between Warburg and Jolles, see Antoine Bodar, 'Aby Warburg en André Jolles: Een Florentijnse vriendschap', *Nexus*, i (1991), 5–18; see also Contarini, ' "Botticelli ritrovato" ' (note 1).
4. GC (draft letter from Aby Warburg to an unnamed mayor, (*c.*1899).
5. See Walter Thijs, 'Uit het leven en werk van A. Jolles', *De Nieuwe Taalgids*, xlvii (1954), 129–37 and 198–208.
6. Jan Kamerbeek, 'Huizinga en de beweging van tachtig', *Tijdschrift voor Geschiedenis*, lxvii (1954), 145–64.
7. Johan Huizinga, *Mein Weg zur Geschichte: Letzte Reden und Skizzen*, trans. Werner Kaegi (Basel 1947), 22–3; and Werner Kaegi, 'Das historische Werk Johan Huizingas', *Historische Meditationen II* (Zurich 1946), 245–86; see also Christoph Strupp, *Johan Huizinga: Geschichtswissenschaft als Kulturwissenschaft* (Göttingen 2000), 39.
8. FC (letter from Aby Warburg to Mary Warburg, 16 Oct. 1902); the following passage is taken from Aby Warburg's letter to Mary of 30 Nov. 1902.
9. Bodar, 'Aby Warburg en André Jolles' (note 3), 8; and Contarini, ' "Botticelli ritrovato" ' (note 1).
10. Bodar, 'Aby Warburg en André Jolles' (note 3), 11.
11. GC (letter from André Jolles to Aby Warburg, 27 Jan. 1901); see also Diaries 10.1 (27 Jan. 1901).
12. AWI, 118, Ninfa fiorentina 1900; see also E. H. Gombrich, *Aby Warburg: An Intellectual Biography* (Oxford 1986), 105–27.
13. Gombrich, *Aby Warburg* (note 12), 129; see also Diaries 10.1 (4 Aug. 1900): 'Discussed with Max the idea of a Warburg library on cultural studies, he wasn't against it.'
14. Friedrich Nietzsche, 'Menschliches, Allzumenschliches', *Werke in drei Bänden*, ed. Karl Schlechta (Munich 1955), i.592–3; see also Walther Rehm, 'Der Renaissancekult um 1900 und seine Überwindung', *Zeitschrift für deutsche Philologie*, liv (1929), 296–328, reprinted in Rehm, *Der Dichter und die neue Einsamkeit: Aufsätze zur Literatur um 1900* (Göttingen 1969), 34–77, esp. 42–3; and Julius Hart, 'Individualismus und Renaissance-Romantik', *Der neue Gott* (Florence and Leipzig 1899), 73–116.
15. Lea Ritter-Santini, 'Maniera Grande: Über italienische Renaissance und deutsche Jahrhundertwende', *Deutsche Literatur der Jahrhundertwende*, ed. Viktor Zmegac (Königstein 1981), 242–72; see also Italo Michele Battafarano, 'Genese und Metamorphose des Italienbildes in der deutschen Literatur der Neuzeit', *Italienische Reise, Reisen nach Italien* (Gardolo di Trento 1988), 13–101, esp. 94–5.
16. Thomas Mann, *Gesammelte Werke in dreizehn Bänden* (Frankfurt 1974), viii.381; see also Helmut Koopmann, 'Renaissancekult in der deutschen Literatur um 1900', *Storia dell'arte e politica culturale intorno al 1900: La fondazione dell'Istituto Germanico di Storia dell'Arte a Firenze*, ed. Max Seidel (Venice 1999), 13–24, esp. 21.
17. See Ritter-Santini, 'Maniera Grande' (note 15), 251–2; and Rehm, 'Der Renaissancekult um 1900' (note 16), 54.
18. Van Wyck Brooks, *The Dream of Arcadia: American Writers and Artists in Italy 1760–1915* (New York 1958), 256.

19. Anke Hufschmidt,' "Zwischen Luxus- und Schundwaare": Überlegungen zur bürgerlichen Wohnung in der zweiten Hälfte des 19. Jahrhunderts', *Renaissance der Renaissance: Ein bürgerlicher Kunststil im 19. Jahrhundert*, eds G. Ulrich Großmann and Petra Krutisch (Munich 1992), 95–111; the quotations from Hirth and Mothes appear here on pp. 100 and 95–6.
20. Nikolaus Pevsner and others, *Historismus und bildende Kunst* (Munich 1965), 89.
21. Rehm, 'Der Renaissancekult um 1900' (note 14), 58–9.
22. Walburga, Lady Paget, *In My Tower*, 2 vols (London 1924), i.130–31.
23. Heinrich Mann, *Die Göttinnen oder Die drei Romane der Herzogin von Assy* (Berlin 1969), 610–11.
24. Koopmann, 'Renaissancekult in der deutschen Literatur' (note 16), 23.
25. Enrico Castelnuovo,' "Primitifs" e "fin de siècle" ', *Storia dell'arte e politica culturale intorno al 1900* (note 16), 47–54, esp. 47.
26. Rehm, 'Der Renaissancekult um 1900' (note 14), 75.
27. AWI, 118, Ninfa fiorentina 1900. (This shelfmark includes the whole correspondence.)
28. For the modern view of Ghirlandaio, see Ronald G. Kecks, *Domenico Ghirlandaio und die Malerei der Florentiner Renaissance* (Munich 2000).
29. The word *'geilen'* ('lecherous') has been altered in Warburg's hand to *'begehrlichen'* ('covetous').
30. This and the following quotations are taken from AWI, 188, Ninfa fiorentina and from the passages already published by Gombrich, *Aby Warburg* (note 12), 111.
31. Gombrich, *Aby Warburg* (note 12), 241.
32. Arthur Moeller van den Bruck, *Die italienische Schönheit* (Munich 1913), 581; see also Gombrich, *Aby Warburg* (note 12), 240.
33. FC (letter from Aby Warburg to Mary Warburg, 17 Nov. 1903); see also Gombrich, *Aby Warburg* (note 12), 110, n. 1.

Chapter 16 A farewell to Florence

1. Klinger's letter to his parents in Rome was written before February 1893 and is quoted here from a copy in the archives of the Villa Romana. The original is in the Naumburg Municipal Archives, siglum 286.
2. Diaries, 10.1 (5 Feb. 1900).
3. Ibid. (20 Jan. 1900).
4. Walburga, Lady Paget, *In My Tower*, 2 vols (London 1924), i.55.
5. On Böcklin's death, see *La Nazione*, xlviii/17 (17 Jan. 1901); *Fieramosca*, xxi/17 (17/18 Jan. 1901) xxi/19 (19/20 Jan. 1901).
6. AWI, 52,4: Im Cimitero degl'allori, als Böcklin heimging (In the 'Cemetery of laurels', when Böcklin went to his final resting place).
7. The following words were deleted: 'Only those who lie here are all so weary of looking and deathly quiet.'
8. Diaries 10.1 (19 Jan. 1901).
9. DLA, A: Kurz (letter from Aby Warburg to Isolde Kurz, 11 Feb. 1901): 'Kindly forgive me for showing you the Böcklin reminiscence yesterday evening. It is far from adequate. Quite the opposite, I was fully prepared to hear your expert and perceptive criticism, something I sorely lack in matters of artistic and literary taste. Here I feel to be an amateur who is all too happy to be criticized, if it is not already too late.' For Isolde Kurz's reply of 13 Feb. 1901, see FC.
10. Karl Marx, *Outline of the Critique of Political Economy*, trans. Martin Nicolaus (Harmondsworth 1973).
11. The words 'impertinent' and 'photographic' have been deleted. The remainder of this text is quoted from a second, revised version; see E.H. Gombrich, *Aby Warburg: An Intellectual Biography* (Oxford 1986), 152–3.

12. The words 'of actuality' have been deleted after 'hyena's laugh'.

13. Otto Brahm, *Karl Stauffer-Bern: Sein Leben, seine Briefe, seine Gedichte* (Berlin 1911), 316.

14. Filippo Tommaso Marinetti, *Selected Writings*, trans. R. W. Flint and Arthur A. Coppotelli (London 1972), 39–40.

15. The words 'from their homeland' have been deleted here.

16. Paget, *In My Tower* (note 4), i.56–7.

17. See AWI, 52.3; Diaries 10.1; *La Nazione*, xlviii/29 (29 Jan. 1901); and *Fieramosca*, xxi/28 (29/29 Jan. 1901).

18. Heinrich Brockhaus, *Arnold Böcklin: Rede der Gedächtnisfeier zu Florenz im Palazzo Medici-Riccardi am 27. Januar 1901* (Leipzig 1901).

19. Ron Chernow, *The Warburgs: The Twentieth-Century Odyssey of a Remarkable Jewish Family* (New York 1993), 114. It cannot, however, be denied that other observers saw an idyllic picture which does not square with the usual accounts of Warburg's state of health in Florence. Tilli Mönckeberg, for example, describes a very different Warburg, a calm, thoughtful husband living in perfect harmony with his wife: 'I find him a very refined, altogether splendid man,' she wrote. 'How well he knows how to raise your spirits, give you advice, take an interest in you. One feels comfortable with him. They are also happy together, so happy that it seems to me to be an ideal marriage! You see, they don't revel in the lap of luxury, they don't always sit opposite each other in tail coat and low-cut dress, and yet they conform to my ideal. One really notices the extent to which they know and understand each other and how indispensable they are to one another. At the same time, they share the same refined tastes, have common artistic interests and create the impression of a harmonious whole'; see Antoine Bodar, 'Aby Warburg en André Jolles: Een Florentijnse vriendschap', *Nexus*, i (1991), 5–18, esp. 11.

20. Chernow, *The Warburgs* (note 19), 114.

21. FC (letter from Aby Warburg to Mary Warburg, 13 June 1902).

22. Diaries 10.1 (7 Feb. 1900).

23. FC (letters from Aby Warburg to Mary Warburg, 7 Nov. 1902 and 25 May 1900).

24. Diaries 10.1 (8 Jan. 1901).

25. FC (letter from Aby Warburg to Mary Warburg, 2 June 1902).

26. NL Bode, 5251/274.1 (letter from Aby Warburg to Wilhelm von Bode, 23 June 1920).

27. FC (letter from Aby Warburg to Max Warburg, 13 Feb. 1901).

28. FC (letter from Aby Warburg to Charlotte Warburg, 14 Dec. 1899).

29. FC (letter from Aby Warburg to Mary Warburg, 16 Oct. 1902).

30. FC (letter from Aby Warburg to Mary Warburg, 18 Oct. 1902).

31. Gertrud Bing, *Aby M. Warburg: Vortrag anläßlich der feierlichen Aufstellung von Aby Warburgs Büste in der Hamburger Kunsthalle am 31. Oktober 1958* (Hamburg 1958), 9–32; see also Diaries 10.1 (22 Feb. 1898).

32. FC (letter from Aby Warburg to Mary Warburg, 15 Nov. 1915).

33. Diaries 10.1 (12 Jan. 1901).

34. Diaries 3.1 (16 June 1899).

35. GC (letter from Alice Hallgarten to Aby Warburg, 4 Dec. 1897).

36. FC (letter from Aby Warburg to Mary Warburg, 28 May 1900).

37. FC (letter from Aby Warburg to Mary Warburg, 28 May 1900).

38. NL Bode, 5251/1 (2 Oct. 1902).

39. Diaries 10.2 (4 Sept. 1902), fols 77–8.

40. See AWI, Mary Hertz's Diary, entry by Aby Warburg (7 Nov. 1902) and FC (letter from Aby Warburg to Mary Warburg, 7 Nov. 1902).

41. FC (letter from Mary Warburg to Aby Warburg, 12 Nov. 1902).

42. FC (letter from Mary Warburg to Aby Warburg, 5 Dec. 1902).

43. FC (letter from Mary Warburg to Aby Warburg, 12 Nov. 1902).

44. FC (letter from Aby Warburg to Mary Warburg, 18 Nov. 1902).

45. NL Bode 5251/1, 23.1 (letter from Aby Warburg to Wilhelm von Bode, 4 June 1904).

Chapter 17 In the new century

1. See NL Bode 5251/1, 3.1 (4 March 1902):'Every word of encouragement is welcome to a private scholar like him and is necessary because he otherwise receives no direct word from the real world; in this necromantic art the dead absorb one's present personal life almost to the exclusion of all else: resurrection can be achieved only by sacrificing one's own life. But that is all perfectly in order; it is certainly one of the more respectable ways of allowing oneself to be consumed.'
2. See Robert Michels, *Italien von heute: Politik, Kultur, Wirtschaft* (Zurich and Leipzig 1930), 140–41, 150 and 153.
3. Michels, *Italien von heute* (note 2), 159.
4. See Valerio Castronovo, *La storia economica* (Turin 1975), 164–5; and Effren Magrini, 'L'industria automobilistica italiana nel 1907', *L'Italia economica: Annuario dell'attività nationale*, ii (1908), 137–53.
5. *Il Marzocco*, iv (25 June 1899), 4.
6. *Il Marzocco*, vi/42 (20 Oct. 1901), 3.
7. *Il Marzocco*, vii/37 (14 Sept. 1902), 1–2; vii/44 (2 Nov. 1902); on Morasso, see Otto Weiss, 'Staat, Regierung und Parlament im norddeutschen Bund und im Kaiserreich im Urteil der Italiener', *Quellen und Forschungen aus italienischen Archiven und Bibliotheken*, lxvi (1986), 310–77, esp. 360–61; and, more generally, Roberto de Mattei, *Cultura e letteratura antidemocratica dopo l'unificazione* (Florence 1937).
8. See Mauro Pratesi and Giovanna Uzzani, *L'arte italiana del Novecento: La Toscana* (Venice 1991), 89; more generally, see Christa Baumgarth, *Geschichte des Futurismus* (Reinbek bei Hamburg 1966); Hansgeorg Schmidt-Bergmann, *Futurismus: Geschichte, Ästhetik, Dokumente* (Reinbek bei Hamburg 1993); and, on Futurism in Florence, Marcello Vannucci, *Firenze futurista* (Florence 1976).
9. Schmidt-Bergmann, *Futurismus* (note 8), 60.
10. Mario Morasso,'La sfida dei giganti', *Il Marzocco*, viii/29 (19 July 1903).
11. Filippo Tommaso Marinetti, *Selected Writings*, trans. R.W. Flint and Arthur A. Coppotelli (London 1972), 39–42.
12. Ibid., 55 ('Against Past-Loving Florence').
13. Claudia Naber, ' "Heuernte bei Gewitter": Aby Warburg 1924–1929', *'Ekstatische Nymphe, trauernder Flußgott': Portrait eines Gelehrten*, eds Robert Galitz and Brita Reimers (Hamburg 1995), 104–29, esp. 111.
14. Peter van Huisstede, 'Der Mnemosyne-Atlas: Ein Laboratorium der Bildgeschichte', *'Ekstatische Nymphe, trauernder Flußgott'* (note 13), 130–71.
15. E. H. Gombrich, *Aby Warburg: An Intellectual Biography* (Oxford 1986), 288.
16. NL Bode, 5251/1, 24, 1–4 (12 Nov. 1904).
17. Aby Warburg, 'Austausch künstlerischer Kultur zwischen Norden und Süden im 15. Jahrhundert', *Sitzungsberichte der Kunstgeschichtlichen Gesellschaft zu Berlin*, ii (1905), 7–12; reprinted in *Deutsche Literaturzeitung*, xxvi (1905), cols 1145–8.
18. Aby Warburg, 'Italienische Kunst und Internazionale Astrologie im Palazzo Schifanoja zu Ferrara', *L'Italia e l'arte straniera: Atti del X congresso internazionale di storia dell'arte, 1912* (Rome 1922), 179–93.
19. Gombrich, *Aby Warburg* (note 15), 303: 'Sometimes it looks to me as if, in my role as psycho-historian, I tried to diagnose the schizophrenia of Western civilization from its images in an autobiographical context. The ecstatic "Nympha" (manic) on the one side and the mourning river-god (depressive) on the other.' See also Karl Königseder,'Aby Warburg im "Bellevue" ', *'Ekstatische Nymphe, trauernder Flußgott'* (note 13), 74–98, esp. 76.
20. Anne Spagnolo-Stiff, 'L'appello di Aby Warburg a un'intesa italo-tedesca – "La guerra del 1914–15. Rivista illustrata" ', *Storia dell'arte e politica culturale intorno al 1900: La fondazione dell'Istituto Germanico di Storia dell'Arte a Firenze*, ed. Max Seidel (Venice 1999), 249–69, esp. 254.

21. FC (letter from Aby Warburg to Mary Warburg, 15 Nov. 1915).
22. See AWI, 111.1, fol. 78: Fritz Saxl, 'Biography of Warburg' (1939E/40).
23. Fritz Saxl, 'Three "Florentines": Herbert Horne, Aby Warburg, Jacques Mesnil', *Lectures* (London 1957), i.331–48, esp. 342.
24. FC (letter from Aby Warburg to his family (11 Aug. 1918).
25. AWI, 110.11.2 (Max Warburg's speech of 5 Dec. 1929).
26. Königseder, 'Aby Warburg im "Bellevue" ' (note 19), 81–2. Königseder also ventures a possible diagnosis from a modern standpoint, arguing that Warburg suffered from a 'schizo-affective psychosis or mixed psychosis . . . in which symptoms of manic behaviour or depression are also found alongside symptoms of schizophrenia' (82).
27. Michael Diers, 'Professor V. Aby Warburgs Krankenakte', *Frankfurter Allgemeine Zeitung*, clxxx (5 Aug. 1992).
28. Ron Chernow, *The Warburgs: The Twentieth-Century Odyssey of a Remarkable Jewish Family* (New York 1993), 7–8. In Warburg's family, his grandmother, Sara Warburg, married her second cousin, Aby S. Warburg. Cases of psychiatric disorders occurred frequently among their descendants. Aby Warburg's sister Olga committed suicide in 1904, and his son Max Adolph suffered from depression throughout his life, spending months at a time in psychiatric institutions.
29. See Königseder, 'Aby Warburg im "Bellevue" ' (note 19). Many doctors regarded opium as the only effective cure for 'neurasthenia'; see Joachim Radkau, *Das Zeitalter der Nervosität: Deutschland zwischen Bismarck und Hitler* (Munich and Vienna 1998), 105.
30. Diaries 10.1 (1 June 1906).
31. Klaus Mann, *André Gide und die Krise des modernen Denkens* (Reinbek bei Hamburg 1995).
32. Steffi Roettgen, 'Dal "Börsencourier" di Berlino al "Genio" di Firenze: Lo storico Robert Davidsohn (1835–1937) e il suo inedito lascito fiorentino', *Storia dell'arte e politica culturale intorno al 1900* (note 20), 312–58, esp. 316–17.
33. Ibid., 316.
34. Sylvia Sprigge, *Berenson: A Biography* (London 1960), 251.
35. DLA, A: Isolde Kurz (letter from Heinrich Brockhaus to Isolde Kurz, 25 Oct. 1924).
36. Mesnil's letters to Warburg are lodged at the Casa Buonarotti in Florence.
37. '*Puis mon souvenir va à l'ami défunt, au compagnon de ces belles années toscanes, à Aby Warburg*' ('Then my memory goes to my dead friend, the companion of these beautiful years in Tuscany, Aby Warburg').
38. Saxl, 'Three "Florentines"' (note 23), 342.
39. Marion Ónodi, *Isolde Kurz: Leben und Prosawerk als Ausdruck zeitgenössischer und menschlich–individueller Situation von der Mitte des 19. bis zur Mitte des 20. Jahrhunderts* (Frankfurt am Main 1989), 31–5; Isolde Kurz, *Florentinische Erinnerungen* (Stuttgart and Berlin 1920), 244–5, although she did retain the passage: 'I also remain eternally indebted to her most erudite husband [Davidsohn], who so often showed me the shortest way to my sources on the strength of his unfathomable knowledge.'
40. DLA, A: Kurz, Briefwechsel mit Robert und Fini Davidsohn. The last surviving letter dates from 3 Aug. 1937.
41. Isolde Kurz, *Pilgerfahrt nach dem Unerreichlichen: Lebensrückschau* (Tübingen 1938), 102.
42. DLA, A: Isolde Kurz, 'Rede in der Deutschen Akademie', fol. 9.
43. Henry James, *Italian Hours* (New York 1968), 395–6.
44. Heinrich Mann, *Pippo Spano* (Berlin 1976), 288.

Bibliography

Unpublished Sources

Berlin, Staatliche Museen zu Berlin – Preußischer Kulturbesitz/Zentralarchiv: Nachlaß Bode 5251, 1543/1 (correspondence between Bode and Warburg and between Bode and Thode)

Florence, Archivio Comunale: Inv. no. 2650; Demografia fiorentina (1862–1914)

Florence, Archivio Corsini: Tommaso Corsini, Diari (1896–1901) (Stanza V)

Florence, Biblioteca Comunale: Atti del consiglio comunale (1896–1904)

Florence, Biblioteca Nazionale: Fondo Chiappelli: Cass. 3, N. 81; Fondo Foscolo: Fosc. XIII, 17e; Fondo de Gubernatis, C.V., 457, 25; Cass. 64, 68, 70; 133, 3; 133,6

Florence, Biblioteca Ricciardiana: Carteggio Fucini, Cass. 4/7

Florence, Casa Buonarotti: Fondo Mesnil

Florence, Gabinetto Vieusseux, Archivio: Loan journals (1896–7); Il Marzocco (1896–1904); Fondo Orvieto, Carte Cantoni Orvieto Laura Ca. 300 (unnumbered)

Florence, Kunsthistorisches Institut (Art Historical Institute), archives: Das Kunsthistorische Institut in Florenz (1888–1897–1925) (Leipzig n.d.)

Florence, Museo Horne: Carte Horne. H X I: List of signatories objecting to the destruction of Florence; H X II: 'Fine dell'Associazione à la tutela del carattere e del patrimonio storico di Firenze'; Articoli estratti; letters; K I 6 Carteggio Horne, 7, Bernard Berenson, 9 Jan. 1899

Florence: Ufficio Toponomastica: Land register of Florence

Florence, Villa I Tatti, Harvard Center for Renaissance Studies: Correspondence of Bernard Berenson

Florence, Villa Romana: Archives of the Villa Romana: Fred Robert von Klement, Bei Lapi in Florenz (Salo 1911); letters from Max Klinger copied from originals in the Naumburg Municipal Archives, 286

Hanover, Stadtbibliothek: 40.4105 (Hartlebeniana)

London, University of London, The Warburg Institute, Archives: Family correspondence, family reminiscences, reminiscences of Max Warburg, with corrections in his hand; General correspondence; 8, 10.1–3, Aby Warburg, Diaries; Diary of Mary Hertz; 20.3: Expenses for flat in Florence; 23: Address books; 43.1: Grundlegende Bruchstücke zu einer monistischen Kunstpsychologie I (1888, 1903); 50.1.1.: Leonardo da Vinci, Lecture I, Lecture II (both in typescript); 50.11: Notes on Leonardo and Verrocchio; 50.3.1, after 5.2.1: Leonardo lectures I–III (all in typescript); 51.1: Untitled. Ghirlandaio in S. Trinità

(24 Oct. 1901); 52.4: Poems and dramatic works, including Im Cimitero degl'Allori, als Böcklin heimging; 52.6: Position regarding Bismarck Monument in Hamburg; 62.5: Hamburg conversations about art; 72: Henry Thode and Gabriele D'Annunzio; 75.2: Hamburg lectures, 1909, IV; 76.1.1: Hamburg lectures 1908/9, Ghirlandaio (typescript); 88.2: The entry of the classicising ideal style in the painting of the early Italian Renaissance; file-card boxes 50, Böcklin; Thode/Liebermann; 110.11.2: Max Warburg's speech (5 Dec. 1929); 111.1: Saxl, Biography of Warburg (1939/40); 118: Ninfa fiorentina (1900); 50: Box of notes, Modern art

Marbach, Deutsches Literaturarchiv/Schiller-Nationalmuseum: Nachlaß Isolde Kurz, A: Isolde Kurz, Rede in der Deutschen Akademie; 'Menschenleugner' (manuscript); letters; correspondence between Kurz and Warburg, between Kurz and Davidsohn and between Kurz and Brockhaus; Nachlaß Maria Kurz

Munich, Bayerische Staatsbibliothek, Department of Manuscripts: Nachlaß Hartleben; Nachlaß Heyse, I, 22

Published Sources

Acton, Harold. 'Stranieri a Firenze all'alba del Novecento', *Nuova Antologia*, cxii/532 (1978), 64–72

Adorno, Francesco (ed.). *Accademie e istituzioni culturali a Firenze* (Florence 1983)

Agosti, Giovanni. *La nascita della storia dell'arte in Italia. Adolfo Venturi: Dal museo all'università* (Venice 1996)

Altgeld, Wilhelm. 'Das Deutsche Reich im italienischen Urteil 1871–1945', *Das Deutsche Reich im Urteil der Großen Mächte und europäischen Nachbaren*, ed. Karl Hildebrand (Munich 1995), 107–21

Angiolini, Alfredo. *Socialismo e socialisti in Italia* (Florence 1900)

Ara, Angelo and Rudolf Lill (eds). *Immagini a confronto: Italia e Germania dal 1830 all'unificazione nazionale* (Bologna and Berlin 1991)

Artom Treves, Giuliana. *Anglo-Fiorentini di cento anni fa* (Florence 1953)

Artom Treves, Giuliana. *The Golden Ring: The Anglo-Florentines 1847–1862* (London and New York 1956)

Artusi, Luciano and Silvano Gabrielli. *Le feste di Firenze* (Florence 1991)

Artusi, Luciano and Vincenzo Giannetti. *'A vita nuova': Ricordi e vicende della grande operazione urbanistica che distrusse il centro storico di Firenze* (Florence 1997)

Balfour, Lady Betty. *Personal and Literary Letters of Robert First Earl of Lytton* (London 1906)

Bargellini, Simone. *Antiquari di ieri* (Florence 1981)

Barth, Hans. *Est! Est! Est! Italienischer Schenkenführer* (Oldenburg and Leipzig 1902)

Barth, Hans (ed.). *Osteria: Kulturgeschichtlicher Führer durch Italiens Schenken vom Gardasee bis Capri* (Stuttgart 1911)

Bassignana, Lucia. 'La manifattura di Signa: Dai frammenti di una storia', *La manifattura di Signa*, eds Andrea Baldinotti and others (Florence 1986)

Bätschmann, Oskar and Pascal Griener. *Hans Holbein d. J.: Die Darmstädter Madonna. Original gegen Fälschung* (Frankfurt am Main 1998)

Battafarano, Italo Michele. 'Genese und Metamorphose des Italienbildes in der deutschen Literatur der Neuzeit', *Italienische Reise, Reisen nach Italien* (Gardolo di Trento 1988), 13–101

Baumgarth, Christa. *Geschichte des Futurismus* (Reinbek bei Hamburg 1966)

Bayersdorfer, Adolf. 'Nachruf auf Karl Eduard von Liphart', *Münchner Neueste Nachrichten* (20 Feb. 1891)

Bayersdorfer, Adolf. *Leben und Schriften: Aus seinem Nachlaß*, eds Hans Mackowsky, August Pauly and Wilhelm Weigand (Munich 1902)

Bennett, Arnold. 'Night and morning in Florence', *English Review*, v (1910), 442–55

Bennett, Arnold. *The Journals*, ed. Frank Swinnerton (Harmondsworth 1971)

Berenson, Bernard. *The Passionate Sightseer* (London 1960)

Berresford, Sandra. 'Preraffaellismo ed esteticismo a Firenze negli ultimi decenni del XIX secolo', *L'idea di Firenze: Temi e interpretazioni dell'arte straniera dell'Ottocento*, eds Maurizio Bossi and Lucia Tonini (Florence 1989), 191–210

Beyer, A. 'Blicke auf die Kunst und Kultur der Renaissance: Der Eugen Diederichs-Verlag im kunsthistorischen Diskurs des Jahrhundertbeginns' (unpublished typescript)

Biester, Björn. *Der innere Beruf zur Wissenschaft: Paul Ruben (1866–1943). Studien zur deutsch–jüdischen Wissenschaftsgeschichte* (Hamburg 2001)

Bing, Gertrud. *Aby M. Warburg: Vortrag anläßlich der feierlichen Aufstellung von Aby Warburgs Büste in der Hamburger Kunsthalle am 31. Oktober 1958* (Hamburg 1958), 9–32

Bizzozero, Giulio. 'Le macchine da scrivere dal punto di vista dell'igiene', *Nuova Antologia*, iv/72 (1897), 45–68

Blochmann, Georg M. *Zeitgeist und Künstlermythos: Untersuchungen zur Selbstdarstellung deutscher Maler der Gründerzeit, Marées – Lenbach – Böcklin – Makart – Feuerbach* (Münster 1991)

Boccia, Lionello Giorgio. *Firenze: Illuminazione pubblica e ambiente urbano* (Florence 1983)

Bodar, Antoine. 'Aby Warburg en André Jolles: Een Florentijnse vriendschap', *Nexus*, i (1991), 5–18

Bode, Wilhelm von. 'Stefano Bardini', *L'antiquario*, x (1923), 1–2

Bode, Wilhelm von. *Mein Leben*, eds Thomas W. Gaehtgens and Barbara Paul (Berlin 1997)

Boehm, Gottfried. 'Hildebrand und Fiedler im Florentiner Kontext', *Storia dell'arte e politica culturale intorno al 1900: La fondazione dell'Istituto Germanico di Storia dell'Arte a Firenze*, ed. Max Seidel (Venice 1999), 131–41

Boglietti, Giovanni. 'L'evoluzione della democrazia socialista in Germania', *Nuova Antologia*, iv/78 (1898), 612–37

Borgese, Giuseppe Antonio. *La nuova Germania* (Torino 1909)

Borghese, Lucia (ed.). *Karl Hillebrand: Eretico d'Europa. Atti del Seminario* (Florence 1984)

Borghese, Lucia (ed.). *Karl Hillebrand: Mostra di documenti* (Florence 1984)

Bossi, Maurizio. 'Cultura tedesca al Gabinetto Vieusseux tra Otto e Novecento', *Storia dell'arte e politica culturale intorno al 1900: La fondazione dell'Istituto Germanico di Storia dell'Arte a Firenze*, ed. Max Seidel (Venice 1999), 381–90

Bossi, Maurizio and Lucia Tonini (eds). *L'idea di Firenze: Temi e interpretazioni dell'arte straniera dell'Ottocento* (Florence 1989)

Brahm, Otto. *Karl Stauffer-Bern: Sein Leben, seine Briefe, seine Gedichte* (Berlin 1911)

Brewster, Harry. *The Cosmopolites: A Nineteenth-Century Family Drama* (Wilby 1994)

Brockhaus, Heinrich. *Arnold Böcklin: Rede der Gedächtnisfeier zu Florenz im Palazzo Medici-Riccardi am 27. Januar 1901* (Leipzig 1901)

Buckler, William E. *Walter Pater: The Critic as Artist of Ideas* (New York and London 1987)

Bullen, J. B. *The Myth of the Renaissance in Nineteenth-Century Writing* (Oxford 1994)

Burckhardt, Jacob. *Briefe*, ed. Max Burckhardt, 10 vols (Basel 1949–86)

Burckhardt, Jacob. *Der Cicerone: Eine Anleitung zum Genuß der Kunstwerke Italiens* (Basel 1855, R1986)

Burmeister, Joachim. 'Turismo in Arcadia: Un "panoptikum" delle presenze tedesche a Firenze nell'Ottocento, per il 75° anniversario di Villa Romana (1905–1980)', *Arnold Böcklin e la cultura in Toscana* (Rome 1980), 66–82

Burmeister, Joachim. 'Überlegungen zu den Ursprüngen des deutschen Künstlerhauses Villa Romana in Florenz: Eine schriftliche Geisterbeschwörung', *Storia dell'arte e politica culturale intorno al 1900: La fondazione dell'Istituto Germanico di Storia dell'Arte a Firenze*, ed. Max Seidel (Venice 1999), 391–413

Burmeister, Joachim (ed.). *L'Arcadia di Böcklin: Omaggio fiorentino* (Livorno 2001)

Cambieri Tosi, Marie-José. *Carlo Placci: Maestro di cosmopoli nella Firenze fra Otto e Novecento* (Florence 1894)

Campbell, Margaret. *Dolmetsch: The Man and His Work* (Seattle 1975)

Canavero, Alfredo. *Milano e la crisi di fine secolo (1896–1900)* (Milan 1976)

Cantoni, Carlo. 'Le università tedesche: Descritte e giudicate da professori tedeschi', *Nuova Antologia*, iv/75 (1898), 417–42

Capitini Maccabruni, Nicla. 'Gli scioperi delle trecciaiole toscane del 1896–97 e l'azione della Camera del Lavoro di Firenze', *Movimento operaio e socialista*, x (1964), 121–36

Cary, R. 'Aldous Huxley, Vernon Lee and the "genius loci" ', *Colby Library Quarterly* (June 1960)

Castelli, L. *La popolazione e la mortalità del centennio 1791–1890: Studi e raffronti con la salute pubblica nel biennio 1891–92* (Florence 1893)

Castelnuovo, Enrico. ' "Primitifs" e "fin de siècle" ', *Storia dell'arte e politica culturale intorno al 1900: La fondazione dell'Istituto Germanico di Storia dell'Arte a Firenze*, ed. Max Seidel (Venice 1999), 47–54

Castronovo, Valerio. *La storia economica* (Turin 1975)

Ceccuti, Cosimo. 'Un parlamentare fiorentino in età giolittiana: Giovanni Rosadi', *Rassegna storica toscana*, xxvii/1 (1981), 73–96

Checchi, Eugenio. 'La popolarità del teatro in Italia', *Nuova Antologia*, iv (1897), 341–3

Chernow, Ron. *The Warburgs: The Twentieth-Century Odyssey of a Remarkable Jewish Family* (New York 1993)

Chiappelli, Alessandro. 'I poeti paesisti de nostro secolo', *Nuova Antologia*, iv/158 (1899), 78–99

Chiappelli, Alessandro. 'Sul confine dei due secoli', *Nuova Antologia*, iv/86 (1900), 620–39

Charney, Leo and Vanessa R. Schwartz. *Cinema and the Invention of Modern Life* (Berkeley and Los Angeles 1995)

Clark, Ronald W. *The Life of Bertrand Russell* (London 1975)

Colajanni, Napoleone. *L'Italia del 1898: Tumulti e reazione* (Milan 1898, R1953)

Colapietra, Raffaele. *Il Novantotto: La crisi di fine secolo (1896–1900)* (Milan 1959)

Contarini, Silvia. ' "Botticelli ritrovato": Frammenti di dialogo tra Aby Warburg e André Jolles', *Prospettiva*, lxviii (1993), 87–93

Conti, A. 'L'affresco di Andrea del Castagno', *Il Marzocco*, iv/21 (25 June 1899)

Conti, A. ' 'L'educazione artistica', *Il Marzocco*, v/4 (8 April 1900)

Conti, Elio. *Le origini del socialismo a Firenze (1860–1880)* (Rome 1950)

Conti, Giuseppe. 'Feste e usanze tradizionali', *Firenze Ottocento: Dalla dominazione 'illuminata' dei Lorena all'elezione a capitale d'Italia, fino agli ultimi anni del secolo, in un clima di generale rinnovamento: Cento anni di storia rivistati anche alla luce delle dirette testimonianze degli scrittori del tempo*, ed. Marcello Vannucci (Florence 1992), 266–83

Cooper, Robyn. 'The popularization of Renaissance art in Victorian England', *Art History*, i/1 (1978), 263–93

Corradini, Enrico. 'Lo sciopero nella città dei Ciompi', *Il Marzocco*, vii/36 (7 Sept. 1902)

Corsini, Carlo A. 'La demografia', *Firenze 1815–1945: Un bilancio storiografico*, eds Giorgio Mori and Piero Roggi (Florence 1990), 3–20

Corsini, Umberto. 'Il problema tedesco nell'immagine italiana tra il 1848 e il 1870', *Immagini a confronto: Italia e Germania dal 1830 all'unificazione nazionale*, eds Angelo Ara and Rudolf Lill (Bologna and Berlin 1991), 129–67

Cresti, Carlo and Silvano Fei, 'Le vicende del "risanamento" di Mercato Vecchio a Firenze', *Storia urbana*, i/2 (1977), 99–126

Cresti, Carlo. *Firenze 1896–1915: La stagione del Liberty* (Florence 1978)

Cresti, Carlo. *Firenze, capitale mancata: Architettura e città dal piano Poggi a oggi* (Florence 1995)

Curtius, Ernst Robert. *Maurice Barrès und die geistigen Grundlagen des französischen Nationalismus* (Bonn 1921)

Da Siena, M. 'La "Primavera di Sandro" ', *Il Marzocco*, iv/9 (2 April 1899) and vi/11 (16 April 1899)

Däubler, Theodor. *Das Nordlicht* (Munich and Leipzig 1910)

De Forest, John William. *European Acquaintance: Being Sketches of People in Europe* (New York 1858)

De la Ramée, Louise *see* Ouida
De Mattei, Roberto. *Cultura e letteratura antidemocratica dopo l'unificazione* (Florence 1937)
Del Buono, Oreste, Gherardo Frassa and Luigi Settembrini. *Gli anglo-fiorentini: Una storia d'amore* (Florence 1987)
Del Soldato, A. *Luoghi e ricordi dei macchiaioli* (Florence 1985)
Delay, Jean. *La jeunesse d'André Gide*, 2 vols (Paris 1956–7)
Dentler, Clara Louise. *Famous Foreigners in Florence 1400–1900* (Florence 1964)
De Rosa, Stefano (ed.). *Heinrich Ludolf Verworner: Il colore del dubbio* (Milan 1997)
Diers, Michael. *Warburg aus Briefen: Kommentare zu den Kopierbüchern der Jahre 1905–1918* (Weinheim 1991)
Diers, Michael. 'Professor V. Aby Warburgs Krankenakte', *Frankfurter Allgemeine Zeitung*, clxxx (5 Aug. 1992)
Dipper, Christof. 'Helden überkreuz oder das Kreuz mit den Helden: Wie Deutsche und Italiener die Heroen der nationalen Einigung (der anderen) wahrnahmen', *Jahrbuch des Historischen Kollegs 1999* (Munich 1999), 91–130
Djikstra, Bram. *Idols of Perversity: Fantasies of Feminine Evil in fin-de-siècle Culture* (New York and Oxford 1986)
Durkheim, Emile. *Le Suicide* (Paris 1897)
Dwelshauvers, Jacques *see* Mesnil, Jacques
Eckardt, Julius von. *Lebenserinnerungen*, 2 vols (Leipzig 1910)
Eilers, Egon. 'Perspectiven und Montage: Studien zu Thomas Manns Schauspiel "Fiorenza" ' (diss., University of Marburg 1967)
Esch, Arnold. 'L'esordio degli istituti di ricerca tedeschi in Italia: I primi passi verso l'istituzionalizzazione della ricerca nel campo delle scienze umanistiche all'estero 1870–1914', *Storia dell'arte e politica culturale intorno al 1900: La fondazione dell'Istituto Germanico di Storia dell'Arte a Firenze*, ed. Max Seidel (Venice 1999), 223–48
Esche-Braunfels, Sigrid. *Adolf von Hildebrand (1847–1921)* (Berlin 1993)
Fantoni, Marcello (ed.). *Gli anglo-americani a Firenze: Idea e costruzione del Rinascimento* (Rome 2000)
Fattori, Giovanni. *Scritti autobiografici editi e inediti*, ed. Francesca Errico (Rome 1980)
Fei, Silvano. *Firenze 1881–1898: La grande operazione urbanistica* (Rome 1977)
Ferraris, C. F. 'La disoccupazione e l'assicurazione degli operai', *Nuova Antologia*, cxxvii (1897), 73–103 and 322–47
Ferrazza, Roberto. 'Elia Volpi e il commercio dell'arte nel primo trentennio del Novecento', *Studi e ricerche di collezionismo e museografia a Firenze 1820–1920* (Quaderni del Seminario di Storia della Critica d'Arte 2) (Pisa 1985)
Firenze d'oggi (Florence 1896)
Fischer, Paul David. *Italien und die Italiener am Schlusse des neunzehnten Jahrhunderts: Betrachtungen und Studien über die politischen, wirtschaftlichen und sozialen Zustände Italiens* (Berlin 1899)
Fleming, John. 'Art dealing in the Risorgimento I', *The Burlington Magazine*, cxv (1973), 4–17
Fleming, John. 'Art dealing in the Risorgimento II', *The Burlington Magazine*, cxxi/917 (1979), 492–508
Fleming, John. 'Art dealing in the Risorgimento III', *The Burlington Magazine*, cxxi/918 (1979), 568–80
Fletcher, Ian. 'Some aspects of aestheticism', *Twilight of Dawn: Studies in English Literature in Transition*, ed. O. M. Brack Jr (Tucson 1987), 1–31
Fletcher, Ian. *Rediscovering Herbert Horne: Poet, Architect, Typographer, Art Historian* (Greensboro 1990)
Fontana, Ferdinando. *In Tedescheria* (Milan 1883)
Fontane, Theodor. *Erinnerungen, ausgewählte Schriften und Kritiken*, 3rd edn (Munich 1994) (= Werke, Schriften und Briefe iii/3)
France, Antatole. *Le Lys rouge* (Paris 1923) (= Œuvres xvi/2)

Franciosi, Giovanni. 'Il "misterio della passione" di Oberammergau', *Nuova Antologia*, iv/89 (1900), 300–11

Fraser, Hilary. *The Victorians and Renaissance Italy* (Oxford and Cambridge, MA 1992)

Freud, Sigmund. *Unser Herz zeigt nach dem Süden: Reisebriefe 1895–1923*, eds Christfried Tögel and Michael Molnar (Berlin 2002)

Freud, Sigmund. *The Interpretation of Dreams*, trans. Joyce Crick (Oxford 1999)

Friedländer, Max J. *Erinnerungen und Aufzeichnungen: Aus dem Nachlaß*, ed. Rudolf Moritz Heilbrunn (Mainz and Berlin 1967)

Fry, Roger. 'Mr. Horne's Book on Botticelli', *The Burlington Magazine*, xiii (1908), 83–7

Fry, Roger. 'French Post-Impressionism', *Vision and Design* (London and New York 1981), 166–70

Fuchs, Dominque Charles. 'Acquisti dalle collezioni Demidoff e Favard nelle raccolte del Museo Stibbert', *L'idea di Firenze: Temi e interpretazioni dell'arte straniera dell'Ottocento*, eds Maurizio Bossi and Lucia Tonini (Florence 1989), 147–51

Fuchs, Dominique Charles. 'Il museo di Frederick Stibbert', *La città degli Uffizi* (Florence 1982), 121–30

Fuld, L. 'Die Zunahme des Selbstmordes', *Über Land und Meer*, lxiii (1890), 148

Fuller, Margaret. *Memoirs* (Boston 1852)

Gabardi, G. 'Un teatro *sui generis*', *Firenze Ottocento: Dalla dominazione 'illuminata' dei Lorena all'elezione a capitale d'Italia, fino agli ultimi anni del secolo, in un clima di generale rinnovamento: Cento anni di storia rivistati anche alla luce delle dirette testimonianze degli scrittori del tempo*, ed. Marcello Vannucci (Florence 1992), 136–43

Galitz, Robert and Brita Reimers (eds). *'Ekstatische Nymphe, trauernder Flußgott': Portrait eines Gelehrten* (Hamburg 1995)

Galli, Giorgio. *I partiti politici* (Turin 1974)

Garin, Eugenio. 'Note sulla cultura a Firenze alla fine dell'Ottocento', *Giornale critico della filosofia Italiana*, 6th series, v/1 (1985), 1–15

Garoglio, Diego. 'Il metodo storico e la specializzazione', *Il Marzocco*, i/50 (10 Jan. 1897)

Gauld, Alan. *A History of Hypnotism* (Cambridge 1992)

Gay, Peter. *The Bourgeois Experience: Victoria to Freud*, iv: *The Naked Heart* (London 1996)

Gay, Peter. *The Bourgeois Experience: Victoria to Freud*, v: *Pleasure Wars* (London 1998)

Gelli, Iacopo. 'Il duello in Italia nell'ultimo ventennio (1897–1899)', *Nuova Antologia*, iv/91 (1901), 151–60

Gennari Santori, Flaminia. 'James Jackson Jarves and the diffusion of Tuscan painting in the United States', *Gli anglo-americani a Firenze: Idea e costruzione del Rinascimento*, ed. Marcello Fantoni (Rome 2000), 177–206

Gentilini, Giancarlo. 'Arti applicate, tradizione artistica fiorentina e committenti stranieri', *L'idea di Firenze: Temi e interpretazioni dell'arte straniera dell'Ottocento*, eds Maurizio Bossi and Lucia Tonini (Florence 1989), 155–76

Germer, Stefan. *Historizität und Autonomie: Studien zu Wandbildern des 19. Jahrhunderts im Frankreich des 19. Jahrhunderts. Ingres, Chassériau, Chenavard und Puvis de Chavannes* (Hildesheim, Zurich and New York 1988)

Gianni, Oliva. *I nobili spiriti: Pascoli, D'Annunzio e le reviste dell'estetismo fiorentino* (Venice 2002)

Giedion, Siegfried. *Bauen in Frankreich, Bauen in Eisen, Bauen in Eisenbeton* (Leipzig 1928)

Gioli, M. 'A proposito dell'arte moderna', *Festa dell'Arte* (10 Feb. 1897)

Goldschmidt, Adolph. *Lebenserinnerungen 1863–1944*, ed. Marie Roosen-Runge-Mollwo (Berlin 1989)

Gombrich, E. H. *Aby Warburg: An Intellectual Biography* (Oxford 1986)

Gombrich, E. H. *Ornament und Kunst: Schmucktrieb und Ordnungssinn in der Psychologie des dekorativen Schaffens* (Stuttgart 1982)

Gombrich, E. H. 'Aby Warburg und der Evolutionismus des 19. Jahrhunderts', *'Ekstatische Nymphe, trauernder Flußgott': Portrait eines Gelehrten*, eds Robert Galitz and Brita Reimers (Hamburg 1995), 52–73

Gregor-Dellin, Martin. *Richard Wagner: Sein Leben, sein Werk, sein Jahrhundert*, 2nd edn (Munich and Zurich 1989); trans. J. Maxwell Brownjohn as *Richard Wagner: His Life, his Work, his Century* (London 1983)

Grifi, Elvira. *Saunterings in Florence: A New Artistic and Practical Hand-Book for English and American Tourists* (Florence 1896)

Gunn, Peter. *Vernon Lee: Violet Paget, 1856–1935* (London 1964)

Hamilton, Olive. *Paradise of Exiles: Tuscany and the British* (London 1974)

Hart, Julius. 'Individualismus und Renaissance-Romantik', *Der neue Gott* (Florence and Leipzig 1899), 73–116

Hartleben, Selma. *'Mei Erich': Aus Otto Erichs Leben* (Berlin 1910)

Haskell, Francis. *Rediscoveries in Art: Some Aspects of Taste, Fashion and Collecting in England and France* (Ithaca, NY 1976)

Hering, Ewald. *Über das Gedächtnis als eine allgemeine Funktion der organisierten Materie*, 3rd edn (Leipzig 1921)

Hesse, Hermann. *Italien: Schilderungen, Tagebücher, Gedichte, Aufsätze, Buchbesprechungen und Erzählungen* (Frankfurt 1996)

Heydenreich, Titus. 'Politische Dimensionen im literarischen Italienbild: Die zweite Hälfte des 19. Jahrunderts', *Immagini a confronto: Italia e Germania dal 1830 all'unificazione nazionale*, eds Angelo Ara and Rudolf Lill (Bologna and Berlin 1991), 283–303

Hildebrand, Adolf von. *Gesammelte Schriften zur Kunst*, ed. Henning Bock (Cologne and Opladen 1969)

Hillebrand, Karl. 'Gino Capponi', *Zeiten, Völker, Menschen* (Straßburg 1873–85), iv.266–90

Hofmann, Werner. *Die Moderne im Rückspiegel: Hauptwege der Kunstgeschichte* (Munich 1998)

Holt, Elizabeth Basye Gilmore. *The Expanding World of Art 1874–1902*, i: *Universal Expositions and State-Sponsored Fine Arts Exhibitions* (New Haven and London 1988)

Horne, Herbert P. 'The battle-piece by Paolo Uccello in the National Gallery', *The Monthly Review*, v (1901), 114–38

Horne, Herbert P. *Alessandro Filipepi Commonly Called Sandro Botticelli: Painter of Florence* (London 1908)

Howells, William Dean. *Tuscan Cities* (Leipzig 1891)

Hubert, Hans W. *Das Kunsthistorische Institut in Florenz: Von der Gründung bis zum hundertjährigen Jubiläum (1897–1997)* (Florence 1997)

Hufschmidt, Anke.' "Zwischen Luxus- und Schundwaare": Überlegungen zur bürgerlichen Wohnung in der zweiten Hälfte des 19. Jahrhunderts', *Renaissance der Renaissance: Ein bürgerlicher Kunststil im 19. Jahrhundert*, eds G. Ulrich Großmann and Petra Krutisch (Munich 1992), 95–111

Huizinga, Johan. *Mein Weg zur Geschichte: Letzte Reden und Skizzen*, trans. Werner Kaegi (Basel 1947)

Hutton, Laurence. *Literary Landmarks of Florence* (New York 1897)

Hutton, Patrick H. *History as an Art of Memory* (Hanover and London 1993)

Hyde, H. Montgomery. *Oscar Wilde* (New York 1973)

Jachmann, Günther (ed.). *Adolf von Hildebrands Briefwechsel mit Conrad Fiedler* (Dresden 1927)

Jaffe, Irma B. (ed.). *The Italian Presence in American Art, 1860–1920* (New York and Rome 1992)

James, Henry. *Italian Hours* (New York 1968)

James, Henry. *Transatlantic Sketches* (Freeport, ND 1972)

James, Henry. *Autobiography*, ed. Frederick W. Dupee (Princeton 1983)

James, Henry. *Complete Stories 1864–1874* (New York 1999)

Jepson, Edgar. *Memories of a Victorian*, 2 vols (London 1933)

Jonas, Klaus Werner. *Die Thomas Mann-Literatur: Bibliographie der Kritik*, 3 vols (Berlin 1972–80, R1997)

Kaegi, Werner. 'Das historische Werk Johan Huizingas', *Historische Meditationen II* (Zurich 1946), 245–86

Kamerbeek, Jan. 'Huizinga en de beweging van tachtig', *Tijdschrift voor Geschiedenis*, lxvii (1954), 145–64

Kaplan, Fred. *Henry James: The Imagination of a Genius. A Biography* (London and Sydney 1992)

Kaplan, Fred (ed.). *Travelling in Italy with Henry James* (London and Sydney 1994)

Karo, Georg. *Selbstgespräche: Aus Heinrich Hombergers Nachlaß* (Munich 1928)

Käss, Siegfried. *Der heimliche Kaiser der Kunst: Adolf Bayersdorfer, seine Freunde und seine Zeit* (Munich 1987)

Kecks, Ronald G. *Domenico Ghirlandaio und die Malerei der Florentiner Renaissance* (Munich 2000)

Kilmurray, Elaine and Richard Ormond (eds), *John Singer Sargent* (exhibition catalogue) (London 1998)

Klee, Paul. *Briefe an die Familie 1893–1940*, ed. Felix Klee (Cologne 1976)

Klee, Paul. *Tagebücher 1898–1918*, ed. Wolfgang Kersten (Stuttgart 1988)

Klement, Fred Robert von. *Bei Lapi in Florenz* (Salo 1911)

Klotz, Heinrich. *Neuzeit und Moderne* (Munich 2000) (= Geschichte der deutschen Kunst, Vol. 3)

Koller, Angela. 'Südsehnsucht und Süderlebnis bei Isolde Kurz' (diss. University of Zurich, 1963)

Königseder, Karl. 'Aby Warburg im "Bellevue" ', '*Ekstatische Nymphe, trauernder Flußgott': Portrait eines Gelehrten*, eds Robert Galitz and Brita Reimers (Hamburg 1995), 74–98

Koopmann, Helmut. 'Renaissancekult in der deutschen Literatur um 1900', *Storia dell'arte e politica culturale intorno al 1900: La fondazione dell'Istituto Germanico di Storia dell'Arte a Firenze*, ed. Max Seidel (Venice 1999), 13–24

Krahn, Volker. ' "Ein ziemlich kühnes Unterfangen . . .": Wilhelm von Bode als Wegbereiter der Bronzeforschung, seine Erwerbungen für die Berliner Museen und seine Beziehungen zu Sammlern', *Von allen Seiten schön: Bronzen der Renaissance und des Barock*, ed. Volker Krahn (Berlin 1995), 34–55

Krohn, Helga. *Die Juden in Hamburg: Die politische, soziale und kulturelle Entwicklung einer Großstadtgemeinde nach der Emanzipation 1848–1918*, 2 vols (Hamburg 1974)

Kuchenbuch, Thomas. *Die Welt um 1900: Unterhaltungs- und Technikkultur* (Stuttgart and Weimar 1992)

Kuhn, Philipp. 'Villa Romana: Geschichte eines Künstlerhauses in Florenz 1904–2000' (typescript)

Kurz, Isolde. 'Unsere Carlotta', *Der Ruf des Pan: Zwei Geschichten von Liebe und Tod*, 2nd edn (Tübingen n.d.)

Kurz, Isolde. *Deutsche und Italiener* (Stuttgart and Berlin 1919)

Kurz, Isolde. *Florentinische Erinnerungen*, 7th/8th edn (Stuttgart and Berlin 1920)

Kurz, Isolde. *Meine Mutter* (Tübingen 1926)

Kurz, Isolde. 'Neue deutsch-florentiner Erinnerungen: Abdruck eines Vortrags vor den "Freunden der Deutschen Akademie in Florenz" ', *Münchner Neueste Nachrichten* (2/3 May 1927)

Kurz, Isolde. *Der Meister von San Francesco* (Tübingen 1931)

Kurz, Isolde. *Die Nacht im Teppichsaal: Erlebnisse eines Wanderers* (Tübingen 1933)

Kurz, Isolde. *Pilgerfahrt nach dem Unerreichlichen: Lebensrückschau* (Tübingen 1938)

Kurzke, Hermann. *Thomas Mann: Das Leben als Kunstwerk. Eine Biographie* (Munich 1999)

Lago, Mary M. and Karl Beckson (eds), *Max and Will: Max Beerbohm and William Rothenstein. Their Friendship and Letters 1893–1945* (London 1975)

Lamberini, Daniela. 'Residenti anglo-americani e *genius loci*: Ricostruzioni e restauri delle dimore fiorentine', *Gli anglo-americani a Firenze: Idea e costruzione del Rinascimento*, ed. Marcello Fantoni (Rome 2000), 125–42

Landucci, Giovanni. *Darwinismo a Firenze: Tra scienza e ideologia* (Florence 1977)

Langner, Johannes. ' "Gegensätze und Widersprüche – das ist unsere Harmonie": Zu Kandinskys expressionistischer Abstraktion', *Kandinsky und München: Begegnungen und Wandlungen 1896–1914*, ed. Armin Zweite (Munich 1982), 107–32

Lee, Vernon. 'The imaginative art of the Renaissance', *Renaissance Fancies and Studies* (London 1895, R1977), 67–133

Lee, Vernon. 'Charcoal and ice', *Genius Loci and The Enchanted Woods* (Leipzig 1906), 73–8

Lee, Vernon. *Vernon Lee's Letters*, ed. Irene Cooper Willis (London 1937)

Leland, Charles Godfrey. *Etruscan Magic and Occult Remedies* (New York 1963)

Lenmann, Robin. *Die Kunst, die Macht und das Geld: Zur Kulturgeschichte des kaiserlichen Deutschland 1871–1918* (Frankfurt and Paris 1994)

Levey, Michael. 'Botticelli and Nineteenth-Century England', *Journal of the Warburg and Courtauld Institutes*, xxiii (1960), 291–306

Lichtenstern, Christa. 'Der "Bildhauer" Hans von Marées und seine verborgene Aktualität in der Plastik des 20. Jahrhunderts', *Hans von Marées*, ed. Christian Lenz (exhibition catalogue) (Munich 1987), 163–78

Lill, Rudolf. *Geschichte Italiens in der Neuzeit*, 4th edn (Darmstadt 1988)

Löher, Franz von. *Das neue Italien* (Berlin 1883)

Lönne, Karl-Egon. 'Relazioni tra la vita culturale della Germania e dell'Italia', *Annali della Facoltà di Lettere dell'Università di Napoli*, xxv (1982/3), 231–43

Lombroso, Cesare. 'Il ciclismo nel diletto', *Nuova Antologia*, iv/86 (1900), 5–14

Lubbock, Percy. *Portrait of Edith Wharton* (London 1947)

Lumière, Louis. 'The Lumière cinématographe', *Journal of the Society of Movie Pictures*, xxvii/1 (1936), reproduced in *Technological History of Motion Pictures and Television: An Anthology from the Pages of the Journal of the Society of Motion Picture and Television Engineers*, ed. Raymond Fielding (Berkeley, CA 1967), 49–51

Luzzatto, Gino. 'Necrologio Roberto Davidsohn', *Nuova Rivista Storica*, xxi (1937)

Luzzatto, Gino. *L'economia italiana dal 1871 al 1914*, i: *1861–1894* (Milan 1963)

McComb, A[rthur] K[ilgore] (ed.). *The Selected Letters of Bernard Berenson* (Boston 1964)

McEwan, Dorothea. *Ausreiten der Ecken: Die Aby Warburg–Fritz Saxl-Korrespondenz 1901–1919* (Hamburg 1998)

Magrini, Effren. 'L'industria automobilistica italiana nel 1907', *L'Italia economica: Annuario dell'attività nazionale*, ii (1908), 137–53

Mann, Heinrich. *Die Göttinnen oder Die drei Romane der Herzogin von Assy*, ed. Alfred Kantorowicz (Berlin 1969)

Mann, Heinrich. *Pippo Spano* (Berlin 1976)

Mann, Klaus. *André Gide und die Krise des modernen Denkens* (Reinbek bei Hamburg 1995)

Mann, Thomas. *Gesammelte Werke in dreizehn Bänden* (Frankfurt 1974)

Mann, Thomas. *Briefe an Otto Grautoff 1894–1901 and Ida Boy-Ed 1903–1928*, ed. Peter de Mendelssohn (Frankfurt 1975)

Mann, Thomas. *Notizbücher*, eds Hans Wysling and Yvonne Schmidlin, i: *Notizbücher i–vi* (Frankfurt 1991)

Manzi, A. 'I teatri di musica', *Firenze Ottocento: Dalla dominazione 'illuminata' dei Lorena all'elezione a capitale d'Italia, fino agli ultimi anni del secolo, in un clima di generale rinnovamento: Cento anni di storia rivistati anche alla luce delle dirette testimonianze degli scrittori del tempo*, ed. Marcello Vannucci (Florence 1992), 119–28

Mariano, Nicky. *Forty Years with Berenson* (New York 1966)

Marx, Karl. *Outline of the Critique of Political Economy*, trans. Martin Nicolaus (Harmondsworth 1973)

Mascilli Migliorini, Luigi. *L'Italia dell'Italia: Coscienza e mito della Toscana da Montesquieu a Berenson* (Florence 1995)

Mascilli Migliorini, Luigi. 'Stranieri a Firenze', *Firenze 1815–1945: Un bilancio storiografico*, eds Giorgio Mori and Piero Roggi (Florence 1990), 465–85

Masini, Pier Carlo. *Storia degli anarchici italiani da Bakunin a Malatesta* (Milan 1969)

Matini, Ugo. 'Gli artisti (impressioni del vero)', *Firenze Ottocento: Dalla dominazione 'illuminata' dei Lorena all'elezione a capitale d'Italia, fino agli ultimi anni del secolo, in un clima di generale rinnovamento: Cento anni di storia rivistati anche alla luce delle dirette testimonianze degli scrittori del tempo*, ed. Marcello Vannucci (Florence 1992), 241–65

Mauser, Wolfram. *Karl Hillebrand: Leben, Werk, Wirkung* (Dornbin 1960)

Meriggi, Marco. 'Italienisches und deutsches Bürgertum im Vergleich', *Bürgertum im 19. Jahrhundert*, i: *Einheit und Vielfalt Europas*, ed. Jürgen Kocka (Göttingen 1995), 147–65

Mesnil, Jacques. *En Italie – G. d'Annunzio* (Brussels 1894)

Mesnil, Jacques. *Le Parti socialiste italien* (Brussels 1896)

Mesnil, Jacques. *Les Mouvements anarchistes* (Brussels 1897)

Mesnil, Jacques. *Massaccio et les débuts de la Renaissance* (The Hague 1927)

Mesnil, Jacques. *Botticelli* (Paris 1938)

Meyer, Michael A. *Response to Modernity: A History of the Reform Movement in Judaism* (Oxford and New York 1988)

Michels, Robert. *Italien von heute: Politik, Kultur, Wissenschaft* (Zurich and Leipzig 1930)

Miller, Lillian B. 'Celebrating Botticelli: The taste for the Italian Renaissance in the United States, 1870–1920', *The Italian Presence in American Art, 1860–1920*, ed. Irma B. Jaffe (New York and Rome 1992), 3–22

Milza, P. *Les Fascismes* (Paris 1985)

Moeller van den Bruck, Arthur. *Die italienische Schönheit* (Munich 1913)

Monti, Raffaele. *I macchiaioli* (Florence 1987)

Monti, Raffaele. 'Böcklin e la pittura in Toscana', *Arnold Böcklin e la cultura artistica in Toscana: Hans von Marées – Adolf von Hildebrand – Max Klinger – Albert Welti* (exhibition catalogue) (Fiesole and Rome 1980), 56–60

Morasso, Mario. 'L'arte moderna alla III esposizione di Venezia', *Nuova Antologia*, iv/83 (1899), 123–53

Morasso, Mario. 'L'estetica della velocità', *Il Marzocco*, vii/37 (14 Sept. 1902)

Morasso, Mario. 'La sfida dei giganti', *Il Marzocco*, viii/29 (19 July 1903)

Mori, Giorgio. *La Toscana* (Turin 1986)

Mori, Giorgio and Piero Roggi (eds). *Firenze 1815–1945: Un bilancio storiografico* (Florence 1990)

Münz, Sigmund. *Italienische Reminiszenzen und Profile* (Vienna 1898)

Musil, Robert, *Tagebücher* (Reinbek bei Hamburg 1983)

Naber, Claudia. ' "Heuernte bei Gewitter": Aby Warburg 1924–1929', *'Ekstatische Nymphe, trauernder Flußgott': Portrait eines Gelehrten*, eds Robert Galitz and Brita Reimers (Hamburg 1995), 104–29

Naumann, Michael. 'Bildung und Gehorsam: Zur ästhetischen Ideologie des Bildungsbürgertums', *Das wilhelminische Bildungsbürgertum: Zur Sozialgeschichte seiner Ideen*, ed. Klaus Vondung (Göttingen 1976), 34–52

Neal, T. 'Morale e arte', *Il Marzocco*, i/50 (10 Jan. 1897)

Nencioni, Enrico. *Impressioni e ricordi* (Florence 1923)

Nesti, Arnaldo. *Vita di palazzo: Vita quotidiana, riti e passioni nell'aristocrazia fiorentina tra Otto e Novecento* (Florence 1994)

Nettlau, Max. *Bakunin e l'Internazionale in Italia dal 1864 al 1872* (Geneva 1902)

Nettlau, Max. *Elisée Reclus* (Berlin 1928)

Nietzsche, Friedrich. 'Menschliches, Allzumenschliches', *Werke in drei Bänden*, ed. Karl Schlechta (Munich 1955)

Nipperdey, Thomas. *Deutsche Geschichte 1800–1866: Bürgerwelt und starker Staat*, 2nd edn (Munich 1984)

Nittke, Charlotte. 'Isolde Kurz und ihre Verleger: Geschichte der Buchveröffentlichungen einer Erfolgsautorin zwischen 1888 und 1944', *Archiv für Geschichte des Buchwesens*, xxxiv (1990), 1–115

Nurdin, Jean. *L'idée d'Europe dans la pensée allemande à l'époque Bismarckienne* (Metz 1977)

Oettermann, Stephan. *Das Panorama: Die Geschichte eines Massenmediums* (Frankfurt am Main 1980)

Ogliari, Francesco and Franco Sapi. *Segmenti di lavoro: Storia dei trasporti italiani* (Milan 1971)

Ohlsen, Manfred. *Wilhelm von Bode: Zwischen Kaisermacht und Kunsttempel. Biographie* (Berlin 1995)

Ojetti, Ugo. 'Diritti e doveri del critico d'arte moderna', *Nuova Antologia*, iv/96 (1901), 734–42

Ónodi, Marion. *Isolde Kurz: Leben und Prosawerk als Ausdruck zeitgenössischer und menschlich–individueller Situation von der Mitte des 19. bis zur Mitte des 20. Jahrhunderts* (Frankfurt am Main 1989)

Osborne, Carol M. 'Lizzie Boott at Bellosguardo', *The American Presence in American Art 1860–1920*, ed. Irma B. Jaffe (New York and Rome 1992), 188–99

Osborne, Harold. 'Expressionism', *The Oxford Companion to Twentieth-Century Art* (Oxford 1981), 179–82

Ottati, Davis. *Storia dell'illuminazione pubblica a Firenze* (Florence 1988)

Ottati, Davis. *Firenze pulita: Il problema dei rifiuti urbani dal medioevo ad oggi* (Florence 1990)

Ottati, Davis. *L'acquedotto di Firenze dal 1860 ad oggi* (Florence 1992)

Ouida (i.e. Louise de la Ramée). 'Pescarel', *Nuovo Osservatore Fiorentino* (Florence 1885)

Paget, Violet see Lee, Vernon

Paget, Walburga, Lady. *Scenes and Memoirs* (London 1912)

Paget, Walburga, Lady. *In My Tower*, 2 vols (London 1924)

Panizza, Oscar. *Das Liebeskonzil und andere Schriften*, ed. Hans Perscher (Neuwied 1964)

Panzacchi, Enrico. 'L'arte e il progresso', *Nuova Antologia*, iv/70 (1897), 393–404

Paolini, Claudio. 'Oggetti come specchio dell'anima: Per una rilettura dell'artigianato artistico fiorentino nelle dimore degli anglo-americani', *Gli anglo-americani a Firenze: Idea e costruzione del Rinascimento*, ed. Marcello Fantoni (Rome 2000), 143–64

Parravicini, Giannino. *La politica fiscale e le entrate effettive del Regno d'Italia (1860–1890)* (Turin 1958)

Parronchi, Alessandro. *Momenti della pittura toscana dal neoclassicismo ai postmacchiaioli* (exhibition catalogue) (Florence 1977)

Pater, Walter. *The Renaissance: Studies in Art and Poetry*, ed. Adam Phillips (Oxford and New York 1998)

Pazzagli, C. 'La vita sociale', *Firenze 1815–1945: Un bilancio storiografico*, eds Giorgio Mori and Piero Roggi (Florence 1990), 55–75

Petersen, Jens. 'Risorgimento und italienischer Einheitsstaat im Urteil Deutschlands nach 1860', *Historische Zeitschrift*, ccxxxiv (1982), 63–99

Pevsner, Nikolaus and others. *Historismus und bildende Kunst* (Munich 1965)

Pica, Vittorio. 'L'arte europea a Firenze, i: I pittori inglesi', *Il Marzocco*, ii/4 (28 Feb. 1897)

Picone Petrusa, Mariantonietta (ed.). *Le grandi esposizioni in Italia 1861–1911* (Naples 1988)

Pinzani, Carlo. *La crisi politica di fine secolo in Toscana* (Florence 1963)

Pratesi, Mauro and Giovanna Uzzani. *L'arte italiana del Novecento: La Toscana* (Venice 1991)

Praz, Mario. *La filosofia dell'arredamento: I mutamenti nel gusto della decorazione interna attraverso i secoli dell'antica Roma ai nostri tempi (1981)* (Milan 1993)

Preyer, Brenda. 'Renaissance "art and life" in the scholarship and palace of Herbert P. Horne', *Gli anglo-americani a Firenze: Idea e costruzione del Rinascimento*, ed. Marcello Fantoni (Rome 2000), 225–47

Probst, Susanne E. L. 'La fortuna del museo "inglese" a Firenze: Il Museo Stibbert', *Gli anglo-americani a Firenze: Idea e costruzione del Rinascimento*, ed. Marcello Fantoni (Rome 2000), 223–34

Proust, Marcel. *In Search of Lost Time*, trans. C. K. Scott Moncrieff and Terence Kilmartin, rev. D. J. Enright, 6 vols (London 2000)

Radkau, Joachim. *Das Zeitalter der Nervosität: Deutschland zwischen Bismarck und Hitler* (Munich and Vienna 1998)

Ragionieri, Ernesto. *La storia politica e sociale* (Storia d'Italia iv/3) (Turin 1976)

Rava, Luigi. 'Il telefono in Italia', *Nuova Antologia*, iv/93 (1901), 705–12

Redgrave, Richard. *A Memoir*, ed. Frances Margaret Redgrave (London 1891)

Rehm, Walther. 'Der Renaissancekult um 1900 und seine Überwindung', *Zeitschrift für deutsche Philologie*, liv (1929), 296–328; reprinted in Rehm, *Der Dichter und die neue Einsamkeit: Aufsätze zur Literatur um 1900* (Göttingen 1969), 34–77

Reitmayer, Morton. *Bankiers im Kaiserreich: Sozialprofil und Habitus der deutschen Hochfinanz* (Göttingen 1999)

Reumont, Alfred von. *Charakterbilder aus der neueren Geschichte Italiens* (Leipzig 1886)

Richter, Irma and Gisela Richter, *Italienische Malerei der Renaissance im Briefwechsel von Giovanni Morelli und Jean Paul Richter 1876–1891* (Baden-Baden 1960)

Ridolfi, Enrico. 'Un grande scoperta artistica: Ritrovamento della "Pallade" di Sando Botticelli', *La Nazione*, xxxvii/61 (2 March 1895)

Rietzschel, Thomas. *Theodor Däubler: Eine Collage seiner Biographie* (Leipzig 1988)

Rilke, Rainer Maria. *Das Florenzer Tagebuch*, eds Ruth Sieber-Rilke and Carl Sieber (Frankfurt am Main and Leipzig 1994)

Ritter-Santini, Lea. 'Maniera Grande: Über italienische Renaissance und deutsche Jahrhundertwende', *Deutsche Literatur der Jahrhundertwende*, ed. Viktor Zmegac (Königstein 1981), 242–72

Roeck, Bernd. 'Psychohistorie im Zeichen Saturns: Aby Warburgs Denksystem und die moderne Kulturgeschichte', *Kulturgeschichte Heute*, eds Wolfgang Hardtwig and Hans-Ulrich Wehler (Göttingen 1996), 231–54

Roeck, Bernd. *Der junge Aby Warburg* (Munich 1997)

Roelcke, Volker. *Krankheit und Kulturkritik: Psychiatrische Gesellschaftsdeutungen im bürgerlichen Zeitalter (1790–1914)* (Frankfurt am Main and New York 1999)

Roettgen, Steffi. 'Dal "Börsencourier" di Berlino al "genio" di Firenze: Lo storico Robert Davidsohn (1835–1937) e il suo inedito lascito fiorentino', *Storia dell'arte e politica culturale intorno al 1900: La fondazione dell'Istituto Germanico di Storia dell'Arte a Firenze*, ed. Max Seidel (Venice 1999), 312–58

Roh, Fritz. *Der verkannte Künstler* (Munich 1948)

Röhl, John C. G. *Wilhelm II.: Die Jugend des Kaisers 1859–1888* (Munich 1993)

Romby, C. 'Immagine urbana, presenze industriali, divenire della città', *Arte e industria a Firenze* (Florence 1983)

Romeo, Rosario. 'La Germania e la vita intellettuale dall'Unità alla prima guerra mondiale', *Momenti e problemi di storia contemporanea* (Assisi and Rome 1971), 153–84

Ross, Janet. *The Fourth Generation* (London 1912)

Ross, Margery (ed.). *Robert Ross: Friend of Friends. Letters to Robert Ross, Art Critic and Writer, together with Extracts from his Published Articles* (London 1932)

Rossi, Lea Nissim. 'Vita fiorentina', *Rassenga storica toscana*, xii (1966), 71–90

Rothenstein, William. *Men and Memories 1900–1922* (London 1932)

Rumohr, Carl Friedrich von. *Italienische Forschungen*, 3 vols (Berlin and Stettin 1827–31)

Runkel, Ferdinand. *Böcklin-Memoiren: Tagebuchblätter von Böcklins Gattin Angela* (Berlin 1910)

Ruskin, John. *Val d'Arno: Ten Lectures on the Tuscan Art Directly Antecedent to the Florentine Year of Victories* (London 1873)

Ruskin, John. *The Works*, 39 vols (London 1903–12)

Russell, Bertrand. 'A free man's worship', *Contemplation and Action 1902–14* (London 1985)

Russell, Mark A. 'Aby Warburg and art in Hamburg's public realm 1896–1918' (diss., University of Cambridge 2000)

Samuels, Ernest. *Bernard Berenson: The Making of a Connoisseur* (Cambridge, MA and London 1979)

Sattler, Bernhard. *Adolf von Hildebrand und seine Welt* (Munich 1962)

Saxl, Fritz. 'Biography of Warburg' (see Unpublished Sources)

Scalia, Fiorenz. 'Il patrimonio artistico del Comune', *La città degli Uffizi* (Florence 1982), 43–51

Schmidt-Bergmann, Hansgeorg. *Futurismus: Geschichte, Ästhetik, Dokumente* (Reinbek bei Hamburg 1993)

Schneider, Friedrich. 'Robert Davidsohn als der Geschichtsschreiber von Florenz', *Deutsches Dante-Jahrbuch*, xxviii (New Series xix) (1949), 165–72

Schoell-Glass, Charlotte. *Aby Warburg und der Antisemitismus: Kulturwissenschaft als Geistespolitik* (Frankfurt am Main 1998)

Schopenhauer, Arthur. *Die Welt als Wille und Vorstellung*, 2 vols (Stuttgart and Frankfurt am Main 1968); trans. E. F. J. Payne as *The World as Will and Representation* (New York 1969)

Schram, Albert. *Railways and the Formation of the Italian State in the Nineteenth Century* (Cambridge 1997)

See, Klaus von. *Deutsche Germanen-Ideologie* (Frankfurt 1970)

Seidel, Max (ed.). *Storia dell'arte e politica culturale intorno al 1900: La fondazione dell'Istituto Germanico di Storia dell'Arte a Firenze* (Venice 1999)

Semon, Richard. *Mnemic Psychology* (London 1923)

Shackelford, Lynne P. 'The significance of the Raphael references in Henry James's "The madonna of the future" ', *Studies in Short Fiction*, xxvii (1990), 101–4

Sheridan, Alan. *André Gide: A Life in the Present* (London 1998)

Singer, C[harles] J[oseph], E[ric] J[ohn] Holmyard, A[lfred] R[upert] Hall and Trevor I[lltyd] Williams. *A History of Technology* (Oxford 1982)

Smith, Bernard. *Modernism's History: A Study in Twentieth-Century Art and Ideas* (New Haven and London 1998)

Smyth, Ethel. *What Happened Next* (London 1940)

Soffici, Ardengo. 'Paul Cézanne', *Vita d'arte*, i (6 June 1908)

Soffici, Ardengo. *Passi tra le rovine: Autobiografia d'artista italiano nel quadro del suo tempo*, ii: *Adolescenza* (Florence 1952)

Soffici, Ardengo. *Il salto vitale*, iii: *Giovinezza* (Florence 1954)

Spadolini, Giovanni. *Firenze fra Ottocento e Novecento: Da porta pia all'età giolittiano* (Florence 1983)

Spagnolo-Stiff, Anne. 'L'appello di Aby Warburg a un'intesa italo-tedesca – "La guerra del 1914–15. Rivista illustrata" ', *Storia dell'arte e politica culturale intorno al 1900: La fondazione dell'Istituto Germanico di Storia dell'Arte a Firenze*, ed. Max Seidel (Venice 1999), 249–69

Spalding, Albert. *Rise to Follow: An Autobiography* (New York 1943)

Sprigge, Sylvia. *Berenson: A Biography* (London 1960)

Steegmuller, Francis. *The Two Lives of James Jackson Jarves* (New Haven 1951)

Stirling, Monica. *The Fine and the Wicked: The Life and Times of Ouida* (London 1957)

Stockhammer, Robert. *Zaubertexte: Die Wiederkehr der Magie und die Literatur 1880–1945* (Berlin 1999)

Strappini, Lucia. 'Angelo De Gubernatis', *Dizionario biografico degli Italiani* (Rome 1988), xxxvi.227–35

Strozzi, Beatrice. 'Degas e Firenze', *L'idea di Firenze: Temi e interpretazioni dell'arte straniera dell'Ottocento*, eds Maurizio Bossi and Lucia Tonini (Florence 1989), 85–92

Strupp, Christoph. *Johan Huizinga: Geschichtswissenschaft als Kulturwissenschaft* (Göttingen 2000)

Sturge Moore, T. and D. C. Sturge Moore. *Works and Days: From the Journal of Michael Field* (London 1933)

Styles, G. 'Suicide and its increase', *American Journal of Insanity*, lvii (1900), 97–102

Sutton, Denys (ed.). *Letters of Roger Fry* (London 1972)

Szylin, Anna Maria. *Henry Thode (1875–1920): Leben und Werk* (Frankfurt am Main 1993)

Tagliaferri, Cristina. *Olschki: Un secolo di editoria 1886–1986*, i: *La libreria antiquaria editrice Leo S. Olschki (1886–1945)* (Florence 1986)

Temple, Ruth Z. 'Truth in labelling: Pre-Raphaelitism, aestheticism, decadence, fin de siècle', *English Literature in Transition*, xvii/4 (1974), 201–22

Thieme, Ulrich and Felix Becker (eds). *Allgemeines Lexikon der bildenden Künstler von der Antike bis zur Gegenwart*, 36 vols (Leipzig 1907–47, R 1999)

Thijs, Walter. 'Uit het leven en werk van A. Jolles', *De Nieuwe Taalgids*, xlvii (1954), 129–37 and 198–208

Thoenes, Christof. 'Geschichte des Instituts', *Max-Planck-Gesellschaft: Berichte und Mitteilungen*, iii (1991), 9–35

Tittel, Lutz. *Arnold Böcklin: Leben und Werk in Daten und Bildern* (Frankfurt am Main 1977)

Tögel, Christfried. *Berggasse – Pompeji und zurück: Sigmund Freuds Reisen in die Vergangenheit* (Tübingen 1989)

Tomasetti, Fabio. 'Trasporti pubblici nella città e nel territorio di Firenze 1860–1915', *Storia urbana*, iii/7 (1979), 115–62

Tommassini, Luigi. 'Firenze operaia all'inizio del XX secolo', *Il socialismo in Firenze e Provincia (1871–1961)*, eds Stefano Caretti and Maurizio degl'Innocenti (Pisa 1987), 76–83

Trollope, Frances Eleanor. *Frances Trollope: Her Life and Literary Work from George III to Victoria* (London 1895)

Trollope, T. Adolphus. *La Beata*, 2 vols (London 1861)

Twain, Mark. *Pudd'nhead Wilson* (New York and London 1922)

Van Huisstede, Peter. 'Der Mnemosyne-Atlas: Ein Laboratorium der Bildgeschichte', *'Ekstatische Nymphe, trauernder Flußgott': Portrait eines Gelehrten*, eds Robert Galitz and Brita Reimers (Hamburg 1995), 130–71

Vannucci, Marcello. *Firenze futurista* (Florence 1976)

Vannucci, Marcello. *L'avventura degli stranieri in Toscana: Ottocento e novecento: Fra cronaca e storia* (Aosta 1981)

Vannucci, Marcello (ed.). *Firenze Ottocento: Dalla dominazione 'illuminata' dei Lorena all'elezione a capitale d'Italia, fino agli ultimi anni del secolo, in un clima di generale rinnovamento: Cento anni di storia rivistati anche alla luce delle dirette testimonianze degli scrittori del tempo* (Florence 1992)

Vasari, Giorgio. *Le vite de' più eccellenti pittori, scultori ed architettori*, ed. Gaetano Milanesi (Florence 1906)

Vidari, Ercole. 'Gli scioperi in Italia nel 1897', *Nuova Antologia*, iv/86 (1900), 103–13

Vierhaus, R. 'Zeitgeschichte und Zeitkritik im essayistischen Werk Karl Hillebrands', *Historische Zeitschrift*, ccxxi (1975), 304–25

Vischer, Friedrich Theodor. *Das Schöne und die Kunst* (Stuttgart 1898)

Visentin, Claudio. *Nel paese delle selve e delle idee: I viaggiatori italiani in Germania 1866–1914* (Milan 1995)

Volkov, Shulamit. 'The dynamics of dissimulation: Ostjuden and German Jews', *The Jewish Response to German Culture*, eds Jehuda Reinharz and Walter Schatzberg (Hanover, NH and London 1985), 192–211

Volkov, Shulamit. 'Selbstgefälligkeit und Selbsthaß', *Antisemitismus als kultureller Code*, 2nd edn (Munich 2000), 181–96

Waetzold, Wilhelm. *Das klassische Land: Wandlungen der Italiensehnsucht* (Leipzig 1927)

Wagner, Cosima. *Die Tagebücher*, ed. Martin Gregor-Dellin and Dietrich Mack, 2 vols (Munich and Zurich 1976–7)

Walter, Eva. *Isolde Kurz und ihre Familie: Eine Biographie* (Mühlacker/Irdning 1996)

Warburg, Aby. 'Sandro Botticelli', *Das Museum*, iii (1898), 37–40

Warburg, Aby. 'Austausch künstlerischer Kultur zwischen Norden und Süden im 15. Jahrhundert', *Sitzungsberichte der Kunstgeschichtlichen Gesellschaft zu Berlin*, ii (1905), 7–12; reprinted in *Deutsche Literaturzeitung*, xxvi (1905), cols 1145–8

Warburg, Aby. 'Italienische Kunst und Internazionale Astrologie im Palazzo Schifanoja zu Ferrara', *L'Italia e l'Arte Straniera: Atti del X congresso internazionale di storia dell'arte, 1912* (Rome 1922), 179–93

Warburg, Aby. 'Piero della Francescas Constantinsschlacht in der Aquarellkopie des Johann Anton Ramboux', *L'Italia e l'arte straniera: Atti del X Congresso Internazionale di Storia dell'Arte* (Rome 1922), 326–7

Warburg, Aby. *Gesammelte Schriften*, 2 vols (Leipzig and Berlin 1932)

Warburg, Aby. *Schlangenritual: Ein Reisebericht. Mit einem Nachwort von Ulrich Raulff* (Berlin 1995)

Weaver, William. *Legacy of Excellence: The Story of the Villa I Tatti* (New York 1997)

Wehler, Hans-Ulrich. 'Deutsches Bildungsbürgertum in vergleichender Perspektive – Elemente eines "Sonderwegs"?', *Bildungsbürgertum im 19. Jahrhundert, iv: Politischer Einfluß und gesellschaftliche Formation*, ed. Jürgen Kocka (Stuttgart 1989), 215–37

Weil, Hans. *Die Entstehung des deutschen Bildungsprinzips* (Bonn 1930)

Weinberg, Gail S. 'Ruskin, Pater, and the rediscovery of Botticelli', *The Burlington Magazine* ccxix/1006 (1987), 25–7

Weiss, Otto. 'Staat, Regierung und Parlament im norddeutschen Bund und im Kaiserreich im Urteil der Italiener', *Quellen und Forschungen aus italienischen Archiven und Bibliotheken*, lxvi (1986), 310–77

Weiss, Otto. 'Deutschland, Dreibund und öffentliche Meinung in Italien (1876–1883)' *Quellen und Forschungen aus italienischen Archiven und Bibliotheken*, lxxi (1991), 548–624

Weizmann, Chaim. *Trial and Error*, 2 vols (Philadelphia 1949)

Wernbacher, Isolde. 'Maria Janitscheks Persönlichkeit und dichterisches Werk' (diss., University of Vienna, 1950)

White, Horatio Stevens. *Willard Fiske: Life and Correspondence. A Biographical Study* (New York and Oxford 1925)

Whiteside, James. *Italy in the Nineteenth Century* (London 1848)

Whiting, Lilian. *The Florence of Landor* (Boston 1905)

Willemsen, Roger. *Der Selbstmord in Berichten, Briefen, Manifesten, Dokumenten und literarischen Texten* (Cologne 1986)

Williams, Carolyn. *Transfigured World: Walter Pater's Aesthetic Historicism* (Ithaca, NY, 1989)

Willis, Nathaniel Parker. *Pencillings by the Way* (London 1864)

Wilton, Andrew and Robert Upstone. *The Age of Rossetti, Burne-Jones and Watts: Symbolism in Britain 1860–1910* (London 1997)

Winterfeld, Anna Maria von. 'Arnold Böcklin und Florenz', *Storia dell'arte e politica culturale intorno al 1900: La fondazione dell'Istituto Germanico di Storia dell'Arte a Firenze*, ed. Max Seidel (Venice 1999), 143–77

Wissmann, Jürgen. *Arnold Böcklin und das Nachleben seiner Malerei: Studien zur Kunst der Jahrhundertwende* (Münster 1968)

Wissmann, Jürgen. 'Zum Nachleben der Malerei Arnold Böcklins', *Arnold Böcklin 1827–1901*, ed. Wend von Kalnein (exhibition catalogue) (Düsseldorf 1984), 28–38

Wohlfarth, Irving.' "Construction has the role of the subconscious": Phantasmagorias of the master builder (with constant reference to Giedion, Weber, Nietzsche, Ibsen and Benjamin)', *Nietzsche and 'An Architecture of Our Minds'*, eds Alexandre Kostka and Irving Wohlfarth (Los Angeles 1999), 141–98

Wölfflin, Heinrich. *Renaissance und Barock* (Munich 1888, R1970)

Woodress, James Leslie. *Howells and Italy* (New York 1952)

Wunberg, Gotthard and Stephan Dietrich (eds), *Die literarische Moderne: Dokumente zum Selbstverständnis der Moderne um die Jahrhundertwende*, 2nd edn (Frankfurt 2002)

Wyck Brooks, Van. *The Dream of Arcadia: American Writers and Artists in Italy, 1760–1950* (New York 1958)

Wyß, Bernhard. *Erinnerungen an Böcklin* (Basel 1921)

Index